D1475128

Rise of the Bourgeoisie,
Demise of Empire

Rise of the Bourgeoisie, Demise of Empire

Ottoman Westernization and Social Change

Fatma Müge Göçek

New York   Oxford
OXFORD UNIVERSITY PRESS
1996

Oxford University Press

Oxford   New York   Toronto
Delhi   Bombay   Calcutta   Madras   Karachi
Kuala Lumpur   Singapore   Hong Kong   Tokyo
Nairobi   Dar es Salaam   Cape Town
Melbourne   Auckland

and associated companies in

Berlin   Ibadan

Library of Congress Cataloging-in-Publication Data
Göçek, Fatma Müge.
Rise of the bourgeoisie, demise of empire : Ottoman westernization
and social change / Fatma Müge Göçek.
p.   cm.   Includes bibliographical references and index.
ISBN 0-19-509925-7
1. Social change—Turkey.   2. Middle class—Turkey—History.
3. Turkey—History—Ottoman Empire, 1288–1918.   I. Title.
HN656.5.A8G63   1995
306'.09561—dc20   95-10331

1 3 5 7 9 8 6 4 2

Printed in the United States of America
on acid-free paper

Acknowledgments

This book is the end product of a long search into the origins of social change in one contemporary non-Western society, namely, Turkey. My interest in these origins led me back into Ottoman history, specifically, the eighteenth and nineteenth centuries, during my undergraduate and master's years in the sociology department at Bosphorus University, İstanbul. Among my many valuable friends and teachers, I am most indebted to Faruk Birtek for teaching me sociological analysis, to Şerif Mardin and İlkay Sunar for introducing me to the intricacies of historical sociology. I owe my interest in Ottoman history to Murat Çizakça, Mehmet Genç, and Heath Lowry. I thank them all for their support and enthusiasm.

The sociology department and the Near Eastern Studies program at Princeton University greatly contributed to my intellectual development. I am grateful to Bernard Lewis, Suzanne Keller, and Bob Wuthnow, who were most generous with their time and attention in directing my dissertation, upon which the empirical research for this book is based. I benefited from long discussions with many friends, in particular Cemal Kafadar, Shaun Marmon, Paula Sanders, Amy Singer, Leslie Peirce, Matthew Price, and Nilüfer İsvan.

I completed the transformation of the dissertation into a book in the congenial and stimulating intellectual environment of the University of Michigan's sociology department, which I joined as a faculty member. The year I spent at the university's Institute for the Humanities was very significant in that it gave me the time to reflect on some of my theoretical formulations. Many of my colleagues patiently listened while I elaborated endlessly on the many problems of the Ottoman social transformation. I would like to thank, in particular, the members of our sociology reading group—Julia Adams, Eduardo Bonilla-Silva, Howard Kimeldorf, Rick Lempert, Mark Mizruchi, Jeff Paige, and Sonya Rose—for their invaluable comments. I am particularly grateful to Jeff Paige who provided constant support and encouragement through all the manuscript drafts. Bill Sewell, Ron Suny, and Geoff Eley were very influential in the development of my ideas.

The archival work for this book required the mastery of the Ottoman language. Had it not been for the wonderful guidance and support of Halil İnalcık, I would not have been able to decipher and understand the Ottoman documents I worked with. I am indebted to him and to Mehmet Genç for generously sharing their vast knowledge of Ottoman history; they helped me see the patterns behind the hundreds of archival documents I based my analysis on. I worked in three Ottoman archives: the Prime Minister's Archives, the Topkapı Palace Archives, and the Archives of the Office of Islamic Religious Ruling. I would like to thank the administrators who helped me, particularly Ülkü Altındağ, Filiz Çağman, Veli Tola, Abdülaziz Bayındır and Ömer Özkan.

In preparing the final version of this book, I wish to acknowledge, with deep appreciation, the support of Bernard Lewis and Jeff Paige. Always demonstrating in deed as well as in thought what it means to be a true scholar and mentor, Bernard Lewis read the final two drafts with utmost care and insight. Jeff Paige provided me with invaluable guidance in elucidating and articulating my sociological arguments; he also suggested the title of this book. Their feedback, as well as that of the two anonymous readers designated by Oxford University Press, greatly improved the final version of this book. All the imperfections that remain are unquestionably mine. Lastly, I would like to thank Gioia Stevens, my editor at Oxford, for her support and encouragement; Henry Krawitz, my associate editor, for his careful oversight of the editorial and production process; and my freelance copy editor, Marian Schwartz, for her excellent editing.

It is with deep gratitude that this book is dedicated to the one person who, from the beginning, shared the delights and the strains of my work and supported me without reservation: my husband, Charles Hammerslough.

Contents

Rise of the Bourgeoisie, Demise of Empire

Introduction: Class Formation and the Ottoman Empire

The Ottoman state evolved from an Anatolian frontier principality in 1299 to become a world empire extending from Eastern Europe and the Arabian peninsula to North Africa in the sixteenth century; it gradually receded before disappearing in 1922, when, on its central lands, the Turkish nation-state emerged. How and why did the Ottoman empire decline, eventually to be replaced by the Turkish nation-state? The argument that follows focuses on the eighteenth and nineteenth centuries, when Ottoman wars and commerce with the West interacted with the existing social structure to create a segmented bourgeois class formation. It contends that this segmentation of the Ottoman bourgeoisie, dividing into its commercial and bureaucratic class fragments, accounted for the decline of the Ottoman empire.

More specifically, it argues that the effects of war, commerce, and the Enlightenment concept of "civilization" shaped the parameters of Ottoman social change. The response of the Ottoman sultan, also shaped by these parameters, was cast within the context of Ottoman Westernization and deeply influenced by the eighteenth- and nineteenth-century adoption of Western goods, institutions, and ideas. The sultan increased efforts at confiscation as a means of control and introduced Western-style education to train a new social group loyal to his person. Yet his actions produced the unintended consequence of transforming three Ottoman social groups—merchants, officials, and intellectuals—into an emergent bourgeoisie segmented along religious and ethnic lines. In time, the bureaucratic element of this segmented bourgeoisie obliterated the commercial minority bourgeoisie, leading to the formation of the nation-state. As the Turkish nation-state consolidated itself at the expense of the bourgeoisie, Turkey was relegated to the margins of the world economic and political order.

Social Change Analyses of Non-Western Societies

Karl Marx's words of caution about the universalization of social change models is an appropriate starting point for critically analyzing theories of social change as they are applied to non-Western societies. Marx, who provided sociology with one of its most analytically rigorous paradigms of social change, stated:

3

[T]o change my sketch of the origin of capitalism in Western Europe into an historico-philosophical theory of a Universal Progress, fatally imposed on all peoples, regardless of the historical circumstances in which they find themselves, ending finally in that economic system, which assures both the greatest amount of productive power of social labor and the fullest development of man . . . is to do me both too much honor and too much discredit. (Wada 1983:59)

Yet few have heeded Marx's caution. The often uncritical application of social change based on the Western European experience to non-Western societies lays bare certain problematic assumptions embedded in them. In particular, most extant theorizing on social change defines two factors—the West and the bourgeoisie—as the source or instigator of change. If and when these factors are absent in non-Western contexts, social change often appears incomplete, nonexistent, or only externally introduced by the West, and narratives often become predicated on the "chaotic" and/or "static" nature of the non-West.

For some, this has led to totally abandoning existing social change analyses as irrelevant to non-Western societies. If we choose this route, we have to note that new analyses have been difficult to come by. Even though Edward Said, dependency theorists, and subalternists have vigorously criticized Western paradigms, they have not yet come up with adequate alternate formulations. This book assumes a less radical stance. It advocates a critical rehabilitation of extant theorizing on social change, seeking to apply this evolving model to analyze change in one non-Western society, the Ottoman empire, in the eighteenth and nineteenth centuries. In doing so, it critically reviews the dominant social change analyses of non-Western societies and then, based upon them, defines the parameters of social change, which are subjected to a critical analysis based on Ottoman archival sources.

The West and Social Change

Two historical factors contributed to the establishment of the implied connection between the West and social change. First, eighteenth- and nineteenth-century Western Europe often provided the model case for most social change analyses. Second, many assumed this pattern to have become universal as Western influence rapidly expanded to the rest of the world through its two unique ingredients, capitalism and democracy, and created structures that, on first examination, mirrored the original.

Even though the meaning of capitalism and democracy varied from context to context, Western European societies, spearheaded by the bourgeoisie, often tended to imagine and define both as universal categories. These categories were then usually employed to legitimize Western expansion to the rest of the world. As social change analyses of Western European origin tended to become universalized and utilized to measure levels of "civilization," the connection between the West and social change deepened. Also, as the eighteenth- and nineteenth-century Western European expansion continued into the twentieth century, and as the West became the center of accumulated knowledge, the relations of Western Europe with the rest of the world came to the forefront, once more privileging the role of the West as the "engine" of social change.

Emerging social change analyses thus elevated a particular historical conjuncture, eighteenth- and nineteenth-century Western Europe, into an almost universal theoretical construct. Only recently, with new political and economic realignments, has the scope of this hegemonic relation between the West and social change become so clearly visible as to require a major reassessment of extant theorizing. The first step in this rethinking is to understand the West itself as a social construction.

The roots of the concept of the West are related to the concept of Europe that preceded it and set the ground for its emergence. The concept of Europe was initially tied to Christianity (Hay 1957, 1968); its crystallization as a concept occurred in opposition to the Muslim attacks against Europe,[1] and in contrast to the overseas discoveries.[2] As European perceptions expanded geographically and physically, and as Christianity in Europe divided into warring factions, "Christendom" slowly became an archaic word and was replaced by "Europe" (Hay 1968: 122). It was this overseas expansion and the concomitant European control over other societies that later added a qualitative dimension to the concept of Europe: the superiority of the Europeans. The Europeans started to view the world in terms of "Europe" versus the "others." "Europe" became the term the Europeans attributed to themselves as they encountered the rest of the world; the "West" was the term attributed to Europe by the societies that came into contact with it. The "West" acquired its present connotation in Russia (Von Laue 1987: 35). Although the "West" was never a well-defined, single entity but entailed many social and economic dimensions, it had, nevertheless, an imagined unity, one fostered by a new physical image.

Two elements transformed[3] eighteenth- and nineteenth-century Western European society: political state-making in France and England,[4] and the economic development of capitalism in England.[5] Capitalism mobilized the economic resources of Europe; political state-making provided it with a centralized, internally coordinated public organization that was in possession of the major concentrated means of coercion. A new independent social group, the bourgeoisie, emerged to gain control over these political and economic developments. The social era that emerged was equipped with new political and economic resources, spearheaded by the bourgeoisie, and was constructed on a new image of society, an image physically represented in a novel material culture.

This new material culture was established on the concepts of civilization, space, and fashion. The European self-evaluation that started during and after the overseas expansion generated the concept of "civilization"; the term expressed the self-consciousness that resulted from technological innovations and changing economic and political conditions in Europe, coupled with the self-definition through negation as the Europeans encountered more and more societies other than their own (Elias 1978: 3–4). These economic and political processes, accompanied by an eighteenth-century population increase, triggered a reorganization in the use of space. Living arrangements changed as the rooms within the residence became separated according to their functions.[6] The separation of the dining room and the ceremonial of the meal spread to the whole of France and England in the eighteenth century; a new definition of good manners and a new code of behavior of meals developed subsequently.[7] A distinction between three types of space followed: reception rooms became required for society, public rooms for ostentation and displays of magnificence, and private rooms for comfort. This spatial restructuring was accompanied by the development of new furniture, and the decoration of the house became an end in itself.[8] The house now contained many more material artifacts than had been used in Europe ever before; the redefinition of the material culture fostered a new conception of fashion as certain artifacts (furniture, glass windows, clocks) produced and used in Europe came to be defined as "European goods."

This new fashion differentiated societies, defining those that set the tone and image of Europe while excluding others; it also gave an illusion of change, of progress, as one style replaced another. After 1700, keeping up with the times, being fashionable and modern by matching the fast pace of changing material artifacts, became an end in itself. France became the European center of high culture and fashion because it provided most of the elements of the new image of Europe. The French language became the medium of diplomacy, scholarship, letters, and polite society (Rudé 1985: 143–44). France became a reference society by which to assess change in others (Bendix 1988: 138). This new image was so radically different from what preceded it that, around 1765, Duclos claimed that "if people who died sixty years ago came back, they would not recognize Paris as far as its tables, costumes and customs are concerned" (Braudel 1981: 206). England contributed to the reproduction of the new image of Europe by providing it with a new economic organization that mass-produced the new, fashionable material artifacts in large quantities. France and England[9] both started to export this material image to other European countries and overseas.

The rulers in the rest of Europe—Joseph I of Portugal, Christian VII of Denmark, Charles III of Spain, Joseph II of Austria, the Margrave Charles Frederick of Baden, and Archduke Leopold of Tuscany—all attempted to imitate France and England. When two new rulers, Frederick the Great of Prussia and Catherine II of Russia, joined in on this demeanor, a debate ensued as to whether Prussia and Russia were, or could ever be, "European." Hence, as the new image of society spread to other countries in Europe, the social boundaries of who should be considered a part of Europe were negotiated. Those who were left outside the European boundaries started to refer to Europe as the "West." Increasing contact with the rest of the world through the expansion of markets solidified a monolithic image of Europe as the "West" in the eyes of the rest of the world. This European expansion produced fleeting counter-effects; contact with China, for example, fostered the vogue for orientalism and the cult of chinoiserie in art, literature, and philosophy of the age. This led to the alteration of gardens in the oriental fashion and the reproduction, in Europe, of Chinese pottery, furniture, and lacquer painting (Clark 1939: 39). The main difference between this contact and the contact Europe was about to have with the rest of the world was that the former generated a brief fashion, whereas the latter seemed to alter irretrievably the structures of the societies with which it came into contact. What ascertained the diffusion of the West was the political, economic, and military power of Europe.

Westernization marked the first stage of Europe's permanent impact on the rest of the world; it evolved to refer to the transformations societies underwent to become like the West. What these transformations were and how one became like the West never became clear, however. All too often, "Westernization" alluded to an imagined transformation and had at best, as empirical evidence, the adoption of the physical attributes of the West, namely, its mode of dress, aesthetics, or material culture. What was Westernized was simply what appeared Western; what appeared Western in turn was a measure of social change. This was partially the consequence of the expanding role of science and technology in defining the West—achievements in material culture became "measures of men" (Adas 1989). The ambiguity of the term "Westernization" was mostly due to the fact that it appeared as an imagined construct, which each receiving society defined according to its own experience (Berdyaev 1947; Pak 1974; Darling 1979; Maruyamo 1980).

In spite of its ambiguity, "Westernization" was nevertheless used in differentiating those who "developed and progressed" after the Western mode from those who had not. It became a very significant force in human history, one that united, for the first time in human experience,[10] the whole world under a single imagined social construct and thus provided a single, worldwide framework for understanding and assessing human activities. Westernization spread, or was imagined to have spread, for the first time, to the world in its entirety. At one historical juncture, it gave Europe the imperial control of some 85 percent of the world's land surface (Von Laue 1987: 25).

The Westernization process, prevalent in the eighteenth and nineteenth centuries, gave way to the concept of modernization in the twentieth century. "Modernization" replaced "Westernization" after World War II, when the latter term was deemed "too parochial to comprehend the communication mode that had spread regularly patterned social change so swiftly and so widely as to require a global referent" (Lerner and Coleman 1968: 386). "Westernization," this viewpoint argued, referred solely to the relations of Western societies with other societies; "modernization," however, presumably covered a global phenomenon and included relations between non-Western societies as well. In reality, what "modernization" actually did was to eliminate the reference of the process to the unique experience of a number of European societies (i.e., "West"-ernization), and make the European political and economic transformations of the eighteenth century a universal experience (i.e., "modern"-ization).

Daniel Lerner defined modernization as "the current term for the process of social change whereby less developed societies acquire characteristics common to more developed societies; the process is activated by international, or intersocietal communication" (1968: 386–409). Two aspects of this definition are noteworthy, namely, the set contrast between developed and less developed societies, and the evolutionary process by which one proceeds from one to the other. What was meant by developed societies was the West, the yardstick for the rest of the world. How this yardstick could then be employed throughout the world had no set pattern. Modernization assumed that all aspects of modernity were up for adoption simultaneously by the follower "traditional" societies, which then "naturally" transformed into "modernized" ones. Traditional society as a sociological construct appeared to be all that a modern society was not, and tradition became a totalizing category comprising "all" that prevented a society from modernizing, from changing.[11] "Modernization" became a blanket term for contemporary social change.[12] One can even conjecture that "modernization" was no more than a culturally neutral, contemporaneous term for "Westernization."

In discussions of Westernization and modernization, these processes often became synonymous with social change. It was the processes emanating from Europe, continually changing and "progressing," that formed the origin of social change; what came to be referred to as social change was often little more than what had occurred in Europe. Similarly, in non-Western contexts, all that was associated with the West causally marked the origin of social change. "Westernization" had at least identified the West as the source of change; yet "modernization" assumed that such a relation no longer existed, or, if it did exist, that it was insignificant.

A reconsideration of the historical impact of the West forms the first stage in developing a critical, theoretical engagement. Eric Wolf (1982), who has been a leader in this effort, cogently argues that the worldwide process of European commercial and industrial expansion cannot and should not be studied without taking into account the common people in the West and the non-West.[13] He also notes that Europe itself was never as homogenous as it was purported to be (379), that the unity of the West was an imagined unity. Similarly, Michael Adas (1989) illustrates how, after the industrial revolution, the

Europeans used science, technology, and material culture as a standard to justify their domination of the rest of the world. This scientific legitimation soon led to the establishment of causality between the West and social change. Adas states:

> As the pace of scientific discovery and technological innovation quickened in Europe and North America, while societies in other areas appeared to stagnate or break down, growing numbers of writers sought to determine the causes of Europe's unique transformation and the meaning of what they viewed as the failure of non-European peoples to initiate their own scientific and industrial revolutions. (1989: 153–54).

Hence scientific and technological accomplishments quickly became the criterion for Western superiority independent of their historical roots. Such technological achievements were even defined as the cause of change itself. Models of social change became ahistorical; scholars assumed that the same economic and political processes could be replicated anywhere to produce similar results.

How, then, to diminish this bias? Many social scientists have argued for the need to rethink our understanding of social change. Most recently, Immanuel Wallerstein has suggested that we "unthink" all the nineteenth century–based social science paradigms since "many of their presumptions are misleading and constrictive . . . and have too much of a hold on our mentalities" (1991: 1). This proposition reiterates Charles Tilly's argument that the social sciences need "historically grounded analyses of big structures and large processes as alternatives to timeless ones of social change coming from our nineteenth century heritage" (1984: 2). Indeed, in his work Tilly demonstrates the contextuality of social science theories by delineating the assumptions that needed to be dismissed.[14] Yet the alternative he proposes, that the neutral boundaries of change can be articulated by differentiating historical levels of change (1984: 61), still cannot easily escape its historical determination and contextual boundedness by the West.

Where, then, to turn for guidance in overcoming this Western bias? The natural starting point could be the words of Karl Marx, the social thinker who defined the discourse on social change in both the Western and non-Western contexts. His work on the transition from the feudal to the capitalist mode of production highlighted Western European change, and his formulation of the Asian mode of production is often employed to analyze the seeming absence of change in non-Western contexts. It should be noted, however, that Marx himself would probably have been the first to critique the historicity of his formulations. He openly states, for example

> No credit is due to me for discovering the existence of classes in modern society, nor yet the struggle between them. Long before me bourgeois historians had described the historical development of this struggle of the classes, and bourgeois economists the economic anatomy of the classes. What I did that was new was to prove . . . that the existence of classes is only bound up with *particular historical phases* in the development of production. (Althusser and Balibar 1970: 202; emphasis mine)

Indeed, Marx's works, especially the 1844 manuscripts, are laden with careful references to the historicity of the change he depicts.[15] Not only did historical events structure Marx's thinking, but his model of change explained best those events he knew and cared about the most, namely, the development of capitalism in Western Europe.[16] This line of reasoning also reveals why his much celebrated Asian mode of production model ran into problems (Bailey and Llobera 1981), if only because his knowledge of the non-Western system was limited.[17] Given this limitation, it is not surprising that he located change outside the Asian mode as emanating from the West.

Yet in his formulation of the Asian mode, Marx echoed the highlights of an ancient European tradition of social thought on the Orient. From its roots in Hellenic times to Machiavelli, to Hobbes and Montesquieu, this tradition portrayed the Orient as despotic and socially stagnant. Two interrelated factors transformed this depiction from conjecture to imagined fact. One was European imperialism. The portrayal of the Orient as stagnant, thus incapable of change and progress, and as despotic, thus in need of "enlightenment" and "civilization" at all costs, justified Western penetration (Said 1978). The other factor was the concomitant expansion of capitalism. As capitalism expanded, it did not unify the history of the world but instead universalized the history of Western Europe (Vilar 1973). Hence the cause and consequence sequence of social change paradigms reversed. As scholars observed the consequences of the capitalist expansion on indigenous non-Western societies, they identified these consequences, rather than indigenous social processes, as change.

This traditional connection between social change models and the West also clearly influenced studies in non-Western contexts. The West developed and believed in a model of change based on its own historical experience and used the non-West only as a mirror to view its own image. Moreover, the West did not use this reflection much for self-improvement but as a justification for the exploitation of the non-West. From the perspective of the non-West, not only were its societies not studied for what they were, but they were, more seriously, misjudged and mistreated for what they were not and could never be.

The Bourgeoisie and Social Change

Most scholars who debate the specific role of the bourgeoisie in eighteenth- and nineteenth-century Western European transformations often recognize the agency of this class in generating social change. Once transported into non-Western contexts, however, this implied connection between the Western European bourgeoisie and change often leads to an unsuccessful search for such a bourgeoisie. If by chance such a group is found, it appears to be fractured or fragmented.[18] Then, the search for an intact agent of change in the non-Western context leads many to the only organized, publicly visible, effective, and rational institution—the state. Once the state replaces the bourgeoisie as the key social actor, it weighs upon the society and structures change. Subsequent social change models almost always become static.

How, then, are we to problematize this latent causal connection between the bourgeoisie and social change in order to prevent the formation of static models? A good starting point is a brief survey of the historical formation of the bourgeoisie in Western Europe and its subsequent spread to the rest of the world. In the study of the bourgeoisie, the etymology of the term "bourgeoisie" seems to be one of the few points of agreement among scholars, who (Brinkmann 1968: 654–56; Wallerstein 1989: 91; Pillbeam 1990: 4) trace the Western European origin of the term first to the Latin form *burgensis* in 1007 and then to its French record as *burgeis* in 1100, where "bourgeois" evolves to denote the inhabitant of a *bourg,* an urban area. The main unifying characteristic of this bourgeoisie as a social group is the Western European bourgeois experience; it becomes extremely difficult to separate the abstract term from its historical occurrence. The image of the bourgeois emerges as a composite picture including a new style of life based on novel consumption patterns, a new way of accumulating capital founded on distinctive financial activities, and a new mode of participating in public life grounded in a unique definition of democracy.

Most scholars agree (e.g., Sewell 1979: 49, 1980: 283–84; Aminzade 1981: 281; Calhoun 1982: 215; Seed and Wolff 1984: 39; Hobsbawm 1989: 20; Wallerstein 1989: 92; Koditschek 1990: 17) that this image becomes a historical reality only by the late nineteenth century. How does this class formation occur? Western European studies on the bourgeoisie concur that this class forms not on its own merits,[19] but instead in opposition to the working class.[20] Wallerstein, summarizing this view, skeptically comments: "And yet, to my knowledge, virtually [no one] writes a book on the making of the bourgeoisie. . . . It is as though the bourgeoisie were a given, and therefore acted upon others: upon the aristocracy, upon the state, upon the workers. It seems not to have origins, but to emerge full-grown out of the head of Zeus . . ." This predetermined active role is predicated upon that famous description of the bourgeoisie in Marx and Engels' *Communist Manifesto*:

> The bourgeoisie cannot exist without constantly revolutionising the instruments of production, and thereby the relations of production, and with them the whole relations of society. . . . All fixed, frozen relations, with their train of ancient venerable prejudices and opinions, are swept away, all new ones become antiquated before they can ossify. All that is solid melts into air, all that is holy is profaned, and man is at last compelled to face with sober sense, his real conditions of life, and his relations with his kind. (Marx 1978 [1848]: 83)

Hence the bourgeoisie sweeps and transforms all in its path. Marx and Engels, agreeing on the cruelty of the bourgeoisie and its exploitation of mankind, focus their attention on the creation of the only force that could overthrow the bourgeoisie—the working class. Most of the subsequent literature on class formation is on working-class formation (e.g., Thompson 1963; Przeworski 1977; Mann 1977; Burawoy 1979; Stedman Jones 1983; Katznelson and Zalberg 1986; Hanagan and Stephenson 1986; Kimeldorf 1988).

What can we reconstruct about bourgeois class formation from the Western European bourgeois experience? Before the French revolution, the bourgeoisie comprised, "in every city, wealthy commoners living on their investments [including] judicial administrative officers, lawyers, notaries, doctors, merchants, apothecaries, innkeepers, grocers, shopkeepers, artisans" (Sewell 1980: 19). This social stratum developed in contradistinction to the major division in feudal Europe between the aristocracy on one side and the commoners on the other.[21] An individual worth based on status and income[22] was the most significant attribute along which this stratum developed (Hobsbawm 1989: 23–24, 26). This stratum probably started to transform into a class with the French revolution (Sewell 1979: 49), which made property the basic institution of social and political order; yet, even though the French revolution made the bourgeoisie, it may not have been made by them.[23]

The problems with the concept of the bourgeoisie increase when it is studied within the context of England, the Western European society that spearheaded eighteenth- and nineteenth-century economic transformation.[24] If similar structural elements unite the bourgeoisie, they ought to be found in both France and England, since the French and English revolutions occurred under comparable conditions. An eminent English historian argues, however, that English society could "not be called a bourgeois society because entrepreneurial landed elite continued to dominate" (Stone 1985: 53–54).[25] Yet another scholar notes that this "failure" of the British bourgeoisie is due to the "idealized notion of an immutable, monolithic bourgeoisie" (Gunn 1988: 25).

Subsequent analysis of the concept within the context of German society reveals further particularities that almost make the definition of a uniform bourgeoisie untenable. Given the emancipatory stance of the bourgeoisie in France and England, the assumed role of the German bourgeoisie in assisting fascism often leads to the treatment of the German case as an "exception" to the rule.[26] Yet the most convincing critique of the German exceptionalism argument specifically points out that this misinterpretation is due to "'western,' most particularly Anglo-American and French developments [being] taken as a yardstick against which German history is measured and found wanting," (Blackbourn and Eley 1984: 10). Eley in particular (1984: 40–41) questions the set of assumptions[27] about the historical agency of the bourgeoisie that lead to the assessment of the German bourgeoisie in such a negative light. He suggests instead that one needs to study each historical process in its own context and focus not on the German peculiarity but on "the French, British and German particularities" (1984: 154).

The location and role of the bourgeoisie in non-Western contexts has been heavily influenced by Barrington Moore's (1967) path-breaking work on the social origins of dictatorship and democracy. Moore compares the Western cases of England, France, and the United States with the non-Western, exceptional cases of Japan, Germany, China, and Russia. The bourgeoisie assumes a very significant role in structuring the conditions leading to a specific political outcome. The strong bourgeoisie in England, France, and the United States guarantees a democratic route; the combination of a weak bourgeoisie and a strong state, as in Japan and Germany, leads to fascism; and the coalition of a weak bourgeoisie with a strong peasantry, as in Russia and China, results in communism. Theda Skocpol's (1979) subsequent analysis on revolutionary change adds to the transformatory role of the bourgeoisie that of the state.

The assumed relationship between the bourgeoisie, the state, and social change also becomes significant in Third World contexts. Analyses of social change in, for instance, the Arab world (Berger 1950), the Sudan (Mahmoud 1984), Algeria (Lazreg 1976), India (Chibbar 1967), Pakistan (Weiss 1991), China (Bergere (1986), Peru (Becker 1983), and Latin American (Allahar 1990) assume, de facto, the existence of a fractured bourgeoisie that never measures up to the imagined Western role, a bourgeoisie often overshadowed by a strong state. Yet in no case does the bourgeoisie adequately fulfill its historical role, as imagined in the French context. As Peter Evans aptly observes, such depictions of the bourgeoisie often obfuscate rather than explain Third World social change:

> For analysts of the original Industrial Revolution, the conquering bourgeoisie may be a useful ideal type. For students of peripheral capitalism, it distracts attention from the actual role of local owners of capital and leads to a focus on what the local bourgeoisie is *not* rather than on what it is. . . . Empirical analyses of the local bour-geoisie . . . have established that local industrialists boast neither the economic nor the political characteristics required by the ideal type. (1982: S212–21)

Obviously, the bourgeoisie has spread throughout the world, and still more obviously, other countries have attempted to replicate the Western experience, often with the support of the state. But the manifest similarities of outcome do not imply corresponding affinities in internal dynamics or social processes. Comparative work needs to be validated by an in-depth analysis of each case, on its own merits.

It is for this reason that I focus on social change in a non-Western society, the Ottoman empire, at exactly the time when Western European models of change emerged. The first step in this project is to analyze the existing paradigms of Ottoman social change.

Existing Analyses of Ottoman Social Change

Analysts of Ottoman social change often search for elements of success in Ottoman society during its formation into an empire, for causes of weakness during its reign, and for seeds of destruction during its decline. Also, most explicate this rise-and-fall model of Ottoman change in relation to the transformations in the West. In assuming this stance, most students of Ottoman transformation build on an intellectual foundation provided by Max Weber and Karl Marx, to which I now must turn.[28]

Weberian Analyses

In Max Weber's[29] classification of societies in terms of rational, traditional, and charismatic authority, Ottoman society would fall under traditional authority,[30] where obedience is owed to the ruler, who in turn is bound by tradition and law (1978, I: 215–16, II: 942–43). Weber specifically places the Ottoman political system under "patrimonialism and, in the extreme case, sultanism [which] tend to arise whenever traditional domination develops an administration and a military force which are purely personal instruments of the master" (1978, I: 231–32). Weber assumes that this combination of an inviolable traditional prescription with a personal one implies "completely arbitrary decision making" on the part of the sultan; sultanism thus serves as a substitute for "a regime of rational rules" (1978, II: 1041). The personal and arbitrary exercise of power,[31] which distinguishes the Ottoman case, also inhibits the development of an Ottoman bourgeoisie, which could have spearheaded social change.[32] In another context, Weber refers to the "Turkish feudal system" and adds another variable—religion—to his depiction. Capitalism fails to develop in Ottoman society due to the combination of the religion of Islam as the source of traditionalism and the assumed arbitrariness of the ruler.

Weber's analysis of patrimonialism develops as a negative case to his study of the development of rational rule in Western Europe. Weber uses what patrimonialism "lacks" to explain the absence of its transition to capitalism;[33] traditionalism and arbitrariness are cited as the two obstacles to this transition.[34] He then analyzes in detail the elements[35] that obstruct the development of capitalism. Yet, how does social change ever take place within such a system? The source of change is embedded in the household[36] of the ruler; it is the continuous conflict between the master and his administrative staff over the control of sources of power that creates change.[37] Yet Weber does not specify what is behind this continuous conflict or how it gets reproduced.

Weber's dichotomization of societies[38] into those with rational authority (viz. the West) and those with traditional authority (viz. the non-West) has augmented some social scientists' analysis of non-Western societies as "traditional." In its attempt to analyze the non-West, the functionalist school adopted Weber's characterization of patrimonial arbitrariness and personal rule. For instance, in his evolutionary and comparative evaluation of societies, Talcott Parsons classified the Islamic empires as a "historic" intermediate. His description of Islam, which is at best a caricature of Weber's depiction, extends Weber's arbitrariness of rule to the arbitrariness of the Islamic religion.[39]

Samuel Eisenstadt's search into the roots of the patrimonial model identifies different patterns of change in traditional societies.[40] He also follows Weber's definition of the source of change closely as he also identifies the ruler and religion as the source of change[41] in empires: the very organs the ruler creates to implement his goals and policies develop contradictory results, and the "strong otherworldly attitude and political passivity" of Islam hinder change and instead sustain the despotic character of existing regimes (Weber 1978, I: 138–39). In his analysis of power and privilege, Gerhard Lenski (1984: 276, 284) also adopts Weber's location of change in traditional societies within the ruler's household. Classifying the Ottoman empire as an agrarian society, Lenski argues that its main struggle is enacted between the ruler and the "governing class" over control of the resources of land and office.

Weber's emphasis on religion has led some scholars to identify Islam as a primary factor separating Middle Eastern and Western models of social change.[42] Many have focused, in particular, on Weber's conjecture about Islam and the nondevelopment of capitalism. For instance, Maxime Rodinson (1972, 1987) has argued that Islam is not necessarily incompatible with capitalism; Stephen Turner (1978) has compared Protestant and Islamic thought to conclude that the elements constraining the emergence of capitalism are embedded not in Islam but instead in the military bureaucratic structures that dominate Islamic societies.[43] Ernest Gellner (1981) has argued that Islam would have led to capitalism had it not been for certain historical conjunctures.

Bernard Lewis (1962, 1979, 1982, 1986) applies this implied connection between Islam and social change to the Ottoman empire and argues that Islam affects the nature of the Ottoman interaction with the West. The Islamic division between the House of Islam and the House of War (i.e., the West) hindered Ottoman access to the West,[44] and the Islamic tradition against the adoption of innovation or novelty impeded Ottoman adoption of the West.[45] Lewis also points to how the Ottomans took exception to this tradition and adapted the European practice in warfare by referring to another saying of the Prophet, that it was just "to fight the infidels with their own weapons" (Lewis 1982: 224–25). Even though religion is based on prescriptions rather than actual practices, societies often interpret these prescriptions to suit their own interests.

Following Weber, Sabri Ülgener (1981a, 1981b) uses the internal dynamics of Islam to explain Ottoman nonchange in the eighteenth and nineteenth centuries; this "retrogression" stems from the emergence of heterodox Islam and the mystical tradition contained within it (1981b: 30–31, 82–83, 98, 101–9, 197). As Islamic mysticism replaces the dynamic perception of life with a static one based on patience and resignation, the Islamic civilization starts to wane; as Muslims lose interest in economic production, retrogression ensues.[46] Yet Ülgener, like Lewis, often treats the texts' prescribed causes as real ones. He overlooks the fact that interpretations of social change by religious texts fail to reflect the multiplicity of causes that the social actors involved in the transformation provide.[47]

Still other studies categorize Ottoman social groups on the basis of religious attitude, as reformist Westernizers or traditionalist reactionaries. Niyazi Berkes (1964: 23–30), for instance, states that Ottoman traditionalists and reformists negotiated the West; one wanted new techniques of military art, while the other realized that a seemingly insignificant innovation had the capacity to destroy the harmony of the whole. According to this formulation, Ottoman social change[48] was located in this constant tension. Şerif Mardin (1960) lends support to this argument by describing how Ottoman reformists eventually won over the conservatives and how reason replaced religion as the panacea for the problems of Ottoman society.

Weber's emphasis on the transformative role of the state has also alerted scholars to cases that, like the Ottoman empire, formed outside the inherent blueprints of France and England. For instance, in their analyses of social change in the Prussian and German empires, some scholars (Dahrendorf 1967; Mann 1986, 1993; Gorski 1993) have articulated the complex role of the state on contemporary social change. In the German case,

Dahrendorf notes how, because of the active role the state assumed in industrialization, Germany remained a "mixture of free trade and state bureaucracy, private economy and interventionism, bourgeois and military order" (1967:59). Like the Ottoman empire, Germany industrialized mainly in the second half of the nineteenth century and at a very high rate; Dahrendorf argues that the speed and lateness of state-sponsored industrialization, coupled with inherited social structures, produced a small and powerless bourgeoisie. The German feudal elite coopted this bourgeoisie, and the state bureaucracy joined with the military to produce "an elite [that] was the state" (Dahrendorf 1967: 221). Dahrendorf thus analyzes the formation of a state-dominated bourgeoisie, but the monolithic presence of the "state" seems to swallow up the agency of the social group comprising it.

Michael Mann (1986, 1993) provides a textured analysis of the nineteenth-century transformation of the European state and civil society. Mapping out four sources of social power—ideological, economic, military, and political—that interacted to produce this transformation, Mann argues that in Europe, after 1660, a transformation occurred from "intensive feudal dynamic" to "extensive power of the state," whereby the state with coordinated but decentralized power relations gave way to a novel organic, centralized state (1986: 450, 458). Particularly after 1850, he notes how states "vastly extended their civilian scope and, quite unintentionally, this integrated the nation-state, fostered national classes, and weakened transnational and local-regional power actors" (1993: 4). Mann's willingness to go beyond economic and political power to include the ideological[49] and the military enables him to capture the complexity of the European transformation in state and civil society.

Halil İnalcık employs state documents to study the role of state tradition in structuring Ottoman social change. He specifically analyzes Ottoman justice decrees[50] to document the Ottoman decline,[51] where changing military tactics and mounting inflation[52] emerge as the main causes (1972: 342, 345–46). İnalcık then documents the ensuing Ottoman historical transformation whereby a new Ottoman social group, the provincial notables, emerges from these military and economic changes the West had induced[53] to sap the strength of the Ottoman state. These notables[54] emerge at the expense of the state until the sultan slowly and systematically suppresses them in the mid-nineteenth century.[55] Western military and financial transformations lead to the devolution and deterioration of Ottoman state power; as the dissipation of power from the centralized state fails to produce alternate political organizations, the demise of the Ottoman empire ensues.[56]

The analytical framework of Weberian analyses thus colors the approach to Ottoman society: societal processes are observed only insofar as they affect religion and rule. Such a stand often relegates the cornerstone of Marxian analysis—economic processes and conflicts—to an ancillary position.

Marxist Analyses

Marx's depiction of non-Western social change appears analytically weak when compared to his rigorous analyses of Western European change.[57] The Ottoman empire, according to his formulation of non-Western change, would be based on the Asian mode of production,[58] defined as a static system with no intermediate forces between self-reproducing villages and the state. Marx argues that significant change, comprising the economic transformation of society and the emergence of classes, could come to such a system only from the outside (Turner 1984: 23). He argues, in the case of Asia, for instance, that Asia has "no history at all, at least no known history. What we call its history is but the history of successive intruders who founded their empires on the *passive* basis of that *unresisting* and *unchanging* society" (Marx 1978 [1848]: 81; emphases mine). Indeed, not only is the society static, but the Asian state also acts as the major internal inhibitor of change.[59] The strength of the state inhibits the development of indigenous agents of change such as the bourgeoisie (Turner 1984: 51). Not surprisingly, what we are left with is the colonizing West as the source of all change. Even though Marx does not approve of the Western capitalist exploitation of the rest of the world, he is willing to tolerate it for the forces of change Western penetration would introduce to the static East.

Marx's conception of the Asian mode of production ought to be critically analyzed within its own historicity. After Marx, scholars like Perry Anderson demonstrate (1979: 361–94) how, throughout history, the West only studied Asia to better understand its own social structure. This long "Western" tradition of thought extended back to Aristotle, who was the first to compare the different systems of political rule, in his case, those in the civilized Hellenic world with the barbarian East. In the sixteenth century, Machiavelli used the Ottoman state as the antithesis of a European monarchy; he juxtaposed royal sovereignty in the West to the despotic, lordly power of the East. Jean Bodin also differentiated the royal sovereignty of the European states from the lordly power of the despotic Ottoman state. In the seventeenth century, as the Ottomans exerted their dominance in Europe, Francis Bacon argued that the fundamental distinction that explained Ottoman military success was the social absence of a hereditary Ottoman aristocracy. The Ottoman sultan's juridical monopoly over landed property was emphasized later in the century.

Perry Anderson uses absolutism to explain both the rise of the West[60] and the variations in Western absolutism that center around property and privileges.[61] In contradistinction to the West, in Eastern absolutism, Anderson argues, the institution of fief systems never became entrenched, and public authority never became juridically limited or divided (1979: 221–22). Yet in spite of his very detailed and conscious analysis of Western preconceptions of the East, Anderson himself defines the East as separate and different from the West. He states, for instance, that the Ottoman empire[62] "camped in the [European] continent without ever becoming naturalized into its social or political system." This, according to Anderson, was due not to a lack of effort on the part of the Europeans but to a shortcoming of the Ottomans themselves: the "attempts by the European powers to 'align' the Porte with the different institutional norms of Vienna, St. Petersburg or London were equally futile: it belonged to another universe" (1979: 390, 398). This divide between the East and the West facilitates the emergence of the causal fallacy of using the description of an observed difference between the East and the West as a causal explanation and assumes that there ought to be two different models of change for the Eastern and Western contexts.[63]

Even though Marx and Engels portrayed the state in the Western context as an instrument of the ruling class, with no agency of its own, many scholars (Moore 1967; Anderson 1979; Skocpol 1979; Tilly 1980, 1984) employed Marx's Asian mode of production to generate a state-centered approach to social change.[64] These interpretations focused on political structure and the state in terms of their effect on the forces of production and defined the state as a political organization that, by its very presence and on its own, structured the forces of production. The state as such generated and structured social change.[65] Theda Skocpol (1979) in particular differentiated the state and dominant classes and argued that the tension between these two formations over surplus appropriation generated social change.[66] Yet such a conception cannot foreclose the treatment of the state as a structure that precedes societal formation; it cannot avoid reproducing the conception of state in the Asian mode as a predetermined, monolithic, unchanging social actor that forces change on society but is not transformed by social forces. Indeed, Skocpol's analyses of social change in non-Western contexts, specifically, "Third World revolutions," argue that Third World revolutions succeed only "within the context of direct colonial or sultanistic-neopatrimonial rule" (Goodwin and Skocpol 1989: 503).

State-centered interpretations of Middle Eastern social change have continued to draw heavily on Marx's Asian model. For example, in analyzing the processes of change within "peripheral" capitalism, Samir Amin argues that "the external influences and internal dynamics that came together to produce capitalism never came together as such in the Arab world and Black Africa" (1976: 36–51). Amin also acknowledges the historicity of change when he argues that the conditions that produced Western transformation were not available for the non-Western latecomers to the capitalist system (1976: 203). In addition, he differentiates social groups within the state and without and notes that non-Western change entails the emergence of a "state bourgeoisie" from the strong bureaucracy, which then gains strength at the expense of "the weaker and unbalanced development of the local bourgeoisie" (1976: 345–46). Ellen Kay Trimberger (1978) similarly traces the emergence, in Turkey and Egypt, of the "revolution from above" to an autonomous bureaucratic state apparatus. Both Amin and Trimberger define the social groups affiliated with the state as becoming the major political actors in non-Western social change. Hence, rather than problematizing the stagnant conception of the state, they both append a dynamic social group—the state bureaucracy—to the conception. Similarly, Aijaz Ahmad traces the unsuccessful emergence of a Third World bourgeoisie to the historicity of state formation, in that "the peripheral state emerges before the emergence of bourgeoisie as a politically dominant class" (1985: 48).

Malak Zaalouk (1989) continues this line of reasoning when he argues, in the case of Egypt, that the nineteenth-century Egyptian bourgeoisie, unlike its European counterpart, was created by the state. Robert Sprinborg concurs as he argues that the Egyptian state "continues to retard the development of the bourgeoisie, giving preference to those classes more instrumental to its rule, while simultaneously seeking to fragment all constituencies to facilitate a divide and rule strategy" (1990:467). In the Middle Eastern context, the state seems to have the implied dynamic role of the bourgeoisie in Western social change. Most recent analyses on the state bourgeoisie (Richards and Waterbury 1990; Waterbury 1991) complement this portrayal by bringing in the commercial bourgeoisie, the development of which was hindered in the Middle East by the ethnic[67] nature of the entrepreneurial class: frequently, "entrepreneurial functions were carried out by combinations of large foreign institutions, and non-national intermediaries such as the Armenians, Jews, and Syro-Lebanese in Egypt, or by outright foreigners like the Greeks in Egypt" (Richards and Waterbury 1990: 402). The Middle Eastern state is thus depicted as developing to benefit the state bourgeoisie at the expense of the commercial bourgeoisie. In all, these conceptions do not adequately problematize the process of state formation in the Middle East; the emergence of the state as a major actor is almost spontaneous, similar to Wallerstein's depiction of the bourgeoisie as emerging "full-grown out of the head of Zeus." All these conceptions employ the category of the state not as a social construct but rather as a classificatory tool for dividing society into different social segments.

State-centered explanation of Ottoman social change follow this analytical emphasis on the exceptional role of the state. Mardin argues that even though "controlling strategic positions in the Ottoman state was more significant and profitable than exercising such control on the production apparatus," the Ottoman state and economy were "too interconnected for the development of a bourgeoisie" (1967: 138–39). Keyder also emphasizes this exceptionalism to explain the lack of a bourgeois revolution in Turkey; he points out that it was "the peculiar status of the bureaucracy as a ruling class, which implied the absence of a land-owning commercial oligarchy, and the ethnic differentiation which occluded the class struggle, that prevented Ottoman social development from embarking upon any of the well-known trajectories seen elsewhere" (1988: 200). Indeed, this dynamic role of the state becomes a permanent feature in Ottoman social change analyses at the expense of social classes. Gerber emphasizes the absence of a landed upper class and the presence of a strong, centralized "bureaucratic bourgeoisie" (1987: 171–73); Ahmad stresses the omnipotence of the Ottoman idea of the state, which "hindered the evolution of classes strong enough to press their interests against those of the State" (1980: 329). Yet one first has to problematize the bifurcation of the political and the economic before dismissing the latter at the expense of the former; the privileging of the political encourages the definition of the state as a social actor at the expense of other social groups.[68]

Immanuel Wallerstein (1974, 1979) attempts to improve the static Marxist analyses of the East by introducing the variable of the world economic system. Rather than focusing on the complex process of Westernization in the world, Wallerstein highlights the production process in general and the expansion of the European world economy to the rest of the world in particular. He specifically uses the Ottoman empire[69] as a case to illustrate the process through which different segments of the world were incorporated into such a system. The periodization and process of Ottoman incorporation, which becomes a crucial issue in his research (Wallerstein 1979: 391; Wallerstein and Kasaba 1983), is then analyzed almost exclusively through European historical records, and the actual Ottoman incorporation into the world-economy is dated as circa 1750–1839.[70] Wallerstein, one may argue, privileges in his analysis of change the nature of Western economic expansion over the dynamics of incorporated societies;[71] even though the world-system approach claims to reveal the dynamics of change outside Europe, it does so within the parameters set by Western models of change. Inescapably, the origin of change once more lies in the West.[72] In Wallerstein's analysis, the bourgeoisie outside Europe is still perceived as a natural expansion of the European bourgeoisie that seemed to spearhead this change. Hence, even though Wallerstein does use a conception of the European world-economy that is as pervasive in its effects as the Westernization process and takes into account the role of the bourgeoisie in actualizing this change, his model, one may argue, still focuses on economic change and almost exclusively on the role of European actors.

Wallerstein's model has been specifically applied, in conjunction with Marxian analysis, to Ottoman history by İslamoğlu and Keyder (1977), who characterize Ottoman social formation by a dominant Asian mode of production and define the state as the dominant vertical element integrating the social system. In this formulation, the origin of change lies in the decrease of state control,[73] hence the state is once more identified as the agent of change. This formulation improves Wallerstein's model because it spatially and temporally differentiates the Ottoman incorporation into the world-economy; it argues that different Ottoman regions joined the world-system at different times, with the Balkans leading in the eighteenth century, Egypt and the Levant in the nineteenth century, and Anatolia after the 1830s. Also, different modes of peripheralization existed in different regions, from commercial farms in the Balkans to large cotton estates in Egypt to petty commodity production in peasant farms in Western Anatolia (İslamoğlu and Keyder 1977: 53–54; İslamoğlu 1987:11). Works by Şevket Pamuk (1987) and Reşat Kasaba (1988) also employ the world-system analysis to Ottoman social change; they define Ottoman peripheralization within the world economic system as the major problematic of Ottoman social change and often emphasize the role of the West in bringing about this change.

Because world-system analysis does not adequately study the internal dynamics of Ottoman change, it cannot differentiate the process of state formation from the decline of state control. One may argue, for instance, that the structure of the Ottoman state is actually much more resilient than it is portrayed in this analysis[74] and that the Ottoman state does not become "a colonial state when it starts to serve the needs of merchant capital" (Wallerstein 1977: 54–55). Instead, one could maintain that it structures merchant capital. The state and its control are once more treated as a constant throughout the incorporation process and the state's capacity to transform itself is overlooked.

To summarize, the Weberian and Marxian analyses both problematize the roles of the state and social groups in producing social change and, in non-Western contexts, privilege the role of the state and the interaction with the West in explaining this change. In the context of the Ottoman empire, the Marxian and Weberian analyses help identify three significant elements of Ottoman social change: households as the units of analysis, the sultan and his state as the significant social actor, and war and commerce with the West as the external catalyst. It is on this framework that this book builds its analysis of Ottoman imperial decline.

War, trade, and a new conception of "civilization" constitute the three social processes analyzed in this book with respect to their effect on Ottoman society. Each chapter on Ottoman social change starts with an analysis of the effect of each process on Ottoman social structure, continues with an analysis of the role of different Ottoman social groups in interpreting and patterning these effects, and concludes with an assessment of the boundaries of transformation in that particular historical conjuncture. A multiplicity of historical sources, ranging from archival documents to chronicles to memoirs, illustrates the process of Ottoman social change. Each chapter closes with a section on the social contours of the new class, the Ottoman bourgeoisie, that starts to emerge from this change process.

Chapter 1 delineates the Ottoman social structure, Ottoman social groups, and the process of eighteenth- and nineteenth-century Ottoman Westernization. It focuses on the sultan's household as the basic organizational unit of Ottoman society, a unit that cuts across formal institutional and class boundaries and contains within it the diverse activities of economic production, religious observance, political administration, and domestic affairs. This household, ranging in size from a hundred to thousands of members symbolically residing under one roof, comprises kin, retainers, and servants, all drawn from different segments of society. The officials imitate the society's basic organizational unit, the sultan's household, and form their own households, through which, in alliance with the sultan's subjects, they keep the sultan's revenues from him. As the competition between the sultan's household and the office-household intensifies, both try to mobilize subjects to rally to their side.

Chapter 2, on Ottoman wars, officials, and Western-style institutions, traces the effects on the Ottoman social structure of its continuous wars during the eighteenth and nineteenth centuries. It then analyzes the process through which the households of the officials established initially to assist the sultan in governance ended up challenging him instead. The sultan's response was to adopt Western-style educational institutions to train a new corps of officials loyal to his person. The graph of the foundation of Western-style state schools in the empire demonstrates the pattern by which the Ottoman sultan attempted to develop a new official corps and produced, instead, the origins of the Ottoman bureaucratic bourgeoisie. As future officials trained in these Western-style educational institutions cultivated allegiances to each other, they developed a social vision of the empire based on a constitutional system of rule and formed secret organizations against the sultan to actualize this vision.

Chapter 3, on Ottoman commerce, merchants, and Western goods, studies the effects of escalating commerce with the West on the Ottoman social structure during the eighteenth and nineteenth centuries. Ottoman minority merchants emerge as the principal Ottoman social group to form social resources that escaped and eventually challenged the sultan's control. The analysis of the spread of Western goods within Ottoman society during the eighteenth century demonstrates how the urban populace increased their accumulation of these goods at the expense of officials and their households. A logistic regression on a stratified random sample of 124 inheritance registers of Ottoman officials, military, and populace reveals a difference in the propensity of members of different Ottoman social groups to own Western goods at the time of their death. Whereas the propensity of officials and the military to have Western goods did not change throughout the eighteenth century, the propensity of the other group, the urban populace, increased greatly. The graph signifies how the social group of Ottoman religious minorities trading with the West entered the protection of Western powers and formed independent economic resources; they thus shaped the cornerstone of a new urban-based social group, the Ottoman commercial bourgeoisie.

Chapter 4, on the concept of "civilization," intellectuals, and Western ideas, focuses on the effect of Western ideas on the Ottoman social structure and the new visions they produced. New conceptions of a civilized society introduced new organizational elements, such as ministries, specialized bureaus, and military units, that emphasized not loyalty to the sultan and his households but efficiency and allegiance to the Ottoman state. As Ottoman social groups came to terms with these new concepts, their disparate interpretations created chasms between them. The most significant divide emerged along religious lines as the Muslims and minorities developed separate visions as a consequence of their differential location in the Ottoman social structure. An analysis of the establishment of newspapers through the nineteenth century illustrates the pattern of the circulation of Western ideas in Ottoman society. These ideas further polarized the Ottoman bourgeoisie along religious lines into its bureaucratic and commercial elements.

Lastly, the concluding section argues that it was this polarization within the newly emerging Ottoman bourgeoisie, this segmentation, that led to the demise of the Ottoman empire. The bureaucratic bourgeoisie, which identified with ethnic and secularist elements, developed into the Turkish national bourgeoisie; the commercial bourgeoisie, which contained the Greek, Armenian, and Jewish minorities, slowly disappeared through migrations, forced and voluntary. Indeed, this segmentation into the bureaucratic and commercial bourgeoisie determined the future trajectory of the newly founded Turkish nation-state.

1

Ottoman Structure, Social Groups, and Westernization

In 1866, the Ottoman statesman Cevdet Pasha and the French ambassador Moustier had a long discussion on the nature of the Ottoman empire during a voyage from France to Constantinople. The ambassador complimented Cevdet Pasha by saying that never in all his years of residence in Constantinople had he ever had access to such thorough information on the empire. Recounting the incident in his memoirs, Cevdet Pasha comments on how limited the foreigner's knowledge of the Ottoman empire is:

> I told [the ambassador]: "Your residence in the Ottoman empire was in the European quarter. [There, y]ou could not even learn about the affairs of Constantinople, let alone the nature of the Ottoman lands. The European quarter is an interval between Europe and the Ottoman lands. From there, you see Constantinople through a telescope; but all the telescopes you use are crooked. (1872: 103–4)

This witty appraisal of the European quarter conceals a deep-seated criticism of the nature of Western knowledge of the Ottoman empire. Just as European social theorists based their interpretation of the East on scanty evidence, even Westerners residing in the empire itself rarely grasped the nature of the Ottoman empire. In order to move beyond these "crooked telescopic images," we need to present a full description of the Ottoman empire based on indigenous sources. This chapter examines the Ottoman empire within a multicausal framework of change, namely, in terms of its social structure, social groups, and the process of Westernization.

Ottoman Social Structure

The Ottoman empire, founded in the late thirteenth century in Asia Minor, ruled over parts of the Balkans, Crimea, Asia Minor, the Fertile Crescent, and North Africa in the eighteenth and part of the nineteenth centuries. Due to its geographical proximity to the West, the Ottoman empire, together with the Russian and Persian empires, was among the first societies to encounter the rising West.[1] Ottoman historians term Ottoman rule from the fifteenth to the seventeenth the "classical age"; the main components of Ottoman social structure are widely accepted as having formed during this time period.

The Ottoman social structure was based on the personal delegation of authority by the sultan.[2] Those who administered the sultan's delegated authority were the "rulers," the

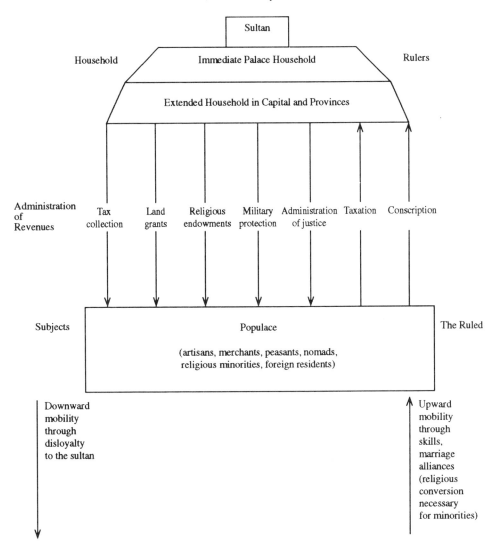

Figure 1. Ottoman Social Structure

literal meaning of the Ottoman term,[3] *askeri,* being "soldiers." The sultan symbolically combined all the rulers within his household. The sultan's extended household performed four services for the empire: political administration, defense, tax collection, and dispensation of justice. Through his household, the sultan administered justice, governed the provinces, recruited an army, to which he often allocated land in newly conquered areas or the right to collect taxes from it as reward, and maintained the system through tax collection. These services formulated the Ottoman institutions: a fiscal institution for tax collection and financial administration; a political institution for governance; military institution for control and warfare; and a legal institution for the administration of justice as well as the administration of religious duties and obligations and of religious education. In return for carrying out these services, household members received grants and revenues, did not pay taxes, wore distinctive clothing, carried arms, and had an exclusive educational and legal system. The sultan monitored this household structure by separating the fiscal, political, military, and judicial services and by manning them with different officials, who submitted separate reports to the sultan on their own and each others' activities. The rest of society without the sultan's delegated authority made up the "ruled," the literal meaning of the Ottoman term, *reaya,* being "the flock." The ruled had no access to the sultan's authority or any of the privileges associated with it.

The social structure reproduced itself through recruitment from among the ruled. Religion was the fixed requirement for joining the ranks of the rulers; being a Muslim was an important requirement for reaching the highest echelons of the Ottoman social structure.[4] Then there were two channels available for the ruled to join the ranks of the rulers: demonstrating the possession of outstanding skills (meritocracy), and forming alliances with households through marriages. Such special skills, often displayed during warfare, led some to be upwardly mobile; others such as merchants and artisans accumulated enough wealth to make successful marriage alliances. The sultan alone had the right to bestow privileges and elevate individuals to the ranks of the rulers or take away their privilege and banish them to the position of the ruled.

The indigenous Ottoman perceptions of this social structure held by the rulers and the ruled were very different. The only domain common to both were the revenues they both drew from, one to administer, the other to subsist. The rulers perceived the system outside of the household structure[5] as resources to be administered. The rulers interacted with the ruled within five social spheres: tax collection, land grants, religious endowments, military protection, and the administration of justice. The services required by the rulers patterned the Ottoman subjects' view of the social structure. The subjects took notice of the empire in terms of the demands it made on them; otherwise, they perceived the sultan and his vast household as one undifferentiated whole. The subjects interacted with the rulers in three social spheres: taxation, military conscription, and the dispensation of justice. In return for labor and services, the subjects obtained military protection and justice.[6]

These spheres also determined the power structure of the empire. Those in charge of warfare and justice, namely, members of the military and legal establishments, controlled and regulated the distribution of resources in the empire in the name of the sultan. Although these two spheres initially corresponded to two separate social groups that functioned independently of one another, in the late eighteenth and nineteenth centuries the members of the two groups had become structurally similar through social networks, especially intermarriage, and through the sultan's centralization of control.

Unit of Analysis: The Household

The sultan's household[7] was the basic organizational unit[8] of Ottoman society. It contained within it all the necessary elements to govern an empire. Household members trained at the palace administered the sultan's immediate household and his domain, that is, the empire. As they moved to the provinces as military and administrative officials, these members formed households of their own patterned after the sultan's. The size of such an Ottoman household ranged, in the sultan's case, from tens of thousands to, in his officials' case, from a couple of thousand down to a couple of hundred members (Uzunçarşılı 1984b: 168–71). In the seventeenth century, the households of top-level Ottoman military and administrative officials fluctuated between three hundred and a thousand members, not including their military retinues. The complete list of the members of the grand vezir's household, for example, reveals the variation in its composition (Göçek 1987: appendix E). The household cut across lines of social stratification and connected people from diverse social origins. Some household members were slaves purchased at the market to run domestic chores (İnalcık 1968b: 242), others were relatives of existing household members, and still others were uprooted peasants or artisans who tried to attach themselves to these households. In addition, there often was a large retinue of private soldiers who maintained the security of both the household and the provinces to which the official was appointed (Uzunçarşılı 1984b: 210). In his attempt to control the growing power of the household, the sultan abolished the military attachment to the office-household in 1827 and annulled the household retinue system in 1829.

The Ottoman word for household included both the public and private, the official and domestic: "gate" *(bab)* defined the setting of the household and/or office.[9] The office of the grand vezir was called "the exalted gate" *(bab-ı ali)* of the grand vezir; this term was fashioned after that of the sultan's household "the imperial gate" *(bab-ı hümayun)*, which literally denoted the principal entrance of the outer wall of the sultan's new palace. All the household members were united symbolically "behind the gate of the household head," with most members physically residing in the building complex comprising the household. This complex often consisted, for example, in the case of the Ottoman grand admiral Kaymak Mustafa Pasha, of "a large mansion for the official and his harem, with two smaller houses near it, in addition to a bath house, coffee room, cellar, some additional buildings for household members on a higher bank, flower and fruit gardens, and yet another house at a corner of the garden" (Aktepe, 1969: 16–18). The inheritance registers of the Ottoman military and administrative officials, especially of those whose inheritances were confiscated by the sultan, list all their goods as they were present in each room of their residence. Such a delineation provides a spatial and physical map of each household[10] and shows that there was no distinction with respect to living, dining, or sleeping quarters. The same space was used for a variety of activities.

The Ottoman sultan concentrated all imperial functions within his palace household. To administer the empire, he replicated his household structure in the capital and provinces. He centralized the system of rule through a communication network[11] that collected all pertinent information in his palace in the capital, Constantinople. The sultan and his palace thus dominated the capital; except for the sultan's palace, apart from the mosque complex, there were no official buildings accessible to the ruled. The members of the sultan's immediate and extended household formed around him and expanded out into the empire through concentric circles. The gate of the grand vezir, which was at the same time his personal dwelling, lost its residential character in the eighteenth century as the Ottoman administration expanded out of the sultan's palace. These new administrative offices comprising the households of the top-level administrators were also all termed "gates." The gates of finance *(bab-ı defteri)*, of war *(bab-ı seraskeri)* and of religious administration *(bab-ı meşihat)* are a few such examples. Needless to say, ministries such as those of finance and war evolved from these structures. Through the eighteenth and nineteenth centuries, the gate of the grand vezir expanded at the expense of the imperial gate to include many government units, including the ministries of the interior and foreign affairs and the council of the state.

IMMEDIATE PALACE HOUSEHOLD

The members of the sultan's household were recruited (İnalcık 1968a: 1087; Findley 1980b: 228–29) from his one-fifth share of the prisoners of wars, gifts, purchases at slave markets, sons of the local nobilities (taken as hostages), and Christian boys levied and converted to Islam (levied from villages in the proportion of one to every forty houses). The relative proportion of the Christian levies was particularly high during the earlier centuries of the empire; they comprised the main element of the sultan's household. This system of levies reflected a macroeconomic policy of labor planning that subjectively diverted the human resources available to Ottomans from certain sections to others (Ergin 1939: 21–28; Kafadar 1981: 23). It also served a social control function as these youths were wrested from their social power bases and made to rely solely upon the sultan for power and resources. The best-looking and most capable were reserved for service in the sultan's household; they received education and training in the Turkish language and customs, writing, law, warfare, and crafts. The rest were sent as apprentices to farmers to be exposed to rural life and culture and then joined the Janissary corps of the Ottoman army.

Training and education in the sultan's household aimed to recreate the social identity of these pages (Uzunçarşılı 1984b: 308–39), who were first and foremost taught loyalty and obedience to the sultan, their sole provider. The eunuchs in the palace kept these pages under strict discipline, supervised all their actions, and refined their manners. The trainers noted the personal qualities and abilities of the pages and developed their aptitudes. In addition to this training and socialization, the formal education of the pages also took place within the palace (Ergin 1939: 2–16, 209). Palace teachers and officials as well as teachers from schools in the city came to give special instruction.[12] Instruction included such topics as religious subjects,[13] Ottoman, Persian, and Arabic literature, history, music, and math, and physical and vocational training.[14] The libraries in the palace helped advance the state of knowledge of the pages. The aim of the palace education was to transform these pages into administrators loyal to the sultan.

The sultan's household was organized into inner and outer sections (Kunt 1983: 6). These sections together comprised the core of the state apparatus; the royal household and state organization were synonymous. The palace pages served the sultan's person in the inner section as they trained for positions in the outer section. As the pages completed their training and left the palace, the sultan allocated them administrative offices in accordance with their abilities and dispositions. These positions often entailed posts within or outside the palace. A post within the palace would be such as that of a palace gatekeeper or pursuivant, where the pages would be in close proximity to the sultan. The responsibilities of a post outside the palace included personal services to the sultan, such as serving as the sultan's private messengers and envoys to the Ottoman provinces. These appointments within and outside the palace often led to administrative posts in the provinces, a post outside the palace usually being the commandership or governorship of an Ottoman province.

The organization of the women within the sultan's household mirrored that of the men in many ways. These women were often recruited (Uluçay 1957: 394–95; 1985: 18–22) through slave markets, were given as gifts, or, early on, were regarded as war booty. As recruits, these women were also socially recreated in the palace within the sultan's household. They too were not able to bring in any external sources of power that could possibly divert their allegiance to the sultan. Women recruits also had to rely solely on personal talent. The most beautiful and talented among them were selected and especially trained in the service of the sultan. Their training was conducted by the women officials of the harem, who taught them reading and writing, music and dancing, handwork, needle-work, and good manners. The sultan's mother supervised their training. The number of women varied from four hundred to more than eight hundred, with approximately 90 percent of them being employed solely in menial labor. If these women became a part of the sultan's intimate circle, in order to prevent the emergence of possible contenders to the throne and the dynasty, they were not permitted to remarry if the sultan died or was dethroned (Uluçay 1957: 396). Their relative position within the harem was contingent on the sons they produced for the throne. A large proportion of these women did not become a part of the sultan's intimate circle, however. The sultan married these women off to the pages he sent to the provinces as his administrators. In this manner, he extended his social network beyond the palace and maintained a double allegiance with many of his administrators. Thus symbolically he concentrated all the human capital of the empire in his household.

The system thus described totally overlooks the agency of the recruits. Although the structure created exceptionally able and loyal household members, it did so at a cost to the recruits, who often had to recreate their identities.[15] The success of the sultan's household depended on how successfully it could forge consistent, constructed identities for the recruits; the ties and networks that formed among groups of individuals through friendship, patronage, marriage, gift exchange, and other social interactions thus gained exceptional significance. The patronage ties[16] between the sultan and his household members formed through the members' recruitment, training, and appointment. Once recruits were accepted into the sultan's household, their social origins faded. They symbolically adopted a new lineage and a new social identity that was associated exclusively with the sultan. In exchange for their services and personal allegiance, the sultan delegated them authority to administer the revenues of the empire. The personal character of the patronage tie provided loyalty to the person of the sultan rather than his position. The patronage network reproduced itself insofar as the sultan was able to maintain this personal character of the patronage.[17]

The significance of these patronage ties can be observed in the career patterns of two Ottoman officials, grand vezir Derviş Mehmed Pasha and sheik-ül-islam Feyzullah Efendi, whose social positions dramatically altered through their association with the sultan (Kunt 1977: 197–214; Türek and Derin 1969). The grand vezir was originally the Circassian slave of the sultan's chief black eunuch. He acquired administrative and financial skills through managing the eunuch's vast property. These skills helped the slave obtain for himself a vast fortune and a large household of ten thousand members; the sultan then appointed him head of the administrative affairs of the empire. The sheik-ül-islam was initially a religious scholar in Eastern Anatolia who gained an introduction to the sultan's palace household through his father-in-law, who was a member. This young scholar so impressed the sultan during religious debates at the palace that the sultan appointed him tutor to his sons. Once his favorite student succeeded the Ottoman throne, the scholar was made head of the religious affairs of the empire.[18]

The seventeenth-century chronicles of Naima ([1863] 1969, vol. V, VI) document another tie that was generated within and through the sultan's household: marriage. After freeing female slaves from the palace household after two or three years of service and bestowing upon them large dowries of jewelry, clothing, and cash, the sultan and his mother then married them off to high-level Ottoman officials. These former female slaves continued to visit the palace during religious holidays and ceremonies, all the while communicating their views, impressions, and problems to the sultan. Through this marriage tie, the sultan doubly secured and rewarded the loyalty and gratitude of the Ottoman official as well. For example, it was the petitions of one such official's wife, formerly sultan's slave, that got him the governorship of Baghdad (V: 2376; V: 2157). The sultan sometimes acquired the allegiance of officials who rose outside the palace by having them divorce their former wives and marry a female member of the palace household, sometimes even one of the sultan's daughters (VI: 2876). Similarly, the sultan married off his former pages to the daughters of important Ottoman officials. Upon the subsequent assignment of these pages to administrative posts, the sultan also gave each one hundreds of slaves and servants. This formed the core of the page's own household, which was structured after the sultan's (V: 2223, 2227; VI: 2876). It is interesting to note that the female's resources stagnated after marriage, whereas the male's expanded.

Gift exchange created the other social tie within the sultan's household. Members regularly exchanged gifts on events such as accessions, holidays, circumcisions, and marriages. These enhanced the ties and social commitments of the household members. The sultan often indicated his approval or disapproval of the members through the nature and size of the gift he exchanged with them. The bestowal of a royal gift often meant reward; it usually consisted of a ceremonial fur coat *(hil'at)* and some gold purses. The sultan's punishment entailed sending the official a dismissal order with his soldiers that often included deportation and/or execution. Needless to say, upon punishment, in addition to the valuable items belonging to the official, the sultan also took away all the gifts he had given.

Household members thus invested in each other's positions and reproduced the organizational structure through social resources—by forming networks, giving gifts and slaves, and proposing marriage alliances. In this reproduction process, the social ties formed by the sultan's household with the rest of society eventually started to challenge the sultan's control over society. The sultan's household, while reproducing itself through social resources, created the prerequisites for its own demise.

EXTENDED HOUSEHOLD IN THE CAPITAL AND PROVINCES

The sultan's palace provided a model for his military and administrative officials, who patterned their own "office-households" throughout the empire after the sultan's (İnalcık 1973: 76–78, 85, 87; Findley 1989: 58–59). Fictitious kinship ties were very significant in constructing and reproducing these households as well.[19] Once these officials left the sultan's palace household, the nature of their ties with the sultan changed, however. In the seventeenth and eighteenth centuries, the sultan's household grew as the empire expanded, bifurcating into the sultan's immediate household in the palace and his extended household outside the palace in the provinces. The ties the sultan maintained with his extended household mostly formed around his delegation of authority. These ties with his officials both reproduced and at the same time challenged the sultan's control over the empire. The loyalty of the officials propagated the sultan's rule, yet the officials also developed ties within the palace household that escaped the sultan's control.

Similar to the ties forged between the sultan and his household, the officials formed ties with one another while being trained in the sultan's palace. If the official was married into the sultan's household, he used his wife's ties to cultivate friends and supporters in the palace. Such ties outside the sultan's control were necessary. Since one's social position in the administrative hierarchy depended on the proportion of one's access to the sultan and his immediate household, the official sent out from the sultan's household to the provinces kept "spies" back in the palace who informed the official about his standing in palace circles, relayed complaints made against him, provided news about other candidates vying for the same offices, and lobbied, through constant petitions to the sultan, in the official's favor. Sometimes the official inverted the process: he used his palace ties to stop the sultan from appointing him to an office. One such person, for example, upon being appointed director of the state financial office, "for being rich, having earned people's trust, and being skilled in collecting revenues," tried to stop this appointment when he foresaw "the future problems [such as death as punishment for the poor state of finances] he might have had during his tenure" (Naima [1863] 1969, VI: 2627). He gave money to members of the sultan's immediate household to stop the appointment and succeeded.

The sultan's delegation of authority to his officials quickly became a double-edged sword. Although it enhanced the sultan's control over his empire, it also severely constricted the sultan's options by making him dependent on the information relayed to him through his household. The sultan was no longer able to retain his monopoly over the distribution of offices; many groups, extending from the provinces to the palace, indirectly intervened in the decision-making process. The frequent historical references to appointments that were changed or quickly annulled reveal how influential these interventions had become: the sultan had to rely more and more on the information the competing parties provided him about the candidates. The candidates with "strong backers" often won out (Naima [1863] 1969, VI: 2570, 2603).

One seventeenth-century case demonstrates the intensity of this competition (Naima [1863] 1969, VI: 2634, 2705). The chief architect of the palace, himself under the sultan's mother's protection, approached the grand vezir and asked him to dismiss some corrupt officials. The vezir, although agreeing that the request was appropriate, turned him down nevertheless. His reason was that "each of those offices were in the dragon's mouth" and that he did not have the power to dismiss the officials "for fear of retribution from their protectors." He stated, moreover, that he could not even interview new candidates for these offices. There were spies even within his own household who immediately informed the officials about his actions, who then immediately started to work slandering and deposing the grand vezir himself. The grand vezir, in order to maintain his own position, then proposed his own trustworthy men as candidates for the offices. Yet the sultan then accused the vezir of nepotism and of attempting to expand his own power base at the expense of the sultan's.

This severe competition among officials eventually affected the basis of sultan's legitimacy in Ottoman society: the administration of justice. Initially, the sultan severely punished those officials who erred, often by death. Yet the "backers" of these officials in the palace started to intervene and secure the sultan's pardon. As a consequence, an errant official was merely exiled from office, and not for long: his backers kept in touch through letters and continued petitioning on his behalf for new offices that became available (Naima [1863] 1969, VI: 2707, 2739). As the social ties of officials became stronger and stronger, the legitimacy of the sultan became more and more problematic. By training his household members and reproducing his own household, the sultan had invested in his officials by training them for office; now he was not finding out that this investment was irrevocable. Upon dismissal of an official, the sultan could and did seize the office and the revenues with it, but he could not take away the skills the official had acquired. This inalienable source of knowledge escaped the sultan's control to come back and haunt his decision-making process in future appointments.

The official's own social bonds with the palace were also inviolable. The networks he had formed with the palace members he had trained with, the social ties of the wives he had married, and the economic and social ties he formed during his office tenure provided the official with power to affect the sultan's decision-making process. The sultan could not take these bonds away upon the official's dismissal; the only way to expurgate these bonds was through execution. Yet, by executing the official, the sultan diminished his human capital. Hence, the Ottoman empire successfully organized itself around the unit of households, which both reproduced the sultan's rule and, at the same time, sowed the seeds of its destruction. The inalienable human capital that the officials accrued eventually led to the destruction of the sultan and his household.

The household as the Ottoman unit of analysis thus united the public and private spheres, family and government, rulers and the ruled, in a way that concepts such as "feudal" or "patrimonial"[20] fail to capture. The household cannot be termed an institution because it was not organized around a clearly defined action or purpose. It also was not a formal organization because it contained a domestic component. Likewise, it could not be termed a domestic organization because it included an official function. The household cut across various social functions and social groups to structurally unite the sultan and his officials with their families, slaves, administrators, and laborers. The household reproduced itself through a combination of material and cultural capital. In its reproduction, social ties and networks, knowledge and skills were as important as material land, labor, and capital. The sociological employment of this concept especially unfolds the internal dynamics of Ottoman social change. The replication of the household as the main organizational structure of the empire accounts for the successful reproduction of the imperial, and, at the same time, also sows the seeds for its demise.

Revenues of the Empire

Ottoman revenues[21] of the seventeenth and eighteenth centuries included those accrued to the agricultural lands of the sultan, the poll taxes collected from religious minorities within the empire, and the extraordinary taxes levied at irregular intervals.[22] Since all the resources of the empire belonged, in theory, to the sultan, the Ottoman financial structure did not differentiate the sultan's revenues from those of the state.[23] In fact, the sultan's household contained the state; his treasury included all the state revenues (Barkan 1940; Tabakoğlu 1981, 1985; Cezar 1986: 308). Ottoman financial policy comprised the collection of all revenues at the sultan's treasury and their redistribution in accordance with the needs of the empire.[24]

Ottoman revenues were collected within a complex fiscal organization that varied according to type of land tenure and geographical region. The agricultural land in most of the Ottoman provinces in the Balkans and Asia Minor either belonged directly to the sultan[25] and was cultivated through his representatives or was given as fiefs to the sultan's officials. The taxation system in these provinces consisted of two taxes, one collected from the subjects, the other from the fief-holders (İnalcık 1990: 2–3). Taxes from the subjects were gathered over cultivated land, over the individuals engaged in cultivation, or over the produce. Taxes from the fief-holders were collected in return for the right to hold feudal tenure, the cost of mounted cavalries if the fief-holders did not join campaigns, and the extraordinary levies imposed upon those who were not tending to their fiefs. Natural resources such as mines formed another revenue source and were either directly operated by the state or farmed out to individuals.[26] Urban centers generated revenues in that the state collected taxes on stamp duties, commodities sold in the markets (market customs), and industrial production units such as wax houses, dye houses, oil presses, and brick kilns (Özkaya 1985: 299–300; Tabakoğlu 1985: 117–18). The most distant Ottoman provinces, such as Egypt, Yemen, Ethiopia, and parts of North Africa, paid taxes directly to the sultan. The states that accepted Ottoman sovereignty, namely, the Crimean khanate, the principalities of Moldavia and Wallachia, the Ragusan republic, the Transylvanian kingdom, some kingdoms in the Caucasus, and nomadic tribes, instead paid annual tributes (Tabakoğlu 1985: 48–67). All these revenues, with the exception of the fiefs, were collected at the capital, at the abode of the sultan.[27] War spending, the salaries[28] of the sultan's household, and investments in the military infrastructure were the principal expenditure categories.

The Ottoman fiscal system functioned effectively insofar as the sultan was able to control the revenue collection and distribution procedure. The relative proportion of revenues from land decreased in the eighteenth century as the empire stopped expanding.[29] The sultan's immediate need for cash revenues for the wars and the substitution of tax-farming and freeholds for fiefs accelerated this revenue depletion. By the end of the eighteenth century, three-quarters of total state revenues were being diverted away from the sultan. This diversion of revenues took two forms: gifts in kind that the sultan gave his household members; and religious endowments that officials and prosperous subjects established (Tabakoğlu 1985: 18–19).

Much archival information exists on how agricultural land and farms were diverted from the sultan's treasury to palace household members. In 1779, for example, two farms (including two houses, one bakery, three hay storage buildings, eight roofed sheds, and four slaves working there) and five thousand acres of land near Constantinople were given to the chief lady *(başkadın)* in the sultan's harem (MM9770/384–85). In 1790, again, thirteen villages on the island of Morea were sold to the sultan's daughter (MM3365/306). In 1793, sixteen farms near Constantinople were confiscated from an administrator and bestowed upon the sultan's mother (MM9770/500–501). In 1808, a deputy in the palace listing his sources of revenues included the income from a number of customs houses and agricultural land (MM6349/116). This land and property, which the sultan's household members accrued as gifts, became entrenched in certain members' households over generations. Separated from the sultan, these fiefs were then often bought and sold among the members; the fiefs themselves, the sultan's most significant source of revenue, thus eventually became commodified[30] and escaped the sultan's control. Although the sultan legally could and did confiscate, within his lifetime, all revenues accruing to these fiefs, this possibility decreased with each subsequent generation (Cezar 1986: 110; Tabakoğlu 1985: 295).

Ottoman religious endowments[31] constituted the other venue by which revenues were diverted from the sultan. The sultan originally encouraged these endowments, which performed very significant civic functions for Ottoman society.[32] Officials could divert funds away from the sultan's control by first investing their wealth in an endowment and then assigning their family members to its executive board as salaried employees on a lifetime basis until their genealogical line died out. The scope of these diversions multiplied by a third in the eighteenth century, when six thousand additional religious endowments were established, bringing the total number of endowments in the empire up to twenty-six thousand. Around 1795, their revenue base matched up to approximately one-third of the sultan's revenues (Yediyıldız 1984: 15, 26). Analysis of a sample[33] of eighteenth-century cases reveals that most of the endowers were officials and that in three-quarters of the endowments some assigned part of revenues was retained by the endower's family (Yediyıldız 1982a: 146; 1982c: 26–28).[34] One case in point is the endowment of Tekelioğlu Hacı Mehmed Agha, the official governing Teke *(mütesellim)*, who in 1815 owned 117 pieces of urban property and endowed 85 of them (CM9026, KK2457). As these religious endowments were drawn up by a judge and confirmed by the sultan, however, the sultan retained some power to oppose[35] the establishment of an endowment. The sultan's position as the protector of Muslims often made it hard for him to turn down most such pious bequests. Once approved, the endowment became financially and administratively autonomous in perpetuity (İnalcık 1973: 132–35, 142). Upon attaining this independent source of income, the descendants became more autonomous financially and socially. Some used the income to expand their own households; others even mobilized the employees of the endowments against the sultan. Yet this potential challenge to the sultan was to some degree offset by the struggles among the descendants.

The revenues of the empire thus portrayed the constant tension over collection and distribution procedures. By the eighteenth century, more and more revenues escaped the control of the Ottoman sultan. The administration of these revenues further fractured the sultan's control.

Administration of the Revenues

The most significant principle guiding the Ottoman administration of revenues was justice. Drawing upon Islamic law and following the Turkic and Persian state traditions, the Ottoman considered justice the foundation of a powerful state and a circle of justice as the foundation of societal order (İnalcık 1985). According to this circle of justice, to control the state required a large army, to support the troops required great wealth, to obtain this wealth the people had to be prosperous, and for people to be prosperous the laws had to be just. If any one of these precepts was neglected, the state would collapse. The sultan had to exercise strict supervision over his administration in order to maintain this circle. The parameters set by Islamic law also affected the sultan's legitimacy.[36] One ruling explicitly stated that "there can be no decree of the sultan ordering something that is illegal according to Islamic law" (Heyd 1967: 9). The Sultan's failure to issue such a decree could lead to his deposition as well. In order thus to administer revenues justly, the Ottoman sultan kept an advisory council in the capital where petitions were heard, constantly checked his governors' conducts and gave summary punishment to violators of law, and periodically promulgated rescripts of justice for the Ottoman lands. Another legal recourse the subjects had to the sultan's justice was during Friday prayers (İpşirli 1991: 462–66), when the populace either put their petitions on a stick and extended them to the sultan, or, if they could not reach the sultan, tied a burning piece of straw to a stick to let the sultan know they had a "burning" request, or they turned their complaints into the sultan's officials who visited all the mosques on Fridays to collect such petitions.[37] In the nineteenth century, the sultan also took trips into the provinces to oversee the administration of justice (Özcan 1991: 361–62).

The boundaries of the sultan's authority in administering justice were set by Islamic religious law and the traditional ordinances and practices of the previous sultans. The latter gave the sultans "the discretionary right to inflict capital punishment on offenders liable, according to Islamic law, to lighter penalties" (Heyd 1967: 13). Yet even then the punishment could only be inflicted "as an administrative measure, for the sake of the order of the country, to protect the people, or to give a warning example to others." In instances where neither set of laws set a precedent, legal case registers were studied to form a decision within the legal boundaries. The alleged arbitrariness of Ottoman rule, so often claimed by Western sources, was thus a false construct;[38] it did not correspond to historical reality (İnalcık 1965: 49–53; 1973; 65, 70; 1985: 2–3). Islamic law often provided parameters within which one could both enforce and, at the same time, challenge the sultan's legitimacy. It was in this context that religious scholars and their interpretations attained social significance in the empire.

The Ottoman administration was organized around three separate departments: the political-military, the judiciary, and the financial. The sultan's officials[39] had the delegated executive authority of the ruler, and religious dignitaries oversaw the administration of law, including the supervision of all legal and financial matters. The vezirs, governors, and military commanders preserved state authority and maintained the internal and external security in each administrative unit. The military judges upheld and practiced judicial authority. The treasurers had financial authority.[40] Along with a representative of the chancery keeping records, these departments represented the royal authority in the imperial council; they had direct personal access to the sultan and were responsible only to him. The heads of these departments comprised the top-level Ottoman administrators. These people, after attending the imperial council, held councils in their own residences to discuss their own office business. The office–residence distinction was not yet present: all state affairs were conducted within the sultan's palace and executed in the residences of the top-level administrators. Formal institutions had not crystallized; these administrative households embodied the functions of numerous institutions within them.

The grand vezir was the sultan's representative and absolute deputy in civil administration. All administrative officials had to report to him, with the exception of the commander of the Janissary soldiers and the highest religious official—these two had direct access to the sultan (İnalcık 1973: 99–100). The power of the grand vezir increased through the centuries as the Ottoman state expanded, and the vezir's household members expanded their power bases with him. The origin of the Ottoman bureaucracy was embedded in the grand vezir's household: his was the first office-household to pattern itself after the sultan's household. This was soon followed with the establishment of similar households by lower-level administrators. The chief secretary of the imperial council, the secretary receiving complaints and lawsuits at the imperial council, and his agent in political and military affairs formed their own households and trained their own secretaries through the apprenticeship system. All these administrators within the central government were theoretically included in the sultan's household. Yet they had started acquiring separate households of their own by the late seventeenth century. Outside the central administration, the commissionerships such as the mint, customs, or cereals, the military organizations such as the Janisssary corps, gun foundry, or arsenal, and the provincial governments and fortresses all had their own secretarial staff (İnalcık 1973: 101). The provincial government replicated the center in its structure: the governor had the sultan's executive authority, the judge his legal authority, and the treasurer looked after the interest of the sultan's treasury.

Agency of the Ottoman Social Groups

Ottoman social groups were structured around the delegation of the sultan's authority. The sultan and his administrators formed one social group (the rulers), and the rest of society formed the other (the subjects). The rulers were all those who were directly in the sultan's service, all military groups not engaged in production, the men of religion and bureaucrats, and their families, relatives, dependents, and slaves.[41] The subjects—all those who had no part in government—were subdivided along the lines of religion and settlement into Muslim and non-Muslim, townspeople and peasants, and sedentaries and nomads. Each subdivision had different tax obligations. The sultan carefully maintained these social divisions; the peace and prosperity of the state depended on keeping the members of each group in their own place. Among these social groups, the social composition of the Ottoman officials, artisans, merchants, and minorities needs to be illustrated in more detail since it was their agency that structured eighteenth- and nineteenth-century Ottoman social change.

Ottoman Officials

Ottoman military and administrative officials became a significant social force in Ottoman history when they started patterning their households after that of the sultan's. In this book, the households of the officials are called "office-households" to distinguish them both from the sultan's and from the urban or rural nuclear household of the Ottoman subject. Three types of members thus coexisted in an office-household (Ergin 1939: 52–53): the official's immediate family within the private quarters; his retinue, including all individuals working on his land and properties scattered throughout the empire; and his officials conducting state business in the public quarters.[42] All three combined often exceeded fifteen hundred members. The term "office-household" captures the duality of the official and the domestic within the Ottoman households. These households managed, within the same unit, both domestic matters and the administrative affairs of the empire— the same household members often participating in both affairs. There were no separate public buildings for the offices. Official business was conducted out of the private residences of the administrators.

The office-households challenged the sultan's household by imitating his palace training and by thus producing household members who could and did compete with the sultan's household members for public office. Starting at age twelve, sons of officials and household members would be privately taught to read and write in their residence. They would then attend the courses offered on religious sciences in mosques. Their training for offices would culminate in the official quarters of their residences; they would learn bureaucratic correspondence, bookkeeping, and other administrative skills (Naima [1863] 1969, V: 2379). These men would be a part of the household and, through living and interacting within the domestic residence, increase the expertise and knowledge of the household members. They would train these members for office. In addition to this training, those interested would also be taught Arabic and Persian by instructors who would come to their residence. Nomads, peasants, and artisans who were not affiliated with households, or those social groups such as the Janissaries who eventually lost their affiliations with the sultan's household, could not adequately survive into the nineteenth century as a social group capable of change.

The new Ottoman bureaucracy of the late eighteenth and early nineteenth centuries formed from within this group as a consequence of education and training both within the office-households and without in the recently established Western-style schools. This new bureaucracy also contained the elements of a social group of Ottoman intellectuals who, through the Western-style development of newspapers and printing, acquired resources outside the sultan's control. This group was separate from the pre–eighteenth-century group of Ottoman religious scholars who based their source of knowledge on Islamic texts and monitored and manned the legal and educational systems of the empire.

Religious Dignitaries

What was the difference between the households of the military and administrative officials and religious dignitaries,[43] who were the interpreters and executors of Islamic religious law and education? The Ottoman training centers for studying the Qur'an and learning to read and write, which were founded and maintained by religious endowments, continued into a two-tiered college system for those who wanted to specialize. The graduates of these institutions, who were recruited into the position of religious dignitaries, had a dual role as interpreters and executors of Islamic law. From its inception, there was a clear attempt to differentiate this office and the authority of Islamic religious law "from the taint that became associated with dignitaries in state service" (Repp 1986: 123). The dual hold of this independent group on Ottoman society through law and education was strengthened through their establishment and administration of religious endowments and their exemption from the sultan's confiscation. Yet the households of officials and religious dignitaries started to lose their distinctiveness especially in the nineteenth century, after the abolition of the Janissaries, the emergence of Western-style courts and schools, and the withdrawal of revenues from religious foundations, the control of which had given the religious institution its autonomy. These developments undermined the social strength of the religious dignitaries and slowly brought them under state control.[44]

The beginning of the eighteenth century, before the advent of Western-style schools and courts, certainly indicates the presence of a strong religious dignitary group overseeing the dispensation of justice, the regulation of education, and the administration of religious endowments. The sultan did not control the religious organization as directly as he did the military one. In addition, the religious organization was able to develop independent resources through its association with religious endowments. This religious organization reached its fully elaborated form in the eighteenth century as one more category was added to the administrative hierarchy, both the judgeships *(mevleviyet)* and the schools *(medrese)*. Although this development created more offices for the religious dignitaries, it nevertheless brought them more under state control as appointments to these offices became politicized (Repp 1977: 278, 286; 1986: 28).

Ottoman Artisans

Within the category of producers, artisans were subject to a code of regulations because of the state's concern with the volume of goods in the internal market so that the people and artisans in the cities would not suffer a shortage of necessities and raw material. Urban production and distribution in the Ottoman empire was therefore organized through a very well-articulated guild system.[45] Guild members included apprentices, journeymen, masters, veterans of the guild, officers, guild council, and guild head (Baer 1970b: 177–90). The sultan's control over the system consisted of confirming the guild regulations, fixing fair prices in markets, controlling weights and quality, regulating purchase and sale, and preventing possible profiteering. The guild was internally administered by an elected guild council, which ensured quality, enforced price regulation on manufactured goods, gave examinations for promotions from apprentice to journeyman to master, issued licenses,[46] investigated and settled disputes and malpractice in the guild, represented the guild in its dealings with the government, and, most importantly, prevented competition and under hand practices in the employment of workmen and purchase of stocks (İnalcık 1970: 216–17; 1973: 54, 57; 152–53; Baer 1970a; 1980).

Although information on the social composition of guilds is limited, religion does not seem to have been a major stratifying factor[47] until 1768, when guild membership started to distinctively separate into Muslim and non-Muslim organizations (Baer 1970b: 193–94; R. Lewis 1971: 148). In the eighteenth century, guilds lost their exclusivity as the strict state control over production and the number of artisans lost all connection with craft or craftsmanship. Guild membership simply became a matter of legal ownership. Increased demand for goods fostered competition over these ownerships: they became commodified. In addition, masters who worked outside guilds to meet growing demand for goods at popular prices destroyed the guild boundaries (İnalcık 1970: 153, 217). The guilds of Constantinople were officially abolished in 1910, and the abolition of those in other towns of the empire followed in 1912 (Baer 1970a: 25).

Ottoman Merchants

The sultan controlled all the methods of production and profit margins in reproduction, with the exception of the merchants. The merchants comprised the only group whose fortunes matched those of the top-level Ottoman administrators. Since urban property and activities[48] were outside the sultan's control,[49] Ottoman merchants were able to form vast fortunes. Such merchants were subdivided into the traveling merchants engaged in trade by overland caravan or by sea, and residing merchants running affairs from a center, where they lived (İnalcık 1973: 161–62; 1969: 100–3). Cotton, Mediterranean foodstuffs, wool, and silk were their main items of trade.[50] Merchants used the wealth they accumulated to organize the despatch of caravans and ships, to station their commercial agents abroad, to form joint trade ventures with Ottoman administrators, to make investments in producing areas, to collect products for distribution elsewhere, and to lend money to people. They also engaged in tax-farming for the state.[51] Yet the social status of Ottoman merchants was significantly lower than that of the administrators, who had the sultan's delegated authority for two reasons. First, the Islamic religious attitude toward making large fortunes through usury was negative. Second, compared to the skilled labor of the artisans, the merchants' profits from charging interest were regarded as unearned gain, profiteering. The shortage of precious metals within the empire also fostered disdain toward all those who accumulated and maintained cash fortunes.

The social composition of merchants was not distinct with respect to religion during the classical age, when Muslim merchants were as prominent as non-Muslim ones. The dominance of Ottoman merchants as a single social group persisted until the effects of the trade capitulations[52] granted to the European countries privileged Western and minority merchants at the expense of Muslim ones.[53] It was only after the eighteenth century that Ottoman merchants became a distinct subgroup that was more and more exclusively comprised of the non-Muslim minorities of the empire. This was due to the ability of the minority merchants to enter Western trade protection to the detriment of the Muslim merchants.

Ottoman Minorities

Ottoman religious minorities[54] mainly comprised the Greeks, Armenians, and Jews, and Arab Christians[55] in the provinces. Even though the separation between Islamic and non-Islamic was the social basis of Ottoman stratification, this became a religio-ethnic separation as the cultural elements identifying these minority groups combined with religious ones. The sumptuary and legal codes and codes on the use of space carefully defined and reflected this basic separation. Minorities had to obey restrictions in the way they dressed and interacted in society. These restrictions prevented them from developing social ties with Muslims through marriage, inheritance, or attending the same places of worship and bathhouses. Instead, they developed social ties with other non-Muslims, who were either members of other Ottoman minorities or foreign residents of the empire, who were often connected to European embassies. It was this religious divide in Ottoman society that was going to be a significant factor in the gradual fragmentation of the empire.

Knowledge of the social practices that shaped Ottoman minority communities is still fragmentary. Ottoman minorities enjoyed protected legal status as an ethnic-religious community. Each was granted some internal autonomy and had to pay for special protection and military exemption in return. This internal autonomy often comprised the right to designate communal administrators to oversee communal property, to adjudicate conflict within the community, and to represent the community to the Ottoman state at large. The legal adjudication of disputes was often perceived as the most significant right and responsibility of the community.

Specific studies analyzing the social position of Ottoman minorities within the society at large are mostly based on analyses of imperial decrees and law codes (Ercan 1983), land surveys and population registers (Özkaya 1985), poll tax registers (Bağış 1983), statistical surveys (Eryılmaz 1990), and, later, constitutional law (Bozkurt 1989). Some others concentrate on the interaction of non-Muslim minorities with foreign merchants (Mantran 1982; Davison 1982), or with Muslims (Findley 1982). Among these sources, imperial decrees and religious opinions concerning minorities, which usually outline the restrictions placed upon them, have often been taken as indicators of their communal behavior. This scholarship and the sources it utilizes produce the following portrait. Imperial decrees[56] throughout the eighteenth century (Refik 1930: 30–31, 83–84, 88–89) state, for instance, that "Christians and Jews should have lower buildings than Muslims," or "Christians should not reside in the vicinity of mosques," but, if they do indeed have property near mosques, "it should be purchased from them at fair value." The religious opinions of the distinguished scholars of their times cover a wider spectrum of possible social practice. Ebussuud Efendi (Düzdağ 1993: 99), for instance, gives opinions on questions such as, "if Zeyd the Jew goes from Istanbul-proper to Galata to conduct business and if Amr the Christian, claiming (Zeyd the Jew) needs to settle a transaction, takes him to the Islamic court of Galata, would Zeyd the Jew have the right to state that he wants the case heard instead by the Islamic court in the neighborhood of Galata-proper." His answer is affirmative.

These decrees also highlight the significance of dress as a social marker, possibly differentiating Ottoman minorities from the rest of society and also from each other. The imperial decree of 1568 (Ercan 1983: 1140–2) carefully spells out,[57] for instance, that minority males have to wear dustcoats of gray broadcloth, with a sash around the belt, the total value of which could not exceed 30–40 aspers, made out only from a specific mixture of silk and cotton, a short headgear only made from the Denizli muslin, and flat-topped black footwear[58] with no inner lining. Similar restrictions were stated for minority women as well.[59] These possible spatial and physical boundaries extend to social ones as decrees employ Islamic law to specify that (Barkan 1940: 327) minority men could not marry Muslim women, inherit from them, or leave them property in their wills. Muslim men could, however, marry non-Muslim women.[60]

It is difficult to assess the extent to which these legal restrictions were enforced. There was probably an increasing degree of Muslim tolerance as one proceeded from legal to social regulations. The few existing historical instances convey a mixed picture. There are only occasional references, such as the 1696 correspondence that mentions a Jewish physician Moses, who cured Muslim patients, being harassed by some people for wearing a sable cap and riding a horse within the city. The sultan ordered these people to stop bothering him (Refik 1930: 29–21). Yet it is not possible to assess the frequency of such cases of harassment. Nevertheless, such restrictions, whether present in theory or in practice, delineated the boundaries of minorities as a separate social group and inhibited their interaction with the Muslim population.

Minorities could escape these restrictions through one channel: conversion. Ottoman religious minorities sometimes converted to Islam either to enjoy the social rights of the Muslims or sometimes to marry a Muslim. Upon such conversions, top-level Ottoman office-households ceremonially bestowed a total Muslim outfit on these former minorities. The new outfit symbolized the cessation of restrictions. Eighteenth-century expense registers of office-households document such bestowals. In 1708, for example, a "new Muslim" woman was given a complete Muslim wardrobe: two dustcoats, a caftan, a robe, slippers, underwear, and head cover, totaling 57 piasters; the amount was paid by the household (MM2488/173). In 1745, the expense register of the grand vezir contained entries on the clothing given to a "new-Muslim" Armenian woman (costing a total of 1,455 aspers), to a "new-Muslim" Jewish man (525 aspers), and to a "new-Muslim" Greek (MM3699). Once again, it is difficult to assess the scope of these conversions to Islam.

Other Ottoman Groups

The other groups in the empire, which did not form a significant force in eighteenth- and nineteenth-century Ottoman social change, consisted of the peasants, nomads, and slaves. Within the category of producers, peasants were subject to a code of regulations due to the state's concern with the volume of goods in the internal market so that the urban populace would not suffer a shortage of necessities and raw material. Since agricultural land belonged to the sultan,[61] the peasant working it had the status of a hereditary tenant with a usufructuary right in return for labor.

Nomads existed mostly in Eastern Anatolia well into the eighteenth century, and the Ottoman state policy of settlement of the nomads continued throughout the empire's history. Although nomads formed a volatile force in the earlier centuries of the empire, they were also significant as vanguards of Ottoman colonization of newly conquered lands. For example, in the fourteenth and fifteenth centuries, the Ottomans repopulated the newly conquered Balkans through the resettlement of Eastern nomadic tribes.

Slaves mostly comprised two categories, those engaged in agricultural production and those placed in households in various capacities (Toledano 1993). Although slave trade was permitted in the empire until the nineteenth century, it was considered an honorable and pious deed to free one's slaves after one's death (Barkan 1940: 397). The children by slaves retained slave status unless recognized by the household head.

Apparent Boundaries of Ottoman Westernization

The historically agreed upon parameters of Ottoman Westernization must be established first in order to problematize[62] the concept in the succeeding chapters. The apparent boundaries of Ottoman Westernization encompassed the consumption of Western goods and the adoption of Western forms in art and architecture. These goods and forms diffused into Ottoman society through the mediation of Ottoman social groups; they then became a part of the social tradition[63] as Ottoman art, architecture and material culture reproduced them within the empire.

Western Goods

Western goods were the first component of the newly emerging West to penetrate eighteenth-century Ottoman society. In the previous centuries, such goods had only been one among a multiplicity of Ottoman status objects of foreign origin.[64] In the fourteenth and fifteenth centuries, for example, Italian states imitated Ottoman design in their silk manufacturing and tile designs; looms in Venice produced cloth specifically for the Ottoman palace and officials. Europeans also brought clocks, musical instruments, porcelain, and delicate fabrics to the Ottoman court as gifts (Renda 1983: 10–12). Yet the consumption of these goods remained very limited in scope; it was mostly Eastern items, particularly those from China (wares) and India (cloth), that were defined as luxurious. In the eighteenth century, owning Western goods and using Western forms acquired a significance of their own that surpassed the value of other status items.

Goods make and maintain social relationships and fix public meanings; social consumption continually redefines all social categories and constantly produces and reproduces society.[65] By offering, accepting, refusing, or being offered goods, social groups utilize consumption to reinforce or undermine existing social boundaries in their societies. The goods assembled together in ownership make physical, visible statements about the hierarchy of values to which their consumer subscribes. Thus, goods that are neutral as objects become social in use; consumption attaches meaning to the goods. The sultan promulgated sumptuary laws to bring the Ottoman use of Western goods and forms under his personal control. Yet it was ultimately the Ottoman perception of material culture, not the sultan, that structured the apparent boundaries of this Westernization process.

The Ottoman perception of material culture[66] was embedded in the Islamic maxims, which saw goods[67] as a means to an end, as a means to support oneself and one's dependents without burdening others. It was not the social art of procuring goods or the number of goods so procured that the Qur'an objected to.[68] Rather, it was the use to which these goods were put, the interpretations attached to them, that the Qur'an often took issue with: the goods had to be used piously, with modesty, for the benefit of society. The pertinent verses in the Qur'an that support this interpretation are as follows. The Qur'an dictated the social parameters for the consumption of earthly goods as it warned believers "not to eat up their property among themselves in vanity" (Bakara II: 188; Al-i imran III: 29), "to lower their gaze and be modest" (Nur XXIV: 30), and "to walk upon the earth modestly" (Furkan XXV: 63). It was up to the believer to perform these duties to the best of his or her ability, "to keep his duty to Allah as best as he can and listen and obey and spend; that is better for his soul" (Tegabun LXIV: 16). Yet this modesty did not imply that the believers should not spend their wealth—they just had to be careful about the manner in which they spent it. The Qur'an advocated, "let him who has abundance spend of that which Allah has given him" (Talak LXV: 7). A shameful doom awaited those "who hoard their wealth and enjoin avarice on others, who spend their wealth in order to be seen of men" (Nisa IV: 37, 38). The proper way was "not to covet the thing in which Allah has made some of you excel others. Unto man a fortune from that which they have earned; envy not one another but ask Allah for His bounty" (Nisa IV: 32).

Even though the Qur'an recommended modesty in the use of goods to decrease the social potential of the goods in creating inequalities among Muslim believers, throughout Islamic history, the social practice of individuals and social groups did not adhere to this prescription.[69] Individuals and social groups have always employed goods to demarcate and enhance their social positions within their societies, and the Ottomans were no exception. The status symbols of an Ottoman official were superior quality cloth, fur coats, bejeweled items, furniture made from precious cloth, carpets, households goods made of gold or silver, valuable slaves, horses and their equipment, and precious arms (Tietze 1982: 578). Although the Ottoman legal opinion on cases involving the consumption of goods used the Qur'an to instigate modesty in consumption and thus ruled against the usage of silk robes or clothing with gold and silver threading (Düzdağ 1983: 186–87), competition among households fostered Ottoman luxury consumption,[70] including many Western goods.

The Ottomans followed the Qur'anic maxim mostly in defining what comprised luxury, which they defined as the display of the life style of a social group higher than one's own. Such a definition called for strictly specified consumption patterns for all social groups, where any deviation from such patterns was interpreted as luxury. The critical writings of one sixteenth-century Ottoman chronicler and official, Mustafa Ali, demonstrate the Ottoman concept of luxury consumption. One quotation in particular sums up the goods that the Ottomans considered luxurious:

> [V]elvet and brocade, gold-embroidered beauties like the gold brocade made in Istanbul, in particular, jackets of sable and lynx fur, belt set with jewels, gem-studded daggers and knives are not proper for anyone but for high notables and privileged personages. Especially Persian and Egyptian rugs and carpets, gold-laced and gold-embroidered sofa spreads, precious cushions and table mats, silver basins and candlesticks, gilded platters, silver censers, likewise golden and silver pen-and-ink case, gilded chiming clocks—to decorate [their dwellings] with these and their likes and to gain fame [in this manner], moreover [to dress] their servants, menials and dependents in princely garb and turbans that would befit the great and the descendants of the Prophet *[seyyid]*—especially if these are rogues from the Balkans or boors from Anatolia, and if what they wear from head to foot are sable and lynx fur coats covered with gold brocade—further choice, gracious [slave] girls, each one worth a thousand florins and slave boys, worth to die for, each one a second Joseph [in beauty], horses worth three or four hundred gold pieces, saddlecloths embroidered with needlework, gem-crusted girths and, certainly, gold-decorated horse harnesses, jeweled stirrups, shields dripping of sweet-smelling oil, six-edged battle-axes, precious swords—all these have to be the privilege of those glorious ones at the highest peak, the vezir and generals of wide fame. If men with lower status than these have the audacity to make use of them, sharp-tongued critics will lash them and will punish them severely by their abuse. (Mustafa Ali 1587; 139, in Tietze 1982: 579)

Officials thus diffused luxury goods into their households as they adorned their household members in them. This highly criticized practice eradicated the well-defined social boundaries within and among households. To procure some service or loyalty, these officials also started to bestow valuable goods as gifts on the ruled; hence the distinctions among the rulers and the ruled began to fade. The social practice of the officials rather than the sultan's laws started to determine the status of these household members and subjects, thus eroding, indirectly, the authority of the sultan.

The sultan introduced sumptuary laws curbing the consumption of foreign goods for two reasons, one financial and the other social. The vast Ottoman expenditure on foreign goods meant a loss of revenues to the treasury. For example, seventeenth-century chron-icler Naima [1863] 1969, IV: 293) stated that the import of "luxury goods" (he did not make a distinction between Western and Eastern goods) led to the flight of cash and goods from the empire to other states. Although such transactions generated customs duties, he argued, if those who brought luxury goods into the empire bought Ottoman goods, wealth was kept in the empire. The social reason for these sumptuary laws was to preserve the "natural order" of Ottoman society. The sultan thus subjected any visible act of consump-tion, be it clothing, food, or housing, to regulation. A 1788 decree (Cevdet 1872: 293), for example, prohibited the luxury consumption of the officials and those who tried to imitate them. The cited reason for the ban was that "such consumption had become a source of oppression." The sultan further stated that the prohibition would also decrease "the trade deficit which was the source of poverty among people." A similar 1792 imperial decree (MM10234/17) prohibited luxury items from being presented as gifts to the palace and from being exchanged among the officials. It suggested that cash exchanges ought to replace these gifts and exchange items, often comprising very valuable cloth, watches, and other similar luxury goods. Such a measure, it maintained, would "remove the recent innovations and squandering which disturbs the ancient order of the exalted state." These laws would stop the huge flow of money out of the empire in the purchase of these luxury items and also help the Ottoman sultan to regain control over the symbolic forms of exchange, which had evaded his scrutiny.

Other Ottoman sumptuary laws focused specifically on fashion[71] and its disruptive blurring of social stratification among Ottoman social groups. Two such laws were de-creed in 1729, for example. One forbade "some useless women who have seized the opportunity to lead the people astray about their social stations"[72] from continuing "to imitate infidel women." The other was addressed to Ottoman turban-makers, banning the practices of those "who have invented turbans which look, Allah forbid, like turbans of the Jews and have caused sin and evil consequences to many Muslims by mistake" from making such turbans (in Refik 1930: 86–88, 103–4). An imperial decree of 1784 (MM182/46) chastized those who dressed like the social groups they aspired to join; "some subjects in the Balkans have started to dress like soldiers and officials without holding any official posts; they should be notified that such an act is prohibited." Accord-ing to the sultan, the disturbing element in both these instances was the imitation by one social group of another. Ottoman women imitated foreign ones, men's turbans copied those of the Jews, and some subjects' clothing resembled those of the rulers. The Ottoman sultan was particularly wary of people crossing the social boundaries between the rulers and the ruled; he speedily tried to control any such attempts to blur social distinctions.

The Ottoman perception of Western goods changed during the eighteenth century as these Western goods became more desirable as luxury items. The latent antagonism of the earlier Ottoman perceptions of the West is recounted by one seventeenth-century chron-icler who stated, for example, how an Ottoman governor who wanted to kill a religious official was "lynched by the people and hanged in a Christian cemetery upside down"

(Naima [1863] 1969, V: 2340–1). In another instance, the artisans, oppressed by the market controller, "nailed a Westerner's hat on his door to allude to his inhumanity and cruelty" (V: 2174). In the eighteenth century, the use of Western goods, although still spurned, nevertheless started to spread. A late eighteenth-century source recounted, for instance, that "rich Ottoman officials, who used Western furniture such as chests, console-tables, lustres, chandeliers and tables in their houses" (d'Ohsson, in Yenişehirlioğlu 1983: 159), felt the necessity to hide these when the current Ottoman sultan turned against the Western way of living and ordered all Western furniture to be thrown away from the palace. The change in the sultan's attitude and the practice of the officials both lead one to observe that the consumption of Western goods had indeed become a significant social issue[73] in eighteenth-century Ottoman society.

During the nineteenth century, the flow of Western goods into Ottoman lands continued at an increasing rate.[74] With the advent of steamships during the same decade, Western goods reached Ottoman ports steadily to replace domestic products eventually. This perceived Ottoman interest in Western goods and the rate of replacement were not uniform, however. Nineteenth-century European travel accounts refer to variations in this Western material penetration as follows. The provinces along the Mediterranean and cities with access to ports experienced this Western influx more strongly: Syria imported leather and furniture (Julliany 1842: 282), Beirut imported Manchester cotton cloth (Farley 1859: 28). One account (White 1845; III: 216; II: 41, 118) stated that in 1844 the most prominent article in the bazaar in Constantinople was cheap imitation Western shawls, both cotton and woolen. These manufactures from the West were largely imported by the Greek and Armenian merchants, who themselves increasingly adopted Western customs. In Antioch, in 1850 (Langlois 1856: 275), the townspeople imported leather to make European foot-wear, glassware, and chairs; competitively priced Swiss and English prints displaced the clothes of Bursa, Aleppo, and Damascus (Rolland 1854: 312; Guys 1862: 250–3). Hence, in general, Western goods were much more readily available at the Ottoman urban centers and ports than inland; their inland spread took another century (Fowler 1854: 269; Dutem-ple 1883: 11; Enault 1855: 388).

Western Art and Architecture

Eighteenth-century Ottoman art also started to explore Western forms as miniature art incorporated the Western innovation of the third dimension, tried new uses of space after the Western mode, and altered its techniques to include new European techniques employing guache, watercolor, tempera (Renda 1977: 10–11, 77). The most significant aesthetic transformation was in the development of a new form of art after the Western mode, however. These were Ottoman wall paintings, mostly of scenery (not figures, as human representations were often scorned in Islamic art), exploring the use of perspective and scale.

Western baroque form diffused into Ottoman architecture during the same time. Yet the influence of baroque forms was not initially visible from the outside. For example, although the living quarters of Sultan Selim III (1789–1807) were internally decorated with fanciful rococo motifs, carved and gilded ceilings, and painted landscapes, the building itself appeared thoroughly traditional from the outside (Renda 1983: 18; Kuran 1977: 325). Yet, throughout the century, as the sultans' building activities increased, the external use of the baroque form expanded with it. As they constructed private residences in the city for their personal use, and as they bestowed funds to construct large complexes for the new Western-style military institutions, the sultans gradually diffused Western-style architecture throughout the capital as well. Western forms proliferated as the Ottoman officials imitated the sultan in building private residences for themselves. In these residences, as officials copied Western forms in the use of space, the first manifestation of a style called "alla franca," *alafranga,* in Ottoman, came about (Esin 1986: 74).

Western forms of the baroque penetrated the rest of Ottoman society as the sultan and his officials constructed public fountains within the city. Ottoman baroque architecture, reproducing itself from the Ottoman form and Western baroque, did not have an intricate space conception or a strong sense of movement because it emphasized outward presentation and decoration rather than inner use of space. Ottoman architecture was not a part of the historical development that led to the production of the baroque; its reproduction of Western baroque therefore simply borrowed the forms: Ottoman attempts in this architectural reproduction were "not to become Western but rather to resemble the West" (Kuran 1977: 327). This is a very significant distinction; indeed, Ottoman art and architecture interpreted the West in an Ottoman context. The Nuruosmaniye mosque, completed in Constantinople in 1755 (Kuran 1977: 309), demonstrates the extent of this aesthetic experimentation with Western forms. For the construction of this mosque, the sultan had pictures and models of the most famous religious buildings brought from Italy, England, and France, and he had a mosque plan drawn accordingly. Yet this plan was never applied because Ottoman religious scholars, upon seeing the plan, stated that the building looked more like a Christian temple than a mosque—they suggested that a more Islamic shape be adopted to prevent unrest among the populace. Another plan that united Western and Ottoman styles more to the liking of the religious scholars was drawn up. Buildings for the new Western-style military institutions did not suffer from such restraints of Ottoman traditional architecture, however. They could be and were built to strict Western standards. Military barracks and shops, houses for the resident officials, bathhouses, and printing houses around the barracks were all planned and constructed according to building plans brought from Europe. The Western-style military institution thus had an aesthetic reverberation in Ottoman society as it reconstructed and redefined space in Ottoman architecture (Denel 1982: 28).

Western aesthetic forms in the Ottoman capital were then reproduced in the provinces through the circulation of builders and artisans. The Ottoman practice of constructing large monumental mosques, bridges, and large forts was to bring skilled workers from the diverse parts of the empire to the site in question. The mosque of Nuruosmaniye, for example, was built by workers brought from Asia Minor and Aegean islands such as Rhodes, Chios, and Mytilene (Göyünç 1983: 328, 333). The process worked in reverse as well; the sultan sometimes sent laborers and journeymen from Constantinople to the provinces to undertake similar constructions there. For example, workers from Constantinople were sent to help restore the Dome of the Rock in 1720–21 (MM7829/12-22) and to construct the fort of Azov on the Black Sea against the Russians. The groups of artists who worked outside the palace adhered to a strict system of apprenticeship, and these also toured the provinces at times. Indeed, there were some itinerant builders and craftsmen who took commissions throughout the empire (Renda 1977: 189; 1983: 18). Through them, Western forms spread from the capital to the provinces.

How much Western form did these constructions in the provinces employ? A brief survey of eighteenth-century Ottoman architecture in Asia Minor reveals substantial penetration of Western aesthetic forms (Arık 1976). For example, the provincial mosques, all built by local notables, reproduced baroque forms in the wall paintings, inscriptions, and decorations; the private residences of these notables also replicated Western forms. Scenes from Constantinople were most popular in wall decorations; the image of the capital was frequently reproduced in the provinces.[75] By the nineteenth century, the Western style had become dominant in Ottoman art and architecture in both form and internal design. The art of painting underwent an additional transformation: following the new fashion in the West, wall paintings of the eighteenth century gave way to oil paintings on the ceilings and walls of Ottoman officials' nineteenth-century residences (Renda 1983: 20–21).

Through their activities, nineteenth-century Ottoman sultans helped reproduce and maintain the Ottoman interest in Western style. Sultan Mahmud II (1808–39) patronized painting; he had his portraits hung in the official buildings that were being built during his reign.[76] Another Ottoman sultan, Abdülaziz I (1861–76), visited the three cultural centers of nineteenth-century Europe: Paris, London, and Vienna. He went to museums and attended concerts and opera performances in these Western cities. Upon his return in 1871, Abdülaziz had his equestrian statue made. Hence, throughout the nineteenth century, Ottoman sultans commissioned massive Western-looking palaces, employed European and minority architects and artists to build and decorate them, and furnished those palaces with imported European furniture and art objects. The new public buildings, such as those housing Western-style schools and hospitals, and the new offices of the Ottoman ministries were also built in the Western style. Western styles of clothing and forms of etiquette were gradually adopted, first by the sultan and his officials, and then slowly by the rest of society.[77] By the end of the century, Western forms had so penetrated Ottoman society that the daughter of a nineteenth-century Ottoman official had "a French woman teach her French, a Hungarian girl dancing, while Jewess Mademoiselle Goldenbourg came for piano lessons, an American dressmaker made a dress from a gold crepe sent from England and a hairstylist arrived from the foreign quarters to arrange the hair of all the ladies" (Haidar 1944: 37, 44).

With such agents of Westernization, Western manners also started to filter into Ottoman society. Yet the net effect of these manners is hard to depict since the historical information is mostly negative, sketchy, and highly selective. The following account from an Ottoman newspaper in 1869 demonstrates the nature of these complaints:

> Most elite families have left the purity, honor, manners, and modesty of Islam. [The women] almost abandoned their dustcoats *[ferace]* and veils *[yaşmak]*; women's petticoat *[fistan]* have replaced the loose robe *[entari]*. It has become good breeding for women to peddle refinement with a few French words such as "bonjour, monsieur, merci," and to dance arm in arm with Europeans[78] in [the foreign quarter of] Beyoğlu, skimpily dressed. It has become gracious for women to engage in all kinds of such disgraceful behavior. . . . And these "alla franga" manners have infected the entire society, from individuals to their families and household members. [This new state of affairs] has driven many decent and honorable families to disarray. (in Sungu 1940: 815)

This kind of anger, often connected to any process of social change, nevertheless reveals the internal frictions that start appearing in Ottoman society over Western practices.

As Western forms penetrated Constantinople and reproduced themselves throughout the capital and the provinces, Western diffusion was transformed into Western influence. Foreign residents, minorities, and Ottoman embassies introduced the use of Western goods; the sultan and his household reproduced them through their consumption. Similarly, Western art and architectural forms were first adopted in the capital to then gradually spread to the rest of the empire. This depiction of Ottoman Westernization in "visible" forms acquires meaning only when it is interpreted by Ottoman social groups. The narrative of Westernization acquires analytical power only when it is situated in relation to the Ottoman social structure and the agency of Ottoman social groups.

2

War, Ottoman Officials, and Western Institutions

In 1872, an Ottoman intellectual and writer, Namık Kemal, made the following comment on the social transformations the empire was undergoing:

> If, ten years ago, at a time when the state, having decided to publish a military journal, could not find among the officers more than two or three ex-clerks [competent enough to do the job], an angel had descended from Heaven and announced that within ten years, officers of the age of 20 and 22, even our own pupils, were to become the heads of the nation . . . who could have believed it? (Mardin 1962: 216)

Indeed, a new Ottoman social group of military officers, physicians, and civil servants educated in the newly founded Western-style schools transformed the empire and themselves. This new social group did indeed lead the empire, but not in accordance with the terms dictated by the sultan and the households. Instead, as the social group produced, segmented, and reproduced itself within Ottoman society on its own terms into the "bureaucratic"[1] bourgeoisie, it determined the future trajectory of social change. And these terms stipulated the demise of empire.

The major eighteenth- and nineteenth-century Ottoman social transformation was the emergence of the Ottoman bureaucratic and commercial bourgeoisie. The main distinguishing trait of this bourgeoisie was its ability, for the first time, to wrest resources away from the sultan's control. The effect of war and trade on the Ottoman social structure, the agency of Ottoman officials and merchants, and the medium of Western institutions and goods adopted by Ottoman society interacted to separate the bourgeoisie into its bureaucratic and commercial components. Two types of resources had been wrested from the sultan's control in the eighteenth and nineteenth centuries: the social resources acquired through Western-style education, and the economic resources attained through commerce with the West. The bureaucratic bourgeoisie drew its strength from the knowledge and expertise taught at Western-style schools and was then able to reproduce this inalienable social resource outside the sultan's control into an alternate source of power. Similarly, the commercial bourgeoisie materialized as Ottoman minority merchants engaged in trade with the West entered the legal protection of major Western powers, thereby avoiding the sultan's control over their economic resources. Even though these two groups could have potentially joined to form the Ottoman bourgeoisie, they remained segmented because of their separate social locations within the Ottoman social structure along ethnic and religious lines. The segmentation had further polarized by the late nineteenth century; almost autonomously, and certainly at the expense of the sultan and his empire, Ottoman Muslims developed primarily into the bureaucratic bourgeoisie and Ottoman minorities predominantly into the commercial bourgeoisie.

The eighteenth- and nineteenth-century Ottoman wars were marked by frequent military defeats and escalating financial problems in provisioning wars. The empire often had to fight on both fronts, east and west, and most frequently with the new power trained in Western-style warfare, the Russian empire. Three consequences ensued from this social pattern to alter the Ottoman social structure. First, as the sultan needed immediate funds to provision these military campaigns, he had to delegate more administrative power to his office and provincial households and had to grant more land tenure rights and private property status to promptly acquire cash revenues. Second, by personally financing many of the Western-style reforms to win on the battlefield, the sultan drained both his own resources and also those of his household and the empire. The large loans he then acquired from European banks led, within a few decades, to the financial bankruptcy of the empire. Third, wars often polarized relations between Ottoman Muslims and non-Muslims as the latter grew and gained power at the expense of the former. The effect of these wars and the concomitant changes in the Ottoman social structure thus varied across Ottoman social groups. Even though office-households and provincial households rapidly accumulated economic resources at the expense of the sultan, they ultimately were not able to wrest these away from his control. Through various measures, such as levies, confiscations, and military obligations, the sultan was eventually able to consolidate these resources.

The most significant measure the sultan resorted to against the challenge of the official and provincial households was his introduction of Western-style schools to generate a new social group that would be loyal to him in his struggle. This new social group would not be dependent on the households and would thereby be able to undermine their power networks. Yet, contrary to the sultan's expectations based on the successful fifteenth-century experience with the Janissaries, this new social group did not develop an allegiance to the sultan. The systematic Western-style education they acquired as a group fostered social networks and allegiances with one another. Also, embedded in the Western scientific knowledge and expertise they acquired through education was the Enlightenment social vision of a just and equal society and state. This group therefore developed allegiance not to the sultan but instead to the abstract notion of an Ottoman state. Empirical analysis of the establishment pattern of Western-style schools in eighteenth- and nineteenth-century Ottoman society demonstrates the wide range of the impact of these institutions. When the students educated in these schools in increasing numbers could not find around them the state and society they envisioned, they started to form secret organizations to reform the empire. Through these organizations and with their continuous political opposition to the sultan, the students acquired a consciousness of their boundaries within the empire and developed into military officers, physicians, and civil servants all intent on reforming the empire. The seeds of the Ottoman bureaucratic bourgeoisie, aimed at reforming Ottoman society and the state, were thus formed.

Effects of Wars on Ottoman Society

The primary reason behind the frequent Ottoman military losses in wars was the development of the professional army in Europe during the eighteenth and nineteenth centuries (Parry 1975: 218–56; Yapp 1975: 330–43, Anderson 1979: 29). Specifically, the size of the armies grew considerably[2] during the eighteenth and nineteenth centuries, and equipment and tactics underwent significant changes as the infantry, for instance, switched from fighting in a phalanx to the line system, which also necessitated constant drilling and discipline, a transformation perfected by Maurice de Saxe. The disciplined infantry reached its epitome with the automata of Frederick the Great, whereby the army maintained parade ground discipline on the battlefield. The introduction of mobile field artillery by Gustavus Adolphus and of horse-drawn field artillery by Frederick the Great and the standardization of guns all changed the pace and intensity with which wars were fought. The new technological innovations in warfare necessitated a small, long-service force trained constantly in barracks; the mercenary soldiers of pre–eighteenth-century Europe were gradually replaced by universal and compulsory conscription, for instance, in France in 1793 and Prussia in 1813.

The increased size of the army, complex tactics, and sophisticated artillery, and other technological developments also necessitated a well-trained officer corps. Officer schools throughout Europe, such as at Saint Cyr, Ecole Polytechnique, and Potsdam, expanded to provide training specifically in the scientific study of warfare. This training also enabled the perfection of unitary vertical command, an innovation introduced by Wallenstein. The enormous increase in firepower in the mid-nineteenth century made this scientific training even more crucial; as the breech-loading, magazine rifle replaced the musket and the machine gun made its debut in 1870, open-order attacks and constant training became essential. Officers trained in these schools also learned to make use of new technological developments such as the telegraph, telephone, and railway in planning and executing the mobilization of troops, maintaining their food and other supplies, and designing warfare strategies and tactics and rapidly deploying troops once the war was over. The nature of the relationship between warfare and peace, between the army and the rest of society, became more complex and involved.

War, warfare, and the necessary training they entailed penetrated and altered societal structures more and more. European kings started to drill their armies continuously, and, as war remained the only art expected from kings, they invested all their resources to shape and prepare the entire social structure for the battlefield: the treasury to regularly pay military salaries; the ministry to regulate the affairs of war; retirement funds for old soldiers, who now devoted their lifetime to fighting; veteran's hospitals and barracks. Manufacturing plants established for the soldiers' clothing and for ammunition created a new public space and a new social location for the army within the Western European system at large. As a consequence of these transformations, the amount of expenditure per soldier increased twofold in Europe in the period 1874–94.[3] Western-style warfare thus necessitated large cash revenues.

The Ottoman empire rapidly started to encounter these professional armies in the late seventeenth century,[4] and their encounter persisted throughout the eighteenth[5] and nineteenth[6] centuries. Even though the size of the Ottoman army and its equipment were not significantly different from that of the European armies, the Ottoman lack of discipline and the constant training that had led to societal transformations in Europe led to frequent Ottoman defeats.[7] During a period spanning 206 years (1703–1909), the Ottoman army fought a total of sixteen wars, most with adverse outcomes. The Ottoman wars with Iran were also debilitating as they were often very long and usually ended without a clear conquest. The mountainous parts of Iran often provided a natural refuge to the Iranian rulers and a natural barrier to the advancing Ottoman forces. The continuous employment of the Ottoman army in these wars also affected internal security, as many revolts[8] occurred throughout the Ottoman provinces.

These Ottoman wars were unlike those in earlier centuries in that they did not bring military and material success or geographical expansion. They also marked significant symbolic and territorial loss to the Ottoman empire (Lewis 1982: 51); specifically, the 1768 war with Russia that ended with the treaty of Küçük Kaynarca in 1774 gave significant territorial, political, and commercial advantages to Russia. The 1783 Russian annexation of the Crimea marked the first loss of Ottoman territory with a Muslim majority population and was followed by a similar incursion against Ottoman lands in 1798, when Bonaparte occupied Egypt, which had been an Ottoman province since the sixteenth century. The 1854 Crimean war fought against Russia with the help of France and Britain also demonstrated to the Ottomans firsthand the pivotal tactical edge the deployment of new Western warfare tactics provided.

Internally, the eighteenth- and nineteenth-century wars drained the resources of the empire, and the subsequent fiscal crises caused transformations in the Ottoman military, fiscal, and land tenure systems. As the contemporary state of military warfare outdated the Ottoman mounted cavalry provided by the military fiefs, these cavalry had to be replaced by drilled infantry, which required salary payments in cash. The military fiefs, however, entailed payments in kind, whereas the sultan needed urgent cash revenues for his campaigns. Since tax-farms rather than fiefs could provide the cash revenues needed to pay the salaries of these new military units, the sultan accelerated the replacement of military fiefs with tax-farming and freeholds, where payment was made in cash.

The pattern by which the effects of war reverberated throughout the Ottoman social structure can be observed within the context of the Ottoman financial system. The two fundamental assumptions of this system were that wars would always be won and that war expenses would not be financed in cash. These assumptions had structured the Ottoman fief organization, whereby posts were distributed in return for loyalty and allegiance and fief-holders made their payments in kind. In addition, the fief organization, the sultan's treasury, and Ottoman finances[9]—and hence the military, agricultural, political, economic practices of the empire—were all interlinked within the structure of the sultan's household. When the Ottoman wars changed from being a source of income to a source of expense, the Ottoman financial system started going through a series of crises, and, because of these linkages, the effect of the crisis escalated and affected the whole Ottoman structure.

By the late eighteenth century, the Ottoman sultans were meeting with frequent difficulties in the payment of the military salaries; one sultan in particular, Selim III, noted time and again that he "would gladly send his own revenues if there were any money in the treasury. He spent many sleepless days and nights thinking of what to do" (in Özkaya 1985: 248). The effect of these wars on the Ottoman economy became more severe throughout the late eighteenth and nineteenth centuries (Genç 1984: 53–61). During the first half of the eighteenth century, the Ottoman economy was in a state of expansion: artisans throughout the empire in Constantinople, Damascus, Ankara, Bursa, Tokat, Salonica, and Adrianople were active, cotton cloth production and printed cotton manufactories grew, and goods were manufactured for foreign markets. The Ottoman state itself bolstered this investment in the Ottoman economy by founding three large printed cotton manufactories in Tokat, Crete, and Chios. The second half of the eighteenth century demonstrated an immediate drop in all economic production, however. Revenues from textile production to cotton prints to soap production decreased 25–60 percent. The agricultural sector suffered a similar fate. By the nineteenth century, the Ottoman state, in order to meet domestic needs, had to set more and more export restrictions on cereals, leather, wool, silk, olive oil, soap, manufactured leather, silk, and cotton cloth. Since the goods and services demanded by the sultan for war often coincided with those demanded by merchants for trade, with each soldier, consumption increased at the expense of production. As goods and services thus became scarce, prices rapidly escalated and inflation ensued. During war periods, the decline in the maintenance of security within the empire also affected trade routes and markets negatively. In addition, Ottoman land losses in the wars contributed to the decline in agricultural production and commerce. The sultan often increased taxation to recover his financial losses, yet, since the Ottoman taxation system was based on production, this practice made it more profitable for taxpayers to produce less to pay fewer taxes. Hence the quantity and quality of goods and services in the empire declined rapidly. This development led to the increased replacement of economic production with imports.[10]

There were many Ottoman attempts to recuperate the large financial losses suffered during these wars. The three traditional fiscal methods the Ottoman sultan resorted to were compulsory donation, confiscation, and currency debasement. In the eighteenth century, the Ottomans tried to apply these methods and added a few new ones to raise the necessary cash for the wars (Berkes 1964: 74; Genç 1984: 60; Tabakoğlu 1985: 261–99; Cezar 1986: 33, 135–36). When the Ottoman state administration needed funds, it usually requested loans from the sultan's treasury. If and when that proved insufficient, the administration, under the tutelage of the sultan, then initiated a system of internal debts, whereby rich Ottoman notables and officials were asked for cash revenues and then given shares in return for their cash loans to the state.[11] Usually, the administration sent requests for loans from rich individuals whose names were periodically collected to each administrative unit of the empire; they then allotted state poll tax revenues as collateral and explained that the loans would be paid after the war. This system of raising funds quickly depleted the sultan's treasury and made him financially dependent on his administration. Also, when the administration raised money through domestic loans, it emphasized that it was the state that needed the money, not the sultan, thus contributing to the escalating structural separation between the sultan and the Ottoman state. Another measure that replenished state revenues at the expense of fueling inflation was confiscation, mostly upon death, of the wealth of those wealthy individuals who usually had some financial transaction with the treasury. Debasement of the coinage constituted the other measure the state used to raise money; this practice was often accompanied by the mandatory collection of gold and silver goods from society in exchange for payment in debased coinage. All Ottoman subjects who owned goods in these valuable metals were required to sell them to the Ottoman mint. To set an example to the rest of society, the sultan and his palace household often led in this measure, donating, in addition to cash contributions, many gold and silver wares in their possession. Other extraordinary measures, such as the confiscation of the one-year equivalent of the pensions of retired religious scholars, orphans, and widows, were quickly discontinued when they met with the severe criticism of religious scholars.[12] The net effect of all these measures was the depletion of the resources of the sultan's household, which became increasingly cash-poor as the costly wars continued.

During the period 1783–87, before starting a new military campaign against Russia and Austria, Ottoman statesmen actually discussed, for the first time, whether they could afford such a war, given the difficulties the sultan encountered in paying soldier's salaries.

When domestic fiscal measures proved insufficient to meet the growing need for revenues, the Ottoman administration considered, for the first time in their history, the idea of cash loans from other states (Cezar 1986: 89–92, 137–38; Özkaya 1985: 248; Kuran 1968: 40). Initially considered as potential lenders were France, Spain, and the Dutch Republic, countries with which the Ottoman state had a history of relatively peaceful interaction. Yet some Ottoman statesmen opposed the idea of borrowing money from a Christian state and proposed that Muslim states such as Morocco, which would gladly contribute to this holy war against the Christians, should be approached first. Although a Moroccan ambassador arriving in Constantinople in 1783 promised such a loan, the Moroccan ruler stalled the Ottomans for years, and, in the end, the loan never materialized. When the Ottomans, assuming that it was in the interest of Ottoman protectorates such as Algeria and Tunisia to support such a holy war, requested help, all sent encouragement, apologies, and no money. In 1789, after all internal revenue sources and all other possibilities within the Muslim world were exhausted, as a final recourse, the Ottoman state decided to borrow money from the Dutch. Yet this loan also fell through when the Dutch, who had suggested that the Ottomans borrow from a wealthy merchant of theirs, could not find such a merchant. In 1799, the Ottoman sultan had to ask for a loan from England. The English promised the Ottomans one million sterling at 6 percent interest and asked the placement of Ottoman customs-duty revenues as collateral. Although an agreement was reached in principle, the loan did not materialize when the English minister argued that a budgetary difficulty in England had made the payment of such a loan impossible. It was more than fifty years after this request that the first Ottoman loan from a foreign state, followed by many internal loans, materialized, with disastrous consequences to the Ottoman empire.

It was again a war, in this case the 1854 Crimean war with the Russians, that provided the occasion for the first Ottoman foreign loan (Suvla 1940: 270–5). The French and the English, who allied themselves with the Ottomans, suggested that the Ottoman sultan could finance this long and costly war by borrowing money from European markets. Indeed, the sultan did indeed borrow, for the first time, 2.5 million gold coins *(Osmanlı altını)* from English banks at 6 percent interest and designated, as collateral, the taxes accruing from the province of Egypt. As the war continued,[13] the Ottomans rapidly needed another loan and a year later borrowed 5.65 million gold coins from the English banks at 4 percent interest, this time specifying the customs duties from Syria and Smyrna as collateral. In all, between 1854 and 1877 the Ottoman sultan made a total of nineteen loan requests—almost one request every year—and borrowed a total of 251,209,758 Ottoman gold coins. Of this amount, however, only 135,015,751 gold coins, that is, approximately 54 percent, made it to the Ottoman empire. The rest were retained by Western powers as interest on the loans. The sultan's designation of Ottoman revenue sources as collateral irretrievably transformed them into commodities and also delegitimated his claims to protect them. A new loan arrangement emerged in the context of another war, this time the 1877 war with the Russians. When the Ottoman sultan could not find credit in the European markets to finance this war, he borrowed 10 million gold coins from Ottoman minority bankers of Galata and from the Ottoman Bank in Constantinople founded by European and Ottoman minority financing. Ottoman minorities had always been involved in the sultan's financial transactions with the West; they had often cashed the receipts with which the sultan had paid Ottoman debts (Suvla 1940: 265). It was their participation in currency exchanges that had generated the large profits that they then started to lend directly to the Ottoman sultan. Yet the Ottoman sultan was soon unable to pay these vast foreign and domestic loans and the Ottoman state had to declare bankruptcy. In 1881, the Western powers, with the participation of the Ottoman minorities, established the Ottoman Public Debt Administration (Düyun-u Umumiye)[14] to collect, in return for outstanding loans, the revenue accruing from the main tax sources of the empire, such as customs duties and tobacco production. During the twenty-eight years between 1886 and 1914, the sultan continued to make a total of twenty six—almost yearly—loan demands, borrowing a total of 120,314,473 gold coins.[15] The symbolic and physical control of the sultan over the empire rapidly eroded as the Ottoman sultan kept parceling out revenue sources that had always been considered sacred and that had been entrusted to his protection by God. Western protection of Ottoman minorities and the disparate economic development among the Muslims and the minorities to the advantage of the latter also polarized the Ottoman populace (Maoz 1982: 95). For instance, in 1799, when Napoleonic troops invaded Palestine, Muslims in Damascus rioted against their Christian neighbors. Similarly, when a Greek revolt broke out in 1821, many parts of Syria and Palestine witnessed Muslim animosity toward Christians.

The Ottoman sultan made his first attempts to raise money by internal loans in the late eighteenth and early nineteenth centuries.[16] First, certain treasury issues *(esham),* variously described as bonds, assignats, and annuities on the proceeds of customs and other revenues, were issued to creditors with an annual income of 5 percent. Most of the proceeds accruing through this measure were spent in the 1768 war with Russia. Similar issues on provincial revenues were reported around 1783. The needs and opportunities of the Crimean war brought a new type of loan *(kaime),* which floated on the money markets of Europe and carried with it a high rate of interest. Even though substantial cash resources were raised through these internal and foreign loans, the continuous wars fought prevented their use for successful structural change.

In summary, the Ottoman wars in the eighteenth and nineteenth centuries depleted the revenues of the empire and caused transformations in its financial, military, and agricultural structures. It was particularly the technological change necessitated by new warfare, the need to switch to a technologically more complex army, that required large amounts of cash revenues for maintenance, especially of artillery, and engineers. As the Ottoman sultan sought out these cash revenues for military campaign financing, he ended up losing significant resources, both social and economic. Military provisioning depleted the Ottoman sultan's vast financial resources, and as the Ottoman need for cash revenues was phrased not in terms of the distress of the sultan but rather that of the Ottoman state, the public space within which the sultan and the state existed as one household unit started to break down. Escalating domestic and foreign loans did not prevent but actually accelerated the demise of empire. In the words of Ottoman statesman Ziya Pasha, "if from 1592 to 1839 the empire had advanced on the road to decline at the pace of a two-horse carriage, from 1839 to 1869 it had rushed with the speed of a railway train" (in Lewis 1979: 172).

Responses of Ottoman Social Groups to Wars

Given the sultan's increasing dependence on his household to finance the costly wars of the eighteenth and nineteenth centuries, the Ottoman office-households, their successors the provincial households, and the households of religious scholars ideally would have been the three social groups eventually to challenge the sultan's control. When financially strained to finance more troops, the sultan did indeed resort to using the military retinues of the office-households as regular soldiers—a practice that enhanced the social power of the office-households. Later in the eighteenth century, when Ottoman administrative power further extended from the office-households to include provincial notables *(ayan)*, the household still remained the organizing principle of the empire (Özkaya 1983: 7–9). The sultan maintained his control over the social structure insofar as the household remained the organizing principle. This condition also explained the failure of both office-households and provincial households to challenge the sultan: neither could generate an alternate organizational structure to the household, which formed a tightly bound, well-trained, and efficiently run social unit. Yet the complex social and moral ties that developed in them did often elude the sultan's control, thereby making his rule precarious. Hence, ironically, in successfully responding to this challenge from the households, the sultan decided to train a new social group in his new Western-style educational institutions with which to replace them.

This new group acquired the scientific knowledge and expertise necessary to replace the administrative functions of the office-household and provincial household. Western-style educational institutions, which were under the sultan's jurisdiction but not his direct control, provided a new social practice that emphasized efficiency in the organization of work and expertise in the acquisition of skills. This often contradicted existing Ottoman practice, which had emphasized thoroughness in work organization and experience in skill acquisition.[17] Because of this shift in emphasis, students in the Western-style schools could challenge the authority of the Ottoman administrators based on their newly acquired scientific knowledge.[18] Also, the organizing principle of this group was not the household but instead the institution. As this emerging Ottoman bureaucratic bourgeoisie built on its networks and applied its new knowledge to the organization of the empire, it marginalized the control over the empire by the households.[19] The new Western-style institutions replaced the office-households, and once stripped of their household organization,[20] household members were reduced to salaried personnel and absorbed into the Ottoman bureaucratic system (Heyd 1961). Ultimately, this social group successfully challenged the Ottoman sultan to transform into the Ottoman bureaucratic bourgeoisie. As the household organization of the empire waned, however, the sultan and his empire dwindled with it.

Ottoman Officials and Office-Households

In the seventeenth century, as administrative authority devolved from the palace, the metaphor of the sultan's household[21] as the organizing principle of the empire started to lose its symbolic and spatial significance. In 1654, the grand vezir was the first Ottoman administrator to move his household from the sultan's palace to a residence within the city (Ergin 1939: 52). This first spatial separation was soon followed by other administrative offices, such as that of the chief Ottoman official of finance *(defterdar)*,[22] who, in 1676, also started to conduct business in his residence in the city (Tabakoğlu 1985: 40–44). By the eighteenth century, the imperial council had ceased to meet in the palace and was now transacting all governmental business in the grand vezir's residence. Yet, even with this physical separation of offices from the sultan's household, the household remained the organizing principle of the empire. As the office-households started training their own household members for the administrative posts of the empire, they appropriated and accumulated resources at the expense of the sultan's household. Candidates from the office-households eventually surpassed the palace graduates in acquiring important central and provincial appointments. In the eighteenth century, half of the sultan's appointments for high office were filled by men who had been either raised or trained in or attached to office-households (Abou-el-Haj 1974: 438, 443). A study of the tenure pattern among top-level Ottoman offices during the same century (Itzkowitz 1962; 1977) corroborated the monopolization of these offices by certain households. Hence, these office-households constituted the first challenge to the sultan's control.

How did the challenge of the office-households to the sultan emerge, and why could it not succeed? The sultan considered household size a significant criterion in assigning offices, because those officials with large households usually performed administrative duties more thoroughly (Kunt 1983: 84). Yet, the sultan's incentive, namely, the thorough collection of resources by the households for the center, ultimately conflicted with that of the official, who had to retain resources himself for the upkeep of his large household. As officials retained more resources for their own upkeep, the sultan accelerated the transfor-mation of the fiefs[23] he had allocated to these households into tax-farms and freeholds (for the latter point, see Cezar 1986: 45; Özkaya 1985: 39, 92, 115). The office-households responded to the sultan's challenge by developing and relying more and more on their own social and economic resources. In order to sustain his control over them, the sultan responded by fostering competition among the office-households.[24] Due to this competi-tion, upon being appointed to an administrative post, the official now had to stay at the capital to guard his appointment and, in his stead, trained and sent his household members as deputies.[25] These household members, once established in the provinces, often formed their own households and became a segment of the provincial notables. If he could not avoid leaving the capital, the officeholder often maintained a representative in the capital to look after his interests in the fierce competition among the households. Hence, the pattern that emerges in this process is one of tension, as different groups contested one another's social boundaries and developed contingent strategies to challenge their re-source control. In the case of the office-households, they inventoried their expenses, developed transactions to supplement their incomes, and formed complex social networks through measures such as gift exchange and marriage to maintain and reproduce their social boundaries. The sultan countered by depleting their resources through levies and confiscations and by instigating competition among them. Each such contingent strategy had consequences for each group, however. As the office-households trained more of their members to participate in the increasingly competitive administrative system, they lost social power to their members, who then formed their own households and often joined the ranks of the provincial notables. As the sultan and his immediate palace household utilized Western-style educational institutions to prepare a new social group with which to replace office-households and provincial households, they in turn were forced to relin-quish their power to this new group of Ottoman bureaucratic bourgeoisie. This internal social transformation was a significant component of eighteenth- and nineteenth-century Ottoman social change, a component that has often been overlooked because of the undue explanatory power placed on Western influence.

Yet how to illustrate this Ottoman social transformation from within? A systematic analysis of pertinent archival documents and historical chronicles illustrates the internal dynamics of Ottoman social change. Through such empirical sources, one is able first to delineate the formation and reproduction of office-households and then to outline the measures undertaken by the sultan to curb their immanent challenge. An analysis of eighteenth-century expense and inheritance registers of Ottoman officials documents maintenance to be the main expense of the office-household, followed by that of the expense accrued through travel and campaign costs. For instance, Elhac Yusuf Pasha, the governor of Jidda (MM9725/257–9), and the grand vezir Şehid Ali Pasha (MM6266/402–20) both had households of considerable proportions; the grand vezir's household comprised 112 household members receiving monthly salaries and 234 personal slaves, including 180 male slaves, 49 female slaves and 5 eunuchs. Another pasha (KK7454) paid his 56 household *ağas* 11 piasters[26] per month, while the 43 orderlies received 6 piasters each. He also had a large private army; his 241 Albanian soldiers with their 5 officers received 9 piasters each, 2 of which were for provisions. In a different office-household (CD11122), a vezir paid his 211 members a total of 1,372.5 piasters in monthly salaries.[27] The inheritance registers of some of these household members also indicate that they received periodic gifts from the household head.[28] In 1795, the cash bonus given by a vezir to his 46 men during a religious holiday reached a total of 4,765 piasters (CD11122). The second largest source of expense of the office-household was transportation. The travel expenses of a vezir from Trebizond to Erzurum, a relatively short distance, documents the extent of this expense (MM2628/12–21); the vezir spent thousands of coins on provisions and on gifts to the local notables. During campaigns, officials also had to join the sultan's army with their households, soldiers, and the men they recruited from their provinces specifically for the campaign. Hence the size of the office-household and, of course, its expenses increased during military campaigns: a vezir's expense register (CD15970) drawn in 1808 at the frontier revealed a household of approximately twenty-five hundred men. During such campaigns, the official, unable to recover his amplified expenses from the sultan, often ended up in debt (Göçek 1994b).

Archival documents depict three measures officials used to generate and maintain their resources. One was to levy additional duties from the subjects, and such duties did indeed become very frequent in the eighteenth century. Another was for officials to generate income by personally investing in agricultural and industrial production and in urban property. Returns from such investments often did form a very large portion of the office-household's income. For instance, in the expense register (D2823) of a grand vezir in 1764–65, only two-thirds of the vezir's revenues accrued from the sultan's allocations: one-third comprised his own economic investments. Two additional expense registers portray the possible scope of an official's personal investments. These investments ranged from industrial products, as in the case of Şehid Ali Pasha (MM6266/402–20), who, around 1716, built 11 soap manufactories in İzmir, to Esad Pasha (MM9770/326), the governor of Damascus, whose confiscated wealth in 1763 contained 54 looms of striped *(alaca)* and 24 looms of silk-cotton *(kutni)* cloth, 2 inns, 236 shops, 42 vegetable gardens, 3 bathhouses, 7 farms, 20 houses, 2 mills, and 4 coffee houses.[29] Elhac Ali Pasha, the governor of Konya, similarly possessed a large number of properties, land, and livestock near Constantinople (MM9770/525). Such investments were widespread throughout the Ottoman administrative system. For instance, an Ottoman official, Battal Sadık Agha, died in 1788, leaving behind a large number of rented-out urban property (MM9719/254–7): 2 mills, 41 pieces of cultivable land, 23 shops, 2 coffee houses, 16 fruit-and-vegetable gardens, and 3 olive oil presses—amounting to a total of 89 pieces of property. The third measure the officials resorted to was money lending, both as suppliers and as receivers. For instance, Elhac Yusuf Pasha, governor of Jidda and former commander of Morea (MM9725/257–9), left behind large inheritances comprising mostly cash totaling 286,769 piasters. Such large amounts of cash, and often the lists of debtors accompanying it, suggest that many Ottoman officials might have engaged in moneylending.[30] The records are more explicit in other cases, including that of one sheik-ül-islam who, in 1846, had lent money, with interest, to a judge and a soldier (CA654). Many officials also attempted to maintain their households through continuous borrowing from moneylenders. For instance, the inheritance registers of two such officials (CM15918, A170/102) contain large debts.

Another much understudied practice the office-households used to reproduce and secure their resources was the employment of social networks. Through such networks, officials established ties, commitments, and alliances that often countered the sultan's control. These networks ranged from informal interaction through visits to gift exchanges to the formal establishment of allegiance through marriages. Eighteenth- and nineteenth-century Ottoman documents often reveal a high degree of social interaction among office-households. For instance, inheritance registers and religious endowment deeds, which contain the names of people assigned as legal guardians over minors or as witnesses and which also cite the nature of the relationship between the parties, demonstrate the strength of social ties in Ottoman society. In the inheritance register of the fief-holder *(zaim)* Mehmed Agha (A127/73), the legal guardian appointed over his minor children was "a family friend" who also happened to be the Ottoman chief architect *(ser mimaran-ı hassa)* Elhac Ahmed Agha. The religious endowment deed of the grand admiral Kaymak Mustafa Pasha contained, as witnesses, many religious scholars and old Ottoman officials residing in Constantinople (Aktepe 1969: 35). The witnesses to the endowment deed of the grand vezir Damad İbrahim Pasha were an even more exalted set (Aktepe 1960: 155). In addition to the above-mentioned grand admiral, the chief palace physician *(ser etibba-ı hassa)*, the agha of the Janissaries, the apportioner of military inheritances *(askeri kassam)*, the former military judge *(kadıasker)*, and the chief secretary of state *(reisülküttab)* all witnessed the deed.

Eighteenth-century chronicles supplement this documentation of Ottoman social networks. They reveal that the most common medium of social interaction for officials in Constantinople[31] was attending each other's informally held courts *(divan)* and receiving days (Naima [1863] 1969, VI: 2047; 2527; 2620; 2631). On these visits, they discussed state matters, campaigned for their opinions on a particular state matter to gain support for its execution, or exchanged information on the availability of posts and appointments made to them. They also entertained each other to the accompaniment of many musicians and dancers. Through such periodic visits, the office-household formed an information network that helped maintain and improve its position vis-à-vis the other households. Officials who were dismissed from posts or who were discontent with the ones they held tried to gain social support for a new office appointment by visiting "influential" households. In some instances, when these officials were unsuccessful in their attempts to get new appointments, they visited the households of other discontent officials and tried to incite opposition to the sultan who controlled the appointments (Naima [1863] 1969, VI: 2555). Visiting households also produced positive results. Officials appointed to higher, more influential posts would usually nominate officials who visited and associated with them to other posts. In one instance, when one such person, Hüsamzade, became the chief of Islamic legal ruling *(müftü)*, he appointed a friend to a teaching post at a school (Naima [1863] 1969, VI: 2642). This cooperation among officials through their social ties often expanded beyond appointments. These ties that the office-households formed also helped them in times of duress, when they collaborated to neutralize the sultan's challenges. For instance, when one official received the sultan's orders to execute another who happened to be his friend, he would often send his own men ahead to notify the official of the impending order, thus giving him time to escape. Later, when the official ostensibly arrived at the residence of the other to execute the sultan's order, he would find no one there (Naima [1863] 1969, VI: 2764). Other friends would then intervene on behalf of the errant official and often succeed in modifying the sentence.

Another medium that fostered social networks among office-households was gift exchange, through which officials confirmed commitments and allegiances and built alliances. The eighteenth- and nineteenth-century Ottoman inheritance and expense registers again document the large scope of gift exchange among officials. If a good was given as a present, these inventories almost always specified the names of the parties involved in the exchange. For instance, the listed gifts given to Ahmed Pasha, the commander of Hotin, indicated that Abdi Pasha, the commander of the neighboring town, had sent him a mule as a gift (CM30257). Such exchanges probably helped confirm the commanders' mutual reciprocal support of one another in times of need. In the expense register (KK7454) of a vezir, of the 118 horses listed, many were recorded as gifts from other Ottoman officials, such as Yusuf Pasha, Hasan Pasha, and "son of Hafız Pasha."[32] The gifts the vezir sent in return were also recorded: he dispatched four horses to the judge of Hasköy, one to the physician Hekim Pasha, and another to his son-in-law in Constantinople. The vezir's register also contained a list of 26 fur coats that were sewn to be given as robes of honor to many officials. Such gift exchanges reconfirmed the alliances among office-households. Officials constantly made such social investments through gift exchange, even when traveling. For instance, upon traveling from Trebizond to Erzurum during the period 1789–91, probably on his way from one appointment to another, a governor (MM2628/12–21) gave many robes of honor at every town he passed through. Bestowed mostly upon local notables, these presents might have served to procure their allegiance to him as their new governor. Gift-giving incurred a long-term obligation on both the giver and the recipient, establishing a link between them. The return to the gift confirmed the link and often initiated a network between the two office-households. Such gift exchanges also occurred outside the sultan's control.[33] Gifts could establish, maintain, and enhance the social resources of office-households, but their maintenance was costly.

The most significant practice office-households utilized to sustain and reproduce social networks was initiating kinship ties. These were the most resistant to the sultan's attempts to wrest resources away from the office-households and the most enduring to the rise and demise of fortunes. Marriage formed the main channel for establishing such ties between households, often guaranteeing access to information, to new offices, and to resources of other households. Also, fictitious family ties were established through patronage, slavery, and milk brotherhood. The information contained in the eighteenth- and nineteenth-century Ottoman inheritance registers, religious deeds, and chronicles displays the significance of these family ties and marriage patterns in reproducing the social location of office-households. For instance, the inheritance registers often inscribe the names and occupations of the heirs of the deceased, thus revealing the nature of kinship ties. In 1808, all the sons of the deputy-judge *(kadı naibi)* of Dimetoka were listed as being the descendants of the Prophet[34] on their maternal grandfather's side (A856/146). The family thus had religious connections on both sides; the father had a religious post, and the mother descended from a prestigious religious family. In another instance, in 1791, the sultan confiscated the inheritance of Abdullah Pasha, the governor of Erzurum (MM9720/206–9). The governor's wife petitioned, however: she stated that most of the confiscated wealth was not his but hers; it was she who had owned the 2 shops, 3 farms, 1 garden, 621 olive trees, 450 goats, and 61 horses. She proved, through court records, that she had indeed inherited these items from her father. Wives of governors often came from wealthy households themselves and retained their wealth. Women's resources, which could not be confiscated by the sultan,[35] thus formed pockets of resistance. Through social networking, many sons were able to retain and expand beyond the sources they inherited from their parents.[36] Religious endowment deeds also portray the complex kinship ties among the top-level Ottoman officials. The deed of the grand admiral Kaymak Mustafa Pasha (Aktepe 1969: 15), for instance, which listed all his family and kin, demonstrated that the admiral's mother was the daughter of the former grand vezir Merzifonlu Kara Mustafa Pasha; the admiral himself was the grandson of another famous grand vezir, Köprülü Mehmed Pasha. The admiral, in addition to coming from such illustrious office-households, had formed additional networks through marriage. He was married to the daughter of the current grand vezir Damad İbrahim Pasha; his brother-in-law Kethüda Mehmed Pasha was in charge of the empire's internal affairs. Sometimes officials married off their daughters to promising household members, thereby securing the futures of their kin. For instance, Sevünduk Pasha married his daughter to his steward, who then became the governor of Adana and acquired the title pasha himself (Naima [1863] 1969, V: 2230).[37]

Another way officials retained and reproduced their office-households was by establishing religious endowments.[38] Such endowments could be established either as endowments of a definitely religious or public nature, such as mosques, schools, hospitals, bridges, or water fountains, or as family endowments for the benefit of the founder's children, grandchildren, or other relations. The latter, although ostensibly founded to benefit the poor and offer prayers for the family, nevertheless expanded in the Ottoman empire, especially in the eighteenth and nineteenth centuries, to protect officials against the sultan's confiscations (Yediyıldız 1984, 1982a, 1982b, 1982c). As the endowers of such family establishments could stipulate the terms under which their funds could be employed and often appointed their own family members in perpetuity as the administrators *(mütevelli)*, the officials often endowed their vast properties[39] for the upkeep of their office-households. For instance, when Mehmed Agha, the chief correspondent *(telhisi)* of the sultan, left endowments upon his death (A94/16), he designated the terms of the endowments in such a manner that his heirs were able to use the annual income of 370,896 aspers accruing from them to maintain his office-household. Religious endowments often benefited the endowers more than the poor for whom they were ostensibly founded. In another instance in 1814, Tekelioğlu Hacı Mehmed Agha, the deputy governor of Teke, who was listed[40] as owning 117 pieces of property upon death, including 70 houses, 30 shops, 14 gardens and orchards, 2 inns, and 1 granary (CA654), endowed 85 of these. Hence, through such measures, office-households were able to generate and sustain the social and economic resources with which they could potentially challenge the sultan.

In the eighteenth and early nineteenth centuries, the sultan countered the challenge of the office-households through three practices: he depleted their resources by allocating them less than what was needed to maintain their household, confiscated their economic resources, and fostered competition among them. The sultan curbed the officials' resource base by decreasing the fiefs he allocated them. He tried to replace these fiefs with cash payment, thus slowly reverting the officials into salaried employees of the state with no direct access to economic resources (Cezar 1986: 58–60, 64). Yet, during the latter part of the eighteenth century, the sultan also had to allocate additional income to the officials based on household size because he had to keep relying on the administrative and military services provided by such large office-households. By conservatively estimating the cost of maintenance for each household member at 70 piasters, and by systematically providing less than the amount necessary for such maintenance, the sultan was able once more to exercise his control over the households, however. An empirical analysis of the sultan's income allotment pattern to office-households vividly illustrates this resource depletion process by the sultan.[41]

A comparison of the allocated amount for household expenses with the estimated household expense reveals that the household size always exceeded the income allocated on average by 20 percent. Hence the sultan was able to deplete the resources of the office-households by systematically providing them with amounts lower than what was needed for household maintenance. As the officials kept paying the difference from their own funds, they were forced to become dependent on the sultan or borrow funds from moneylenders. Indeed, in one instance in 1827, the confiscated books of four Ottoman Armenian moneychangers, Tıngıroğlu Osib, Kılcıoğlu Kirkor, Davidoğlu Osib, and Sarısimyonoğlu Osib (MM10278/33–6), revealed that they owed money to many officials, including the ex-sheik-ül-islam Mustafa Asım Efendi and the current sheik-ül-islam Yanyalızade Abdullah. They were also owed money by many other officials, including Nurullah Pasha, the governor of Edirne, and Mehmed Pasha, the commander of Limni.

The second practice that the sultan employed to curb the challenge of office-households was confiscation.[42] The sultan confiscated the wealth of the Ottoman officials either when they were dismissed from office or when they died. Archival documents again illustrate this practice in depth. For instance, the sultan confiscated the inheritance of Abbas Agha, the tax collector of Kütahya, upon his death in 1792 (CM2034). His cash and valuables were then sent to the sultan, and his livestock, cereals, farms, and property were

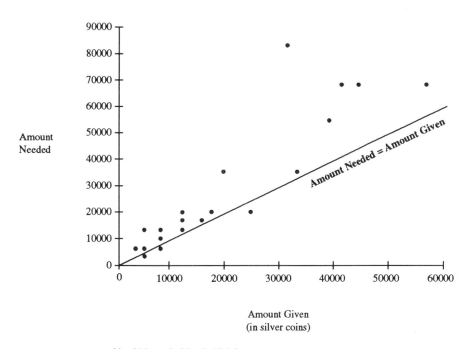

N = 30 households of officials

Figure 2. Fiscal Control as Indicated by the Amount Given by the Ottoman Sultan Versus the Amount Needed for Household Maintenance. (Başbakanlık Arşivi, Hazariyye Defteri [Prime Minister's Archives, Registers of Imperial Aid], no. 4: 180, 280–82.)

auctioned locally; the cash amount accruing from this transaction was then relayed to the sultan's treasury as well. Similarly, when the former chief of finance Mehmed Efendi was exiled from office (Naima [1863] 1969, VI: 2551–54), a total of 50,000 piasters and 100 purses of gold were found buried in various places in his residence: the official had tried, without success, to hide some of the wealth from the sultan's confiscation. Even though the threat of confiscation did indeed provide the sultan with significant power, he could not practice it without justification. The imperial decrees at the end of the eighteenth and the beginning of the nineteenth century frequently assured Ottoman society that the inheritance "of those who did not have any accounts with the Ottoman state would not be confiscated" (Buyruldu 1–2/12 in 1808).[43] Since officials could not escape having accounts with the state and thus the sultan, they were prime targets for confiscation. Among Ottoman social groups, the inheritances of Ottoman officials and provincial notables were confiscated the most, followed by those of wealthy merchants. The 1,033 confiscations in my sample population of eighteenth-century officials support this argument. Throughout the eighteenth century, the Ottoman sultan's attempts to curb the resource bases of the officials and provincial notables became evident as he confiscated more and more inheritances. In 1722, when Mehmed Pasha, the former governor of Tripoli-in-Lebanon, owed money to the treasury, he was told to pay his debts "or his wealth, the wealth of his sons and of the prominent members of his household would all be confiscated" (MM3792/1–6). The sultan used Mehmed Pasha's debts to the treasury to threaten him with confiscation. Similarly, in 1739, Mollacık Mehmed Efendi, the accountant in charge of the collection of the poll tax, also owed money to the treasury (MM10338/309). Although threatened with confiscation, he "asked for the forgiveness of the sultan and settled in his debts with the treasury for a reduced amount of 50,000 piasters." In this case, the official was able to pay a cash amount and forgo confiscation. In 1744, the subjects complained against Mirioğlu Hasan, the voivode[44] of Morea (MM9741/193–94), for overcharging the sheep tax. The voivode had escaped by the time these complaints reached the sultan. Upon the sultan's orders, his wealth was confiscated by Mustafa Pasha, the commander of Morea.

The confiscation of officials' wealth often took place during their life and was due to their misuse of office. In 1750, Mehmed Pasha, former grand vezir and governor of Baghdad, was dismissed and all his wealth confiscated "except an amount sufficient for his sustenance" (MM10194/5). Similarly, in 1804, when another Mehmed Pasha, the governor of Sivas, was unable to pay his debts, he was dismissed from office and his wealth confiscated (CM15871). In 1805, the wealth of a tax-farmer (*mültezim*) Mustafa was seized for "his oppression of the peasantry" (CM6959). Confiscations and their release in cash increased during campaigns when a revenue crisis developed around the payment of the soldier's salaries. For instance, in 1738 an imperial order was issued (MM10338/312 and MM10164/414) to confiscate the wealth of Atıf Efendi, the chief treasurer of the empire, who was able to fend off the confiscation by promising to pay 104,000 piasters in cash. This amount was then used immediately to pay the salaries of the soldiers at the frontier. The confiscation of the inheritances of merchants or officials who were known to have cash stocks particularly escalated during these periods as well.[45]

The other measure the Ottoman sultan used to counter the challenge of the office-households was to foster fierce competition among them. Ottoman chronicles again illustrate the nature of this competition. For instance, in the late seventeenth century, the Ottoman chronicler Naima[46] vividly described the method one dismissed official ingeniously employed to get another post ([1863] 1969, VI: 2622). He borrowed cash and goods worth one hundred purses of gold and gave these as gifts to some well-known men, who then testified as to what an experienced official he had been. Upon this testimony, the chief financial administrator recruited him as a member for his own household and gave him, in exchange for sixty purses of gold the post of collecting revenues from the province of the Horn of Africa.[47] Complaining that the appointment system came to revolve more and more around the investments officials made in one another's resources, the same chronicler stated:

> Sometimes, when a man's talent is recognized by the sultan and high-state officials, the man suddenly acquires a fame. All the people, thinking he is now a man who has a say in everything, in every state affair, flock to his doorstep. Some go seeking self-interest, others try to forestall any harm he might cause them, still others attempt to acquire fame and favor through their association with him. . . . Whatever the reason may be, they try to get nearer him by giving him whatever they own. In return, he solves the problem of one, yet shelves the difficulties of five others. Still, through many tricks, he accumulates a large amount of gold and expensive property. . . . These people who start joining (and forming) the household of the man are all ignorant, mean people burning with the ambition of an administrative post. ([1863] 1969, VI: 2662, 2936)

With time, this competition for posts and the significance of social resources in attaining them had reached such a proportion that a group of "confidence men" emerged in Constantinople. These would make it seem as if they had just been appointed to offices and then sit and gather the wealth of all those adamant office-seekers who wanted to buy their favors.[48] Another reason for the fierce competition among officials was the economic and social difficulties one encountered upon failing to procure a post. Even though the loss of economic resources was less significant than the loss of social resources in terms of the long-range consequences, it became more and more difficult for an official to attain a new post as more and more time lapsed between appointments.[49] There were many others in similar situations. Once the post was lost, the official's position became very precarious: he could not cut his expenses since he needed to retain a large household to keep his chances of attaining a post, and he also had to buy off favors and invest in social ties through gift exchange to maintain his candidacy for a post (Naima [1863] 1969, VI: 2961). This precariousness enhanced the competition for appointments and led office-households to invest more and more in developing their own social ties. In addition to the gifts they gave to maintain posts, officials had to bid for posts and pay large amounts in cash for the right to collect taxes *(iltizam)*[50] on agricultural land.

What was the most significant outcome of this tension between the sultan and the office-households? Both sides trained new personnel with which to counter the challenge of the other. In the case of the office-households, this resulted in the transfer of resources from officials to household members. Household members became the center of inter-household competition as officials tried to recruit able members for their households to improve their competitive stand (Naima [1863] 1969, V: 2045; VI: 2599). Members sought to join those office-households that offered them more opportunities.[51] In the late seventeenth century, many household members started to desert their office-households to join others where the likelihood of attaining posts for themselves was higher. Such desertions sometimes led to conflicts between office-households. For instance, when a few household members of İbrahim Agha, the chief of finance of the empire, ran away and joined the office-household of a military official, the ensuing friction between the officials led to the latter's dismissal from office. Some household members ended up acquiring offices that equalled or surpassed in stature those of the household head. Two elements of the interoffice competition produced this result. Members obtained training within the office-household, which provided them with administrative skills. When they then started managing the properties of the office-household, they often procured economic resources for themselves. Seventeenth- and eighteenth-century Ottoman chronicles abound with the records of top-level officials who were trained in the households of others. The voivode of Wallachia, for instance, was trained within the household of Koca Kenan Pasha; the treasurer of the grand vezir Derviş Pasha, who was also a former slave in the household of the chief eunuch at the palace, became the voivode of Kilis and Ağraz (Naima [1863] 1969, VI: 2917; 2526). Hence, household members were able to devolve resources away from the office-households by accumulating administrative skills. In the case of the sultan and his palace household, this challenge of the office-households resulted in his training another body of potential administrators in Western-style schools. These too acquired knowledge and expertise and gradually sapped resources from the sultan. Yet the competition between the sultan and the office-households also produced a new social group in Ottoman society that challenged them both: the provincial notables and their households.

Provincial Notables and Provincial Households

In the seventeenth and eighteenth centuries, local notables[52] merged with members of office-households who resided in towns and provinces as overseers to form a locally wealthy and influential social group. This group accumulated wealth by administering economic resources and gained influence by forming their own households. The local notables had been the intermediaries between the town populace and the Ottoman administration in the sixteenth century. Their assistance included relaying the subjects' complaints about the administrators to the sultan, helping to guard the town, and informally overseeing the administration of justice,[53] often by acting as experts in monetary adjustments and appraising inheritance values. Town officials relied on them in regulating food provision for the town and food production. In the seventeenth century, many of those participating in the expansion of the empire in the east and west, including officials, soldiers, and religious scholars, also retired[54] to the provinces to join the ranks of these notables (Tabakoğlu 1985: 214–15). Through this addition, the social ties between the provinces, the office-households, and the capital intensified. In the eighteenth century, as competition between the sultan and the office-households escalated and as the Ottoman wars continued, the ensuing Ottoman administrative transformation[55] from military fiefs to tax-farms gave provincial notables access to social and economic resources (Cezar 1986: 306–7; Özkaya 1977: 103). They thus transformed into "provincial households."[56]

The conflict between the sultan and the office-households aided the development of provincial households in that officials could not leave the capital for fear of losing their posts and therefore delegated authority to household members residing in the provinces (Özkaya 1985: 196). As the officials became more and more entrenched in office competition, they remained in the capital and let the provincial notables have more and more authority as their deputies. Also, when officials had to dismiss many household members when their competition with the sultan diminished their resources, some of these members emerged as provincial notables, as they had gradually commanded the skills necessary to oversee production and collect taxes. For instance, in 1808 Kör İsmail, the provincial notable of the Havza and Köprü towns (MM9755/111), who was owed 38,650 piasters by various Ottoman officials residing in these towns, was probably a local resident who had become a notable. The sultan's frequent need for cash to provision his campaigns formed the other reason for the empowerment of provincial notables. When the Ottoman–

Austrian war lasted sixteen years (1682–98), for instance, the sultan raised the necessary cash to provision the war by farming out public revenues and state lands, and the notables emerged as provincial agents of the tax-farmers or as tax-farmers themselves. Similarly, the continuous wars on both fronts of the empire, such as the 1768–74 Ottoman–Russian war, further fostered the authority of the provincial notables as these households maintained security in the provinces.[57] In addition, when the size of the Ottoman army engaged in numerous wars proved insufficient, the auxiliary force of the notables formed a more and more significant part of the Ottoman military (Mutaciyeva 1977: 180–81).

The economic resources of the provincial notables increased significantly after their appointment as tax-farmers. Yet the source of their wealth was, like office-households, tax collection and tenure in a state office. Like the office-households before them, the provincial notables[58] invested this wealth in agricultural land, urban property, or moneylending. Eighteenth- and nineteenth-century Ottoman inheritance registers illustrate this argument. The 1783 inheritance register (MM9741/180-3) of the notable of Hasan, Dimetoka, who had a wheat harvest of 1,645 *keyl*,[59] 390 sheep, many livestock, farms, vineyards, and pastures, documents the agricultural base of the provincial notables. Some of the produce accrued from his tax-farming; some from his own local investments. Yet the wealth was not restricted to agriculture but also extended to urban property. In town, this provincial notable owned a barbershop and a coffee house. The townspeople also owed him a large debt of 66,155 piasters, indicating either that the notable was engaged in moneylending or that many of the townspeople had tax arrears. Indeed, some notables used the wealth they had accumulated from the urban and rural economy to lend money. In 1808, for instance, Kör İsmail, the notable of Havza and Köprü, provided capital and credit to merchants and artisans (Cezar 1977: 65). Hence, although the notables mostly gathered wealth through tax-farming, they invested this capital in a variety of fields, ranging from land to real estate to trade ventures. For instance, in addition to agricultural land and urban property, the inheritance register (CM31689) of Pehlivanoğlu Ahmed Agha, the notable of Samako Bolu, contained two valuable items, a ship with a load capacity of 1,500 pounds, and a third share in another vessel with a load capacity of 3,000 pounds. Another notable of Saruhan (CM20543) who died in 1813 had twenty pieces of urban property, including two tanneries, two grape storehouses, one shoe store, half a share of a kebab house, two mills, and three vineyards. Still another, Kavayalı İbrahim Bey (ME3: 106–10), obviously engaged in trade with the West, since his vast inheritance[60] in 1836 included approximately one and a half million piasters lent to an Austrian merchant at 4 percent interest, and about a million piasters loaned to the Austrian counsul in Draç. In addition, provincial households claimed some fiefs as abandoned and uncultivated and petitioned, often with success, to requalify these holdings as private property *(mülk)*; they also purchased uncultivated land, which they converted to agricultural farms (Cvetkova 1977: 169). Through these measures, notables were able to create large revenue bases for themselves, some of it, like the agricultural lands reverted to personal property, outside the sultan's control.

In the eighteenth century, the provincial households started to collect revenues through tax-farming. They did not relinquish these to the sultan but retained them for the upkeep of their own households, since the largest source of expenditure for the provincial household, like the office-households, was maintenance. Because the notables, like the officials before them, kept and provided soldiers as auxiliaries during military campaigns, they depleted their wealth in their efforts to equip and maintain these soldiers. The large proportions of soldiers under these notables demonstrate their significance as provincial forces. In 1803, for instance, Tepedelenli Ali Pasha had 80,000 provincial soldiers serving under him; at the end of the eighteenth century, Abdülhalim, the notable of Başkar, had 20,000 foot soldiers and 3,000 cavalry. Tirsiniklioğlu, the notable of Rusçuk, had an army of 20,000 at the beginning of the nineteenth century. These large auxiliaries, preying on the notables' wealth, were nevertheless a source of influence for them. In addition to the sultan's campaigns, the notables used these soldiers to track and catch bandits, punish rebels, send food provisions to the capital, provide security, and collect taxes (Özkaya 1977: 146–58). Once more, since it was upkeep expenses that economically endangered the survival of provincial households, they again invested in social networks to reproduce their power. Some provincial notables joined the ranks of the officials through marriage or trade alliances. According to a 1790 inheritance register (CM31691), for instance, the son-in-law of Abdülaziz, the deceased notable of Milas, was the head of the sultan's palace doorkeepers,[61] thus indicating that the daughter of a provincial notable had married an official from the sultan's palace. Trade alliances between notables and officials were also not uncommon. In 1809, the notable of Varna and a former grand vezir, Mustafa Pasha, are listed (MM9755/175) as being partners in suet and wax trade. The pasha's agents in Constantinople sold the wax and suet the notable had processed in Varna. One may conjecture that the pasha had probably served in Varna in the past as an official, whereby he formed this economic tie with the notable.

In addition to patronage ties, marriage, family ties, and gift exchange, the provincial households developed a new social resource: political representation. As intermediaries between local subjects and the sultan, provincial notables were elected by the subjects and approved by the sultan. Ottoman archives document the emergence of the political ties of the notables with the subjects, ties that the sultan could not obliterate. During the eighteenth century, for instance, Ottoman townspeople sent frequent petitions to the sultan, asking him to appoint a provincial notable to maintain security in their towns and to defend them against bandits, and then naming their own candidate for the position. In 1759, the "representatives," comprising "the learned *(ulema)*, the pious *(suleha)*, the subjects *(reaya)*, and the populace *(beraya)*" of the towns of Aska, Serkehe, Aşayır, and Selendi presented such a petition (E7974). They stated that since their towns had had constant attacks from bandits, there was a "dire" need for a courageous notable to protect them. For the position, their candidate was "Elhac İbrahim, a brave man, knowledgeable about the situation, and cherished by the people."[62] Even though the outcome of this particular petition is unknown, such petitions nevertheless set the precedence for the sultan to institutionalize this principle of representation in the late eighteenth century. An imperial decree of November 1790 (HH24893A) spelled out the rules of this elective principle, declaring that "the notable should be elected by the townspeople by popular consent, without the intervention of any official authority. The notable, in return, should not execute his duties without getting the people's approval; he should not decide by himself. The state would take care (and punish) those notables who mix things up." Although the administration of justice and attention to the opinion of the subjects had always been a significant maxim in the Ottoman administration, the acceptance of the subjects' candidates introduced a new dimension that went beyond the regulatory measures in administering justice. For the first time, this representative derived his administrative legitimacy not solely from the sultan but also from the subjects. It was this new social resource that often enabled him to successfully resist the sultan control.

The sultan tried to control the provincial notables in the same manner as the office-households: through confiscations and forced taxation. Yet he had more difficulty supervising the provincial households because they were geographically closer to revenue bases than the sultan.[63] Still, the confiscations the sultan enacted reverted resources to him and prevented their transmission to the next generation of notables.[64] The sultan's justification for the confiscations was the notable's failure to pay taxes, which the sultan often interpreted as an indication of the notable's rebellion against his authority. In 1766, for instance, the sultan confiscated the wealth of the Karaosmanoğlu family, who were the notables of Manisa but were now referred to as "bandits" in the Ottoman documents because of their rebellion against the sultan (D3023). Similarly, the notable of Dimetoka could also not escape confiscation;[65] he was executed in 1783 by the sultan's order for "his defiance" (MM9741/180). One tax-farmer, Halil Bey, was punished in 1783 through confiscation (MM9741/202) when he "behaved against the sultan's order and escaped upon the fear of exemplary punishment." His wealth consisted of sixteen farms and many shops. Katırcızade Mehmed, the notable of Kemerhamid (MM9750/56), was executed and his inheritance confiscated in a similar manner in 1801. The early decades of the nineteenth century also contained many such confiscation orders.[66] Control through exemplary punishment was practiced by the sultan; for instance, when Veli Pasha was beheaded, his severed head was placed in waterskin bags filled with honey and sent to the capital, where it was displayed on the "admonition stone" in front of the sultan's palace (Sakaoğlu 1984: 164). After the 1860s, the center once more established control over the provinces at the expense of the provincial notables, whom they replaced by salaried officials sent from the capital. The confiscations, which peaked in the 1770s, were abolished officially in 1839 with the sultan's reform edict (Yüksel 1992: 400–403).

The sultan could also deplete the resources of the provincial notables through forced taxation. In the eighteenth century, the sultan's demands for soldiers and their provisions increased due to frequent Ottoman military campaigns, mostly against the Russian and Austrian empires. Hundreds of imperial decrees were sent to the provincial notables ordering them to provide soldiers for the 1787–92 wars (Özkaya 1985: 47). In November 1772, for instance, the sultan demanded 15,650 soldiers from 57 notables in Anatolia for the spring campaign of 1773 (CAsk 26021). The real need of the sultan for soldiers often intermixed with his attempts to check the power of provincial notables. Using military campaigns as an excuse, the sultan depleted the economic resources of the provincial households, as demonstrated in the case of the notable of İzmir who belonged to the Karaosmanzade family. The case starts in the Ottoman archives with a 1769 petition (MM9999/57) stating that Elhac Halil, the tax collector of the neighboring town of Saruhan, "having fallen under the influence" of the provincial notable, had failed to perform his duties and correctly report the amount of tax he gathered. The sultan immediately appointed another tax collector and, at the same time, to deplete the resources of the notable, asked him to contribute generously to the ongoing Ottoman campaigns. In 1772, the sultan ordered the notable to join the impending campaign with his retinue and then pardoned him from service, in return for 500 fully equipped and armed soldiers sent as recompense (MM10003/398). The notable also had to pay the salaries of these soldiers, as the sultan's treasury only took care of their food provisions. A similar correspondence (CM7049) followed eight years later in 1800, when the sultan again ordered the notable of İzmir to join his military campaign. Then, although the sultan once more pardoned him from service in return for providing soldiers, the demands were much higher this time. Instead of 500, the sultan asked for 3,500 mounted soldiers and 150,000 piasters for equipment assistance. He then reverted this demand into cash, requiring the notable to pay, in lieu of the 3,500 mounted soldiers, 350,000 piasters. It probably would have been costlier and more dangerous for the notable to join the campaign; he would have spent a fortune maintaining his retinue and might have fallen into disfavor if and when he failed to win a battle. Rather than take such risks, the notable replied that he would pay the 350,000 but not the additional 150,000. The sultan gave his pardon, on the condition that the 350,000 piasters should be sent very speedily within two to three, at most, five days because, he added, soldiers would be recruited from Albania with that money, and these Albanian soldiers refused to join unless they were paid in cash in advance. Included in the imperial letter was a warning: if the notable failed to pay the 350,000 as required, the sultan would punish him for his misbehavior and make him pay the additional 150,000 as well. This case demonstrates the long and intricate negotiations between the sultan and the provincial households as each tried to maintain its social boundaries against the advent of the other.

The reactions of the provincial households to such strict and, at times, impossible demands of the sultan varied, however. Some notables had their resources totally depleted and perished; others formed connections with the officials and activated these connections to revoke the sultan's orders; and still others rebelled against the injustice of the sultan and his administration. In the seventeenth and eighteenth centuries, two rebellions rocked the Ottoman empire; one reached its peak in Western Anatolia during the years 1595–1610, and the other in the Balkans during the years 1791–1808. The sultan had difficulties controlling both rebellions because of cooperation between the bandits and the provincial notables, where the notable's support was either covert or overt, depending on his relationship with the sultan. Ottoman archival documents substantiate the sultan's attempts to control these rebellions, as they list frequent confiscation orders for the wealth of provincial notables, who are often referred to as "bandit" *(şaki)* or "bandits" *(eşkiya)*[67] because they happen to oppose him. In 1749, for instance, an archival document (MM9770/239–40) lists that the sultan executed one such "bandit," Veliefendioğlu Mustafa, his two brothers, and his two nephews and then confiscated their wealth.[68] Similarly, in 1764, a document specifies (MM9991/654-5) that another such "bandit," Sepetçioğlu Mustafa of Gönen, escaped and his house was burned.[69] In 1766, the sultan executed still another "bandit," Karaosmanzade Ataullah of the family of notables of İzmir,[70] along with his brother and his son, and confiscated his wealth (CM29536). The sultan dealt with the "bandits" in the Balkans in a fashion similar to the ones in Western Anatolia. In 1783, for instance, when Beyzade Nureddin, the notable of Priştine (MM9741/176-7), "one of a group of brigands," was sentenced to be executed, he managed to escape, but his inheritance was nevertheless confiscated. Yet since most of his property was burned out, the inheritance was left to his inheritors. Similarly, in 1792, Zaimoğlu Mehmed, the ex-notable of Nevrekob (CM4206), was hanged and his wealth confiscated because of "his banditry and his communication with the rebels."[71] In 1795, the sultan ordered that Abdülhakim Agha, the ex-mufti of Ayas, who "with the intention of becoming a notable turned rebellious and oppressed and committed injustices," be imprisoned in the Kayseri castle and that his wealth be confiscated (CM12065).[72] In 1799, when the tax collector Kürd Mehmed Agha and his forty "clingers-on" *(taallukat)* accumulated a lot of property in Damascus, their wealth was confiscated and sent to the sultan (CM15558). Yet the notables could, and often did, form pockets of resistance to confiscation. For instance, when one provincial notable, Köse Pasha, who rose to prominence after supplying soldiers to the sultan's campaigns, was notified of the impending visit of the sultan's agents to confiscate his wealth (Sakaoğlu 1984: 78), he circulated among the populace the rumor that the sultan was sending the agent to assess the wealth of the populace in order to affix new taxes. The notable suggested, therefore, that they all hide their wealth. He himself replaced the valuable goods in his residence with cheap substitutes and, in addition, served the agent some common wheat soup as a meal to demonstrate the poverty of the region. On the same evening, he orchestrated the populace to come to his residence bearing sticks and stones and crying out to the notable that "they were all hungry, and the notable should share with them whatever he was giving the sultan's agent." Upon these incidents, the sultan's agent left with the impression that the state was misinformed about the wealth of this region and its provincial notable. No confiscation order followed.

Still, confiscations, forced taxation, and executions ultimately did decrease the power of the provincial notables in challenging the sultan's control. The provincial households failed[73] to successfully challenge the sultan for the same reason that the office-households had been unsuccessful: both households had lodged their power base in resources the sultan controlled, mainly agricultural land and the tax revenues accruing from it. These households could not successfully develop and reproduce resources independent of the sultan's control. The households did nevertheless utilize their administratively trained household members to challenge the sultan. In addition, before their slow demise, the provincial households used their new social resource—political representation—to challenge the sultan's authority. In 1808, under the leadership of the grand vezir Bayrakdar Mustafa Pasha,[74] himself a provincial notable of Hezargrad and Rusçuk, the provincial notables joined forces, came to Constantinople, and forced the sultan to sign a Deed of Agreement (Sened-i İttifak) of mutual support, which recognized and confirmed the Ottoman provincial notables as a social group. Of the six clauses in the agreement, three concerned the notables,[75] whereby the notables agreed to obey the terms of the agreement, not to object to the sultan's recruitment of soldiers from their provinces, and also to come to the sultan's aid if there were rebellions among the soldiers in the capital (Karal 1983, V: 92). Even though the effect of the agreement was not long-lasting, in that the sultan soon retrieved most of the privileges he had parted with, the agreement had a significant symbolic impact on the Ottoman notion of sovereignty. Although the sultan ratified this agreement, the Ottoman state, not the sultan, was a party in it. Even though the sultan, by introducing such a distinction, was able to avoid being legally accountable to the notables, the distinction was nevertheless fundamental in foreshadowing the gradual separation of the Ottoman state from the sultan.[76]

Households of Religious Dignitaries

The ascendance and devolution of the influence of the religious scholars followed the pattern of the office-households. The households of religious scholars had been significant because of their ability to escape confiscation, wield economic and social control over religious foundations, the judiciary, and the educational system of the empire, and form ties with office-households through marriages to reproduce their control. Their power had reached such a degree in the fifteenth century, for instance, that when Mehmed II confiscated many of the landholdings of their religious establishments, his successor had to give this land back. Similarly, in 1622, when Mustafa I seized the surplus yield of the religious endowments, this also was a temporary measure not repeated (Gibb and Bowen 1963, II: 32–33). The religious dignitaries could not form social resources that ultimately could escape the authority of the sultan over their resources, however. By gradually forming Western-style courts and educational institutions, Western-style ministries overseeing the administration of religious foundations, the sultan was able also to demobilize the potential of this social group to challenge and delegitimate his rule.

The social strength of religious dignitaries is confirmed by the diaries of Lady Mary Montagu, who resided in Constantinople in the early eighteenth century.

> I had the advantage of lodging three weeks at Belgrade with a principal Effendi, that is to say, a Scholar. This set of men are equally capable of preferments in the Law or the Church, those and Sciences being cast into one, a Lawyer and a preist *[sic]* being the same word. They are the only men really considerable in the Empire; all the profitable Employments and church revenues are in their hands. The Grand Signor, tho general Heir to his people, never presumes to touch their land or money, which goes in an uninterrupted succession to their children. 'Tis true they lose this privelege by accepting a place at Court or the Title of Bassa, but there are few examples of such fools amongst 'em. You may easily judge the power of these men who have engross'd all the Learning and allmost all the Wealth of the Empire. Tis they that are the real Authors, tho the Souldiers are the Actors of Revolutions. They depos'd the late Sultan Mustapha, and their power is so well known 'tis the Emperor's interest to flatter them. (1965: 316–17)

Although many indeed were "no fools" to accept official positions, they did nevertheless enter into networks with the office-households through their administration of religious endowments and through intermarriages. In the seventeenth century, for example, the household of a religious judge included, through marriage ties, other judges, merchants, tradesmen, and military officials. One extreme example of such tie formation is the household of one seventeenth-century head of religious affairs, sheik-ül-islam Feyzullah Efendi, who married his eight sons and six daughters to prominent office-households in the religious, financial, and military administration (Türek and Derin 1969). Through these marriages, his household was able to retain its hold over the allocation of religious posts for decades. Even though dismissed from office and exiled to Eastern Anatolia for almost ten years, this dignitary was able to maintain his household and relative position within the administration. He managed this difficult task by maintaining a residence in Constantinople, corresponding with high-level officials, and sending them frequent gifts. Ten years later, he was appointed back to the office of head of religious affairs.

Religious dignitaries further extended their networks through landholding and education (Baer 1980; Szyliowicz 1973: 59–61). They developed patronage ties through their frequent audiences and discussion circles in the mosque. Upon obtaining administrative posts, these scholars used their ties to form large office-households of their own. The household expense registers of the officials of the religious administration in the archives[77] document their households to be comparable both in size and in activity to those of the officials'. Late sixteenth-century chronicles (Repp 1977: 277) prove that religious dignitaries trained their household members for religious posts in a manner very similar to that of the officials'. Their own sons or the sons of household members thereby got more and more frequently appointed to relatively high posts at a young age. This state of affairs, the concentration of power in a few families, was occurring in the provinces as well as the capital (Ortaylı 1979: 157).

A comparison of the religious post tenures between the seventeenth and eighteenth centuries demonstrates the swift pace of this monopolization of posts by such religious household members (Ortaylı 1979: 156–57). Nine out of twenty heads of religious affairs in the seventeenth century rose from among the subjects (45 percent); in the eighteenth century, only four out of thirty came from the same group (13 percent). Social resources and the ties between office-households became even more significant in monopolizing the post of the head of religious affairs (Zilfi 1983: 320). Between 1703 and 1839, three Ottoman households contributed thirteen of the fifty-three heads of religious affairs (22 percent) and twenty of the seventy-six head of religious affairs tenures (26 percent) in the period. This eighteenth-century monopolization of religious establishment by certain families and their households also facilitated the sultan's encroachment upon their spheres of influence.

The differences between the religious and military organization in control and resources started to wane in the early nineteenth century, however.[78] By the eighteenth century, as the households of religious dignitaries also frequently intermarried with the military, and as the sultan abolished the Janissaries[79] in 1826 and founded Western-style schools and courts that now undermined their legitimacy, the boundaries demarcating them became much more fluid. The inner tensions within the religious establishment due to the swelling of the ranks, monopolization of offices, increasing tension among the wealthy and poor religious scholars, and developing allegiances with the unorthodox religious orders *(tarikat)* hastened this process. Properties of religious foundations also fell into ruin throughout the centuries (Gibb and Bowen 1963, II: 178). The administration of the religious endowments was centralized by the sultan and turned into a ministry after the Western mode in 1840; the establishment of a ministry of education in 1857 and a ministry of justice in 1879 followed. This bureaucratization deprived religious dignitaries of both their financial and administrative autonomy. Adolphus Slade, who visited Constantinople during the reign of Mahmud II, the sultan who instigated these series of reforms, provides a poignant account of this decline in power as he narrates how the sultan overcame the resistance of the religious dignitaries to condone his adoption of Western-style costumes for the military:

> The Scheick Islam [sheik-ül-Islam] of the day refused to issue a *fetwah* [decree] sanctioning the change of costume, on which Mahmoud sent for Meki-zadeh Effendi, a Mollah of great personal influence on account of his wealth and noble descent, his family having furnished several Scheicks Islam to the state, and demanded if auhority for the proposed alteration might not be found in the Koran. "The particular case may not be cited," answered the courtier, "but it is written that the desire of the prophet's successor shall be law." Charmed with the decision, Mahmoud, in order to render it authoritative, deposed the unbending head of the law, and appointed Meki-zadeh Effendi in his place. (1837, I: 493)

Slade's narration of how the sultan could so swiftly and so summarily dismiss the sheik-ül islam exhibits how the structural position and power and the dispensability of religious dignitaries had started to resemble those of the office-households. Ultimately, they were not able to challenge the sultan but instead their power eroded as the sultan coopted more and more of their social strength by creating Western-style schools and courts. By the end of the nineteenth century, they had lost control of both education and justice to the newly created Western-style institutions and had become government officials.

The sultan assumed that the students trained at these Western-style schools would be loyal to him in the way his household members initially were, before the institutionalization of office- and provincial households and the learned hierarchy set in. His assumption proved incorrect: these students developed allegiances to each other, proceeded to expand the state at the expense of the sultan, and formed the origins of a new group, the Ottoman bureaucratic bourgeoisie.

Ottoman Adoption of Western-Style Educational Institutions

The combination of an external factor, the costly Ottoman wars, with the internal dynamics, namely, the challenges of office- and provincial households and religious dignitaries, led the Ottoman sultan to adopt Western-style educational institutions in the eighteenth and nineteenth centuries. The analysis of the effects of the wars on the Ottoman empire and the nature of the challenges of the office- and provincial households now leads to an empirical investigation of the Ottoman sultan's response, namely, his adoption of Western-style institutions. After the eighteenth century, the Ottoman sultan started introducing different types of Western-style schools in order to train a new group of administrators who would be loyal to his person. His efforts escalated the beginning of the nineteenth century only to decline in the latter half, when these newly trained students, rather than professing loyalty to the sultan, began to criticize him and the nature of his rule over the empire. Western-style schools brought with them new epistemological assumptions, new social visions that polarized Ottoman society and caused the emergence, for the first time, of organized political opposition to the sultan. The end result of this process was the formation of the Ottoman bureaucratic bourgeoisie.

The Sultan's Adoption of Western-Style Institutions

As a consequence of the Ottoman defeats, the first sphere[80] in Ottoman society to be transformed, under the control and initiation of the sultan, was military practice. Although the Ottomans had adapted Western practice in warfare from the onset of their empire as they utilized innovations such as artillery and handguns, Western shipbuilding techniques, and Western-style charts (Lewis 1982: 49, 223–25), recent military developments in the West required much more extensive structural changes, ranging from the systematic training of the corps to fully equipped hospitals. The creation of schools and academies for military education had been a notable feature of eighteenth-century Europe (Rudé 1985: 217). In 1731, the Russians had founded the noble cadet corps in St. Petersburg, the French Royal Military School in Paris was established in 1751, and the Austrian military academy at Wiener-Neustadt in 1752. Similarly, schools for engineers, whose role in military warfare had become significant due to technological advances, appeared in Woolwich in 1741, Mezières in France in 1748, and Russia in 1756. Until then, the Ottoman sultan had kept abreast of Western technological developments through the services of a palace group known as the "Western corps" *(taife-i efrenciyan)*. These were paid retainers in the sultan's service who maintained contact with the West; they applied the latest scientific advances for the benefit of the Ottomans in both civil and military projects (Murphey 1983: 287–91).

A number of factors informed the sultan's decision to directly introduce into Ottoman society a military training institution after the Western model. Ottoman defeats against Western armies had necessitated a constructive Ottoman response, and the success of the Russian ruler Peter the Great in adopting Western military practice to defeat Western armies may have served as a positive example. Also, within the context of the empire, Muhammed Ali, the Ottoman governor of Egypt who eventually secured an independent political standing for the province, had successfully introduced Western institutions into Egypt through his household in the early nineteenth century (Hunter 1984). This social practice may have provided the Ottoman sultan with a plausible mode of adoption where he would use his own household to select and introduce such institutions. The Ottoman administrative precedence also enhanced this possibility since the Ottoman sultans had successfully administered the empire through their palace-trained households for centuries. Hence, theoretically, this household organization could recreate a similar success, as Western-style training originating in the sultan's palace replicated itself throughout the empire, thereby transforming it after the Western mode. It may have been this line of reasoning based on structural precedence that led the Ottoman sultan to abolish the Janissary corps in 1826 and to ask, the same year, the governor of Egypt to send him officers to train the Ottoman soldiers. Yet, when the governor stalled on this request, the Ottoman sultan formed a Western-style palace battalion from his household slaves, free Muslim youths, and officials' sons training in the palace (Levy 1971: 27, 32). This was the first Ottoman officer training institution and also the last effort to revive the palace school. The institution then expanded and gravitated out of the palace. The model for the financing of these new "imperial" schools was based on previous Ottoman practice. Because establishing educational institutions was considered a pious Islamic deed, the sultan, officials, and some wealthy subjects founded and maintained schools for the public as religious endowments (Ergin 1939: 68). Hence, when the Ottoman sultan started founding such schools after the Western-model in the eighteenth century, he financed these new schools as if they were religious endowments. Unlike the income-generating, self-sustaining religious endowments, however, these new schools could not finance themselves and needed constant replenishment of funds from the sultan's treasury.

The abolition in 1826 of the Janissary corps,[81] which had been a fundamental military unit of the empire, was a turning point in the Ottoman adoption of Western-style institutions. The main obstacle to the sultan's attempts to found Western-style military training had emerged from the Janissaries, who formed the backbone of the Ottoman army. The Janissaries, although originally a standing army, had become embedded in Ottoman society with time. They acquired additional economic resources and social networks through trade and marriage, so much so that by the eighteenth century they were no longer a strictly military organization with clearly defined goals and boundaries. The new Western-style military training the sultan was now proposing was strenuous, required the acquisition of new skills, and necessitated continuous presence at the barracks—all new social practices the Janissaries did not want to engage in, even though, ironically, continuous presence in the barracks had been an original Janissary practice that was later abandoned. Also, military activity, the one and exclusive core of these new practices, did not tolerate the nonmilitary enterprises of the Janissaries in commerce. Although the Janissaries challenged this Western-style training system,[82] in the end, the sultan removed this alternative form of organization by abolishing them in 1826 (Levy 1982: 232; Berkes 1964: 48; Ergin 1939: 49–50). The introduction of Western-style military practice to Ottoman society thus led to a whole new system of training and organization.

The new Ottoman army built upon the sultan's training corps, which were drilled full time in their own barracks, away from any interaction with the populace. They thus did not develop ties with other Ottoman social groups as the Janissaries had done, but instead fostered allegiances to one another. The adoption of other institutions after various Western models followed an accelerated pace. The first new departments of state to be established were those of war, religious endowments, and Islamic legal ruling; ministries of civil and foreign affairs (1835) and the ministry of finance (1837) followed. The palace school, which had always formed the basis of practical and administrative training, was closed down in 1833 and replaced by a series of translation chambers at the new ministries (Mardin 1962: 208–9, Lewis 1979: 88; Findley 1989: 11). Consultative committees were created within and outside these new institutions to discuss issues of development. The second half of the nineteenth century witnessed the codification of the Ottoman legal system after various Western models, most prominently the French. The promulgation of a new penal code in 1840 was followed in 1858 by new land and penal codes and in 1861 by commercial and maritime codes. The codification culminated in the promulgation of a new civil code in 1870, again using the French as a model (Lewis 1979: 109–10, 118–19, 122). The replacement of the household with the institution as the organizing principle of the empire produced significant reverberations throughout the empire. Western-style institutions, unlike households, were independent organs established to pursue a defined goal with a clearly defined and trained group of individuals. Once they were introduced into the Ottoman military, they quickly penetrated other areas of knowledge and other spheres of activity. The establishment of the naval (1776) and military (1793) engineering schools extended to the medical school (1826) and school for surgeons (1831), and another school in military sciences (1834),[83] until the education provided in the Western-style Ottoman schools reached the same level of instruction. These Western-style Ottoman schools were mostly organized after the French model, and the courses were often taught in French. The courses at the School of Military Sciences in Constantinople, for instance, were organized after the French military academy of Saint-Cyr, and the course outline for the general staff were designed after that of the Ecole d'Etat-Major. The need for high schools that would prepare students for military academies led to the formation of the Galatasaray high school in 1863, a school once more based on the French educational model. Spheres outside education also reflected the influence of other Western forms. Prussian and English practices served as ideal models in cannon foundry and naval order and provisioning, respectively.

Among these adoptions of Western-style institutions, the educational ones were the most significant since they reproduced Western ideas in Ottoman society. Even though Ottoman historical evidence establishes that the Ottoman sultan did indeed adopt Western-style educational institutions, it is difficult to assess scientifically the scope of this adoption from the existing historical evidence. The inability to do so brings issues of validity and representativeness of the historical evidence to the forefront. The contribution of sociological methodology becomes crucial at this juncture: historical sociology provides the venue of systematic observation that makes generalizations beyond one historical case possible. Only the employment of such sociological methodology can determine the *prevalence* of this adoption of Western-style schools over the eighteenth and nineteenth centuries. An exhaustive survey of the historical sources on Ottoman education generates the following figure on the number of types of Western-style schools the Ottoman sultan founded during the eighteenth and nineteenth centuries.

The spread of the sixty types of schools established by the Ottoman sultan generate the following pattern. Such schools were established with relative infrequency in the eighteenth century; it was only in the first half of the nineteenth century that the sultan started establishing new types of schools at an exponential rate. Yet, the increasing costs of supporting these institutions and the sultan's inability to acquire the loyalty of the students trained led to a rapid decline by the end of the nineteenth century. Yet by that period the new structural and epistemological elements had already developed in Ottoman society.[84] The institution had replaced the household as the organizational unit, and the vision of a constitutional government over citizens of an abstract Ottoman state had supplanted the image of a sultan governing over his flock. Indeed, these new elements made possible the formation of the Ottoman bureaucratic bourgeoisie.

N = 60 types of schools started by the Ottoman sultan

Figure 3. Number of Types of Western Schools Founded by the Ottoman Sultan. (O. Nuri Ergin, *Maarif Tarihi* [The History of (Ottoman) Education], 2 vols. İstanbul, 1939, 1941; Mehmed Raşid, *Tarihi- Raşid* [The Historical Chronicle of Raşid], 5 vols. İstanbul, 1865; Cevdet Pasha, *Tarih-i Cevdet* [The Historical Chronicle of Cevdet], 12 vols. İstanbul, 1883–91.)

The penetration into the empire of the Western-style institution as the organizing principle was a long process that originated with the arrival of Western military advisors, continued with the establishment of military schools where these advisors also taught, and culminated in the foundation of Western-style schools and institutions throughout the empire by the second half of the nineteenth century. Since new Western military expertise had been considered the crucial factor in securing future Ottoman military victories, the Ottoman sultan attempted to recruit French military officers, who could train his own soldiers at the palace. Initially, there was no set Ottoman recruitment pattern; refugees, adventurers, the recommendations of various embassies, consuls, and merchants were all utilized to enlist European engineers, architects, and military officials for the Ottoman army (Beydilli 1983: 260–63). By 1795, Ottoman recruitment became more systematized as the government sent lists of vacant officer and technician positions to European capitals, particularly Paris.[85] Originally, the European advisors who were recruited complained about the poor working and living conditions that resulted from the religious restrictions placed upon their participation in Ottoman society, as it had been on that of the Ottoman minorities before them. They could not acquire high status within the Ottoman military without converting to Islam and adopting the Ottoman mode of dress. Only a few advisors, such as the comte de Bonneval (1675–1744),[86] agreed to these conditions, while many others quickly returned to Europe. By the second half of the eighteenth century, when these stringent conditions were relaxed so that Western advisors could assist the Ottoman army without converting to Islam and adopting the Ottoman dress and ways,[87] substantial military assistance, especially from the French, followed. More military experts, technicians for arsenals, construction and foundry workers, carpenters, and ship-wrights came to work in the Ottoman army.[88]

The increase in the arrivals of military advisors coalesced with the expansion of Western-style institutions in the empire. The first Ottoman school to be founded in 1738 after the Western model to introduce new military techniques was a school of military engineering; the foundation of a medical service and a medical school to treat Ottoman soldiers followed. The school of military engineering slowly expanded in 1790 as engineers and officers were recruited mainly from Sweden and France as instructors. In 1792, barracks for the bombardiers, sappers, and miners were set up, and 1795 witnessed the foundation of a land engineering school. Other Western-style corps developed in a similar manner. In 1774, the new unit of artillery corps with 250 recruits drilled in light cannon. By 1782, the Ottoman artillery corps had expanded to 2,000 soldiers in their own barracks where they were kept under constant training (Cevdet 1861, II: 57). In 1776, a new school of naval engineering was founded and, eight years later, a fortification section added to it. As Ottoman ships started to be built after the techniques utilized in English and French naval yards, an Ottoman career naval service kept under constant training developed along this construction activity. The traditional seasonal naval recruits of the Ottoman army were gradually replaced by a permanent, drilled body of sailors. A more visible and dramatic indication of the scope of change was the dress code of 1826, according to which the troops had to wear uniforms consisting of Western-style tunics and trousers; in 1829 the clothing reform was extended to civilians, the new costumes of state officials being especially carefully regulated (Lewis 1979: 99–102).

The large group of French advisors, assisted by many English, Swedes, and Italians, accelerated this development of Western-style institution-building. Originally, lessons in these Western-style military schools were given in French, with Ottoman minorities frequently employed to translate them into Ottoman simultaneously. Yet efforts to translate these lectures and Western technical books into Ottoman commenced simultaneously,[89] and accelerated in the second half of the eighteenth century.[90] Gradually, by the end of the nineteenth century, these translated books and the first cohort of Ottoman trainees replaced Ottoman minorities as translators and Western advisors as lecturers.[91] Now, for the first time, the newly skilled Ottoman "professional" soldiers trained and taught others the expertise they needed.

All these training schools and advisors prepared the organizational framework for the establishment, during 1789–1807, of "an army of the New Order" *(Nizam-ı Cedid),* which contained the new infantry and cavalry units based on the Western model. It was this army and these trainees that eventually transformed the Janissary corps and the household structure; as the sultan established more and more Western-style institutions to sustain this army, he spread the institutional organization to other financial and administrative spheres of activity. To compensate for the lack of funds, he decreed new extraordinary levies *(imdadiye),* and with the proceeds he established a treasury to finance these new institutions and ministries to administer them. Even though the sultan's treasury had been the only one of the empire, in 1793 the Ottoman sultan formed, for the first time, a separate treasury for his new army. This new military treasury co-opted cash revenues from Ottoman tax-farms to build new naval yards, barracks, and schools and to pay Western advisors. This establishment of a separate treasury was significant for two reasons. First of all, it led the sultan to lose the control he had over the distribution of resources in the empire as the other treasuries he established slowly overtook and marginalized his own.[92] Also, the revenues the sultan specifically allocated to these treasuries accelerated the structural separation between the sultan, his military, and his state. By the nineteenth century, the economic resources of the state, the military, and the sultan became totally separated and allocated to different treasuries. The new treasuries founded to finance the Ottoman military altered the Ottoman resource allocation system, however. As the sultan kept financing these military institutions with the intention of training a loyal social group that would help him counter the internal challenge of the households and the external threat of the Western military, his own treasury and wealth started to shrink, and these military institutions wrested his economic resource base away from him. By the early nineteenth century, this shrinkage had reached such a degree that the sultan's expenses exceeded his revenues and he became insolvent. After this resource realignment, the treasuries were compartmentalized and brought together under one single treasury in 1893, with one major difference. It was not the Ottoman sultan but instead the Ottoman state, equipped with Western-style institutions and staffed by newly trained personnel, that emerged to control the resources of the empire. This new Ottoman military and state appropriated the revenues of the sultan for the newly united treasury and allocated to him, in return, "an appropriate salary from the treasury" (Cezar 1986: 289). The Ottoman sultan's control over the resources of the empire thus dwindled.

New Social Vision and Polarization

The introduction of Western-style education into the empire brought with it a significant epistemological disjuncture between Islamic knowledge as it had been practiced in the empire and the new "scientific" knowledge that was being interjected. Whereas the former had been embedded in the moral system of religion emphasizing the significance of the community, the latter was founded on scientific thinking and organized around the rational individual. Legitimation in the former was based on the sacred authority endowed upon the Ottoman sultan as the protector of the believers; legitimacy in the latter hinged, at least in theory if not in practice in some parts of Europe, on the implementation of justice and equality for all individual participants of the system. Although these conceptions presented idealizations, they nevertheless did inform the social practices of the recruits in the Western-style institutions. The nature of this epistemological transformation and the discontent it produced with the earlier Islamic division of knowledge was crucial in structuring the future course of the empire.

The Ottoman educational system had been organized around the Islamic division of knowledge along four dimensions (Findley 1989: 36, 138): the rational concept of knowledge *(ilm)*; the gnosticism of the mystics *(irfan)*; the philosophical-scientific culture (*felsefe*); and the worldly literary culture *(adab)*. Since the Qur'an and the discourse on it had been designated the rational concept of knowledge, Western scientific knowledge had to be situated in another category. The gnosticism of the mystics, namely, the intuitive experience of the divine, formed the basis for the new "modern" world vision, probably due to the assumed link between intuition and scientific observation. The newly emerging group of students made many attempts to integrate Islamic knowledge with its Western forms in order to draw upon this Islamic discourse to legitimate their social stand on issues (Mardin 1962: 81). Yet ultimately all of these endeavors to integrate the two paradigms failed because, unlike the new "scientific" knowledge, the focus on the Islamic discourse was not accompanied by a thorough structural reorganization. As the new scientific knowledge germinated in the empire through Western-style institutions and ideas, they first challenged and then, gradually, marginalized the other. The memoirs of the new recruits in the Western-style schools vividly demonstrate how painfully aware the new students were of how much more individually empowering the new one was, especially compared to the former discourse. In the late nineteenth century, one student wistfully noted:

> Alas! To youth like us who were studying cosmography, trigonometry, engineering, who were more or less reading syllable by syllable Voltaire and Volnay,[93] and who, with the confidence and vanity of youth even aspired to criticize and refute what they learned, [to such youth] the religion teacher who now and then stopped by the school, every two weeks and, at other times, once a month, to inspire the religious ideal in all of us, ceaselessly made and interpreted the following statement in almost all his lectures. "As the Qur'an decrees," he stated, "work during your military training in being a servant to the sultan and always obey his orders." His assistant . . . probably to capture the attention of the students by invoking their curiosity and to make sure the hour was spent with minimum disturbance, kept repeating over and over the Islamic rulings on how to preserve the state of ritual ablution. (Georgeon 1986: 21)

Hence, neither of the two tutors on Islamic knowledge addressed, let alone countered, the challenge of scientific knowledge.[94] Other students repeatedly made many similar comments; one remarked on how the teachers of the religion courses "explained nothing about religion except to utter, at every possible instance, the necessity of blind obedience to the sultan who was the shadow of God on earth" (Nur 1992: 134). Indeed, the students contrasted more and more what they were learning with what they had been taught previously, always to the advantage of the former.[95]

As these students problematized Islamic knowledge within the context of Ottoman society, they also started to question the loyalty they were assumed to impart to the protector and overseer of this knowledge, namely, the sultan. A whole spectrum of symbolic resistance started to develop around the loyalty oath to the sultan that all the students attending the Western-style schools had to repeat, every week. The students started either to fail to repeat the oath or to subvert its meaning in their own renditions. Indeed, the discourse around the oath provided the first public basis of the new resistance to the sultan. The oath, which illustrated the sultan's continuous attempts and expectations in fostering a body of administrators to himself, was phrased as follows: "May God prolong, in good health, the life of our sultan, in whom the whole universe seeks refuge and finds justice and by whose blessed bread we are nourished. And may God render permanent and everlasting his rule on the Ottoman throne. Amen" (Hasan Amca [1958] 1991: 40). The directors of the Western-style school uttered this oath out loud, then cried out, "Long live my sultan," and expected the students to repeat this utterance after him three times. Memoirs of students from this period (Enver Paşa [1913] 1989; Hasan Amca [1958] 1991; Sağlam [1940] 1991; Ahmed İzzet [1924] 1992; Nur [1928] 1992) reiterated, time and again, how increasingly difficult it was becoming for them to observe this ritual. Another ritual where the students professed their loyalty to the sultan was upon their invitation to the palace to break their fast during the month of Ramadhan. After the meal, the sultan complimented them and gave them a gift of one gold coin each and in return expected them to pray for him, their benefactor. One medical student recounting one such event noted how "everyone said amen and shouted long live the sultan, except for the medical students, whose voice was barely heard. Even though their supervisor yelled at them to shout, he was not effective, as they moved their mouths in silence" (Sağlam [1940] 1991: 78–79). As the students kept resisting these rituals, they were repeatedly told that they were being ungrateful to their benefactor and father, the sultan. Two instances demonstrate the nature of the speech the students were given because of their disrespect. In one instance, the student recounted how "these lectures by the [sultan's] pashas started off and ended and were often repeated time and again over the skirtloads of money the sultan, who was the benefactor of the universe, was spending on us" (Ahmed İzzet [1924] 1992: 7). He also noted how, in response, some students yelled "may the sultan go upside down!," an alliteration on "long live my sultan."[96] In another instance a military medical student paraphrased one of the speeches they were given by the minister of education:

> You are ungrateful because you do not know the hand that feeds you. Even a dog would know that. It is our sultan, our benefactor who does not scold one, that feeds you. You vile men! Every part of your school is leaking, you have no decent clothing or food. When it starts raining [at night], you have to keep shifting your beds from one corner to the other. Do not think we do not know of these; but we do not look after you because you are not loyal to the sultan, you traitors! (Nur [1928] 1992: 125)

As a rejoinder to this speech, a few students shouted, "Vile man, damn the sultan!," whereupon the pasha immediately plunged into their midst to try to locate them. But he could not do so and eventually had to leave off without arresting anyone. This resistance to the sultan soon expanded as the sultan's officials attempted to sanction students through their loyalty and as students countered by rallying to one another's support in condemning it. Hence, when a group of students were called in for questioning on the "seditious, free-thinking behavior" of some students at their school, they were asked to report against the others on the grounds that "this was a question of loyalty to the sultan" (Mehmed Rauf [1911] 1991: 66)." The tension between the two groups further escalated when the sultan's officials tried to dismiss the legitimacy of the new forms of Western knowledge the students were attaining by repeatedly stating that "loyalty, which came before everything, was why the sultan took care of them, and one could certainly become victorious on loyalty alone, without resorting to scientific knowledge on warfare" (Enver Paşa [1913] 1989: 255; Hanioğlu 1985: 63) Indeed, it was this contestation of social legitimation between loyalty as advocated by the sultan and meritocracy as implied by Western-style schools that led to a new vision and that restructured the empire.

What did this new emergent social vision among the students of the Western-style schools entail? Societal emphasis on the sacred order, communal loyalty, and the sultan yielded to natural law, individual labor, and the state. Loyalty was now defined in more abstract terms as loyalty to the state, which anyone could individually secure through being fair and just. The Enlightenment concept of knowledge based on positivism and materialism introduced with it a new interpretation of Ottoman society whereby individuals, rather than households, were judged by their contribution to Ottoman society, through their labors rather than their loyalty. Indeed, the Ottoman discourse on this materialism reached such a degree that one Ottoman intellectual, Beşir Fuad,[97] committed suicide to prove that all, including death, could be explained naturally through science (Hanioğlu 1981: 9; Mardin 1983: 42–43). The boundaries of the individual in Ottoman society and the nature of his responsibility to the community thus was speedily redefined.[98] The new vision argued that only an Ottoman constitutional state could unite these ideals of natural law, individual labor, and the state, as it created a body of Ottoman citizens equal under law on their own individual merits. The newly trained Ottoman students applied their recently acquired scientific knowledge to Ottoman society to attain this vision. They reasoned that the scientific method of the positive sciences and the systematic observation it entailed could be used to explain Ottoman societal processes. For instance, on two separate occasions, medical students plotted a course of social action for themselves based on the analogies they drew between what they learned and what they observed:

> We learn that in chemistry . . . two particular elements mix and transform into a novel, valuable compound. Let us all unite to form such an immense power. Then let us attack and destroy, with our own hands, this bastion of the castle of despotism established against us. . . . [It is said that] physicians ought not to get involved in taking the political pulse since their actual profession is medical care. But who will the nation have its pulse taken by [of course, no one] but the physicians. (Hanioğlu 1981: 12, 22)

The Western form of knowledge thus started to provide the students with a course of social action. The new vision emphasized a fresh model for the Ottoman individual that "did not merely push paper, but constantly combatted ignorance and struggled for life . . . and utilized the self-help system of Samuel Smiles" (Hanioğlu 1981: 199). The boundaries of this vision moved across societies and nationalities to unite all men around the ideals of a civilized fraternity. For instance, one editorial by Mehmed Bey on 1 May 1870 called for "brothers across the ocean, as well as across the desert, let us give one another our hand, let us unite to conquer liberty, let us associate to arrive at equality, let us cherish one another so that fraternity might reign on earth" (Mardin 1962: 23). Yet how was this new social group going to establish such an imagined fraternity in Ottoman society, let alone in the universe?

Even though the students imagined a fraternity that would unite them all, the emerging Western-style schools actually polarized the empire along new dimensions. One dimension entailed the choice of strategy for Ottoman social change. The new credentialed group initiated change from above. Rather than investing resources throughout society at the lower levels, they utilized the imagery of the tuba tree in heaven, whereby the roots of a tree grew upward and its branches reached downward to bring fruits, to argue that it would be more enlightening to introduce social change from above (Findley 1989: 132). Yet the major shortcoming of this strategy was the inability to discern the societal demand. School after school had to be closed down due to lack of students. For instance, the Imperial School of Commerce, established in 1882 after the French Ecole des Hautes Etudes Commerciales, had to be closed down in 1888 due to a shortage of students. Even though it was reopened in 1905, the students were more interested in joining the state bureaucracy than engaging in trade (Toprak 1982: 49). In addition, earlier in the century it was reported that even the graduates of the medical school were more interested in secure government jobs than in practicing medicine. Even though new educational institutions had been founded, there were not adequate structural transformations in society, sufficient professionalization that could accommodate these new graduates.

The other dimension entailed the issue of leadership in social change. Even though the Western-style schools were established to provide all students with equal opportunity, preexisting Ottoman social inequalities rapidly spread into this new social context and polarized the student body. Ever since sultan Mahmud II's time, recruitment into the military academies was done from among the populace to stop them from developing ties with the office-households (Mardin 1983: 57–58). Yet in most of the Western-style schools, such as in the military academy in 1889, the sons of pashas held a privileged position as they attended special sections (Hasan Amca [1958] 1991: 33; Mardin 1983: 57–58). In other instances, beautifully groomed elite students would be in the same classroom with the rest of the student body, but they would not sit in rows with the rest of the class but instead occupy the chairs especially placed for them next to the teacher's desk (Mardin 1990: 219–20). The Ottoman elites, namely, the sons of the sultan's house-holds and prominent officials, thus received privileged status and faster promotions than the scholarship students recruited from among the populace.

The student body also resented some teachers' attempts to rectify the poor grades given to the sons of pashas (Amca 1958: 107). Scholarship students started to violently criticize and resent these elite students, who joined and got promoted through connections. In the military academies, it became routine for young officers to caution incoming students not to take the privileges of the sons of pashas seriously and to convince themselves, instead, that they were the true owners of the empire (Mardin 1990: 191). The increasing vengeance against these students was evident in one instance (Ali Kemal [1913] 1985: 64) when all of the students were extremely pleased when the teacher scolded one of the sons of pashas for his failure to answer a question. Tensions also developed between urban students and those from the provinces, leading to fights with large sticks (Temo [1939] 1987: 10). Ottoman social inequality thus acquired a new material and geographical dimension in education.[99] Indeed, one of the first decisions of the group of former students who eventually established a constitutional system was to abolish the ranks of elite officials promoted too soon due to their connections (Mardin 1991: 153–54). In order to foster their own ranks, the same group also established many scholarships for the poor. By marginalizing the elite in this manner, the new social group of students further defined its boundaries, articulated its vision, and challenged the sultan.

Emergence of Organized Political Opposition

The organized political opposition to the sultan in these Western-style schools emerged through a gradual process of increasing social consciousness, a process that is demonstrated well in the memoirs of one of the founders of the first political opposition group to the sultan (Ali Kemal [1913] 1985: 68, 73–76, 89, 95–96, 105). As the author narrated, the inability to discuss certain ideas was the first instance through which they realized "the reality of the absolutist rule on their ideas." During a French lesson where they were using Pelissier's *Morceaux Choisis,* the teacher referred to a poem where a dog named Sultan was mentioned. The teacher, upset by this reference, hastily left the classroom to beckon the director, while "all the students read and reread the poem with glee." Before the break, superintendents and teachers came to collect each and every book from them. The narrator recounted that this was the first incident that "opened his eyes" to the problems with Ottoman rule. He also reminisced on how, under the influence of the different methods of political rule they were learning about, a group of students would get together and reiterate that they ought to "go to Europe, or even to America . . . to leave the world of slavery for the lands of freedom." Indeed, many did go to Europe in search for freedom and gathered periodically at the Café des Thermes on the Boulevard St. Germain in Paris to discuss the affairs of the empire. Many also engaged in the minutest details of the French political debates, such as the Jules Ferry affair, since this was "a luxury they could not practice in the Ottoman empire." Upon his return, the narrator attended the school for civil servants, where he recounted to his friends all he had seen in Europe. One day, as he mentioned "the students organizations like Helvetia, Philadelphia that he had encountered in Geneva," they decided to form a similar organization in their own school where they would all "wear, like the ones in Switzerland did, red fezes with blue tassels." Upon discovery by the authorities of their political activities, however, they were arrested and questioned for four weeks. When the authorities discovered a stanza *(bent)* from a poem by Jean-Jacques

Rousseau in his pocket, they gave the narrator a particularly hard time, repeatedly asking him how he had "become such an apostate." The students were released only on condition that they would not read "thinkers such as Rousseau who were against religion and ethics and therefore disapproved of by the sultan." The narrator wryly noted, however, that the minister of education, Münif Pasha, who was giving this advice was himself one of the first Ottoman translators of Rousseau. Indeed, once sown, the seeds of opposition could not be gathered. The informal opposition gradually transformed into the organized political opposition groups of secret societies.[100]

These secret societies were founded with the aim of bringing liberty and equality to the empire by establishing a constitutional system of rule. The military medical academies were the first foundation of the opposition to the sultan because, one student recounted, "the medical students, as individuals, knew the difference between East and West, and felt the deep sorrow of the [Ottoman] backwardness" (Sağlam 1991: 74). Hence, as the students continually compared the two worlds,[101] their medical school "became the nest of the [Ottoman] efforts to reach as soon as possible the level of those countries which had achieved a high level of civilization; [all students tried] to free [Ottoman society] from Eastern sluggishness and [wanted to] lead it to progress, to the love of freedom and the fatherland." These students read and memorized, by heart, the banned poems of prominent Ottoman writers,[102] who often criticized the sultan (Ali Kemal [1913] 1985: 54; Nur [1928] 1992: 99). The transformation from informal networks discussing freedom literature and the affairs of the empire to secret societies organizing political opposition occurred in the mid-nineteenth century, after the education of the first cohort of Western-style trained students. The first opposition group was organized in 1859 in the military academy with the explicit intent of dethroning the current sultan for his incompetence in ruling; swiftly uncovered, the event was referred to by the Ottoman state as the "Kuleli incident," after the military barracks where they were tried. Soon after, in 1865, the Patriotic Alliance (İttifak-ı Hamiyyet) was created clandestinely by a group of individuals who had all worked in the Translation Office of the Foreign Ministry. The organizational models they had chosen for this alliance were the Carbonari, the early nineteenth-century secret society against the restoration in France and Italy, and the Young Spain, Young France, and Young Italy societies (Mardin 1962: 10–11, 21). The students also articulated themselves as a social group as they participated in and mobilized mass movements. For instance, on 11 May 1876, after the Bulgarian revolt, they took to the streets and rioted to protest the faulty handling of the affair by the heads of the administrative *(sadrazam)* and religious *(seyhülislam)* institutions of the empire (Aktar 1990: 53–54). In justifying their course of action, the students argued that at such seditious and transitional times, it fell upon them to arm themselves and find a solution to the disasters of the empire. They explicitly stated:

> It is not proper to one's religion and national honor to occupy oneself with classes and courses at a time when the jurisprudence and the independence of the Ottoman state and her dominions are trampled upon by her enemies. Everywhere the Muslims are suffering from the tortures and insults inflicted upon them by the hands of the Christians. According to Islamic law, it is our duty and obligation to remove the influential administrators who have caused this state of affairs. (Aktar 1990: 54)

The students, who thus started to participate in revolts as a social group, gradually initiated a series of riots that indeed culminated in the dethronement of the current sultan. The group that marched to the palace to execute the dethronement was comprised of military students under the explicit order of their director "to carry out a sacred duty for the state and the nation" (Aktar 1990: 58–59). For the Western-style trained students, the state and the nation had replaced the sultan as a mobilizing force in Ottoman society.

The first organized opposition to the Ottoman sultan dates back to 21 May 1889, when the medical military students formed a secret organization, the Ottoman Union, which quickly spread into the military *(harbiye)* and medical *(tıbbiye)* academies and the school for civil servants *(mülkiye)*. Due to the influence of Auguste Comte, the name of the organization was then changed to Union and Progress, the title under which it ruled[103] the empire from 1913 to its demise. Ahmed Rıza, who initiated this change and who later became the president of the first Ottoman assembly, had trained with the French positivist thinker Pierre Lafitte in Paris and headed the Paris branch of the committee (Ahmed Rıza [1900] 1988: 23). He stated that such a change of name was called for "to indicate that the rights of all the various nationalities in the empire would be honored by the association." Political opponents in the schools increased in numbers through the 1890s as the students clandestinely wrote and circulated bulletins and issued secret newspapers (Aktar 1990: 60–61). The same period was also marked by the continuous arrests of students due to political opposition activities, under the legal cause of "freedom of thought" *(serbesti-i efkar)*. In 1897, seventy-eight students who coordinated these school activities in the name of freedom were deported to Tripoli when a plot to assassinate the minister overseeing military education was uncovered.[104] The Ottoman Freedom Society, which was formed in Salonica in approximately the same time period, also aimed to establish a constitutional regime in the empire (Bleda [1950] 1979: 22).[105] The pledge ritual for the society entailed taking an oath in a room with a green baize-covered table with a Qur'an and a gun on it. When one gave his oath on the Qur'an, he was told that he would receive a bullet in the head if he disclosed the secrets of the organization.

It was through this political opposition to the sultan that the emerging bureaucratic bourgeoisie acquired a separate consciousness. As they fought and suffered together, they bonded more. As they fused together into a tightly knit group, they helped each other out financially, physically, and emotionally. One Ottoman intellectual noted the strength of the ties that developed in the late nineteenth century among them:

> There was such a discipline established among the students that they acted [as a unity] as if they were one mouth and one body. Even though we openly practiced politics and read newspapers that were banned as harmful and seditious [by the state], no one dared to report us to the administration. During the six years [I was in school], only three spies emerged among us. They [the students] would throw a military cloak over them at night and altogether thoroughly beat them up. No one would talk to these spies. Some even cursed them as they passed by them. The first [punishment] was called "cloak beating" . . . the second was termed "excommunication." . . . [The second] was a weapon more terrible than beating. Nobody would ever speak to them. . . . [In the end, because of this behavior] the spies either would become consumptive[106] or insane. (Nur [1928] 1992: 116)

The students organized among themselves and democratically elected representatives to decide upon what to report to the administration and why. In their private lives within the Western-style schools of the empire, these students were indeed endeavoring to actualize their vision within their limited circles as they debated, elected representatives, and strove for the freedom they thought they did not have in the empire.

The significance of their vision and its mobilizational power became evident only after their graduation and assignment to bureaucratic posts throughout the empire. It was through such posts that they were able to spread their influence throughout the empire, organize social networks, and protect one another whenever necessary. Many became teachers and administrators, using their ties and professional connections "to tirelessly work for freedom" (Bleda [1950] 1979: 41).[107] This course of social action was in accord with the explicit aim of the Committee of Union and Progress to gradually place its members into positions of responsibility within the Ottoman administration. Once mobilized in such a manner, the committee conjectured, they could slowly take over the state and destroy the despotism of the sultan (Mehmed Rauf 1911: 22, 81). The sultan, in need of well-trained administrators, assisted in his own demise as he treated these rebels as errant children, often bestowing upon them, in spite of their divided allegiances, important significant posts in distant Ottoman provinces. It was through these posts that the students could penetrate their influence throughout. For instance, one of the Union and Progress members recounted how they "sent the youth who had escaped and sought refuge in [their] cell to the village branches . . . to farms, or . . . to village schools" (Temo [1939] 1987: 100). In the provinces, they immediately notified one another as to who was with them so that the members would know who to contact for communication or for funds (Temo [1939] 1987: 58). Many committee members continued their political opposition while holding significant government posts since they considered themselves the officials of the Ottoman state, not of the sultan (Hanioğlu 1981: 43). As this social group of Western-style trained students transformed their Western scientific knowledge into social practice through their various posts in Ottoman society, they generated resources independent from the sultan that molded them into the Ottoman bureaucratic bourgeoisie.

Rise of the Bureaucratic Bourgeoisie

On 30 May 1876, when the Ottoman sultan Abdülaziz II was deposed through a popular movement spearheaded by the Western-style trained military officers, the memoirs of the sultan's chamberlain indicated how shocked he was by the rude treatment of the sultan by these young officers.

> The deposed sultan was sent, under the heavy rain, first to one palace and then to another. . . . When I tried to pack the dinnerware set to take with us, the major of the battalion said, "How come the sultan is eating his meals with gold fork and spoon, these are the property of the nation now, it will not be suitable for you to use them anymore." . . . The same major also ordered all the soldiers who were referring to the sultan as "my exalted sultan" to call him "Aziz Efendi" [the shortened form of the sultan's name Abdülaziz, followed by the title often given to all educated Ottoman males]. . . . (Fahri Bey [1880] 1968: 5–7, 12)

This memoir exposed the dramatic divide that had emerged in the empire between the chamberlain, who considered himself a member of the sultan's household, and the army officer, who saw himself as the representative of the Ottoman state. One professed personal servitude to the sultan, while the other claimed loyalty to the state. This army officer and others like him who trained in the Western-style schools of the empire marked the emergence of the Ottoman bureaucratic bourgeoisie with its own independent social resources and its own vision of the future of Ottoman society. This new vision relegated the sultan to being a symbolic figurehead in the background of the Ottoman state. Indeed, literally, the emergence of the photographic technique replaced the sultan in all military and civil bureaus of the empire as they hung his portrait in their office with great splendor (Rasim [1924] 1987: 180–1). The early nineteenth century also marked the removal, when referring to the sultan, of terms such as "the humble servant," "servitude," "orders," supplanting them with a singular word, "benevolence" (Rasim [1924] 1987: 217). This act also functionally removed the sultan from the realm of effective control of the empire to the symbolic domain where his influence was restricted to gift-giving. Another indication of the expansion of the Ottoman state institutions at the expense of the sultan's household entailed the drastic increase in the salaries paid to the new bureaucratic cadre. Before 1839, these had amounted to 130 million aspers,[108] but they increased 50 percent to 195 million in 1850, and an additional 71 percent to 333 million aspers in 1868 (Eldem 1970: 206–7). Similarly, the number of Ottoman civil officials escalated from 2,000 scribes in 1800 to 35,000 civil officials in 1900 (Findley 1989: 25). There was indeed a significant social group with its own vision that emerged in the late nineteenth-century Ottoman empire through Western-style education: the Ottoman bureaucratic bourgeoisie.

In analyses of bourgeois class formation, the emerging bourgeois class is often defined through its relationship to the mode of production and to economic resources. Yet such analyses do not take into account another resource that endows class with a cultural capital that is as inalienable as labor power: social resources acquired through education and connections to the state. The educational system and the social networks a social group accrued by participating in it form a social resource that articulates the social and economic boundaries of the social group, endows them with a vision, and thus transforms the group into a social class. Similarly, the state structure and the nature of the relationship a social group forms with it creates a social resource that trespasses the limitations economic production often places on such a group. Western-style education[109] thus becomes a very significant component of class formation in non-Western contexts. In the development of the Ottoman bourgeoisie, the cultural capital of credentials acquired through Western-style education was as significant as the material capital of wealth attained through commerce and production. Only after being educated in these Western-style institutions did the new social group of students acquire a new vision and construct a social conscience that mobilized them to reform and revolution, and it was only then that they were able to challenge the prominence of Ottoman minorities in the bureaucracy of the nineteenth century. Only through education did they acquire a new set of values, a sense of objectivity and professionalism that separated them from the rest of the populace. Through their cultural credentials, the Ottoman social group created what they termed a "fraternity" and utilized the networks they fostered with one another to eventually access the key positions in Ottoman state and society. This new social tie *(sınıfdaşlık)* created through the Western-style educational experience, through sharing the same experiences not within the household but within the classroom, and through relating to one another not by true or fictitious kin ties but instead by the commonality of political and social goals ultimately succeeded and gradually replaced the structural hold of households over Ottoman society. This common life experience turned those it affected into a "cohort," in its sociological sense indicating a group of individuals bonded through sharing a similar life experience.

The articulation of education as a relation of production and of credentialed skills as labor power builds on current trends in sociological analysis that attempt to go beyond the economic sphere to include the effect of the political and the state structure on class formation. As Poulantzas has argued, for instance, even though the state apparatus is often devoid of class affiliation, at certain times, "functions of the state are precisely circumscribed by its political class power" (1978: 323). Yet Poulantzas could not incorporate the political with the economic because he did not start at the level of resources, before the economic-political differentiation occurred. Miliband (Holloway and Picciotto 1979: 3–5), on the other hand, separated the social functions of the state but failed to identify the structural links between a particular social class and the state. Similarly, the debate on the social location of the professional-managerial class again assumed the economy–polity divide when they differentiated "the common relation to the economic foundations of society" from "the coherent social and cultural existence [as indicated by] a common life style, cultural background, kinship networks, consumption patterns, work habits and beliefs" (Ehrenreich and Ehrenreich 1979: 10). It is the emphasis on social resources as a fundamental category that reveals the new processes in society. In turn, this emphasis on the process, in contradistinction to the preexisting causal argument, explains the formation of a social class such as the bureaucratic bourgeoisie. This "new" class develops (Gouldner 1979: 94) as it owns and controls, not private property in the classic Marxist sense, but instead specialized knowledge, or, if one wants to express in similar terms, "cultural" property. What adds value to this cultural property is not the market but its location within the state structure. In this context, the analogy between becoming class-conscious and learning a foreign language holds, in that "both present men with a new vocabulary and a new set of concepts which permit a different translation of the meaning of inequality from that encouraged by the conventional vocabulary of society" (Parkin 1971: 90). As such vocabularies develop from within and are also introduced from without, one acquires insight into the obscured connection between state, education, and class formation. State activities, forms, routines, and rituals often constitute and regulate social identities. Indeed, "out of the vast range of human social capacities, state activities more or less forcibly 'encourage' some whilst suppressing, eroding, undermining others" (Corrigan and Sayer 1985: 2–3, 4). The agency in this process, the one that structures, mobilizes, and sanctions these activities, belongs to the bureaucratic bourgeoisie. And, as the bureaucratic bourgeoisie engages in this meaning-building, it identifies its own aims and goals with those of the state, and, in the process, claims the power of moral regulation (Corrigan and Sayer 1985: 203). Once it thus sets the official discourse, those interpreted as deviating from the "universal" norms, such as religious minorities, are marginalized. This reconceptualization extends beyond the geographical divide that often portrays non-Western class formation as significantly different from the Western political processes (Amin 1976; Trimberger 1978; Ahmad 1985; Zaalouk 1989).[110]

What, then, were the elements that defined this social group emerging through Western-style education as an Ottoman bureaucratic bourgeoisie? Most studies on Ottoman class formation missed this important segment of the Ottoman bourgeoisie as they focused on economic functions and thus overlooked the disjuncture ethnic segmentation produced in society,[111] while others concentrated on political and intellectual activities and failed to observe the significance of commerce on bourgeois class formation.[112] It is the *combination* of both the bureaucratic and the commercial that illustrated the process of bourgeois class formation in the Ottoman empire. In both cases, it was the capacity and ability of social groups to accumulate and reproduce resources outside the control of the authorities that led to the formation of the bourgeoisie. Western-style education and commerce enabled this new class to define for itself a social position within Ottoman society, independent of and outside the sultan's control. The knowledge and skills they acquired through education gave them both expertise and an inalienable resource with which they successfully challenged the sultan's control over the distribution of social and economic resources in the empire. The crystallization of the social space this group created for itself in the mid-nineteenth century was illustrated by the physical transformation of the capital, whereby more public spaces emerged to accommodate the emerging bourgeoisie (Ortaylı 1983: 173–88). Public parks and tea houses in Tepebaşı, hotels, restaurants, and reading saloons in Beyoğlu, a modern library in 1869, summer residences, a subway, schools, police stations, theaters, separate buildings for the new ministries, regular boat service on the Bosphorus, and even the establishment of boat service specifically for the students developed a new geography of space. The European side of the city became the fashionable districts, as the districts of Istanbul proper, near the sultan's initial palace in Topkapı, declined in significance. Students educated in the Western-style institutions, regardless of their field of specialization or their small numbers,[113] started to form a new vision for the empire at the expense of others.

In addition to this physical space, a new moral space also developed. The boundaries of the private and the professional also became redefined and separated from one another. Hence, for instance, one grand vezir in the early twentieth century, upon being "criticized about appearing in inappropriate public places such as Tepebaşı and Taksim smoking his pipe," had developed enough of a sense of professionalism to retort that "after he performed his duties, he was free and would do whatever he so pleased" (Findley 1989: 199). This vezir was also the first alumnus of the Western-style school of civil servants and appointed five other graduates from his school to his cabinet of thirteen, demonstrating once more the strength of school ties. Such ties were also significant in mobilizing and maintaining political opposition against the sultan, as all like-minded graduates protected one another throughout the empire as if they were "one large family." Of course, this family was different from the previous sultan's household in that there was no omnipotent household head and all the members were theoretically equal in the resources they acquired from education and brought to the relationship. This was evident, for instance, in the new *Civil Administration Journal,* which referred to the image of "a family of professionals," who saw one another individually as brothers, and who constantly discussed issues of efficiency and productivity in terms of how they could serve their country better (Findley 1989: 243). This new sense of professionalism was particularly evident in the school of civil administration (Findley 1990: 876–77) whereby the trainees, based on their newly acquired skills, claimed the authority by themselves that previously the sultan alone had the authority to endow upon them. The concept of administering the empire in the name of the sultan as his slaves dependent on his permission and authorization was replaced by a new approach whereby professionals administered the country in and of itself as responsible citizens, and, in doing so, used their expertise to reach decisions independent of, and without sanctioning by, the sultan. This shift enabled this group to free and reproduce their social resources outside the sultan's control and so to structure the boundaries that defined them as the bourgeoisie. In this sense, one could even argue that they developed "a sense of collectivity and otherness" (Merriman 1979: 14) and "an ethos of professionalization" (Abbott 1988) that distinguished them as a social class.

The first social indication of this social group's visible boundaries emerged with the 3 March 1829 dress code issued by the sultan, which required all civil servants, with the exception of those in religion, to wear the "modern" outfit of a frock coat with a high standup collar, one row of buttons, and an above the knee cut, white collared and starched shirts, neckties, narrow pants, and a fez.[114] In addition, the sultan of the time, Mahmud II, also trimmed his beard, a traditional symbol of authority, and required all civil servants to follow his example. Office furnishings changed (Findley 1989: 212), as European-style desks in rows replaced cushions and writing pads. Yet the most significant change was in the mode and definition of work.[115] The other significant social indication of this group's boundaries comprised its attempts to reproduce itself. In the late nineteenth century, the establishment of a code of regulations to govern their behavior, personnel records to make them all legally equal as professionals, and a retirement fund to sustain them in society defined the bureaucracy as a social group (Findley 1989: 27). The most significant measure among these was probably the establishment of a salary system whereby officials no longer had access to prebendal forms of dispensation (Findley 1980a: 145; 1989: 29). Yet this transition to salaried offices was not an easy one (Findley 1989: 302), as officials "tried to retain income from previous positions, hold more than one office at a time, or supplement salary by doing something else on the side." Another instance demonstrated the resistance of officials to be pegged into such posts (Cevdet 1872: 45), as one civil servant, Hasib Efendi,[116] refused, time and again, the salary increase that came with his promotion, arguing he did not need it. The Ottoman statesman narrating the incident rightfully noted that the civil servant's refusal of the raise that accompanied his promotion demonstrated his inability to distinguish the personal from the professional.[117] When the civil servant still refused, they gave the raise as "yearly gifts" *(atiyye)*.[118] Still another social indication of the social boundaries of this class was its involvement in political activities. For instance, one Ottoman statesman who was also the minister of war noted in his diary how distressed he was when, asking for a report on the improvement of the Greek army, he got a letter from the Ottoman military attaché in Athens that gave the information he wanted in the first paragraph "and then went on for three pages on Ottoman politics, giving me his suggestions on how to formulate a good Ottoman cabinet. . . . I was so distressed at how politicized these officers had become that I could not bring myself to punish this particular one" (Mahmut Şevket [1913] 1988: 132). As a part of their politics, this bourgeoisie, upon attaining power, in turn gave priority to multiplying the number of schools, thus reproducing and expanding their ranks through education. Between 1879 and 1895, it built 4 secondary preparatory schools and 160 secondary schools; it also tripled the Ottoman literacy to 15 percent by the end of this period.[119] Not all segments of Ottoman society participated equally in this new formulation, however. Religion, geographical location, and gender became the significant factors determining one's political participation in the system, as the Muslims and the urban-based populations formed the "nation" to the exclusion of the others.

The inability of the newly emerging institutions to incorporate minorities was evident throughout the social system. For instance, during the period 1859–79, all of the 162 graduates in the school for civil servants were Ottoman Muslims. Also, after 1879, even though the number of graduates increased fivefold, the small number of minorities that had started attending hardly increased (Findley 1989: 114). Another instance that provided insight into why such a divide was reproduced was the "separateness" of the ten Ottoman Jewish students attending the Ottoman medical school. These students had their meat delivered from a special butcher and their own cook appointed by the state to prepare kosher meals; they ate and lived together in a separate barrack (Nur [1928] 1992: 219). This separation of food intake and space undoubtedly restricted social interaction between Ottoman minorities and Muslims in this context as well.[120] Similarly, in the first and only Ottoman school founded abroad in Paris, in 1857, by the Ottoman sultan (Şişman 1986; Chambers 1968: 313–29), even though minorities were actively recruited as students, of the thirty-five minority graduates with identified occupations, only four joined the Ottoman administrative service.[121] Acceptance of minorities in the late Ottoman bureaucracy was also checkered. In the four branches of Ottoman officialdom (Findley 1982: 342–43), there were no minorities in the religious establishment, some in the military in special capacities (although most purchased exemption), and some in palace service, where one had easier access except to the most important immediate entourage of the sultan. Most minorities were concentrated in the last branch, the civil bureaucracy, yet they too were demobilized in the late nineteenth century as they could not partake in factionalism and clientage. Similarly, trust in these minorities never fully developed; most were dismissed on account of "certain causes and circumstances," or, as once put explicitly, "their contact with foreigners would entail difficulties in confidential matters" (Findley 1982: 364). As Ottoman Muslims received an education and subsequent bureaucratic professions to the detriment of minorities, the nascent Ottoman bureaucratic bourgeoisie became an almost exclusively Muslim one.

Even though some Ottoman statesmen did attempt to admit minority children into the military academies, the sultan opposed this suggestion. Similarly, the idea of forming a regiment from the Jews who escaped from Russia in 1891–92 was delayed for fear of an Ottoman Muslim reaction (Bozkurt 1989: 125–28). Also, the 1843 military service obligation placed upon Muslims and minorities alike was later changed by introducing a military service substitute tax *(bedel-i askeri)*,[122] whereby minorities could avoid military service. Indeed, if such a practice had been successful, it could have alleviated the pressure on manpower felt by the Ottoman army. After some unsuccessful attempts, the last attempt to revive the practice after 1908 also "withered under the shadow of ancient prejudice," as these recruits were never fully trusted.[123] The Ottoman sultan certainly tried to actualize minority recruitment into the military and the minorities definitely were initially enthusiastic and willing to serve, but the structural differences that religious segmentation had translated into in Ottoman society (Göçek 1993a) rendered such an option moot.

The most significant attempt to integrate the Muslim and minority populations of the empire was made during the formulation of the Ottoman parliament in 1877. Muslim and minority representatives were carefully selected from each province,[124] and the sultan explicitly reiterated in his speech a principle implied in the imperial rescript of 1852, that "henceforth all his subjects will be considered the children of the same country, and will be placed under the protection of one law" (Karal 1982: 395). The members of the parliament did pledge a secular oath,[125] and the minority deputies enthusiastically participated, both removing all references to differentiation by religion and ignoring communal lines in the parliamentary debates. Even though the Ottoman sultan promulgated equality for all his subjects, which actually meant giving the minorities the rights the Muslims already had, the actual practice of this ruling was limited. The parliament itself could not survive the increasing tension in the empire and was dismissed by the sultan. Hence, the most significant attempt to integrate the minorities in the new social system also failed.

The minorities of the empire did themselves acquire social resources through a Western-style education, but not in the sultan's schools. They attended instead the minority and foreign schools established by the European powers. As the minorities prospered through trade with the West, they started sending their sons to Europe for education in greater numbers. They also established Western-style schools within their own communities, in addition to the preexisting religious schools of the patriarchates and the rabbinates (Ergin 1939). During the nineteenth century, their education was heavily complemented by the European powers that established schools in the Ottoman empire for the explicit purpose of educating the children of European foreign residents and the Ottoman minorities. A 1894 treatise of the Ottoman minister of education, which inventoried all the foreign and minority schools in the Ottoman empire, revealed that there were 413 foreign and 4,547 minority schools, of which 4,049 operated without a permit from the Ottoman sultan (Çetin 1981). According to the report, the number of schools founded in the Ottoman empire by Western powers over the eighteenth and nineteenth centuries was as follows: France founded 115 schools, the United States 83, England 52, Russia and Balkan states (Greece, Serbia, and Bulgaria) 50, Austria and Germany 32, and Italy 25. These figures corresponded to the following in terms of number of students educated. In 1896, at the middle school level, there were 76,000 pupils in minority and 7,000 in foreign schools; at the secondary school level, 11,000 pupils in minority and 8,000 in foreign schools. This compared unfavorably with the 31,000 pupils in the Muslim middle schools and the 5,000 in Muslim secondary schools (Issawi 1982: 277). These Western-style schools educated the Ottoman minorities and accelerated their development[126] into a new social group: the Ottoman commercial bourgeoisie.

3

Trade, Ottoman Merchants, and Western Goods: Rise of the Commercial Bourgeoisie

According to one Ottoman chronicler writing in the late nineteenth century,

> Ever since the emergence of steamboats, telegraph, and railway, and ever since the Europeans became too big for their britches,[1] they have made a habit of assaulting and, upon coming close, of immediately erecting their flags over the harmless and the weak throughout the globe, thereby including [them] in their realm of possessions. They [then] defend [these possessions] against one another by right of conquest.[2] (Ahmed Lütfi 1875: 33)

The close Western connection between trade and diplomacy was noted by Ottoman officials time and again.[3] Indeed, the eighteenth and nineteenth centuries marked the expansion of Western trade and with it the growth of Western political domination over the rest of the world. As in many other non-Western contexts,[4] the Ottoman empire too underwent a dramatic economic change[5] from balanced association to bankruptcy in its trade relations with the West. The Ottoman trade structure, the nature of the Ottoman social groups embedded in it, and the meanings different groups attributed to Western goods all combined to interpret this Western impact. One social group that emerged to benefit from Western trade was the Ottoman minorities. As they accumulated—through their association with the West and due to their specific location within the Ottoman social structure—resources outside the sultan's control, they formed the origins of the Ottoman commercial bourgeoisie. Changing trade patterns, Ottoman social groups, and the penetration of Western goods into Ottoman society interacted to sow the seeds of the Ottoman commercial bourgeoisie as one group accumulated resources at the expense of others through trade with the West. Yet, these seeds did not take root in the empire due to Ottoman ethnic segmentation and surfacing nationalisms and were supplanted, during the twentieth century, by a Turkish-Muslim national bourgeoisie.

Patterns of Ottoman Trade with the West

The discovery of the new world, Western colonial expansion, and the subsequent increase in European production accelerated the pace of European trade with the Ottoman empire.

The nature of the trade changed as well. Trade capitulations the Ottoman empire had granted to the Italian states as early as the fifteenth century to encourage trade[6] were converted into contractual bilateral documents in the eighteenth century as the Ottoman sultan lost his authority to revoke them unilaterally (İnalcık 1973: 55–56). First the French state and then the English successfully strove to attain similar trade privileges, and the Ottoman sultan was eventually forced to extend these terms of trade to the Habsburg and Russian empires. The West started to capitalize on its victories against the Ottoman army to further exploit and expand these trade capitulations, and, as they did so, Western trade with the Ottoman empire expanded as well. A trade imbalance developed as Ottoman exports to the West decreased at the same interval.[7] Most of the goods exported from the Ottoman empire consisted of raw materials and carpets.[8] In 1750, Ottoman imports from the West to Constantinople were mostly manufactured goods or processed products (Braudel 1984: 471).[9] Western traders often brought these goods to the Ottoman ports and carried back Ottoman exports. The distribution of Ottoman exports among these Western states over time, in percentage shares of Ottoman exports, as illustrated in the accompanying table, reflects this transformation in Ottoman trade with the West.

Year	French	English	Dutch	Venetian	Habsburg
1634	26.6	39.8	7.8	25.8	—
1686	19.0	39.0	21.0	12.0	—
c.1784	36.5	9.2	18.3	12.0	24.0
1887	18.0	61.0	—	3.0	18.0
1910	11.0	35.0	—	12.0	42.0

Source: McGowan 1981:18; Ortaylı 1981:31

Whereas the English had been the Ottoman empire's largest trading partner in the seventeenth century,[10] they were replaced by the French during the eighteenth (Owen 1981: 83–85). The 1740 trade treaty between France and the Ottoman empire contributed to increasing French dominance.[11] The expansion of French trade resulted from its massive eighteenth-century reorganization: the French embassies, consulates, posts, and storehouses in the Ottoman empire were all combined under one structure, regulated, and standardized.[12] The French government introduced sets of rules and regulations about the responsibilities of French consuls and merchants in Ottoman trade (Masson 1911: 32, 44). French consuls were also organized for the first time in a strict hierarchical pattern,[13] whereby the French merchants were able to benefit fully from the organized services of the French consuls and ambassadors. This systematization of French trade through cooperation between the state and its merchants enhanced its economic impact on the Ottoman empire. Another financial incentive to the expanding French trade with the Ottomans was provided by the French chambers of commerce. These chambers, particularly that of Marseille, took an active interest in promoting trade with the Ottomans, financed the budgets of French consulates, and participated in the instruction of ambassadors.[14] During the eighteenth century, using the new trade organization and the support of chambers of commerce, French trade expanded into Syria, Egypt, Asia Minor, Persia and the Persian Gulf, Egypt, the Red Sea, the Balkans, and the Adriatic and Black seas.

The socially significant transformation in the Ottoman trade pattern with the West emerged during the eighteenth century. European rivalries emerging during and after the

Seven Years' War and the French revolutionary and Napoleonic wars had affected trade, as the French and the English blockaded one another's commercial activities. The Ottoman empire's neutrality during most of this period promoted the enterprises of merchants trading under the Ottoman flag; the earlier influence of the Italian trading states had also waned by this period. As a consequence of these developments, Ottoman minority merchants[15] gained a very significant opportunity to replace the European traders in the Middle East (Owen 1981: 55). The Napoleonic wars especially led to the rise of the Ottoman Greek merchants,[16] as they overcame both the French and English blockades by collaborating with both, profiting immensely in the process (Frangakis-Syrett 1991b: 392–94). This collaboration often took the form of requesting and usually acquiring foreign protection in trade from more than one Western power. Many such minorities also engaged in economic production. For instance, the biggest textile factory was "established in Smyrna in the 1770s by an Ottoman Armenian under government protection and in imitation of a similar project in Istanbul. It employed up to 500 workers and printed muslin and cloth for export to Switzerland, Germany and England" (Frangakis-Syrett 1985: 39). Since Ottoman trade treaties with the West also made tax-farming significant as a direct way of controlling produce, many minority families also increased their already existing involvement in tax-farming (Frangakis-Syrett 1992: 98). The mercantile activities of the Ottoman minorities remained the most significant consequence of the eighteenth-century shift in Western trade with the Ottoman empire, yet among the Ottoman minorities there was a concomitant shift in commercial involvement and prosperity from Ottoman Jews to Ottoman Christians, including Greeks, Armenians, and Arab-speaking Christians in the provinces.[17]

Location of the Ottoman Social Groups in Trade with the West

The expansion of Western trade with the empire had differential impact on the Ottoman social groups. While the sultan and his office-households suffered from the impact of trade with the West, the Ottoman provincial notables, artisans, Janissaries, and foreign residents of the empire potentially stood to gain from it. Yet, among them, only a specific one, the Ottoman minorities, managed to retain the resources they accumulated through this association, thus forming the seeds of an Ottoman commercial bourgeoisie; the rest could not escape the sultan's control. The Ottoman sultan attempted to directly regulate the expansion of trade with the West through two measures. To curb the demand for Western goods, he promulgated a series of largely ineffective imperial edicts (Özkaya 1985: 142), and, to circumscribe the supply of these goods, he personally financed the establishment of many Ottoman manufactories to compete with them. In 1720, for example, the sultan brought in master workmen from Chios to found a broadcloth manufactory and silk looms in Constantinople. Similarly, in 1729 he financed the organization of Ottoman cloth manufactories, which were established with the explicit intent to imitate foreign prints. In 1777, the Ottoman sultan founded more broadcloth and cloth factories in Constantinople to compete with the European cloth that was entering the Ottoman markets in ever increasing amounts. The sultan's grand vezir and members of his administration also wanted to help in this process of nurturing an indigenous Ottoman industry as they funded the invitation of master weavers from India in 1783 to start cloth production. Although the Ottoman sultan and his officials tried to curb the depletion of Ottoman economic resources caused by Western trade, they were not effective in successfully matching Western production in the empire.[18]

The Ottoman office-households, whose social position in the empire centered around the distribution of administrative posts, did not benefit from the expansion of Western trade either. Since officeholding rather than trade generated prestige in Ottoman society, these households were also not induced to engage fully in trade; instead, they utilized trade solely to generate the additional income they needed to maintain their large households. Unlike the office-households, the Ottoman provincial notables, which had retained their ties with agricultural production in the provinces through tax-farming, benefited from eighteenth-century trade with the West. The notables located in geographical proximity to the West, such as those who had access to the Aegean shores and those in the Balkans, carried on a brisk trade in wheat and cotton outside the sultan's control and against the sultan's sanctions. Even though the Ottoman sultan proclaimed decree after decree fixing the price of wheat and cotton and banning their export outside the empire, he could not control this trade.[19] The frequency of such eighteenth-century edicts issued in 1735, 1747, 1755, 1763, 1765, 1778, 1781, and 1782 demonstrate, indirectly, how widespread this illegal trading had become (Özkaya 1985: 325–27). For instance, a 1782 edict stated that the provincial notables along the Danube "kept provisions intended for Constantinople in their storehouses and sold them to foreigners" (CI2187). The sultan ordered the superintendent to purchase these provisions instead and send them to the capital with haste. Another account by a Western traveler (Leake 1835, III: 202, 207) commenting on how an Ottoman provincial notable sold cotton to Vienna through Greek merchants illustrated the substantial amount of illegal export in another commodity, cotton: these merchants handled 30,000–40,000 bales of cotton every year. Provincial notables who successfully expanded their economic resources through illegal trade with the West could not capitalize on their gains, however. As long as their social position depended on the administrative posts of the sultan, they could not escape his immanent control and generate independent sources of their own.

Ottoman Janissaries, artisans, and religious minorities were the other significant Ottoman social groups in eighteenth- and nineteenth-century Ottoman social change. The Janissaries and the artisans, which had coalesced into a single unit by this time, lacked the necessary resources to challenge the sultan by themselves. Only in alliance with the households could they have provided such a challenge—but such an alliance did not occur because of the structural configuration of households as self-contained and self-reproducing social units. The Ottoman religious minorities were the third social group. Since strict social boundaries delineated the Ottoman religious minorities, their interaction with the rest of Ottoman society and with the households was also limited. Yet, by developing extensive trade relationships with the West during the eighteenth and nineteenth centuries, these minorities were nevertheless able to develop vast economic resources outside the sultan's control. By doing so, they generated the seeds of the emergent Ottoman commercial bourgeoisie.

In the seventeenth and eighteenth centuries, the social and economic boundaries between the Janissary corps and the guilds started to disappear as both lost their exclusivity and monopoly over the provision of urban security and commerce; the newly emerging group of free petty artisans and peddlers had roots in both organizations. Some Janissaries, such as those engaged in military construction and production, acquired artisanal skills that they could then have transferred to the marketplace (Kafadar 1981: 44–47). The historical conjuncture of the sixteenth and seventeenth centuries did indeed necessitate such a transfer as the vast inflation that enveloped the Ottoman empire decreased the real salaries of Janissaries and forced them to look for means of economic support outside the military. The Janissaries utilized the social ties they had developed with urban inhabitants in making this transformation; those patrolling the city for security, having thus established personal contact with many city dwellers, then formed partnerships with them. Also, in their attempt to relinquish the cost of their household expenses, Ottoman officials started to enroll[20] their own household members into the Janissary corps, thereby indirectly charging the cost of their household maintenance to the state (Kafadar 1981: 81). The more direct integration of the Janissaries into the rest of society occurred as they invested in long-term ties by marrying urban dwellers and thus passing their inheritance[21] and social position along to them. As a consequence, in eighteenth-century Syria (Rafeq 1977: 59–60), for instance, the Janissaries blended in with urban society and functioned in a number of urban capacities, such as moneylenders, crop sharers, administrators or supervisors of religious endowments, customs officials, tax collectors, or artisans.[22] The reverse penetration by petty tradesmen into the Janissary corps might have resulted from the cooperation between the two when groups of artisans were selected to accompany the Janissaries to provision them during military campaigns. The Ottoman sultan then invited some of these artisans who had performed an outstanding service during the campaigns to join the ranks of the Janissaries (Aktepe 1954: 19). Also, through their participation in military campaigns, artisans gained the opportunity to form ties with the Janissaries that were easily transferable to commercial ones during periods of peace.[23]

Eighteenth-century Ottoman archival records do indeed document this gradual diffusion of the Janissaries and the artisans into one social group, as more and more artisans appear within the ranks of the "military" category. For instance, within one randomly selected volume (A5–368) of military inheritance registers from 1772, almost a third of the cases belonged to artisans.[24] Although Janissaries could in theory be distinguished by their honorific title, "elder brother," *(beşe),* it became impossible to identify them as such in the actual court cases dating from the eighteenth century. For instance, the court registered inheritance of İzzed Ahmed Pasha, commander of Hotin (CM31051), listed many "artisan-Janissaries" among the creditors, as two, İsmail and Uzun Ali beşe, were bakers, and the others were Seyyid Ali beşe, who was a grocer, Ali beşe, a butcher, Hasan beşe, a candlemaker, Ali beşe, a saddlemaker, Süleyman beşe, a tobacconist, Mehmed beşe, a pastry-maker, and Mahmud beşe, a felt-maker. The emergence of this ambiguous category often led to administrative disputes over matters of taxation and inheritance. For instance, Janissaries who were tax exempt as soldiers tried to retain this privilege when they started to engage in trade. In the eighteenth century, the sultan received many complaints from his administrators on how the tax revenues from the marketplace and the customs fell because of the refusal of the Janissary-traders to pay them. For instance, in 1762, Halil, the superintendent of Sofia, complained that the Janissary-traders did not pay customs duties on goods such as grapes, figs, cotton, leather, and linen that they brought from other provinces and sold in Sofia. The sultan decreed that all traders had to pay the duties regardless of their status (MM9537/34). Similarly, the issue of who had rights over the inheritance of such a person, the military corps or the heirs, also emerged. In 1799, when elhac Abdülaziz Agha, a usurer who was also a Janissary belonging to the 45th Unit, died without heirs, upon the arrival at the capital of the news of his large wealth,[25] the inheritance partitioner and the head of the Janissary corps quarreled over whether the treasury of the sultan or that of the Janissary corps should acquire this wealth (CM7602).

Why was this emergent group of artisan-Janissaries, which had both economic and political resources, unable to successfully challenge the sultan? Unlike the office- and provincial households, most activities of the Janissaries and the artisans were contained within the boundaries of urban centers. Their ownership of capital also often stayed limited to their own craft. In addition, one could argue that they did not have the household organization and administrative skills to penetrate and manage Ottoman resources. Still, there were two exceptions to this pattern, usurers and merchants, who accumulated vast economic resources within and beyond urban centers. The possible extent of this wealth is illustrated by the 1788 inheritance of the usurer, Hacı Hasan, also known as "the son-in-law of Hankallıoğlu" (MM10230/32), whose heirs paid 85,000 piasters to keep his inheritance from being confiscated by the sultan, and by that of another usurer and money-changer elhac Abdülaziz Agha (MM9726/28).

Abdülaziz Agha's loans to many urban dwellers and officials, many with interest and securities, portray the nature and scope of the commercial networks that developed beyond local boundaries. The wealthiest among these usurers and merchants were often those who engaged in commercial activities with Ottoman officials and their households. Yet these activities made the usurers and merchants prone to confiscation by the sultan, who could argue[26] that their wealth had been indirectly amassed through the offices he himself had bestowed upon his household members. He could thus use all indications of misbehavior, misappropriation of funds, or unpaid accounts to the treasury to legitimate such a decision. Indeed, the sultan used this reasoning in 1808, when, in order to pay military campaign debts, he confiscated the inheritances of merchants "who were known to have large amounts of wealth" (CM19875). For instance, the confiscation of the wealth of one such merchant, Hacı Ali, explicitly referred to the severe cash need of the Ottoman state for a military campaign as the reason for this confiscation. In this case, the sultan did, however, give the heirs of the deceased treasury shares in return for the confiscated amount, promising[27] to convert them into cash after the campaign (CM31146). Still, by performing such confiscations, the sultan was able to control the capital accumulation of artisans and Janissaries in general and merchants and usurers in particular. These social groups, like the office- and provincial households before them, failed to escape the sultan's control over the resources they accumulated.

Indeed, throughout the Ottoman empire, it was only the social group of the Ottoman minorities that benefited from the expanding trade with the West and that, unlike other Ottoman groups, could also avoid the sultan's control over their accumulated resources. Their case therefore warrants special analysis.

The Case of the Ottoman Minorities

The Ottoman minorities existed in large numbers in the major cities of the empire, which placed them into close proximity with European foreign residents and Western merchants. For instance, the Ottoman minorities comprised a significant proportion of the urban population of the three major cities within the central provinces of the empire, namely, Constantinople, Smyrna, and Adrianople. In Constantinople in 1833, Ottoman Greek males comprised 29.1 percent of the tax-paying population, Ottoman Armenian males 25.6 percent, and Ottoman Jewish males 6.1 percent.[28] In eighteenth-century Smyrna, varying population estimates divided the population roughly into half Muslim and half minorities, and in Adrianople, of the 20,000 households, 3,000 were Ottoman Greek, 1,000 Ottoman Jewish, 1,000 Ottoman Armenian, and the rest Muslim (Özkaya 1985: 143, 148). The association of these minorities with the escalating number of European foreign residents engaged in commerce and diplomacy increased considerably during the eighteenth and nineteenth centuries. This affiliation was most prevalent[29] in Constantinople, which always contained large European foreign colonies (Mantran 1982: 128–30). The Ottoman minorities resided close[30] to these foreigners and, unlike with the Muslims, faced no social restrictions in associating with them. In addition, the Ottoman minorities had quite a significant cultural capital, proficiency in European languages, which enabled them to serve as translators in the embassies of foreign residents and in their trading activities. As the minorities interacted socially and professionally with the foreign residents, their observance of the social boundaries the Ottoman sultan placed on them started to diminish. For instance, they stopped their close adherence to the strict Ottoman dress code, which limited the range of colors, garments, and accessories minorities could wear. Instead, the minorities started to don "Frankish-style dress" and also occasionally imported yellow shoes, a shoe color confined specifically to Muslims (Özkaya 1985: 155). A 1758 imperial decree addressed the sultan's concern over this innovation in the mode of dress stating that "the harm and inauspiciousness of this abominable state of affairs was the concern of the treasury of the Muslims and the cause of the disturbance of the order and regulation of subjects" (Refik 1930: 188–89). The sultan therefore banned the practice of minorities wearing Frankish clothing. He also prohibited those minorities trading under foreign flags and their servants from dressing in the Frankish mode and limited this privilege specifically to those minorities employed by the embassies.

As the number of foreign embassies, consuls, and residents increased in the Ottoman empire throughout the eighteenth and nineteenth centuries, the Ottoman minorities employed in these units also increased. The nature of this employment brought two significant privileges to the Ottoman minorities. First, by entering the service and protection of a foreign power, they were exempted from paying the poll tax *(cizye),* which had initially developed in compensation for the protection provided to the minorities. Second, they acquired the trade privileges of the foreign residents, among which was the very significant one of trade duties that were significantly lower than those of the Ottoman merchants. Because of these commercial and fiscal privileges, the number of Ottoman minorities employed by the embassies and engaged in trade *(beratlı)*[31] escalated and by the eighteenth century reached such a level that the Ottoman treasury suffered large tax losses and the sultan had to resort to issuing repeated edicts that set quotas on the number of such exempted minorities and their servants (Refik 1930: 74–76) or even attempted to issue such certificates himself (Lewis 1979: 455).

The location of the minorities within the Ottoman social structure restricted them from investing their resources in Ottoman society. During the eighteenth century, minority exchange with Muslims was still largely confined. Although the minorities interacted with the Muslims in the marketplace, shops, and inns, other nuclei of social interaction, such as mosques, sometimes bathhouses, and often coffee houses were restricted to Muslims. Even though the minorities did indeed have their own places of interaction, given the intricate connection between social power and religion in the empire (Göçek 1993a), those of the Muslims were structurally more significant. Also, male minorities could not marry Muslims and form enduring kinship ties with them, which meant that they could not reproduce their social and material resources.

The only exception to this pattern were those few Ottoman minorities who were appointed to official positions as the sultan's translator, treasurer, or governor, thereby developing exceptional ties with officials, notables, and the sultan. These few did indeed have access to more resources than the rest, but this access, unlike that of Muslim officials, was usually limited to their tenure in office. Minority men could not marry other office-household members to transmit their resources to the next generation but were confined to developing one social tie, that of passing their profession onto their sons. Yet in the eighteenth century, minorities started both to generate capital through trade[32] and to retain it through Western protection. Through this interaction of the Ottoman social structure, their agency, and the historical conjuncture of escalating Western trade, the Ottoman minorities became the first social group to accumulate resources outside the sultan's control.

The three groups within the Ottoman minorities in eighteenth-century Constantinople that possessed large amounts of wealth trespassing the confines of their professions[33] and their urban boundaries were, specifically, the minority officials in the sultan's service, money-changers, and merchants. Yet not all of these subgroups had equal opportunity to retain the resources they accumulated outside the sultan's control; minority officials in the sultan's service and the money-changers who often had dealings with the Ottoman treasury could not escape the sultan's control. Only the minority merchants could. The small but powerful group of minority officials who were often in the sultan's employment as administrators or translators dissolved as they were caught between the conflicting expectations of the Ottoman sultan and the rising West. Since they were drawing their power from the sultan, once they challenged that connection, they lost the social power in Ottoman society that came with it. Although there were many such minorities, the career patterns of two of them, one Greek, Demetrius Cantemir, and one Armenian, Mouradgea d'Ohsson, illuminate the process through which this shift in the social position of Ottoman minority officials occurred as they struggled with the conflicting demands that the Ottoman sultan and the Western powers placed upon them.

Demetrius Cantemir came to Constantinople in 1688, when he was fifteen, because his father, the prince of Moldavia Constantine Cantemir, was an Ottoman Phanariot[34] Greek who had been appointed to his post by the Ottoman sultan (Constantin 1968: 59–61). Unlike many other Ottoman minorities, Cantemir, as an official's son,[35] participated in the life of the capital and developed close relations with Muslims. In his historical chronicle of the Ottoman empire, he recounted taking "Musick" lessons from Ottoman Muslim instructors and listed two intimate Muslim friends, "Cherkies Mehemed Aga, the Master of the Imperial Stables," and "Haznadar Ibrahim Pasha, the governor of Belgrade, who was present at all the [sultan's] consults of those times" (Cantemir 1737: 151, 164). Cantemir recounted, for instance, how he used to "invite İbrahim Pasha to his house, and did to gain his good will by treating him with wine . . . so that the Pasha would open his whole mind to him" (Cantemir 1737: 300). This Ottoman Greek thus met with Ottoman Muslim officials socially and was soon himself appointed an Ottoman official, the prince of Moldavia, in 1710. Once at his post, however, he allied with the Russians against the Ottoman sultan and had to escape to Russia when the Ottomans defeated the Russians in the Balkans. One could argue that in spite of all his exceptional privileges, Cantemir's conflicting social and political allegiances between the Ottoman sultan and a Western power eventually led to his downfall as an Ottoman minority official.

The Ottoman Armenian Ignatius Mouradgea d'Ohsson, who was known among the Ottomans as Muradcan Tosunyan, also rose through his employment as a translator, yet this time for the Swedish embassy rather than the Ottoman sultan (Beydilli 1983: 247–314). Like Cantemir, d'Ohsson was also following in the footsteps of his father, who had been a translator in the Swedish consulate in Smyrna for almost forty years; he entered the Swedish embassy in Constantinople as a translator in 1763, when he was twenty-three, and was promoted to the position of the head translator just five years later. A Catholic

Armenian, d'Ohsson kept his ties with the foreign community in Pera and was educated by the Franciscan and Dominican priests residing there. His fast rise within the Swedish embassy continued as many honorary titles were bestowed upon him; he was given the title "royal secretary" when he was thirty-five and was knighted with the title "chevalier" five years later. Because of his assistance during the drawing up of the Ottoman-Swedish Trade-Peace Treaty, d'Ohsson received a medal from the Swedish king and in 1787 the title "d'Ohsson," which was a Swedish approximation of his former Ottoman patronymic, Tosunyan. D'Ohsson's family ties, which had procured him his initial position as a translator, also enhanced his wealth in marriage: he married the daughter of an Armenian money-changer who conducted business with the Ottoman palace.[36]

As Cantemir had entrusted his hopes to the Russians away from the Ottoman sultan, d'Ohsson invested his economic resources outside the Ottoman sultan's control, in Parisian banks. When he traveled to Paris in 1784 to have his book on the history of the Ottoman empire published, he visited the king of Sweden and concluded the Swedish–Ottoman alliance treaty. Upon his return to the Ottoman empire, d'Ohsson was treated very well by the Ottoman sultan, Selim III, who, just as his predecessor had made use of Cantemir's administrative and military skills, utilized d'Ohsson's expertise on the science of warfare and the administration and provision of the military. The sultan specifically asked d'Ohsson for a memorandum expressing his viewpoint on the affairs of science and the military, and upon receiving it[37] approved and asked d'Ohsson "to keep on procuring, engineers, architects and officers from Europe." D'Ohsson rose to his highest rank in the Ottoman empire when, in 1796, he was appointed Swedish ambassador. Yet within a few years, when the French invaded Egypt, whereupon d'Ohsson openly sided with the French, the same Ottoman sultan who had commended his expertise asked the Swedish government for his removal from office. D'Ohsson left the Ottoman empire in 1799 for Paris, where he died in 1807. Like Cantemir, d'Ohsson was eventually estranged from the Ottoman empire as his multiple allegiances conflicted and he sided with Sweden and France against the Ottoman empire.[38] His life, like Cantemir's, vividly illustrates the ambivalent situation of the few Ottoman minority officials, between the conflicting demands of the Ottoman empire and the West. Like these two cases, most of this subgroup of small but powerful minority officials eventually disintegrated under the strain of these conflicting demands; they either left the empire or lost their jobs.

Another subgroup that was able to accumulate wealth beyond the confines of their community and the city they lived in was the minority money-changers. But they too, like the minority officials, could not retain the resources they accumulated outside of the sultan's control. Many archival documents disclose the cause behind this inability: minority money-changers could not escape, as the minority merchants eventually could and did, the sultan's jurisdiction over them. One example of such a money-changer was an Ottoman Armenian, İzavor son of Agasob from Eğin (B77/8), who died in Constantinople in 1763 while visiting, with his two sons, his partners in the capital. His wealth, 900,000 aspers, comprising his share in his partnership with the money-changer in Constantinople, was potentially prone to the sultan's confiscation, however. The sultan did indeed confiscate the inheritances of the Ottoman Greek furrier/money-changer Manol[39] in 1737 (CM8158), and an Ottoman Armenian money-changer Bedros[40] of the Ottoman mint in 1784 (D7217), on the grounds that both had accounts to settle with the sultan's household and with office-households. Unlike Muslim officials and provincial notables, once their wealth was confiscated, these Ottoman minorities often did not have households or social networks to fall back on in order to reverse the setback, or simply to survive. Only one group of minorities managed to develop the social resources necessary to foil the sultan's confiscation: the Ottoman minority merchants.

The minority merchants could retain the resources they accumulated through their interaction with the West by entering into foreign protection. Until the eighteenth century, the trade activities of minority merchants had not been separate from those of Muslim merchants, as all participated equally in Ottoman trade. Many Muslim merchants, for instance, were commercially active[41] in urban centers throughout the world, from Venice and Ancona in Europe to Calicut and Java in Southeast Asia (Kafadar 1990: 194–99). At the same time, many Muslim and minority merchants often had a sister company based in a Western port.[42] Only after the rise of Western trade and the Europeans' exclusive association with the Ottoman minorities did Ottoman merchants differentiate their fields of activity according to religion. Hence, from the eighteenth century onward, the Muslim merchants concentrated in domestic trade[43] and the religious minorities traded with the rising West (İnalcık 1979: 6; Masters 1988: 33). This economic specialization by Ottoman minority merchants at the expense of European and Ottoman Muslim ones emerged from a coalescence of factors that ranged from the structure of trade to the dynamics of Ottoman control over trade.

First, in these centuries the periods of warfare among the major Western powers started to expand quickly into the economic sphere. Commercial blockades often accompanied military warfare so that the European merchants suffered from the effects of political conflict (Frangakis-Syrett 1985: 34–35). As they were increasingly involved in the escalating intra-European conflict, it became immanently rational to designate a social group that was politically neutral to this conflict: the Ottoman minority merchants filled this prerequisite perfectly and increasingly assumed the role of the European merchants in Ottoman trade.

Second, European merchants faced increasing economic barriers in their trade with the Ottoman empire, which led them to prefer employing minority merchants as intermediaries. As a consequence of trade capitulations, European merchants who traded with the Ottoman empire had had to pay only a 3 percent duty, as opposed to Ottoman merchants, who paid duties up to 10 percent. Yet this imbalance did not translate into domestic trade within the empire, so that the European merchants trading in the empire had to pay the same domestic trade duties as the Ottoman merchants did (Kütükoğlu 1974: 64, 71). This reduced the incentive for European merchants to engage in the Ottoman domestic trade and reinforced the prevalence of Ottoman minority merchants as their intermediaries.

Third, competition among the European powers for influence within the Ottoman empire escalated their cultivation of Ottoman minorities as their allies within. They therefore often tried to secure the political allegiance of the Ottoman minorities by offering them legal protection from the Ottoman sultan. For instance, competition between the Austrians and the Russians over political influence in the Ottoman provinces of Wallachia and Moldavia led the Austrians to extend protective status to two hundred thousand Ottoman subjects in Moldavia, and to sixty thousand Ottoman subjects in Wallachia. The Russians countered by distributing their own protection papers for free in order to claim representation and jurisdiction over this protected populace of "citizens" (Bozkurt 1989: 140–41).

The fourth reason entailed the additional restrictions placed on both European and Ottoman Muslim merchants. Until the end of the eighteenth century, as the sultan categorically barred European merchants from trading in the Black Sea region (Braudel 1984

1984: 477), they had to engage Ottoman merchants to trade on their behalf. It was with the peace treaty (Küçük Kaynarca)[44] signed with Russia at the end of 1774 that the Ottomans had to relinquish to the Russians unrestricted privileges in the Black Sea. Yet, in the eighteenth century, the Ottoman sultan had set a quota on the number of Muslim merchants engaged in trade as well,[45] thus leaving only the Ottoman minority merchants capable of accommodating the commercial demands of the West.

Fifth, minority merchants were often coreligionists with the Western ones and also possessed the linguistic skills to communicate with both the Europeans and the Ottomans. This cultural capital gave minority merchants a competitive edge over the Muslims. Sixth, European merchants were afraid that any contract entered into with an Ottoman Muslim would be struck down in a Muslim court. Uncomfortable with this protection, they chose to deal with minority merchants instead (Masters 1988: 102).

Finally, unlike the Muslims, the Ottoman minorities were willing to enter under Western protection to avoid the sultan's confiscation, a measure the sultan used to avert the potential challenge of the vast economic resources of merchants.[46] Initially,[47] the Ottoman sultan did not object to relinquishing his custody over minorities, but he could never have permitted his control over the Ottoman Muslims, whom he considered entrusted to him by God, to be supplanted in a similar fashion.

As a consequence, more and more minorities throughout the empire participated in European trade under foreign flags.[48] The Ottoman Greek community accumulated wealth with the development of European commerce and shipping. The Armenians prospered as they controlled the trade routes leading to Persia, Central Asia, and India and became active in banking. The Arab-speaking Christians[49] of the empire also benefited from the great prosperity in Aleppo that emerged through trade with Europe. In addition to the prosperity in Aleppo, earlier interactions between Middle Eastern and European Christians, especially under the guidance of the Vatican, made a difference. The Vatican increased its Christian missions to the Middle East, and there was a significant preference for Arab-speaking Christians among European Christian traders, who started to dominate Middle Eastern trade in the eighteenth century (Raymond 1974: 282, 463, 490; Lewis 1982: 107–9). Silk cultivation enriched the rural Christian community in Lebanon and Westernized the Maronite community as they renewed contact with the Papacy (Khalaf 1982: 113). Hence, through the nineteenth century, many minorities continued to "easily acquire a foreign nationality, and thus enjoy the advantages of extraterritoriality, while probably maintaining their local contacts" (Frangakis-Syrett 1991a: 198; 1991b: 413–14).

Ottoman Adoption of Western Goods: Evidence from Inheritance Registers

Ample historical documentation and sociological analysis of Ottoman society have demonstrated that there was indeed a process of Westernization. Yet the most crucial problematic, that of the *boundaries* of Westernization, remains. How far had Westernization diffused into Ottoman society? Was it limited to a certain segment of the empire at a certain time and place, or did it represent a larger pattern that affected the entire society at all levels? Hence, how could one extend beyond the visible, the dominant, the privileged to capture, rather than one fragment, the experience of the *entire* society? How could one operationalize Westernization, or, in this particular context, the diffusion of Western goods into Ottoman society at large?

One archival source that could possibly expand the constraints listed above is the vast collection of Ottoman inheritance registers, which cover all segments of Ottoman society and have been collected throughout the centuries in accordance with Islamic law. A systematic analysis through random sampling of this archival source could help us approximate the nature and scope of Ottoman Westernization. Indeed, such an analysis, to be undertaken in this section, demonstrates that Ottoman Westernization was a phenomenon that did not remain limited to the elites in the empire but also emerged among the populace at large. The empirical investigation displays the emergence of an Ottoman bourgeoisie as Ottoman subjects possess Western goods at an increasing rate throughout the century while the Ottoman elite, who have much higher purchasing power, do not change their accumulation pattern during the same time. Figure 4 demonstrates this finding.[50] The graph indicates that Ottoman elites always had a higher probability of having Western goods but the propensity of subjects rose throughout the century, whereas that of the elites stayed the same.

Historical Evidence

The current historical information on the penetration of Western goods into Ottoman society is suggestive but not systematic. Western goods often penetrated Ottoman society, especially at the upper echelons. Among many examples,[51] the diary of Thomas Dallam from the period 1599–1600 narrates how he played "an organ that was in the sultan's palace for him, with his pages in attendance" (1893: 69–71). The eighteenth-century

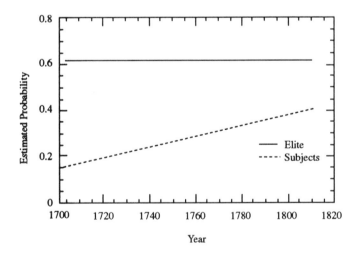

N = 124 inheritance registers

Figure 4. Estimated Probability of an Ottoman Inheritance Register Containing Western Goods. (Başbakanlık Arşivi Muhallefat Defterleri [Inheritance Registers in the Prime Minister's Archives]; Topkapı Müzesi Arşivi Muhallefat Kayıtları [Inheritance Records in the Topkapı Palace Museum Archives]; İstanbul Müftülüğü Askeri Kassam Tereke Defterleri [Estate Registers in the Archives of the Office for Islamic Religious Opinion Drawn by the Military Inheritance Partitioner]; İstanbul Müftülüğü Beledi Kassam Tereke Defterlei [Estate Registers of Constantinople-Proper in the Archives of the Office of Islamic Religious Opinion Drawn by the Municipal Inheritance Partitioner].)

chronicles of Ottomans and foreign residents and Western travelers' accounts broadly outline Western diffusion as they focus on the upper echelons of Ottoman society, the sultan, and top households of the empire. The projected image is one of escalating Western goods consumption at the elite level. Casual documentation from Ottoman archives also tends to support this image.

Historical chronicles and travelers' accounts provide the following depiction of Western goods in Ottoman society. Gift exchange emerges as the most recurrent medium within which Western goods occur. These goods were often given as gifts to the sultan by Western embassies, such as those presented by the Venetian *bailo*[52] as well as the French and English ambassadors.[53] The sultan's officials received some of these Western trade goods as gifts as well.[54] Western embassies also facilitated the use of these trade goods by actively displaying them at their embassies.[55] The European residents in Constantinople facilitated and maintained Western goods diffusion even more in the nineteenth century as their numbers doubled. These exposures to the West through foreign residents helped generate an image of the West, an image that slowly expanded from Western goods to Western entertainment to customs to military institutions. The Ottoman minorities, by virtue of being socially associated with and employed by the European embassies, were the first Ottoman social group to consume Western goods and imitate a Western style of life.[56] They associated with the large group of European residents and with a sizable proportion of the military advisors among them.[57] The overall impression one gets from this depiction of Western good usage is that it was common among the upper echelons of Ottoman society and also present, to a certain degree, among the minorities. Yet the depth or breadth of this impact is not at all specified.

The conventional use of the primary sources, comprising those eighteenth- and nineteenth-century state and municipal archives in Constantinople, often supports this generalization. According to these sources, Western goods usage among the Ottoman elites seem to escalate during the eighteenth and nineteenth centuries. We observe that Western goods consumption first penetrated the Ottoman ports and urban centers and did not fully diffuse into the inland domestic markets until the late nineteenth century, when, as a consequence of the industrial revolution, English textiles flooded world markets.[58] Eighteenth-century Ottoman archival sources portray a large accumulation of luxury goods of both domestic and foreign origin from either Asia or Europe. The 1730 confiscated inheritance register (D2211) of Mehmed Kethüda, the steward of the grand vezir, for instance, contained, in addition to such bejeweled valuable goods as silver and gold belts, arms, watches, and a French table clock, thousands of pieces of cloth from India, Persia, Damascus, France, and Poland. Similarly, the register of a tax-farmer, Ahmed Agha, in 1755 (A170/102), the Ottoman grand admiral Gazi Hasan Pasha in 1780 (D9964), and the sultan's sword-bearer[59] in 1789 (MM9719/113–18) also included hundreds of valuable Western goods, ranging from books, eyeglasses, and watches to bejeweled boxes, daggers, clocks, boxes containing glassware or a tea set from Saxony, telescopes, chocolate boxes, jewelry, French trays, shawls, and walnut chairs. Archival documents also depict how these goods circulated in Ottoman society through confiscations or purchases. Many confiscated estates included imperial orders to transport the valuable goods to the sultan's palace,[60] to auction the rest, and to send the cash revenue to the Ottoman mint. In some archival documents, there is evidence that the confiscated goods were auctioned at "the sultan's market" *(sultan pazarı)* within the palace,[61] with members of the palace and office-households in Constantinople purchasing the goods[62] and thus increasing the circulation of the confiscated goods. Among these purchased goods, many foreign ones of Western and Eastern origin were often listed, such as Indian robes, Frankish maps, Frankish books, English pistols, binoculars, flatware from Saxony and Venice, and Parisian watches. Ottoman chronicles demonstrate how the sultan practiced giving the confiscated valuable goods in his treasury as gifts to officials with new appointments. Archival documents thus demonstrate the presence and circulation of Western goods at the capital. As for the Ottoman provinces, Ottoman inheritance and expense registers indicate that office-households facilitated the circulation of Western goods in that context. Officials often took many of these goods with them when they left the capital for their appointment. Once there, they continued purchasing such goods from Constantinople by periodically sending their stewards to Constantinople with lists of such items for their own use, for their household members, or as gifts to provincial notables.[63] Many scholars[64] have also utilized these registers to highlight different dimensions of Ottoman social life, such as the social position of women and minorities and commercial and legal practices.

Sociological Operationalization

How generalizable is this portrayal of Westernization to Ottoman society at large? Is the portrayal that emerges highly selective, or do Western goods uniformly penetrate from the upper echelons to the rest of society? This, at least, tends to be the null hypothesis one can formulate from the existing evidence: the wealthy Ottoman elite, who have more capital than the rest of society, would accumulate more Western goods at a higher rate than the rest of society throughout the century. A random sample of Ottoman inheritance registers—where such inventories of goods of Western origin were present—was selected to test the spread of Western goods across Ottoman social groups through time.

Why use inheritance registers? Inheritance registers[65] contain inventories of the wealth owned by individuals. The most significant contribution of inheritance registers to historical analysis is the information they provide on the lives of ordinary people.[66] The significance of inheritance registers for sociological analysis centers on the social spectrum they cover. By providing information on the underclasses, these registers disclose the entire social structure and facilitate the analysis of all social groups in a society. By documenting and distinguishing the goods that penetrate and circulate in society through time, they document social diffusion. Inheritance registers also highlight the social and economic reproduction of society as they identify the social stratification pattern and its continuity through generations.[67] Yet, a word of caution is necessary here: in and of themselves, inheritance registers do not have any explanatory power unless they are randomly sampled and interpreted within a theoretical context. Methodologically, these registers only permit inferences into the accumulation pattern of individuals and do not directly reflect consumption patterns.

Historical Contextualization

Ottoman inheritance registers can be used as the unit of historical sociological analysis only after their historical contextualization, that is, their social, spatial, and temporal location within Ottoman society. The origins of these inheritance registers can be traced to the Islamic law of inheritance, which mainly consists of the rules laid down in the Qur'an,[68] the prescriptions of the Prophet in his teachings, and the pre-Islamic customs prevailing among the Arab tribes near Mecca and Medina (Chowdhury 1964; Coulson

1971). One particular section among the Qur'anic verses lays out the basic rules of inheritance where the exact shares of the heirs are specified in detail.

> Allah charges you concerning your children: to the male the equivalent of the portion of two females, and if there be women more than two, then theirs is two-thirds of the inheritance, and if there be one only, then the half. And to his parents a sixth of the inheritance, if he has a son; if he does not have a son and his parents are his heirs, then to his mother appertains one-third; and if he has brothers, then to his mother appertains one-sixth, after any legacy he may have bequeathed, or debt has been paid. . . . And unto you belongs a half of that which your wives leave, if they have no child; but if they have a child then unto you one-fourth of which they leave, after any legacy they may have bequeathed or debt has been paid. And unto them belongs one-fourth of that which you leave if you have no child, but if you have a child then one-eighth of that which you leave, after legacy or debt. And if a man or a woman has a distant heir, having left neither parent nor child, and he or she has a brother or a sister only on the mother's side, then to each of the brother and sister one-sixth, and if they are more than two, then they shall be shares in the third, after any legacy or debt—not injuring the heirs by willing away more than a third of the heritage has been paid. (Nisa IV: 11–12)

Hence, the Qur'an specifies the exact share of each heir as the heirs move from closer to more distant kin. Women inherit one-half of men, and this rule is used to determine shares of distant relatives. The wills the deceased could make before death are limited, and these wills could not exceed one-third of the inheritance value.[69] Three groups are protected in partitioning an inheritance—orphans, minors, and women. The Qur'an prescribes that one should refrain from misusing the shares of orphans who cannot look after their own interests[70] and requires that women's shares should be given to them, in addition to their marriage portions.[71]

In the application of these maxims, as prescribed, first the costs of the funeral and then the debts of the deceased were paid out of the estate. If debts equaled or exceeded the assets of the estate, the assets were distributed among the creditors in proportion to their claims. The remainder was then divided among the legal heirs in proportion to the shares specified in the Qur'an. One particular characteristic of the Qur'an was its nonrecognition of juristic persons, hence there was in theory no institution as heir in an inheritance; one could, however, establish a religious foundation.[72] The Ottomans accepted the Hanefite school of interpretation of the Qur'anic prescriptions and used İbrahim al-Halebi's *Mülteka al-abhur* as the source book in applying the Islamic law of inheritance. Ottoman practice closely followed the general principles laid down by the law, with some practical qualifications.[73] The Ottoman inheritance registers were thus inventories of all the movable and immovable property and goods, receipts, debts, and wills of the deceased. These registers were structured by the Islamic law of inheritance, maintained by the sultan, and administered by the sultan's deputies. After the payment of debts and the execution of wills, the inheritance was divided in accordance with the shares prescribed by the Qur'an. A judge *(kadı)*[74] at the religious court drew up and executed the inheritance.[75] The judge could only intervene in an inheritance distribution under certain circumstances, mainly to protect the shares of orphans or missing heirs, to adjudicate if there were any disputes on the distribution, to settle complex debt or credit transactions, or to referee upon the request of concerned parties (Barkan 1966: 2).

An Ottoman inheritance register[76] commenced with a heading containing the name of the deceased, his father's name, often his occupation and honorific title, the place where he died, the place where he resided in his lifetime, the names and relations of all heirs, and the date the inheritance was drawn up and executed. The second section of the register contained an inventory of all the goods and property and credits owned by the deceased, including their descriptions, quantities, and values. The third section listed all that was subtracted from the total inheritance value: burial costs, debts of the deceased, court duties, wills of the deceased. The final section indicated the distribution of the remaining inheritance value among the heirs; all the heirs and their respective shares were registered separately.[77] The inheritances of different Ottoman social groups exhibited different characteristics. The inheritance of a Janissary (HH14109A) belonged to his heirs. If there were no heirs, the inheritance reverted to the chest of the Janissary corps; in return for the privilege of retaining such unclaimed inheritances, the head of the Janissaries paid a specific yearly amount to the sultan's treasury.[78] Merchant inheritances with no heirs belonged to the sultan's treasury (MM10169/125) only if the amount of the inheritance was above 10,000 aspers. If it were below this amount, the inheritance reverted to the treasurer of the customs house (MM10386/326). Although Ottoman religious minorities had the right to settle their judicial affairs communally in adherence to their own religion, the inheritance registers drawn up at the Islamic court contained many inheritance cases of religious minorities (for example, B27/31, 39).

The legal organization for the inheritance execution reflected the Ottoman stratification between officials and subjects, as separate judges oversaw the sultan's officials and his subjects. Ottoman officials had their own "military" *(askeri)* judges as opposed to the subjects, who had "local" *(beledi)* judges. Military judges[79] did not reside in each judicial district as the local ones did,[80] but resided in Constantinople and heard cases at the sultan's palace on Tuesdays and Wednesdays and at their residences the rest of the week. The execution of the inheritance was alike for both the officials and populace, however: the judges had inheritance partitioners in each court execute and register the inheritance. The inheritance partitioner recorded the total number goods in the inheritance into this register, and the experts then appraised the value of each good and entered this figure next to the description and quantity of goods. After the subtraction of court duties[81] and burial costs, the partitioner divided the total amount among the heirs in accordance with Islamic law. The inheritance execution revealed many abuses on the part of judges and local and military inheritance partitioners. A series of imperial decrees throughout the eighteenth century specified these abuses while delineating the punishments for each one. An imperial correspondence in 1801 (CA173), for example, ordered judges not to interfere with inheritances unless specifically asked to do so by the concerned parties and not to demand inheritance duties of more than twenty-five per thousand. A 1609 imperial decree (Mühimme 78/899) reprimanded judges for breaking the rules of inheritance.[82] The most severe eighteenth-century conflict over inheritance distribution originated in the shifting boundaries between Ottoman officials and subjects.[83] As more Janissaries engaged in trade and more subjects became officials through joining the office-households, the distinctions between subjects and officials eroded. This made the conflicts between local and military judges over the execution of inheritances more severe. The judges argued about the legal status of the deceased as one claimed he was a subject and the other said he was an official. Both wanted to execute the inheritance and get the duty.

Ottoman inheritance registers exist in vast numbers for all segments of the population throughout the Ottoman empire. How then to sample among these? Since we are concerned with three dimensions of Westernization, namely goods, institutions, and ideas, and since we conjecture that empires within which these spread were centrally organized, we focus on the capital of the Ottoman empire, Constantinople, the three archives within which comprise the entire spectrum of Ottoman inheritance registers.

Sampling

The empirical study operationalizes eighteenth-century Ottoman Westernization and social change as the pattern of Western goods diffusion into Ottoman society through 124 Ottoman inheritance registers drawn up between 1705 and 1809. These registers came from three separate samples representing three Ottoman social groups: top-level administrators, the military, and the populace. The sample of Ottoman administrators originated from among the registers of top-level Ottoman officials and others that were confiscated by the sultan. The sample of the Ottoman military came from the registers of the military inheritance partitioner for Constantinople, who was under the jurisdiction of the military judge of Rumelia. The sample of the Ottoman populace was drawn from the court registers of the inheritance partitioner for the district of Constantinople proper. These three random samples were selected in a similar manner.[84] Of the sample of thirty-four registers from the populace, half were religious minorities and three-quarters women. The sample of thirty-seven military members was made up mostly of men richer than those in the populace. The sample of fifty-three top-level Ottoman administrators was drawn from among registers confiscated by the sultan.[85] The main assumption in this analysis was that these samples approximated the characteristics of the eighteenth-century Ottoman social groups. The confiscated registers gathered at the capital represented the registers of Ottoman officials and provincial notables, the military inheritance registers corresponded to those of members of the Ottoman office- and provincial households, and the inheritance registers of the populace of Constantinople translated to those of the subjects.

Using the sample of inheritance registers in such a social scientific manner does have certain limitations, however. First, the sample population: The inheritance registers were drawn only upon the request of the heirs or upon the rise of other complications, and they therefore did not include those inheritances that were distributed without judiciary assistance and probably those inheritances where the deceased was too poor to need any apportioning. The sample population is therefore biased toward large and complicated inheritances and does not cover the target population of all the deceased in eighteenth-century Ottoman society. Since the eighteenth-century population of the Ottoman empire is not known, it is altogether difficult to estimate the target population as well. The sample of subjects is drawn from the registers in Constantinople and may therefore exhibit special characteristics that may not be generalizable to other cities or to rural areas. The capital may contain more wealth and social variation than other Ottoman cities and provinces.

Second, the nature of the inheritance registers: The inheritance registers are often incomplete. All the information about them is sometimes spread out under separate entries within one or more registers.[86] Even if all the entries of the register were gathered together, the information contained may nevertheless be incomplete (Barkan 1966: 74–78) where the registers of those who died while traveling, such as merchants, pilgrims, or soldiers on campaigns, might not have reflected their total wealth. Even if the inheritance registers were complete, the inheritance register reflected only the wealth of the deceased upon death and did not indicate the changing wealth composition of the deceased during different periods of his life.[87] Some individuals might have given their wealth away before death through gifts, donations, endorsements, and false debt avowals to favored heirs. The slaves freed upon the death of the owner, agricultural land, and properties leased out to the deceased by religious endowments are also not included in the registers. Perishable goods are not recorded in the registers either, except for staples such as wheat, barley, olive oil, and the produce from farms in the possession of the deceased. There were other complications that emerged after the death as well. The heirs or other persons close to the deceased often hid or stole the goods of the deceased, thereby obfuscating the complete wealth. The wealth of the spouse[88] was also not included, making it impossible to generalize about the family of the deceased. In addition, inheritance partitioners often tended to make inflated assessments of the inheritance to procure a higher duty for themselves, thus problematizing the comparative use of the total value of the inheritance. In spite of these problems, however, the inheritance registers are the best historical source available to study Ottoman social transformation: they certainly contain more information about Ottoman society than the official state correspondence for and by the administrators or the traveler accounts for and by Westerners.

Empirical Analysis

The empirical analysis undertaken here attempted to link the diffusion[89] of Western goods with Ottoman social structure and the historical context. It specifically drew a sample from three separate groups to capture the variation across social groups and from 1705 to 1809 to capture the variation across time. The two hypotheses tested were that (1) the Ottoman propensity to accumulate Western goods would increase throughout the century for all social groups, and (2) this accumulation would be the highest among the social group that had the most wealth, namely, Ottoman officials, and then decline consequently from the military to the populace.

The analysis employed logistic regression[90] because the dependent variable, comprising the proportion of inheritances containing Western goods, was bound by zero and one. The individual inheritance register was the unit of analysis, categorized as either having or not having Western goods. The logistic regression tested the probability of individuals having Western goods depending on their social group, year, and the interaction between social group and year.[91] The regression equation was fitted to the data to create the graph of estimated probability of owning Western goods. Social group, year, and the interaction between social group and year were the predictor variables in calculating the probability of inheritance registers containing Western goods.

The first regression, with the three different social groups of the top-level officials, the military, and the populace, showed that the difference between the slopes for the top-level officials and the military over the course of the century is not statistically significant. In other words, the inheritance registers of top-level officials and the military did not indicate different Western-goods accumulation propensities. This result supported only half of the second hypothesis, that top-level officials and military did indeed have a higher propensity to acquire Western goods than the populace. Yet, there was no significant difference between the propensities of the top-level officials and the military to acquire Western goods. This part of the hypothesis did not hold. Since there was no statistically significant difference between the propensities of top-level officials and the military, the analysis combined these two into one group and termed them the "Elite." Over the course of the eighteenth century, the slope for the elite (-1.458) was indeed significantly different from that of the "Subjects" (the populace). There was no significant change ($.012880$) when the interaction between year and social group was added on.[92] Hence, the graph did not support the first hypothesis that the Ottoman propensity to accumulate Western goods would increase throughout the century for all social groups. The propensity of the elites did not change during the eighteenth century; only that of the subjects did. The graph did not support the second hypothesis, that the eighteenth-century Ottoman accumulation of Western goods would increase more for the officials than the military and populace. The officials and the military did have a higher propensity to accumulate Western goods, but this propensity did not change during the eighteenth century. On the contrary, the propensity of the populace was higher than that of the elite.

Out of the 124 inheritances, only 59 contained Western goods.[93] When these 59 were analyzed in more detail, variations emerged across social groups and across time. The proportion of Western goods in the inheritances changed from one social group and one time period to another. The accompanying table, constructed from the sampled inheritances, gives the proportion of Western goods in those inheritances that have Western goods.

Period	Administrators	Military	Populace
1703–23	.027186	.009424	.028571
1724–45	.112000	.00	.051282
1746–66	.077851	.031473	.050612
1767–87	.048060	.036517	.036429
1788–1809	.050698	.039071	.057566

Throughout the eighteenth century, the proportion of Western goods increased for members of all social groups who already possessed Western goods. The top-level administrators had the highest proportion of Western goods in the mid-eighteenth century; the populace reached that proportion at the end of the century. The Western-goods proportions among the military increased slowly but steadily after the first half of the eighteenth century. The difference in Western-goods proportions among the three social groups who had Western goods decreased by the end of the eighteenth century.

The proportional value of Western goods within inheritances also changed across time and social groups.[94] The ratio of value of Western goods to the total value increased through the eighteenth century and reached a peak at the end of the century. The accompanying table presents the median proportions (expressed in percent) of Western-goods value to total-goods value (for those inheritances that possessed Western goods with values) throughout the eighteenth century.

1703–23	0.45
1724–45	0.58
1746–66	1.61
1767–87	0.70
1788–1809	3.39

The top-level administrators had more valuable Western goods than did the other two groups. Among those who had values recorded for Western goods, the median proportion of the value of administrators was 3.24 percent. The proportions were lower for the military (1.61 percent) and still lower for the populace (0.58 percent). The overall median proportion of the total value in Western goods was closer to that of the military—1.63 percent.

The registers also provide us with an image of what these Western goods actually were and how the Ottomans termed and recorded them; they contained goods described as "Frankish map," "English pistol," "yellow Venetian satin cloth," "gold Markobi alarm clock *(çalar saat),*" "silver Merkobid watch *(saat),*" "glass-stand which contains glassware," "Frankish carved wooden drawer and spoons," "infidel chair with padded cloth," "Saxonian white bowl with lid," and "Venetian eyeglass with case." In terms of the frequency with which each good appears in these registers, the analysis reveals that clocks and watches were the most popular Western goods, followed by pistols and muskets, textiles, chairs, binoculars and telescopes, glassware and flatware, mirrors, chests and drawers, eyeglasses, beds, books and maps, and miscellaneous items such as parrots. The analysis of Western goods with values revealed significant differences in accumulation patterns across Western good type. In particular, the values of Western pistols and muskets, glassware and flatware had a big spread, probably because there were local equivalents of these available. The values of watches, textiles, and binoculars were mostly around 10,000 aspers. The range was nevertheless spread out for watches and binoculars, whereas textiles seemed to remain a luxury item in the eighteenth century, when the prices of watches and binoculars were reduced due to mass production but the price of textiles was still high.[95] Mirrors and chairs, which usually had values less than 1,000 aspers, did not seem to be luxury items.

The numerical distribution of these Western goods in eighteenth-century inheritance registers was as follows:

Clocks and watches	147
Pistols and muskets	76
Textiles	62
Chairs	57
Binoculars and telescopes	39
Glassware and flatware	38
Mirrors	33
Chests and drawers	21
Eyeglasses	12
Beds	5
Books and maps	5
Miscellaneous goods	5
TOTAL	500

Of the 147 watches in the sample, the registers recorded the values of 67 of them, the highest value being 46,050 aspers, where the watch was often studded with precious stones, and the lowest 70, often referring to a broken or incomplete watch. The median value was 6,150, the mean 9,822, and the distribution of the value of the watches was skewed with many watches (50/67) below 10,000. Of the 76 pistols and muskets in the sample, 40 had recorded values, the highest value being 30,000 aspers, often inlaid with silver and gold and studded with precious stones, and the lowest 240 aspers. The median value was 3,175 and the mean 5,836, with an even distribution among administrators and the military, with the former owning more valuable pistols and muskets than the latter. The populace, forbidden from owning and carrying firearms by imperial decree, did not have any such item listed. Of the 62 Western textiles in the sample, the values of 18 were recorded and the highest value was 92,400, often referring to gold or silver French brocade, and the lowest 200 aspers. The median value was 9,850 and the mean 16,273—hence textiles indeed varied in value. The distribution revealed a large difference between the military and the administrators, where the populace still did not own any Western textiles. Textiles seemed to be a luxury item with a skewed distribution among social groups, as the values of textiles owned by administrators were twice those of the military. Of the 57 chairs in the sample, 29 had recorded values. Since the Ottomans used sofas and cushions until the eighteenth century, chairs were indeed a newly introduced item. The highest value of the chair was 13,200 for chairs that were often gilded and padded with valuable cloth, and the lowest 5 aspers. The median value was 150 and the mean 899, thus chairs also varied in value but were not very expensive. The value distribution revealed the value of most chairs (28/29) to be below 1,000 aspers. The values of chairs owned by the populace, although less, were more evenly spread than the other two groups. The registers recorded the values of 17 of the 39 telescopes and binoculars in the sample, the highest value being 31,100 and the lowest 100 aspers. With a median value of 1,200 and a mean of 7,579, the value range was very large. The distribution among the administrators and the military was even, and the populace did not own any of these goods. Top-level administrators again had binoculars and telescopes that were more valuable than those of the military, and the populace did not own any, as they probably had no need for these instruments, which were often associated with warfare. Glassware and flatware also had a wide spread in value, where out of the 38, the values of 16 were recorded. The highest was valued at 12,050 aspers, the lowest at 240. The mean value of 4,167 and the median value of 3,550 were close to each other. The administrators again owned more valuable glassware and flatware, often from Saxony or France, and the military more plain white flatware from Germany. Of the 33 mirrors in the sample, 13 had recorded values, the highest value being 6,050 aspers and the lowest 60. The mean value was 1,157 and the median 340. The value distribution revealed most (11/14) mirrors to be below 1,000 in value. The administrators again owned more valuable items than the military. Out of 21 items of furniture, the values of 8 were recorded, the mean being 4,122 and the median 2,745 aspers. The value of the furniture also ranged from the lowest at 120 to the highest at 14,050 aspers. The populace did not own any of this Western furniture, and the administrators' were valued at a mean of 5,285 and a median of 2,745. Military groups' had the same mean and median, 635 aspers. Out of 12 eyeglasses in the sample, the value of 3 were recorded, and 2 of these, worth 750 and 960 aspers, belonged to members of the military group and 1, valued at 300, to an administrator. Out of 5 "Frankish printed" books in the sample, the value of 4 were indicated as 300, 2,400, 16,000, and 18,050 aspers. A member of the military group again owned the cheapest one and the others belonged to the administrators. Out of the 5 Western beds, the value of 4 were again recorded as 80, 120, 300, and 360 aspers; 2 belonged to members of the military (80 and 360), and 2 to populace (120 and 300).

In summary, our empirical analysis of Western-goods accumulation by different Ottoman social groups challenged the existing studies, which assumed Western-goods penetration to be homogenous, continuous, and introduced from above. Yet the empirical analysis demonstrated that this was an overgeneralization: different Ottoman social groups had different propensities to possess Western goods throughout the eighteenth century, and this propensity increased for the group least expected for lack of resources: the populace. This finding provides additional proof to our contention on the rise of the Ottoman commercial bourgeoisie during this period.

Rise of the Ottoman Commercial Bourgeoisie

In the Ottoman context, those accumulating primarily social resources outside the control of the Ottoman sultan formed the basis of the Ottoman bureaucratic bourgeoisie, and those similarly aggregating economic resources outside the sultan's control constituted the foundation of the Ottoman commercial bourgeoisie. Since these conceptions of the bourgeoisie as a social class are themselves socially constructed, it is necessary to undertake a critical examination of the emergence of the notion of the commercial bourgeoisie and the multiplicity of meanings it acquired across societies over time. Only then can one make an adequate assessment of the social boundaries of the Ottoman commercial bourgeoisie and its definition in terms of its capacity for resource accumulation and reproduction outside the existing social structure. The analysis of the formation of the Ottoman commercial bourgeoisie thus warrants a historical examination of the emergence of the concept of the bourgeoisie and a subsequent empirical contextualization of the concept in eighteenth- and nineteenth-century Ottoman social change.

The origins of the bourgeoisie[96] can be traced to the French revolution and that of a commercial bourgeoisie in particular to the concomitant emergence of industrialization and Western commercial expansion. It was the dissolution of guild regulations that controlled labor and production (Aminzade 1981: 2) and the emergence of absolute individual property by the Civil Code of 1804 (Sewell 1980: 114–15; 1979: 48) that marked the origins of the bourgeois class based on the concepts of free wage labor and private property.[97] The concomitant change in the meaning structures surrounding the concept of work formed, in turn, the foundation stone of the new bourgeois order (Joyce 1980, 1987; Kaplan and Koepp 1986; Roseberry 1989: 34). Work, which had historically been conceptualized as a social stigma, was now exalted as an essential foundation of human happiness, the lack of which indicated moral degradation (Sewell 1980: 64–65, 226). This moral dimension provided the new conception of social action with the capacity to bind or unbind social groups into classes. Among social groups in Western Europe, the community of craftspeople had the potential to be mobilized into collective social action that envisioned a voluntary association of productive[98] citizens (Sewell 1980: 144; Calhoun 1982: 176). It was the bourgeoisie who provided the leadership for this voluntary association of citizen workers,[99] differentiating themselves as a class through their level of income and the way in which it was acquired (Aminzade 1981: 25–28). Among the factors that could induce bourgeois hegemony in Europe, the French ideology of liberty, equality, and fraternity, significant especially in terms of the concept of nationalism, which contained within it the "imagined" elements that guaranteed this ideology, led to the concomitant emergence of Western civic consciousness (Aminzade 1981: 269–79). This consciousness not only helped the bourgeoisie hegemonize its class position but also pacified the nascent class consciousness of the workers as it turned them into citizens. The social reproduction of the bourgeoisie occurred as it married and thus integrated into the gentry; soon, big business and civic leadership[100] started to go hand in hand (Rogers 1979: 437).

Yet the crucial assumption[101] in this conception of the Western historical experience of the bourgeoisie was an element of ethnic, racial, and religious homogeneity that often did not hold in other contexts.[102] What happened when the "social" homogeneity assumption in class formation did not hold? One of the insights into this consequences of such a scenario can be found in a footnote in Hobsbawm's analysis, where he acknowledges that "where such a stratum consisted of foreigners or strangers, its relation to the indigenous social structure was much more complicated, as the nineteenth century Jews discovered in

Central and Eastern Europe." (1989: 23, note 29). It is on this aside that we can start to theoretically construct the foundations of the Ottoman commercial bourgeoisie as a class. Indeed, one can argue that the Ottoman case was structurally similar to the Central and Eastern European one in that the Ottoman merchant group contained a relatively large contingent of "nonhomogeneous" ethno-religious minorities—Ottoman Greeks, Armenians, and Jews. In addition, like the Central and Eastern European Jews, this group was the first to experience the initial impact of the emerging economic transformation from without. Hence, it was the external[103] impact of changing commercial ties with the West that formed the impetus for the emergence of this social class. Due to the social and religious constraints placed upon them by Ottoman society, however, the minorities failed[104] to convert these economic resources into social power with which to challenge the control of the sultan. How this divide operated can best be understood through analyzing the effects of ethnicity on class formation (Parkin 1974, 1979), a stand that extends beyond the tendency to analyze class relations within an assumed cultural and ethnic homogeneity. According to this conception, communal minorities[105] play a pivotal role in class formation through the processes of closure that surrounds them to enact decisions based on tradition rather than the newly emerging market rationality, which presumably treats all labor as equal.

If we extend this argument to the Ottoman case, we indeed observe that the Ottoman minorities, in defining their social location, turned not to Ottoman society at large but instead to their own communities and often employed education to articulate this new definition. The new minority schools that formed were significant in creating an imagined cultural homogenization. In the case of the Ottoman Greek community, for instance, this new sense of identity stated that "every youngster was responsible to two distinct authorities: his family and the nation *(ethnos)* that 'embraced' him, which was conceived of as the totality of those of the 'same race' *(omogeneis)*, past, present, and future, who were conscious of their rights and responsibilities" (Augustinos 1992: 169). It is significant that this formulation omitted the role of the church and the minority community that was defined by religion. Indeed, this new conception allowed for new loyalties to develop to the abstract notion of the "nation" as defined by the new leaders in contradistinction to the former conceptions developed by the church and its communal leaders. The Ottoman Greek consciousness of this new identity enabled the formation and mobilization of independence movements among the Ottoman minorities. Some of these movements, such as those of the Greeks, were successful, while others, such as those of the Armenians, failed; the Ottoman Muslims also started selecting options of their own. As trade with the West provided Ottoman minorities with economic and educational resources, the communal boundaries of who comprised the Ottoman bourgeoisie became more articulate and often started to include an imagined "ethnic" component that was often fostered by educational institutions. By the early twentieth century, when public debate developed around who comprised the Ottoman bourgeoisie, the ethnic category of Turkish quickly became identified with it. As an Ottoman Muslim thinker stated:

> [T]here was almost no Turkish bourgeoisie during the Ottoman reign. Similar to the situation in the Polish Kingdom, imprisoned elements comprised the Ottoman Turkish bourgeoisie. The Ottomans were only soldiers or officials. Yet the bourgeoisie forms the foundation for our contemporary states; the large modern states have all relied on an artisanal, commercial and banking bourgeoisie in their formation. The Turkish national renaissance can be the honorable ground for the genesis of the Turkish bourgeoisie within the Ottoman state. (Akçura 1911: 102–3)

These attempts by the early twentieth century to form a national bourgeoisie highlight the direction in which the nascent commercial bourgeoisie developed in the Ottoman empire. Indeed, the early years of World War I were replete with state attempts to create a national market as it tried, through cooperatives, to transfer commerce from the minority to Muslim-Turkish elements, thereby attempting to form a "surrogate bourgeoisie" (Toprak 1982: 21; Keyder 1988: 196). The promotion of Muslim merchants and businessmen ensued, and the neutralization of the Ottoman minorities was completed in 1924, in less than a decade.

The gradual transformation in social consciousness from Ottoman minority status to a bourgeois consciousness occurred through the changing nature of the interaction between the Ottoman Muslims and minorities. The objective conditions of nineteenth-century trade with the West and the privileges the Ottoman minorities acquired through their involvement in this trade led to the emergence of this consciousness. The French domination of Ottoman trade ended in the early nineteenth century with Napoleon's invasion of Egypt, whereupon the British once more became the dominant trade partner.[106] Another treaty preceded the French one in 1838, which this time was between the Ottoman empire and the English. This trade treaty has often been regarded by many Ottoman thinkers[107] as the cause of the collapse of the Ottoman economy.[108] As the figures above indicate, it certainly did expand English domination over the Ottoman trade.[109] The Habsburg influence also started to increase during the same time period,[110] when the Germans identified and targeted the Middle East as a potential market for their industrial goods. The period of expansion of foreign trade under the English and the Germans also produced external borrowing and financial dependence, eventually culminating in a period of stagnation and European financial control.

During the nineteenth century, in addition to investing through the Ottoman minorities, the West started to get involved first in the organization and running of indigenous Ottoman industries and then in procuring the necessary infrastructure for their maintenance. The roots of this involvement can be traced back to the 1854 Crimean war, which immensely strained Ottoman financial resources. France and England advocated the Ottoman state seek financing for the war from European markets. Between 1854 and 1881, a period of twenty-seven years, fifteen loan agreements were signed between the Ottoman state and the European banks where the sale value of the bonds ranged between 32 and 98 percent (Eldem 1970: 260). Another source of finance for the Ottoman state was borrowing vast amounts from an indigenous source, the newly emerging Ottoman minorities,[111] also known as the "Galata bankers." This group materialized through arbitrage, that is, the manipulation of the rates of exchange of various currencies circulating in the empire—a condition that emerged due to the Ottoman lack of standardization of exchange values. As these minorities amassed huge wealth, they first started to advance payment on the salaries of Ottoman officials, engage in tax-farming, and discount treasury bills. They then proceeded to lend money to the Ottoman state and established banks[112] to do so. When the concomitant debts of the Ottoman state to these minorities exceeded 8.72 million Ottoman piasters, the Administration of "Six Charges" *(rüsum-u sitte)* was established to organize a payment plan. This administration drew directly upon the significant tax revenues of the empire, such as the fishing taxes of Constantinople, the salt and tobacco monopolies, and the silk production taxes accruing from some Ottoman provinces, to pay back the vast state debts to the minority bankers (Eldem 1970: 262).

This economic-administrative arrangement with minority bankers served as a model for the Ottoman Public Debt Administration, which was established in 1881 to repay the more than two million French franks of Ottoman debts[113] to the West. The Ottoman empire, England, France, Germany, Italy, and Austria were the participants in this arrangement (Eldem 1970: 262; Ortaylı 1981: 22). By the second half of the nineteenth century, these Ottoman debts to the West were more than half of the regular Ottoman budgetary expenditure (Owen 1981: 101). The Ottoman state entered into a cycle of indebtedness as it borrowed more money to pay its debts and, by doing so, gradually reached a point when it could barely pay the interest accruing on these debts.[114] The bankruptcy and the public debt administration that ensued also facilitated the economic resurgence of European foreign residents and Ottoman minorities who created and manned, at the expense of the Ottoman Muslims, the infrastructure of the Public Debt Administration. This administration lasted for thirty-six years, from 1882 to 1918, during which period Ottoman state revenues accruing from six leading resources—tobacco, stamps, spirits, fisheries, and silk—were turned over to them. These revenues increased substantially over the years.[115] Gradually, in the name of efficiency, the foreign-sponsored officials started to collect these revenues themselves. In 1886, the Public Debt Administration employed a staff of 3040, of which 55 were Europeans and the rest Ottoman subjects; by the years 1912–13, the number of personnel had increased to over 5500, spread throughout 720 tax collecting offices, with foreign residents and Ottoman minorities[116] comprising most of the employees (Owen 1981: 194).

The Ottoman state attempted to counter this Western economic penetration by trying to develop an indigenous industry through such policies as establishing state-sponsored factories and firms, founding a school of industrial reform in 1867, and having exhibits for Ottoman products. These measures were not successful due to the Ottoman inability to protect its markets or to match the low production costs of the West. The world market had taken its hold, and mass-produced Western goods had already penetrated Ottoman markets. Nevertheless, the Ottoman state sustained its intervention in industry. During the period 1840–60, it established approximately 160 state-sponsored factories—yet these could not be operated due to a lack of skilled workers, a shortage of capital, and the continuous Western economic presence. From 1860 to 1876, the Ottoman state therefore focused on strengthening indigenous commercial groups (Önsoy 1988: 47). It started a fivefold effort to nurture indigenous commercial groups as it assembled companies on the model of guilds, standardized and regularized the quality and price of products, increased customs duties for the protection of indigenous production, opened schools for business and industry, and inaugurated industrial exhibits[117] to introduce and promote Ottoman goods. Although many of these were indeed initiated, very few of them could be sustained. For instance, firms were established for the guild of jewelers and tanners in 1866, for saddlers in 1867, and for textile manufacturers, blacksmiths, and mold casters in 1868. The gradation of the guild system was also utilized to establish the curriculum of the School for Industry, which was founded in 1868. Similarly, many economic privileges were given to entrepreneurs to establish industries (Eldem 1970: 114). The state promulgated a law in 1873 exempting prospective factory founders from taxes and customs duties; in 1877 this exemption was extended to building materials. A ten-year tax immunity was introduced for new plants in 1897. Yet the inadequacy of financing,[118] the lack of managerial skills, the inability of artisans to make the transition to the new system, and the difficulties in collecting the sales dues from the artisans led to the collapse of these endeavors as well (Önsoy 1988: 95–114).

The vast gap between Western capital investment in the Ottoman empire and the Ottoman state and private investment continued to grow throughout the nineteenth century

(Eldem 1970: 114–15). For instance, between 1883–1913, the forty-six companies founded with domestic investment[119] had a total capital of 110 million Ottoman piasters. In the same period, the total capital of the thirty-nine companies founded through foreign investment during the same period extended 1 billion Ottoman piasters—a tenfold difference.[120] Ottoman state industry also remained limited in its investments.[121] Meanwhile, Western economic penetration continued incessantly in ever increasing dosages as the Europeans, who were first granted rights to carry out retail trade and then to own property or acquire a business license in the empire gradually expanded into almost all the sectors of the Ottoman economy. The following account of European activities in Western Anatolia depicts the pattern of this spread:

> [T]hey established steam operated mills to grind wheat into flour and took part in the growing food processing industry of the city. They also set up silk spinning concerns, factories for printing muslin and dyeing yarns as well as cotton gin factories. They were particularly active in mining and invested heavily in such important infrastructural projects as the building of railways and the establishment and running of utilities such as gas, while not neglecting such complimentary sectors to their traditional trading activities as shipping and insurance. (Frangakis-Syrett 1992: 110–11)

Indeed, by the end of the nineteenth century, Western economic dominance in the Ottoman empire had branched into the spheres of commerce, finance, production, and infrastructural construction. Even though the penetration was not uniform, it nevertheless had an impact on the Ottoman economy. Ultimately, however, it was the agency of Ottoman social groups that structured the nature of Western impact.

As Western European powers acquired economic and concomitant political power over the Ottoman sultan, they started forcing a series of reforms to help the Ottoman empire join the ranks of "civilized" countries. Legal equality for all was one mode through which the Western powers exercised their domination. The Ottoman reforms[122] of 1839 and 1856, both involving imperial decrees guaranteeing equal rights to all subjects, were executed at the encouragement of the Western powers. Indeed, one can argue that it was the Ottoman Muslim and minority responses[123] to these edicts that helped transform the Ottoman minorities into a commercial bourgeoisie. For instance, one of the chroniclers and statesmen of the time, Cevdet Pasha, noted how the 1856 reform "was a day of joy for the minorities, and a day of sorrow for the Muslims who mourned losing the sacred rights they had attained through the blood of their ancestors and forefathers"[124] (1872: 67–68). Similarly, another Ottoman statesmen, Fuad Pasha, argued that the Ottoman state had been founded on four principles, the Muslim community, the Turkish state, the Ottoman dynasty, and Constantinople as the seat of government. He questioned whether they were not demolishing one of these principles by making the minorities equal to the Muslims, who had been the dominant nation for centuries (Cevdet Pasha 1872: 85). Still another chronicler (Ahmed Lütfi 1885: 6–7) remarked how the Muslims, not the minorities, had spilled all their blood, lives, and property for the empire, so the latter would never overcome their subordinate status even if the legal system was unified. He was right. The issue of legal equality further polarized the Ottoman state and made the Ottoman Muslims[125] and minorities more aware of their differences.

This polarization and the redrawing of social boundaries with a new consciousness occurred throughout the Ottoman empire. In Mecca "some rallied for a holy war against the Turks who they thought had Christianized and Europeanized, others insulted the Ottoman governor calling him a Christian, a Jew, and still others wanted to pillage the properties of the ethnic Turks for leaning toward the Christians" (Cevdet Pasha 1872: 113). In Jiddah, the dispute over flying a Muslim or a British flag on a merchant ship led to a Muslim–Christian conflict in which twenty-two Christian merchants were killed along with the British and French consuls, leading to the bombardment of the city by the British and French fleets (Gülsoy 1991: 451). In Manisa, rumors of an impending attack by Muslims on minorities during Easter (İD22739) led the sultan to send a regiment to the area. Ottoman Muslim officials in Denizli who prevented minorities from carrying out their religious rituals were duly punished (Ayniyat 439: 71), as were those in Nazilli about whom the Christians complained for "uttering improper words to them" (Ayniyat 439: 114). In Varna, rumors circulated that a Greek bishop was killed by Muslims, but an examination by two European physicians proved that he had died naturally (İD287/1). In Damascus, as some minorities started to dress like Muslims, were rumored to have Muslim slaves, and openly held religious processions through the streets, the Muslim populace "started to attack them whenever an opportunity arose" (Maoz 1982: 96–97). In Maraş (Gülsoy 1991: 451–58), Muslim–minority polarization occurred through two incidents, one over unequal taxation and the other over a commercial credit. According to the 1856 taxes (İrade 22853/3), the Ottoman minorities had paid 77 piasters per household to the Muslims' payment of 62 piasters per household. When the Muslim officials, rather than compensating for this inequality in accordance with the imperial rescript, decreased Muslim taxation at the expense of the minorities, so that the Ottoman minorities now paid 87 per household to the Muslims' 56, there was a great deal of minority resentment. Upon hearing the reform edict read out at the governor's mansion, the minorities rejoiced while the Muslims protested by shutting down their stores and refusing to fulfill their obligations to the state. The governor had to force these stores to be opened up. In the other instance, a British merchant and a Muslim artisan had a dispute over 4,000 piasters for military provisions that the British merchant claimed he had paid for in full. When the case was brought to court, the judge agreed with the merchant, but the deputy prepared a document in favor of the artisan. When the merchant swore at the deputy for doing so, the deputy gathered a crowd of more than four thousand, stating that the merchant had invalidated the laws of Islam and therefore needed to be punished. All marched to the merchant's mansion, setting it on fire; six demonstrators were killed from the mansion, and the merchant, his wife, and his child perished in the fire. The two American missionary families living with the merchant were saved, as was one of the merchant's children. The following day military troops were sent and all who demonstrated rounded up and imprisoned. The Ottoman state returned the pillaged goods and ordered a salary of 500 French francs to be paid to the surviving child for life. Hence, throughout the empire, increasing tensions between the Muslims and minorities made them more aware of their differences.

Another factor that facilitated the process of consciousness[126] was population movements (Goldstone 1991), specifically, migrations. The nineteenth century saw large migrations of both Muslims and minorities at a historical juncture that was economically and militaristically precarious for both parties. The migrations of Ottoman Greek (Augustinos 1992: 28) and Armenian males (Göçek 1992) comprised the labor migrations from the provinces to the Ottoman capital.[127] Similarly, mass migrations[128] of ethnically Turkish Muslims occurred from the Balkans and Russia during the second half of the nineteenth century (Eryılmaz 1990: 82–83). The impact of these population movements can be observed in relation to the change in the ethno-religious composition of the empire in both the capital and the provinces and in the ethnic division of labor that emerged as a consequence. The two reference years of 1885 and 1897 for which empirical data exist for both the empire and the capital on the population composition (Eryılmaz 1990: 81, 107) indicate the following. The overall population composition of the empire changed[129] from 73.5 percent Muslim and 26.5 minority in 1885 to 74.1 percent Muslim and 25.9 percent minority in 1897. Hence even though both figures represent an overall change of .6 percent in either direction, what is noteworthy was the nature of these population movements—almost all[130] the Muslim migrants arrived at the capital, thereby dramatically changing the population composition of the imperial city.

The advantaging of the minorities over the Muslims led to a significant social polarization within Ottoman society during the nineteenth century. The Ottoman social groups that engaged in internal trade, industry and crafts, and professions started to vary across religious lines. For instance, according to a 1912 Ottoman yearbook (Issawi 1980: 13–14), while Ottoman Muslim participation became limited to 15 percent in internal trade, 12 percent in industry and crafts, and 14 percent in the professions, the share of Ottoman minorities expanded to comprise 66 percent of those engaged in internal trade, 79 percent in industry and crafts, and 66 percent in the professions.[131] Similarly, the European companies involved in establishing Ottoman tobacco monopolies, ports, railroads, and coal mines in the late nineteenth century privileged Europeans and Ottoman minorities for administrative positions. For instance, in the case of the railroad companies that were established, although 90 percent of those employed were Ottoman subjects, Europeans occupied the highest and most lucrative posts, with Ottoman Christians joining them in the middle-level categories, while most Ottoman Muslims were relegated to the lowest ranks as manual laborers. The salary scale was also commensurate, foreign workers earning twice as much as Ottoman ones, and Ottoman minorities earning more than Muslims (Quatert 1983: 79). These pay differences among workers across religious lines escalated the antagonisms between the Ottoman minorities and the Muslims. Yet it was not only the Western powers that fostered the polarization; the Ottoman sultan Mahmud II practiced the same policy in the early nineteenth century in reverse (Özcan 1991: 363, 368). When he made visits to mausoleums and mosques or traveled through the lands, his cash endowments to subjects were segregated along religious lines; Ottoman Muslims each received 51 piasters, while Ottoman Christians and Jews received 31 piasters each. Similarly, when he made endowments to educational institutions in the capital, Muslim schools received 50,000 piasters, Greek schools 20,000 piasters, and Armenian and Jewish schools 7,500 piasters each. Also, in 1845, when the sultan asked representatives from all provinces to be sent to the capital for advice, "all members were reimbursed for their expenses, the Christians at only half the rate of the Muslims" (Augustinos 1992: 60). Hence, the Ottoman differentiation between the Muslims and the minorities from within the empire interacted with the Western privileging of the minorities without to further polarize Ottoman society.[132]

The Western-style educational institutions of the foreign residents and minorities played a significant role in complementing these privileging commercial relations with social ones. Since the Ottoman sultan had not placed any restrictions on the interaction between minorities and foreign residents, the Ottoman minorities often attended Western-style schools established by the foreign residents. Due to expanding trade ties with Europe, the children of some Ottoman minority merchants also began receiving their education in Europe in increasing numbers. There, they were exposed to Western knowledge and to the alternate social, economic, and political organization it proposed (Özkaya 1983: 226–28, 235). Ottoman Greeks and other Christians had started sending their sons to Europe in the sixteenth and seventeenth centuries—usually to Italy—to study and train, especially as physicians. Also from the late sixteenth century, the Vatican had established colleges for Eastern communities in Rome, which affected the development of the Catholic Armenians and the Arabic-speaking Maronites of Lebanon (Lewis 1982: 109). This steady flow of Ottoman minority children to Europe for education increased in the eighteenth century. In the eighteenth and nineteenth centuries, the children of other minorities[133] attended the new academies that were being established in the Russian empire (Minassian 1992: 18–19). In addition, Ottoman minorities further interpreted the impact of this Western knowledge in their communities by establishing similar schools within their own communities. For instance, Greek merchants established such schools in the Peloponnese, Epirus, and Western Anatolia and on the Black Sea coast, Cyprus, and Crete. These Western-style schools[134] provided minorities with Western scientific knowledge, supplied them with the necessary social and economic skills to use this knowledge, and suggested alternate forms of societal organization. By doing so, they provided the crucial social and cultural consciousness that was imperative for the transformation of the minority merchants into a commercial bourgeoisie. The Ottoman minorities established numerous structures of mutual help and brotherhood, such as communal administration, charitable associations, and corporate organizations (Dumont 1982: 229). Rather than relegating control to the sultan, they then espoused to organize, administer, and control their own communities themselves. The minorities geographically closest to the West were the first to start emancipatory movements from the sultan's control: the social unrest in the Balkans commenced in the late eighteenth and early nineteenth centuries and culminated in Greek independence in 1821. The Westernization Russia was undergoing also affected the Balkans, as the local priests who traveled to Russia and other Balkan intellectuals who worked in Russia brought back Western ideas, and also Eastern Anatolia, as Armenian students educated in Russia came back to instigate change.[135] Other Balkan rebellions followed. Revolts in the Arab and North African provinces ensued.[136] Hence, escalating Western trade privileged Ottoman minorities over Muslims and, by offering them foreign protection, helped these minorities accumulate resources outside of the sultan's control. It was on these resources that the seeds of the Ottoman commercial bourgeoisie and subsequent independence movements were sown.

Ethnic segmentation in the concomitant economic division of labor persisted, however, as all divided themselves across religion (Eryılmaz 1990: 107). For instance, in 1885, although the distribution[137] of those employed by the state as bureaucrats ranged across the ethnic-religious divide, comprising 11.41 percent Ottoman Muslim, 0.38 percent Ottoman Greek, 0.59 percent Ottoman Armenian, and 0.44 percent Ottoman Jewish, the ethnic composition of those in "trade, commerce and industry" was dramatically different. While 25.37 percent of these were Ottoman Muslim, the majority were Ottoman Greeks, Armenians, and Jews. Hence, in the Ottoman capital, minorities surpassed Muslims in all economic spheres. The economic predominance of the Ottoman minorities was further documented by the 1912 figures, which cited that (Issawi 1982: 262–63) out of the forty private bankers and thirty-four stockbrokers listed in Constantinople, none were Muslims; and of the thirty-seven large textile importers, only five were Muslims.[138] This economic segmentation, when coupled with the impact of Western-style education and the population pressure of migrations, undoubtedly increased class consciousness across both the religious and the economic divide.

Another factor that contributed to increased polarization was the steady increase of foreign residents in the empire throughout the nineteenth century. The case of the foreign residents in Egypt[139] validates this assertion. Increased European trade with Egypt was accompanied by an increase in European immigration, as 30,000 foreigners came and settled in Egypt each year between 1857 and 1861. In 1862 this figure rose to 33,000, in 1863 to 43,000, in 1864 to 56,500, and in 1865 it reached the peak of 80,000 foreigners per year (Steppat 1968: 283). These Europeans quickly controlled commerce, finance, and industry, so much so that in 1907 they owned approximately 15–20 percent of Egypt's capital, even though they constituted 3 percent of the population (Issawi 1968: 391). Yet, the interaction of these foreign residents with the rest of society was mediated through the Ottoman minorities, who had the linguistic and societal skills of both contexts. Indeed, eventually these minorities came to occupy a significant social position in Egyptian society through their association with the foreign residents, as "the Greeks, Jews, Armenians, Lebanese and Syrians owned most of the petty business, and even the civil service drew heavily on such groups to fill the more qualified positions" (Issawi 1968: 398).

The increasing tension between the foreign residents, Ottoman minorities, and the sultan is demonstrated throughout the nineteenth century, especially in two historical accounts. In one instance (Cevdet Pasha 1872: 226), when unrest occurred at the capital in 1861 due to a financial crisis and the Ottoman currency started losing value, merchants and artisans stocked up on items and refused to sell them to the populace. As the Ottoman sultan had often noted, the provisioning of the populace did indeed became a problem: riots broke out in bakeries as people fought over bread and rumors spread that some had started procuring arms and ammunition. Stores were all shut down and the Ottoman administration met with the sultan until morning. At dawn, town criers were sent out telling people that the sultan has a proclamation and that all ought to come to the mosques for morning prayers to hear it. Indeed, they were all told that the sultan would speedily punish "the seditious" *(müfsid)*. It is noteworthy to see how the mosque, restricted to the Muslims, remained the center of imperial communication, thereby effectively cutting the minorities off from access to this significant source of information. Even though the Ottoman minorities did indeed have their equivalents to which the Muslims did not have access, the Ottoman power structure was nevertheless reproduced in mosques.

The other instance relates to the 1859 protest of Ottoman minority merchants and artisans of the capital when the palace and the sultan failed to pay the debts accrued to them. According to various accounts,

> As many artisans and merchants faced bankruptcy and had to take out large loans as a consequence of the failure of the palace to pay its debts, the merchants and artisans from among the Christian subjects of the empire took their complaints first to the Ottoman government, and when the government refused to accept their petition [for not having any jurisdiction over the sultan's palace], they all marched onto the palace to present their petition to the sultan. When the commander in chief *[serasker]* at the palace got rid of them after uttering vague words about taking care of the matters, a couple of hundred of them rented a boat and went to the French, British and Russian embassies screaming and yelling in protest, and presented a petition to each of them. (Cevdet Pasha 1872: 98–99; [1880] 1980: 20)

This was probably the first of many instances when the Ottoman minorities of the capital rallied around an economic issue to act, for the first time, as a social group apart from the Muslims. They then approached the three Western powers for administrative justice and protection. This internal ethno-religious division separated the Ottoman bourgeois transformation in commerce from that of Western Europe. Because of this internal division, the emergence of the Ottoman commercial bourgeoisie as a social class and the dissipation of the empire went hand in hand.

4

"Civilization," Ottoman Intellectuals, and Western Ideas: Polarization Within the Bourgeoisie

In 1911, from the Ottoman war front in North Africa against Italy, the Ottoman military official who later became Enver Pasha wrote the following to a lady friend in Europe:

> C'est un poison votre civilisation, mais c'est un poison qui reveille et on ne veut, on ne peut plus dormir. On sent que si on refermait les yeux, ce serait pour mourir. (Enver 1913: 186)

> [Your civilization, it is a poison, but it is a poison that wakes one up and one cannot, one does not want to sleep anymore. One feels that if one were to close one's eyes, it would be in order to die.]

Indeed, this pungent but accurate assessment describes the process by which Ottoman society observed and interpreted Western civilization and then had to come to terms with this unavoidable and uncomfortable interpretation. Ottoman interaction with the West through goods and institutions thus combined with a third, powerful component: Western ideas. What were these ideas, who interpreted them, in what context, and to what ends? The concept of "civilization," Ottoman intellectuals, and Western ideas disseminated through newspapers and voluntary associations are examined to respond to these queries.

The concept of Western "civilization" entered Ottoman discourse and led to a reassessment of the Ottoman social structure. As Ottomans observed, interpreted, and, eventually, compared the West with their own society, distinct visions and aspirations formed. The principles and priorities of Ottoman social groups changed accordingly and transformed their visions of what Ottoman society ought to resemble. The other significant development was the increased number of Ottoman social groups with access to material and social resources that escaped the sultan's control. As opposition to the sultan mounted, one group literally escaped the sultan's control and escaped to Europe to live there as political exiles. In addition, as officials acquired cultural capital and as minority merchants accumulated merchant capital, they created the social environment for the emergence of a new social group: Ottoman intellectuals. These intellectuals worked for the new journals and newspapers, wrote novels, taught at the Western-style schools, and, in general, used their newly acquired skills to make their livelihood. Unlike the former Ottoman thinkers, who usually had their sustenance from the sultan and/or the households, this new group, although not always entirely independent of the sultan, did nevertheless have the option, for the first time, of an alternate source of sustenance lodged in the public sphere. They could therefore envision a society that was not centered and legitimated around the office of the sultan. The Western-style schools, newly emerging professional and social organizations, secret societies, and Western and Ottoman books and periodicals, along with the reading rooms and public libraries where they were circulated, created the new cultural environment, the Ottoman "civil society" within which this alternate Ottoman vision acquired meaning.

Newly emerging newspapers and voluntary associations formed the two most significant social and cultural media through which these intellectuals and ideas survived. The rapid circulation of Western ideas and the need for civil contexts where these could be discussed generated an ever increasing demand for Ottoman newspapers and reading rooms, a demand that was only occasionally arrested through the censorship of the sultan. The new Ottoman social groups with cultural and material capital met and organized within voluntary associations, acquiring a consciousness of their common interests meanwhile. Yet one element, the preexisting Ottoman ethnic segmentation among Muslims and minorities, could not be overcome through the visions created by the Ottoman intellectuals, through Western ideas and with the aid of voluntary associations and newspapers. All imagined communities inspired by nationalism split along ethnic lines; the united image of the empire was perpetually shattered.

"Civilization" and the Emergence of a New Ottoman Social Vision

The most significant development of late eighteenth- and nineteenth century Ottoman society was the emergence of a new vision of Ottoman society that was informed by Western ideas of "civilization." Although few agreed on what this concept actually entailed and many argued for disparate interpretations, the concept's ambiguity did not weaken but instead strengthened its effect on the Ottoman social structure. The societal expectations of many Ottoman social groups dramatically altered as a consequence of these diverse and often incompatible interpretations. The succinct late nineteenth-century definition[1] of "civilization" *(medeniyet),* by an Ottoman palace chronicler captured the ultimate meaning the concept acquired in late nineteenth-century Ottoman society:

> The edifice of [Western] civilization is built on two principles, one material and the other moral. The moral principle is devoutness. . . . The material principle comprises the rescue from idleness of the populace by the farmers, merchants and artisans, and the restrengthening of the principles that justify the production of wealth and discipline. (Ahmed Lütfi [1875] 1991: 6–7)

This nebulous definition could well be used to define civilization, capitalism, and/or industrialization, all the Western historical processes that came to the Ottoman empire simultaneously as one undifferentiated whole. It was indeed the combined force of these processes under the rubric of civilization that affected the Ottoman social structure in the eighteenth and nineteenth centuries.

The origins of twentieth-century social change can be traced to this historical conjunction of capitalism, democracy, and industrialization, which affected all spheres of life, from the personal and communal to the national, from the family and workplace to the public sphere. Hence what Raymond Williams would term an "epochal change" occurred with "new meanings and values, new practices, new significances and experiences" (1973: 8, 10), creating a new culture comprising a set of ideas, meanings, and associations that presented an order of equality and reciprocity while giving a product of history the appearance of natural order. Yet the old also survived, albeit in redefined form. Karl Marx, the most astute observer of this epochal change, noted in *The Eighteenth Brumaire*:

> The tradition of the dead generations weighs like a nightmare on the minds of the living. And, just as when they appear to be engaged in the revolutionary transformation of themselves and their material surroundings, in the creation of something which does not yet exist, precisely in such epochs of revolutionary crisis they timidly conjure up the spirits of the past to help them; they borrow their names, slogans and costumes so as to stage the new world-historical scene in this venerable disguise and borrowed language. . . . In the same way, the beginner who has learned a new language always retranslates into his mother tongue. ([1867] 1974: 284)

Hence what resulted was the creation of the culture of Western civilization, at once socially constituted and socially constitutive (Roseberry 1989: 42). In this context, spatial and temporal categories were carefully regulated and the norms of social behavior redefined. The historical conjunction of capitalism, democracy, and industrialization created the concept of class as it differentiated people according to their economic activities. The principles it advocated favored the bourgeoisie at the expense of others, and the bourgeoisie combined three elements contained in this historical conjuncture, namely, the religious, commercial, and scientific ideologies, to create a societal vision based on production, design, and building that advocated a rational, scientific worldview (Davidoff and Hall 1987: 26). It also combined within it "objectivist and subjectivist moments" (Bourdieu 1987: 2) as people, institutions, and organizations negotiated the meaning of the new culture and the emergent social groups, especially the bourgeoisie. Hence Western civilization accumulated within it a mobilizational force.

The diffusion of this force into Ottoman society first became visible through a range of social action, from the adoption of modes of Western behavior, such as clothing made in European fashion, top hats, fancy canes, pet dogs, piano lessons, French language lessons, operas, dances, and balls, to the eventual employment of Western literary forms such as the novel, short story, and newspaper and the print culture it introduced, which had profound effects in creating new visions of Ottoman society and the individuals living within it. These literary forms constructed a new image of an Ottoman as a refined man "introverted, very sensitive, knowledgeable in Western music and literature, conversant in a Western language, positivist, attributing value to human beings, and subscribing to a Western style of life" (Kavcar 1985: 85). Literary topics included Western ideas such as a new conception of the individual, the idea of freedom, women's rights and social justice, education abroad, fashion, and foreign languages and often criticized types of incorrect Westernization. The increasing stature of the visiting Europeans, especially the French and the English, altered norms of behavior, so that, upon the visit of the prince of Wales, for instance, the Ottoman sultan sat down, for the first time, to dine at the same table with his officials (Cevdet Pasha 1880: 41), and Ottoman officials started to regularly attend the embassy balls of Western powers (Cevdet Pasha 1872: 61–62). The presence of the English during the Crimean war also induced comparisons between the Ottoman empire and the West. For instance, the Ottoman statesman Cevdet Pasha lamented that, during this period, the British had sent relief to the fire victims of an Ottoman town weeks sooner than the Ottomans themselves (Cevdet Pasha 1872: 35). Another official, Ahmed İzzet Pasha, unfavorably compared the Ottoman system of rule to that of the Europeans' (Ahmed İzzet [1924] 1992: 8).

The wide spectrum of interpretation which the Western ideas underwent in the Ottoman context can be best illustrated by the changing Ottoman interpretations of the 1789 French revolution (Rasim [1924] 1987; Lewis 1953). The Ottomans first viewed this revolution as a purely internal affair, and then, when it started to spread throughout Europe, as a Western concern that would keep the European powers occupied to the benefit of the Ottomans. Indeed, in 1792, one personal secretary of the sultan prayed that "God cause the upheaval in France to spread like syphilis to the enemies of the [Ottoman] empire, hurl them into prolonged conflict with one another and thus accomplish results beneficial to the empire" (Lewis 1953: 119). This negative image of the revolution intensified with Napoleon Bonaparte's invasion of Egypt. The Ottoman administration interpreted the aim of Bonaparte's 1799 Declaration of Human Rights to the Egyptians as "lowering the human species to the level of wild animals through abolishing all religions, demolishing all cities and countries, seizing the wealth of the populace, and destroying the ties among human beings, and by using the lie of a false freedom to deceive the fools from among the populace" (Rasim [1924] 1987: 87). This Ottoman imagery of "wildness" ensuing from the French revolution reiterated an earlier Ottoman observation that "the leaders of sedition and evil appearing in France, in a manner without precedent . . . prepared the way for the reduction of the people of France to the state of cattle" (Lewis 1953: 121). This interpretation was indeed much different from the later "civilized" one that the Ottomans adopted to advocate the replacement of the sultan's rule with a constitutional one. Such a transformation in the Ottoman interpretation occurred as a consequence of the establishment of Western-style educational institutions, increasing Western trade, and escalating circulation of Western ideas through voluntary associations and newspapers. In only a few decades, with the first generation of Ottoman graduates of the new Western-style schools of the empire, the French revolution became the main mobilizing principle to "burn the Bastilles [of the world], annihilate despotisms, violently tear away the heads of tyrants," and to "offer the social contract as the new organizing principle of society" (Hanioğlu 1981: 162–63). Rather than interpret the West through the Ottoman cultural framework, this new "cohort"[2] of individuals who shared the same life experience gave meaning to their own society through the Western framework.

How extensive was this Western cultural penetration into the meaning structures of Ottoman society? Patterns of Ottoman word usage in the eighteenth and nineteenth centuries demonstrate the extent to which new Western concepts penetrated to the core Ottoman structures of meaning. The diffusion of foreign words into Turkish dated to the eleventh century, when the Turks came to Asia Minor and were exposed to the Greek, Persian, and Arabic languages. Ottoman, an amalgam of Turkish, Persian, and Arabic, developed during Turkish rule in Asia Minor as the vocabularies of these three were incorporated into the written language. The Ottoman encounter with the Aegean Sea and sea trade also coincided with the adoption of navigational words, mostly from Greek and Italian. As the Ottomans expanded west and north, they encountered the Balkan and Slavic languages. In the eighteenth century, Ottoman embassy accounts introduced new Western words to describe various dimensions of European societies. These occasional assimilations became much more systematic in the nineteenth century, when the Ottomans started to adopt Western words from French to express, and attach meanings to, new concepts and ideas, such as freedom, equality, and liberty (Özön 1962: i–v). Unlike this earlier Ottoman usage of foreign words, the Western usage brought with it a powerful vision that ultimately altered the Ottoman social structure.

The Ottomans themselves traced and took notice of their adoption of words of Western origin.[3] In his 1811 dictionary, *Dictionary of Language (Lehçet ül Lugat),* sheik-ül-islam Mehmed Esad Efendi identified 851 Western words and regarded these as having been "Ottomanized," while another, Ahmed Vefik Pasha, specifically marked words of Western origin in his *Dictionary of Ottoman (Lehçe-i Osmani).* In 1880, another *Ottoman Dictionary with an Appendix of Foreign Words (Lugat-ı Ecnebiye ilaveli Lugat-ı Osmaniye)* identified the Arabic, Persian, and Western words in Ottoman. Later in the decade, small dictionaries of Western words in the Ottoman language were published. One of these was a small dictionary of Ottomanized French words published by an Ottoman intellectual, Mustafa İzzet, in 1884, to correct those words that had been adopted incorrectly and provide their accurate French spelling. The Redhouse Ottoman–English dictionary of 1890 combined all previous dictionaries into one large volume. It contained approximately 100,000 words and marked, among them, words of Western origin. Later in the nineteenth century, the first extensive dictionary of Turkish, the *Turkish Lexicon (Kamus-u Türki),* again identified the origins of Ottoman words. Yet Western scientific words were often adapted directly without searching for synonyms in Ottoman. For instance, the 1901 French–Turkish dictionary of medical sciences simply transliterated forty to fifty thousand medical terms into Ottoman without bothering to come up with Ottoman neologisms (Özön 1962: ix–x).

A content analysis[4] of the adoption of Western words into the Ottoman-Turkish language demonstrates the scope of Ottoman adoption of words of Western origin. This analysis is based on one scholar's (Özön 1962) linguistic survey of twelve historical sources from the fifteenth to the eighteenth centuries[5] and the works of twenty-nine authors from the nineteenth and early twentieth centuries. The scholar had constructed the *Dictionary of Turkish-Foreign Words (Türkçe-Yabancı Kelimeler Sözlüğü)* from these sources. The content analysis on the words of Western origin indicates that these comprised approximately 7 percent of all words in the Ottoman language. Among the total of 6,930 Western words, words of French origin predominated: 71 percent of all Western words in the Ottoman language were of French origin. The rest of the Western powers, like the English, came nowhere near the French impact: words of English origin comprised 6.3 percent, and the Balkan and Germanic words each amounted to 1.3 percent of the total words of Western origin. The long Ottoman trade with the Italian and the Greek accounted for the 11.8 percent words of Italian origin and 6.45 percent of Greek origin. The Latin, Spanish, Armenian, and Judeo-Spanish influence were all under 1 percent. These results highlight two significant patterns. First, the French language had a very significant cultural dominance on the Ottoman meaning system. Second, the influence of the languages of the Ottoman minorities who had been associated with the Ottoman empire for centuries was almost nonexistent.

According to the content analysis, how and why did the French language, rather than the languages of the Ottoman minorities, acquire so much symbolic power in the Ottoman language? Social power and its symbolic representations often coalesce. The lack of influence of the languages of the religious minorities substantiates their socially segmented existence; minorities contributed relatively little to the evolution of the Ottoman language in comparison with the subsequent Western powers specifically because of their location in Ottoman society. The French language gained such prominence[6] because it was the language of instruction in the Western-style schools of both Muslims and minorities. The 1896 Ottoman Public Education Regulation stated that the entirety of the courses at the newly established Ottoman university would be taught in French until the completion of the training of students who could deliver such lectures in Ottoman (Esenkova 1959: 4–6). In its correspondence, the Ottoman state also employed French as its principal Western language; French was taught to all members of the Ottoman translation chamber of the Ministry of Foreign Affairs. As Ottoman embassies to Europe increased in the late eighteenth and nineteenth centuries, ambassadors and their retinues also became exposed to the French language and brought some forms and words on their return to Constantinople.[7] The French language also became more accessible after 1840, when the Ottoman students sent to Europe came back having learned the French language and kept up their French by purchasing books and newspapers from the European shops in Constantinople. During the same period, among the foreign residents of the empire, the population of French military advisors, technicians, and engineers surpassed all other Western powers. As some Ottomans exposed to the life style of these residents and returning students adopted elements of Western material culture, they also employed its terminology.

In addition to these institutional and social channels, French penetrated the Ottoman language through another figurative route, literature. The first literary translations into Ottoman were French works, by Victor Hugo, Daniel Defoe, and Chateaubriand.[8] The first Ottoman short story emulating the French model was written in 1870, and the rage of Ottoman novel writing started in 1875. Unlike the topics of French literary works, however, the clash between the Ottoman and Western cultures often constituted the favorite theme of this new narrative form. Popular Ottoman novelists such as Ahmet Mithat and Hüseyin Rahmi Gürpınar also exposed the Ottoman reading public to new Western words. For instance, one 1881 novel, *Karnaval,* contained 115 new, mostly French, words, which were meticulously explained and defined in the footnotes. Yet the nineteenth century also marked the beginning of Ottoman efforts to replace Ottomanized French words with "proper" Ottoman ones;[9] attempts to translate new Western ideas into Ottoman words following French word construction[10] followed. Words of Western origin also provided political opponents of the sultan with a means of symbolic resistance. To escape the sultan's censorship over certain dangerous foreign words, such as liberty, freedom, and the nation, some started using transliterated French words without first translating them. For example, one such intellectual[11] entitled his play based on the execution of a progressive Ottoman official *Liberte*. The names of characters in the play were also French: the fairy of freedom was labeled "Liberte"; the other characters were "Nasyon" (nation), "Despot," and "Press." In addition, the name of the hero was "Liberal" (Özön 1962: 6). This creative Western word usage in particular, and the pattern of the Ottoman interpretation of Western symbols in general, revealed the wide range of Western ideas in Ottoman society. The French revolution had indeed "bequeathed a political vocabulary through which . . . a new generation of visionaries" (Eley 1981: 96) formed, but these visionaries performed within the cultural parameters of their own society.

Ottoman Intellectuals and the Concept of a United Fraternity

The new Ottoman social vision was inspired by eighteenth-century Western Europe, where political participation widened, citizenship ideals crystallized as a consequence of the struggle against absolutism, and a citizenry organized into a public body beneath the

protection of the law. The vision became linked to the demand for representative government and a liberal constitution, together with the basic civil freedoms before the law, such
as speech, press, assembly, association, conscience, and religion (Eley 1990: 13–14). As
the Ottoman bourgeoisie took a political stance against the existing Ottoman social structure and redefined the Ottoman social vision through education, theaters, newspapers, and
other media, they acquired class consciousness.[12] They became fully conversant in a new
language[13] that the sultan and his households could not, and did not, support. As they
attended Western-style schools, scrutinized foreign and local newspapers in the new
reading rooms, and had tea at the newly opened restaurants and hotels, they turned
everything, all social media, into what E. P. Thompson has termed "a battleground of
class" (1963: 832). As they continued to oppose[14] the existing Ottoman social structure,
they articulated an alternative vision.

What comprised this new vision? One Ottoman official's memoirs on how he discovered "a new universe" through Western knowledge hints at the essence of this vision. This
official knowledge hints at the essence of this vision. This official had been a religious
scholar conversant in the traditional languages of Arabic and Persian and knowledgeable
in Islamic sciences. He then encountered "a more simple manner of expression" and a new
language, French, in the company of friends who were fully acquainted with Western
knowledge.

> [The leading] Ottoman statesman adopted [the Western mode of] a plain but eloquent
> style in his new [political] profession, and [other Ottoman statesmen] followed his
> example. I also liked this new method and aspired to compose my style in accordance
> to it. I [therefore] used my time in their company as a training ground for myself in
> adopting their style. [This] felt as if I had started school anew. [In the process] I learned
> quite a lot about the political affairs of the empire and mastered the French language.
> Yet, since people were opposed to the Ottoman religious scholars' learning of the
> French language at that time, I concealed this [fact] from my brethren. [But, through
> such activities], I passed through the religious universe and entered a different one.
> (Cevdet Pasha 1872: 21)

This new universe was indeed one that based its values and beliefs on the Enlightenment
principles of Europe rather than the moral standards of Islamic jurisprudence. The "sim-
plicity" that this official referred to probably reflected the concepts of liberty, freedom,
and equality that were based on the "natural laws of the universe." Indeed, he was fully
conversant in both the Ottoman and Western approaches to knowledge, which led him to
make many astute comparisons between the two systems of knowledge. Yet, such Western
knowledge and behavior became increasingly prominent and problematic in Ottoman
society as the leaders of the empire redefined their social position in relation to it. Some,
like our official, had to hide their mastery of this world. Others who revealed their mastery
were often criticized. For instance, one chronicle chided such people as "scoundrels
returning from Europe acted without restraint in constantly talking about the virtues of
Europe they found agreeable, and adopting the manner of the Franks" (Ahmed Lütfi
[1875] 1991: 51–52).

The Ottoman epistemological transition from such Western imitation to interpretation
occurred through the agency of the newly emergent group of Ottoman intellectuals.
Before the late eighteenth century, such intellectuals had mostly existed within the official
household structure and had an independent standing only within the context of religious
foundations. By the end of the eighteenth century, a sufficient number of new institutional
forms had emerged to sustain their social position independent of the sultan. Employment

as faculty members in the new Western-style schools, as journalists and columnists in the newly emerging newspapers and periodicals both in the empire and abroad,[15] as novelists, essayists, poets, and actors provided them with enough resources[16] to be independent of the sultan and the households. The first cohort of Ottoman military and medical students and faculty trained in the Western-style state schools were taught that the epistemological origins of knowledge were not located in Islamic moral principles but instead in the "secular, rational" maxims of the Enlightenment. Some tried to merge Islamic ethics and Western morality; others became militantly secular and materialist. All constantly debated Western science, philosophy, and its implications for Ottoman society. It was at this historical juncture that the Ottoman Muslims and minorities seemed to unite around an abstract notion of a civilized society that trespassed all ethnic and religious boundaries. Hence, these intellectuals included, for the first time, Ottoman minorities as well as Muslims on the grounds of the theoretical equality of all human beings.

The Ottoman minorities strove alongside the Muslims to create a truly multi-ethnic and multireligious society. Many served as faculty in the newly established Western-style state schools, some wrote novels and plays, others founded and acted in theater companies, and still others founded and managed newspapers.[17] An Ottoman Armenian wrote the first Ottoman novel in 1851 (Vartan Pasha [1851] 1991) describing the lives of the minorities, lives that strongly paralleled the interaction patterns of the Muslims;[18] others founded the prominent theater companies of the empire. In 1856, an Ottoman Armenian, Sırapyan Hekimyan, who had been educated in Venice, established a theater and put on stage a play in Italian for the foreign residents and in Turkish. Aravelyan formed the "Eastern Theater Company" (Şark Topluluğu) in 1861. The Ottoman state intervened soon after to control this new medium. In 1870, it bestowed the theater monopoly to perform "tragedy, drama, comedy, and vaudeville" on one prominent Ottoman Armenian producer and actor, Güllü Agop, for ten years (And 1992: 62–63). This particular monopoly subsequently led to the emergence, in the empire, of opera and popular theater—the two types[19] of performance not covered by the monopoly. Many Ottoman Greeks and Armenians acted and worked for these theater companies. The Ottoman minorities thus created and sustained this new medium of social interaction outside the control of the sultan. This new medium generated three significant consequences in Ottoman society. First, it provided a new public sphere of discussion for the emerging civil society. The plots of the plays often dealt with contemporary social issues such as the mindless imitation of the West,[20] or the many sacrifices one had to undertake in the name of one's country[21] (And 1992: 73). Playwrights, producers, actors, and audience could all participate in, contemplate, and debate the social issues of the time through this medium.[22] The second consequence concerned the actors in these plays, who were mostly[23] Ottoman minorities. The fact that their command of the Turkish language was not considered adequate (And 1992: 57) provoked a serious debate on social identity, on who could and should be considered an Ottoman. It also enunciated the possible linguistic conditions of such an identity, thus fostering one of the many seeds of nationalism. This debate led to pronunciation lessons for the actors, to a discussion of what comprised "true and correct Ottoman" and which groups practiced it, and to the establishment of art associations around issues such as censorship and actors' rights surrounding the newly emerging performance arts. All the involved groups thus became increasingly conscious of the boundaries of social action in the Ottoman empire. The third consequence concerned the audience in these plays, which comprised the military and medical students being educated at the Western-style schools of the empire. This audience was especially pivotal in using this medium to articulate their criticism of the current social order and to debate future scenarios for Ottoman social change. By specifying the rights and responsibilities of the spectators in the audience, the Ottoman state[24] also legally defined the boundaries of this group. Contemporary periodicals further highlighted the social impact of this medium as they critically discussed its pedagogic functions for the populace (And 1992: 55–56). Hence there was for a few brief decades in the early nineteenth century an imagined Ottoman civil society that unified Ottoman minorities and Muslims. Although these Ottoman intellectuals were united around the secular principles of the Enlightenment, they could not prevent themselves from confronting issues of political identity as they defined, justified, and defended the boundaries of the Ottoman empire. The historical conjuncture forced an imagined ethnicity back into this identity: Russian imperial expansion into Central Asia and the Balkan wars sent large populations of ethnically Turkish immigrants into Ottoman territory in the late nineteenth century. This resulted in the formation of a significant group of "nationalist" intellectuals advocating Pan-turkism and Pan-islamism (Georgeon 1986: 15). As these newcomers attempted to create an ethnically and religiously based vision of Ottoman society, the precarious unity of Ottoman intellectuals across ethnic and religious lines was irrevocably shattered.

Ottoman Adoption of Western Ideas: Newspapers and Voluntary Associations

In the West the bourgeoisie had developed their distinct view of the world through two media, the public meeting and the voluntary society (Morris 1990a: 4). In the Ottoman empire, a new social space for Western ideas and their interpretations emerged when the secret organizations established by students in Western-style schools to advocate political freedom and a constitution combined with newspapers to circulate ideas and with voluntary associations to pursue social reforms based on these ideas. These two new channels of communication, newspapers and voluntary associations, created for the Ottoman bourgeoisie a new interaction site and a new vocabulary of self-definition. Through these channels, the bourgeoisie was able to reproduce[25] its social position in Ottoman society. Newspapers guided the bourgeoisie in constructing Ottoman public opinion as readers discussed new ideas, concurred with the interpretation of the bourgeoisie, and often took a stand against the sultan. Voluntary associations enabled the bourgeoisie to organize in a structure outside the sultan's control; in such associations, members translated the Western ideas into modes of social action and reform. Hence the origins of an Ottoman civil society[26] formed through these channels and fostered the identity and social consciousness[27] of the Ottoman bourgeoisie. This civil society[28] acquired an informational capacity through newpapers and an organizational capacity through voluntary associations to successfully challenge the sultan's control over Ottoman society.

If Ottoman print media in general and newspapers in particular had not emerged at this particular historical conjuncture, the abstract vision of an Ottoman motherland would not have been able to replace the historic image of the paternal Ottoman sultan. As the print media created an imagined Ottoman community, conceptualized an Ottoman public opinion, and sanctioned the alleged omnipotence of the Ottoman sultan, the abstract vision of the Ottoman motherland started to take root. Before the eighteenth century, access to knowledge had operated through the organizational structure of the households and through personal social networks. The image of the sultan remained the symbolic core of

Ottoman society insofar as the channels to knowledge, and therefore to social power, remained constricted within the household structure and networks condoned by the sultan. The emergence of the Ottoman printing press in the early eighteenth century followed by the establishment of newspapers and periodicals in the early nineteenth altered the existing relation between knowledge and control. The establishment in 1729 of the first Ottoman printing press[29] using Arabic characters eased the physical restrictions on access to knowledge and escalated the circulation of ideas within the Ottoman empire. Concomitant developments in the postal system in the empire accelerated the rate of the circulation of ideas (Eldem 1970: 172–73).[30] By purchasing and reading an Ottoman or translated Western book, or, if one was illiterate, by attending one of the many reading cum coffee houses in the capital where certain newspapers were read out loud,[31] one could have direct personal access to knowledge outside the household structure. The late nineteenth-century proliferation of newspapers also presented a multiplicity of views, which, in turn, helped produce and reproduce Ottoman public opinion. It is noteworthy that the sultan instituted censorship laws at particularly this juncture; yet even though he was able to materially obstruct the printing of newspapers, he could not decipher or contain the multiplicity of implied meanings in each newspaper. The new, abstract "civil"-ized vision of Ottoman society these newspapers proposed persevered at the expense of the sultan.

The newly emerging nineteenth-century voluntary associations provided the organizational basis for Western ideas as they became interpreted in the Ottoman context. Before the nineteenth century, the large household[32] and the religious endowment (Hatemi 1987: 80) had provided the only two legitimate organizational models in Ottoman society. As ideas and interpretations started to flow outside the sultan's control, individuals interested in them coalesced under the shelter of voluntary associations. By doing so, they trespassed existing Ottoman structures to create a new intermediate one between the individual and the Ottoman state, one that acted "independently of the family, household, neighborhood or the workplace" (Morris 1990a: 167; 1990b: 395, 400). Moreover, they met, debated, and organized together with others who reasoned and acted like themselves.[33] Their discourse facilitated and fostered the publication of even more books and periodicals.[34] In their development, Ottoman voluntary associations paralleled Western ones in that they were either state sponsored or independent. In the West, voluntary associations advocated the values of self-help, thrift, temperance, and mutual improvement (Morris 1990b: 416–17); in the Ottoman context, they upheld technological and social progress, professional ethics, and service to society. They formed and articulated visions that transcended, in theory, the involuntary loyalties of region, kin, or faith.

Western and Ottoman voluntary associations were significantly different on two principles, however, one political and the other epistemological. For one, when the sultan or members of his household wanted to contribute financially to these voluntary associations as they previously had to religious endowments, they were often met with resistance and refusal. Members of the voluntary associations stressed the priority of raising money by the people for their motherland. This political stance further problematized the symbolic connection between the sultan and "his" subjects as voluntary associations wedged themselves between the citizens and "their" homeland. The other difference was an epistemological one. Some Ottoman voluntary associations, especially the earliest ones, had the explicit aim of disseminating and upholding Western ideas in Ottoman society. In the eye of the Ottoman public, this epistemological stand further conflated the process of Westernization and the idea of progress. To Westernize came to be associated with positive change.

Yet the most significant function of the Ottoman voluntary associations remained the social support they provided for social groups such as the Ottoman bureaucratic and commercial bourgeoisie and the intellectuals who could not be contained in the preexisting structures. It was through such associations that the Ottoman bourgeoisie acquired the chance to articulate, test, and perfect their proposed reforms. They also suffered through the shortcomings of voluntary associations as their reforms remained restricted to the few urban poor who were arbitrarily contacted. Their efforts were also often unsystematic and short-lived. Hence, like in the West, Ottoman voluntary associations were more effective in creating social networks among newly emerging social groups than in facilitating reform in society. In periods when the newspapers were censored, the voluntary associations also sustained the opposition to the sultan by providing their members with a social sphere within which to articulate their sense of identity and belonging.

Newspapers

In the late eighteenth century, the complex impact of Western ideas on Ottoman society crystallized through the establishment of newspapers along two dimensions, one epistemological and the other political. Ottoman newspapers were crucial in translating Western ideas into Ottoman discourse as they reported on international news items from European newspapers. They usually retained many of these concepts in the original, since they often experienced a shortage of journalists to write such international news items, as well as a lack of funds with which they could theoretically have hired them. Direct translation was thus easy and cost effective but occurred at the cost of marring the Ottoman discourse on arts, science, and ideas. Western ideas often overshadowed Ottoman critical analyses as a consequence of the considerable scale of such translations. Visions of change these newspapers portrayed were often based on Western ideas, which in turn were founded on the European experiences of change. Yet such visions found a receptive audience in the Ottoman capital as they coalesced the interests of different social groups. The first initiators of newspapers[35] in the Ottoman empire were the European embassies. The print media spread out through the empire as these embassies published books and newspapers in Ottoman.[36] The *Bulletin de Nouvelles* published by the French embassy in Constantinople in 1795 was the first such newspaper; it was distributed to the French colony and to others who knew the French language. Upon its success, *Gazette Française de Constantinople* was established a year later in 1796 (Alemdar 1980: 2–3). Similarly, the first independently owned newspaper in the empire, *Journal of News* (Ceride-i Havadis) was published in 1840 by a foreign resident, Englishmen William Churchill (Lewis 1979: 94–95). Through establishing such newspapers, European embassies and foreign residents facilitated the construction of an imagined Ottoman civil society after the Western model. Although such an image was often restricted to the Ottoman capital, and originally to a cluster of individuals both foreign and Ottoman who were literate, conversant in Western languages, and interested in the West, it became a legitimate image for the expanding newspaper audience. The audience often comprised, in addition to foreign residents concerned with European and Ottoman affairs, the Ottoman commercial bourgeoisie, interested in accessing world markets through Europe, and the Ottoman bureaucratic bourgeoisie, attentive to European models of political participation. As the newspapers circulated Western ideas, the audiences receiving them internalized those visions. They epistemologically conflated the Western vision of Ottoman society presented in these newspapers and the society itself, expecting social processes to happen as imagined.

The establishment of Ottoman newspapers also had a significant political impact: the censorship laws that the sultan promulgated to control the knowledge disseminated through newspapers expounded the increasing polarization between the Ottoman state and the expanding civil society. The Ottoman sultan had to censor repeatedly, and the escalating power of civil society became more evident. As the sultan closed down newspapers to suppress certain ideas, the newspaper audience invented new means and devices to procure such knowledge. By the end of the eighteenth century, Ottoman subjects themselves had started to establish, in increasing numbers,[37] independent printing presses, many of which also undertook newspaper publication (Lewis 1979: 188). The sultan once more strove to maintain his control over the circulation of knowledge by establishing the Ottoman official gazette in 1832. In the introduction of the gazette's inaugural issue, he stated that the gazette would daily inform his subjects on matters of the empire, thus preventing them from "fear and anxiety that sprouts from lack of knowledge" (Nüzhet 1931: 58). Yet gaining access to such knowledge through the gazette did not curb the subjects' pursuit of knowledge in other newspapers and periodicals. By 1877, the sultan and his government had started to interpret the knowledge circulated by some such newspapers as "damaging to the legitimacy of the current Ottoman rule," and the practice of censorship emerged (Çapanoğlu 1970: 14–17). Newspapers of political satire were the specific focus of the sultan's prohibition in this first instance. The debates in the Ottoman constitutional assembly over the issue of the sultan's censorship and the new press law illustrated the magnitude of the tension between the sultan and the newly emerging civil society as represented, in this case, by the Ottoman assembly.

The emerging view of Ottoman civil society was represented by those assembly members who criticized the sultan's decision. (The assembly debates have been published; see Çapanoğlu 1970.) Arguing that newspapers of political satire were printed everywhere, in London, Paris and Berlin with the aim to educate and civilize the audience, these members insisted that censorship would inhibit Ottoman progress and increase its backwardness in relation to Europe. "As rifles cannot be outlawed because of their potential to destroy human lives" (14), they continued, newspapers on political satire could not be banished because of their potential destructive effect on political rule. They also pointed out that the sultan's prohibition only hurt those Ottoman workmen who made their living through such newspapers while European newspapers of political satire were still readily available at the capital. The opposing faction, rallying behind the sultan's decision and thus representing the interests of the state, countered by cynically stating that the empire would be in trouble if it relied on such newspapers to educate and civilize the Ottoman populace. Also, they added, the Ottomans did not have to imitate and adopt such newspapers just because they existed in Europe. These newspapers should therefore be banned as they were banned in Russia. The assembly finally sided with the civil society perspective and struck out the sultan's censorship clause from the new press law. Yet their argument was rendered moot when the sultan soon after abolished the assembly. This debate captured the emerging pattern of interaction between the Ottoman sultan and emerging civil society whereby the sultan tried to control the expanding social influence of civil society by censoring and banning[38] its main channel of communication, the newspapers, and the Western ideas contained in them. Soon after, censorship against newspapers became a widespread practice.[39]

A quantitative analysis[40] of the establishment of newspapers in the Ottoman empire illuminates the complex relationship between the rise in Western ideas, as operationalized by the number of newspapers founded in the empire, and the sultan's attempts to control

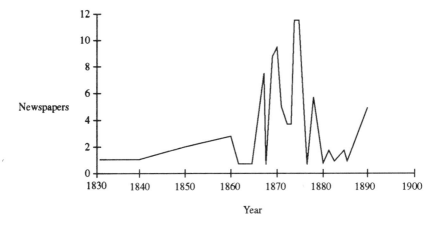

N = 93 newspapers started

Figure 5. Number of Ottoman Newspapers Started in the Late Nineteenth Century (1830–1890). (S. Nüzhet [Gerçek], *Türk Gazeteciliği* [Turkish Journalism], İstanbul, 1931; Bernard Lewis, *The Emergence of Modern Turkey* [London, 1968], pp. 156–94; *Türkiye'de Dergiler, Ansiklopediler* [Journals and Encyclopedias in Turkey], İstanbul, 1984.)

them, as quantified by the number of bans exercised by the sultan. The overall curve demonstrates that after the establishment of the official Ottoman gazette in 1832, the number of newspapers increased in a steady although uneven mode. The numbers of Western newspapers multiplied in the mid-nineteenth century as the sons of Ottoman officials and Western-educated students founded or staffed more Ottoman newspapers. The steady rise in the decade 1850–60 was also due to the effects of the Crimean war, which introduced new practices such as the use of the telegraph, the establishment of the first daily newspaper in Turkish, European war correspondents residing in Constantinople, and an increasing proclivity to receive news on a daily basis (Lewis 1979: 147, 185). The 1870s were a period of expansion[41] in Ottoman civil society in all realms, from newspapers to specialty journals. Political satire journals started in 1873, and many were soon published in rapid succession (Derman 1984: 72). The first Ottoman encyclopedia was published in 1869 on science and knowledge, and others followed throughout the century (Akbayar 1984: 219–27). Journals for children started in 1869 as well (Gencel 1984: 185), and one for women was initiated a year earlier in 1868. The first Ottoman women's journal, *A Garden in Bloom* (Şükufezar) published by women came out in 1886 (İlyasoğlu and İnsel 1984: 164). I conjecture that all these newspapers, the personnel producing them, and the public reading them can be taken as indicators of the emerging Ottoman civil society and the bourgeoisie embedded within it. The decline in the graph set in with the sultan's abolition of the Ottoman constitutional assembly, continuing until 1890, when the sultan himself was deposed by the oppositional Young Turk movement of the Ottoman bourgeoisie. The upturn after the deposition might indicate the effectiveness with which the newspapers were established to secure communication within Ottoman civil society. An in-depth analysis of the graph precisely articulates the nature of the social obstacles to the establishment of newspapers, and thus, as I conjecture, to the circulation of Western ideas. The dips in the 1860s and 1870s probably reflect the effects of the 1867 press law promulgated by the sultan to control the circulation of knowledge and the 1873 decree of the sultan to restrict the freedom of the press. The decline after the 1880s once more coincides with the abolition of the Ottoman constitutional assembly by the Ottoman sultan. Even though the graph does not extend that far, the effects seem to continue until the deposition of the sultan in April 1909, whereupon there is once more a resurgence of serial publications.

The graph has two shortcomings, however, one quantitative and one qualitative. First, the population (N) of ninety-three newspapers does not include those Ottoman newspapers started abroad, mostly in Europe, that were critical of the sultan's role. Exile journalism flourished as many opponents of the sultan, mostly the students or recent graduates of the Western-style state schools, fled to Europe, primarily France, and started publications there. In 1868, the first journal, *Freedom* (Hürriyet) was published abroad, followed by other journals. By the end of the nineteenth century, fifty-seven Ottoman newspapers were in circulation in Europe, and, of these, forty were published in Ottoman, two in Arabic, and fifteen in French (Nüzhet 1931: 79–80). These newspapers were especially significant because of the large number of copies smuggled into the empire.[42] The reasons behind the Ottoman sultan's inability to prevent the expansion of civil society at the expense of the Ottoman state become more evident when this exile journalism and its impact on the empire are taken into account. The second shortcoming is a qualitative one. The graph does not take into account the velocity at which these newspapers were circulated within the empire. Not only were banned Ottoman and European newspapers clandestinely sent to secret addresses in the empire (Temo [1939] 1987: 59, 170), but they and the few that were published legitimately or underground within the empire were swiftly circulated through clandestine networks. Ottoman Muslim students of the Western-style state schools, often the most devout audience of these publications, often invented many ingenious methods of circulation. One memoir, for instance, recounted how, in the late nineteenth century, the military medical students accessed such publications:

> The medical students would get the newspapers from the French postal agencies in the empire, tie them to ropes and dangle them from their dormitory windows until night-time when, upon the return to the dormitory from the classroom, one student would wait at the door to alert for possible incoming officers, while another stood on the bunk bed and read aloud the news to the fifty to sixty students in each dormitory. . . . These newspapers were then hidden in toilets . . . and later taken out of the school and wrapped inside the garments of students [and eventually] abandoned in mosques. (Nur [1928] 1992: 111–12)

Reading salons, where one could read all the newspapers for a minimal amount, also accelerated the circulation of such ideas.[43] Indeed, these instances demonstrate even more strongly the efficiency with which ideas, especially ones of Western origin, circulated throughout the empire within the newly emerging social groups to foster the seeds of Ottoman civil society. Even though they were occasionally obstructed by the sultan's attempts to control the flow of knowledge in the empire, the effects of these obstructions were impermanent.

Voluntary Associations

Before the nineteenth century, the Ottoman religious endowment, as the only public association outside the Ottoman state, provided a large spectrum of social acts that qualified as pious deeds. It was also the only context within which Ottoman subjects could exercise their personal and voluntaristic choice of religious piety by endowing goods, buildings, fountains, schools, or even annual prayers to any social unit of their choice. These religious endowments were organizationally different from the nineteenth-century voluntary associations that succeeded them, however. The benefactors of religious endowments were never a clearly defined group but remained a part of the vast community of Muslim believers. Unlike the members of voluntary associations, these benefactors did not comprise a well-bounded group of individuals that were structurally and ideologically united around a common cause. Voluntary associations have specific criteria for including some individuals and excluding others; as they exercise these criteria, they create new meanings both within the association and also without.[44]

In addition to the religious endowment, the Ottoman household structure and informal gatherings within the context of households provide the other organizational basis that supported the establishment of voluntary associations. Members of Ottoman office-households had always gathered periodically in their residences to discuss the affairs of the empire.[45] Yet such gatherings, as well as those in mosques, marketplaces, and coffee houses were categorized as informal, unintentional social interactions. Indeed, if there was a specific explicit purpose, other than the customary ones such as weddings, circumcisions, and religious holidays, the Ottoman state often interpreted these interactions as seditious activity against the state and banished the members. In the nineteenth century, however, the contexts within which such interactions occurred expanded to include the new Western-style schools, government offices, and public performing art centers, such as the theater. For instance, in the late nineteenth century, one Ottoman official, Nazım Pasha, the father of the poet Nazım Hikmet, remarked upon how "a group of youth who thought of themselves as enlightened met most nights to go to the only theater in town where they would discuss the play and affairs of the empire during intermission" and how "debates on the Ottoman code of laws took place at all meeting locations ranging from offices to schools to residences" (Nazım [1900] 1992: 62–63, 57–58). As these new contexts multiplied throughout the empire, knowledge outside the sultan's control expanded with it.

It is hard to date the Ottoman transformation from such informal affiliations to voluntary associations. In the West, such associations, either state sponsored, such as the French Académie Française, or independent, such as the British Royal Society, were instituted during the seventeenth and eighteenth centuries. Literary and philosophical societies were first created in the 1790s but spread out in the 1820s to foster the bourgeoisie's bid for legitimacy and power (Morris 1990b: 410). The first such independent Ottoman association is asserted (Mardin 1962: 219; İhsanoğlu 1987c: 43–74) to be the "Beşiktaş group," which was founded in 1826 and named after the Istanbul neighborhood where most of the members resided. The members,[46] who were mostly Ottoman state officials and religious scholars, met regularly in the residence of the member İsmail Ferruh Efendi and regularly collected annual dues. The explicit purpose of the association was cited as "learning and teaching among all those individuals longing for science and education" (İhsanoğlu 1987c: 49–50). Also, only those individuals whom the members "personally knew" could be admitted to the association. This selective stance on admission and the ambiguity in defining the purpose of the association soon led the Ottoman state to deport the group "for engaging in unorthodox activity against the state."[47] Indeed, by selecting members according to their own criteria, which were independent from those prescribed and legitimated by the Ottoman state, the group did exercise a power of exclusion. Yet, the vague intended aim of this group as "interest in science and education" disqualifies it as the first Ottoman voluntary association.

The origins of Ottoman state-sponsored associations (İhsanoğlu 1987b: 6–10) can be traced back to the "Law Council" (Meclis-i Valayı Ahkam-ı Adliye) the Ottoman sultan created in 1837 to oversee, in an advisory capacity, the formulation of new legal regulations after the Western mode, and the "Provisory Council" (Meclis-i Muvakkat) formed in 1845 to advise in the reorganization of Ottoman science and education after the Western model. The term "association" (or society) was first used in 1845 by the Provisory Council to refer to the need to establish an "Ottoman Academy of Science" *(Encümen-i Daniş)*, that is "an association of learned men who could produce the books that are most crucial for the populace.[48] As the Ottoman press diffused information on how such associations functioned in the West, European orientalists in the empire founded its first independent association in 1853, the Société Oriental de Constantinople. Taking the French Société Asiatique as its model, this association defined its aim as collecting and disseminating information on the East, particularly the Ottoman empire. Among the twenty-three members of this association,[49] there were no Muslims, and only three Ottoman minority members, two Greeks and one Armenian. Muslim intellectuals formed their own organization in 1861, as the Ottoman Scientific Society (Cemiyet-i İlmiye-i Osmaniye), under the leadership of Halil Bey, Ottoman ambassador to St. Petersburg. The organization defined its goal as "the compilation and translation of all works on science and education, with the exception[50] of religion and politics" (Mardin 1962: 238–40; İhsanoğlu 1987a: 203–14). This goal brought to the fore two issues surrounding Ottoman voluntary associations. First was the type of social activity they chose to engage in, namely, the compilation and translation of all pertinent works in Western languages into Ottoman, which accelerated the diffusion of Western ideas into Ottoman society. The other was the context in which such social activity was explicitly excluded, namely, the much contested spheres of religion and politics. This attempt to limit the boundaries of the social activities voluntary associations could engage in eventually failed, however, as the associations started to provide more and more services to the newly emerging Ottoman civil society. Such services comprised, for instance, in the case of the Ottoman scientific society, a reading room,[51] with a library of more than six hundred volumes and many European newspapers, where free[52] lessons were also provided in English, Greek, and French on topics relating to law, economy, and politics to science students two or three times a week. The association also published a periodical, *The Journal of Sciences* (Mecmua-i Fünun),[53] which translated and popularized Western science among the Ottomans. The Scientific Society (Cemiyet-i İlmiye), founded in 1879–80, was similarly established to diffuse Western science and technology in Ottoman society. State regulations licensing such associations soon followed. In 1889, the Ottoman juridical system licensed the establishment of such associations and in 1909 legislated that all such organizations report their activities to the state (İhsanoğlu 1987b: 4). It was only in 1914, with the establishment of the Turkish Knowledge Society (Türk Bilgi Derneği), that indigenous research for the accumulation of knowledge became a priority over the translation of Western science. The organization defined the areas of knowledge as Turcology, Islam, biology, philosophy, sociology, mathematics, materialism, and Turkism.

The pattern in which Ottoman professional associations formed reflected their proximity to the state. Those professions such as medicine and pharmacy that were closer to civil society than the state organized much sooner than those such as engineering and architecture that were, for long periods, associated with the state. Another attribute of these professional associations was their inability to overcome the ethno-religious divide in Ottoman society; Ottoman Muslims and minorities often formed analogous organizations in each profession. The first Ottoman professional association, the Société Médicale de Constantinople, was established in 1856, during the Crimean war, upon the recommendation of the English army physician P. Pincoffs (İhsanoğlu 1987b: 10–15). The physicians of the allied forces in the capital and the European physicians residing in Constantinople constituted the members of the association. This society, which also put out the *Gazette Médicale d'Orient,* did not have any Ottoman Muslim physicians as members (Cevdet Pasha 1872: 196). The first Muslim attempt to establish such an association in 1865 coincided with the graduation of the first cohort of Western-style medical schools of the empire. These graduates articulated three objectives in founding such a medical association: first, to diffuse medical sciences throughout society; second, to strive to transform the Ottoman medical education conducted in the French language into Turkish; and third, to Turkify the medical language. The conscious attempt of this society to move beyond translation efforts to create an Ottoman body of medical knowledge demonstrates, once more, the aftermath of Western-style education, which had provided its students with skills to undertake such an interpretation of Western knowledge. Before 1921, more than ten such associations were established by Muslim and minority physicians. This emerging ethno-religious divide, which reflected the prior segmentation of Ottoman artisanal groups, became pervasive in professional associations, however. For instance, in pharmacy, minority pharmacists established the Société de Pharmacie de Constantinople in 1879, and the Muslims founded the Association for the Union of Ottoman Pharmacists in 1909. Even though the latter also included minorities at the start, these then separated to form the Société des Pharmaciens de l'Empire Ottoman. Similar divides along ethno-religious lines differentiated Muslim and minority professional associations in other fields as well, including those for veterinarians, agriculturalists, dentists, engineers, architects, geographers, and natural scientists.

How effective were these voluntary associations in fostering Ottoman civil society and the Ottoman bourgeoisie embedded within it? The scant historical evidence on the issue demonstrates that Ottoman voluntary associations had the potential to mobilize society but also that this potential was often carefully controlled and curbed by the Ottoman state. For instance, when the Bosnia–Hercegovina conflict started in the late nineteenth century, some Ottoman students organized into voluntary associations, donning uniforms, forming their own military battalions, and enlisting others—only to be hastily dismantled by the Ottoman sultan, who perceived such mobilization as a potential threat to his rule (Nazım [1900] 1992: 68). Such voluntary associations also rallied to the support of those state officials with whom their interests coalesced. In the mid-nineteenth century, when the popular Ottoman statesman Mithat Pasha, who advocated constitutional rule, was deported by the sultan, voluntary associations and Western-style schools organized, in two or three days, a petition containing eighty thousand signatures on behalf of the statesman (Nazım [1900] 1992: 78). Still, in the end, the petition could not prevent the trial and execution of the statesman. Indeed, one can only conclude that in the Ottoman empire, newspapers and voluntary associations provided a new social sphere for the emerging civil society and the bourgeoisie, yet this sphere was continually contested by the sultan and his state.

Polarization Within the Bourgeoisie: Ethnicity, Capitalism, and Nationalism

The Ottoman bourgeoisie, which could, in theory, organize around a common vision of future society, thus was not able to carry this vision through in practice. Instead, it polarized in the late nineteenth century into different ethnic and religious segments with disparate visions. The combination of the newly emergent capitalism and nationalism with the existing Ottoman social structure determined the nature of this polarization.[54]

The first Ottoman encounter with Western nationalism through the independence movements of the Ottoman minorities had indeed been a negative one. In addition, Ottoman attempts to counter the effects of this nationalism by promoting the concept of "Ottomanism" also failed (Kuran 1968: 109–17), when it was discovered that, beyond its physical borders, there were no strong imagined unifying patterns among the multiplicity of groups comprising the empire. The only other possible pattern based on the dominant religion generated the possibility of "Islamism" as a mobilizing force (Hanioğlu 1985). One Ottoman sultan in particular, Abdülhamid II, did indeed firmly advocate this policy until his overthrow. Yet the emerging separatist movements among the Albanian and Arab Muslims of the empire destroyed this possibility leaving only ethnic Turkish nationalism as a viable alternative. "Turkish nationalism" (Georgeon 1986) slowly grew in the late nineteenth century after the Crimean war and the invasion of Central Asia by the Russians. These historical events increased Turkish self-awareness as many Turkic people immigrated from the Russian to the Ottoman empire. The new Turkish immigrants actively studied the linguistic and historical "homogeneity" of the Turks and advocated a Turkish-Islamic identity, the plausibility of which rapidly increased after the Ottoman–Greek war of 1897. The emergent Ottoman bourgeoisie therefore also divided along this ethnic line.

Why could the Ottoman bourgeoisie, as a class, not surmount the ethnic divide? After all, it could, in theory, have socially reproduced itself along the parameters advocated by the intellectuals and the civil society within which they were embedded. The origins of such a failure need to be located in Ottoman intra-bourgeois relations,[55] in the segmentation along ethno-religious lines. The Ottoman Muslims and minorities drew upon disparate elements in constructing[56] their "imagined" political communities. Hence, the transition from ethnicity to nationalism, from religious community to nation, occurred differently in different parts of Ottoman society. This construction also initially obfuscated[57] class inequalities and individualized class relations at the level of politics and ideology; people of different economic locations "all appeared in politics as undifferentiated 'individuals,' or 'citizens'" (Przeworski 1985: 13).

Memoirs of Muslim Ottoman intellectuals and officials[58] often provide instances of this gradual polarization. One such instance exists in the late nineteenth-century reflections of an Ottoman military physician,[59] a graduate of the Western-style school and a political antagonist of the sultan. The case centers around the deportation of his cohort to Tripoli for treason, his subsequent debates with the locals there, and his later visions of Ottoman social change (Mehmetefendioğlu 1897: 23–25, 27, 40–42). Upon being arrested for "treason against the state," the physician first recounts his discussions with the soldiers as he explains that he and others fought to liberate their motherland from oppression:

> In order to anathematize us, they [the sultan's men] had told the naive soldiers [who arrested us] that we were Greek spies. This blow by the vile, tyrannical [Ottoman]

government was the most difficult one for me to accept. My eyes teared up. "No, my brother, no," I shouted, "they have deceived you, they lied to you— we are not spies, we are not traitors to our motherland. We, like you, fought *for* our country. You battled those who attacked our homeland from outside [our borders] and won. We declared war on those inside our motherland and we are sure we will also be victorious." (1897: 23–25)

It was this image of the Muslim patriots against the tyrannical sultan that dominated most of the discourse of late nineteenth-century Ottoman society. The fight was always "to save their nation, their motherland from this band of brigands . . . and tyrants who tear down houses, grab earnings, and suck the blood of the motherland dry" (1897: 25). How would such a fight eventually succeed and what would happen then were rarely discussed. Like all visions of change embedded in the Enlightenment tradition, they all assumed that their morally just cause would "naturally" succeed[60] and progress toward a civilized society would then "naturally" follow. Hence, Enlightenment ideas, often combined with Islamic ideals of social justice, provided the patriots with a unified yet abstract vision. Deposing the current Ottoman sultan became defined as the immediate, common, tangible goal.

The fervor of both sides, the "tyrants" and the "patriots," was continually displayed in symbolic rituals. In this case, during the deportation of the seventy-six patriots to Tripoli, the Ottoman band representing the sultan played the tune of a military parade song, "The impious cruel traitor who invented a thousand evils from one evil," while the banished responded by shouting three times, in return, "Long live the motherland! Die tyranny!" and then bursting into the tune of a popular song, "Everywhere I turn, there are sighs and tears, compassion, affection have disappeared" (Mehmetefendioğlu 1897: 11, 27). The reason for the deportation was the active mobilization of the newly skilled bourgeoisie to bring constitutional rule to the empire. The successful revolution that occurred eleven years after their departure brought to the surface, however, the conflicts among the subjects of the empire that had stayed concealed during the united opposition to the sultan. In this case, the debate between the deported patriots and the members of the Tripoli municipal council, who wanted to send them back to the capital immediately, centered around who was looking after the interests of the empire and how. This debate illustrated the conflicts developing from within the Muslim bourgeoisie, conflicts that eventually led to the dissolution of the empire and the emergence of local nationalisms. First, debate ensued around defining the political identities of the two parties. The local Tripoli notables started to oppose the patriots, insisting:

We will never [engage in a dialogue with you] because you are, like the Young Turks, all atheists. By declaring freedom, they [the Young Turks] want to turn us into infidels, make us accept the customs of the infidels, coerce us to be brothers with the Jews, and parade our women naked in the streets. . . . Now freedom has been restored. Do not meddle in our affairs and go back to your country. This country is ours, not yours. We have been here for centuries, our ancestors are buried here. You are foreigners. (1897: 39–40)

The community of Muslim believers, once united as the "dominant group" (*millet-i hakime*) under the Ottoman empire, thus started to crumple as local communities employed different criteria in constructing their identities. The response of the Ottoman physician to this devastating criticism portrays the dwindling Ottomanist vision of the patriots. This vision had a very different definition of motherland, one that trespassed the geographical borders the locals were so stubbornly clinging to; it also illustrated how disparate the boundaries of imagined communities within the Ottoman empire had become.

> First, this is not your country but the country of all the Ottomans. The difference
> between us is that you consider only Tripoli as motherland, whereas we consider her,
> Anatolia, the Balkans and Arabia as motherland by virtue of all being a part of the
> lands of the Ottoman empire. . . . If we, like you, had only considered as our mother-
> land the place where we were born and provided for, we would not have trampled on
> our careers, our families, our freedom to come here. [Hence] there is not one person
> among you who, during our [eleven years of] exile here, has served our country as
> much as we have [done]. . . . [Also] you misinterpret constitutionalism. [It does] not
> intervene in anyone's beliefs or force them to abandon their religion. . . . Do you know
> what the method of political consultation [meşveret] means? [It means that] no one will
> be able to tyrannize you, and you will be able to insist on what is due to you . . . the
> law will be equal for all. (1897: 40–41)

It was this promise of the notion of equality that, had it actually been delivered, might have united the Ottoman bourgeoisie. Yet, instead, social groups constructed and pursued definitions of equality that different latent assumptions embedded in them.

Muslim patriots envisioned sharing equality with all, but only under the rules they themselves determined. The minorities wanted equality to erase all social differences among them and the Muslims and were frustrated when this did not occur. Hence, the existing differences within Ottoman society became further polarized. The Ottoman Muslims, rather than developing alternate, mutually beneficial cosmopolitan rules and regulations that would guide social and political behavior, increasingly blamed the minorities for their lack of participation in the causes of freedom as they, the Muslims, had defined them. Not adequately recognizing the structural persistence of the constraints that Ottoman society had placed on the minorities, the Muslims derided apolitical or separationist minority behavior and excluded them from their vision. More and more of them started to take notice of the inadequacies in the minority response to the "united march to freedom" (Mehmed Rauf [1911] 1991: 90). The initial deliberations on the secret political organization of the Union and Progress party, which eventually emerged victorious at the expense of the reigning sultan to govern the empire, showed the extent of this polarization. During the debates on who should qualify as a member of the organization, one of the founders, after noting that some minorities could not adequately serve the cause "for many reasons," argued for "all trustworthy Ottomans regardless of religion or nationality" to be included in the ranks. His argument was immediately disputed by others who argued that "only Muslims should qualify" (Temo [1939] 1987: 17). Even though this historical anecdote did not specify which viewpoint eventually prevailed, in the end, there were no minorities among the founding members of the organization.

Soon after, the increasing contrasts of the minority behavior with that of the Muslims commenced to result consistently in a negative assessment of the former. For instance, in one late nineteenth-century article on the concept of equality, a leading Ottoman intellectual, Namık Kemal, undertook the following comparison of who sacrificed what for the motherland:

> Let us not forget that our society demonstrates the most strange form of equality. We,
> who are Muslims, serve our motherland both with our money and our lives. Our other
> fellow citizens, the minorities, only expend money. Is it a divine decree that we per-
> form the function of watchguards while they act as moneychangers?[61] (Chmielowska
> 1990: 235)

There was no longer a sultan that all the Ottomans were subject to, but instead an abstract motherland toward which all somehow fulfilled their obligations differently. The Ottoman Muslims first started to become increasingly aware of these disparate images of motherland surrounding them. They then realized that other ethnic Muslims in the Ottoman empire, such as the Arabs, also had different future scenarios in mind. Most agreed that such images were the unintended consequences of eighteenth- and nineteenth-century Ottoman social change alone. As one Muslim army physician noted in the late nineteenth century,

> We saw that a Circassian club had opened in our neighborhood. Then an Albanian association was formed. Soon after, an Arab philanthropic society appeared! . . . Circassians wanted their freedom, as did the Albanians. The members of all these clubs were graduates of our own schools. . . . Hence the Bulgarian . . . Albanian . . . Arab independence movements were all manned by those reared and educated in our country, our schools. . . . (Nur [1928] 1992: 268)

Yet the effect on the empire of the Ottoman Muslim ethnically Turkish subjects rallying around such a specific nationalism would have been dire. The same army physician noted, at a later point in his memoirs, what the consequence would have been:

> I am dying for the Turkish cause, but I am carrying this cause like a secret bowl in me. I do not tell about it to anyone. For I know that if we do that, our action will legitimate the explication of the inner thoughts of the others. And that would mean the fragmentation, the extinction of the empire. (330)

Yet, once formed, it was hard to eliminate the "we" versus "the others" discourse that is already evident in the quotation. As the Ottomans scientifically convinced themselves that their Turkic language and civilization had developed much earlier than those of the Europeans, they became more affirmative in their pride for a "glorious national heritage" (Georgeon 1986: 28). Indeed, the new early nineteenth-century findings in Turcology[62] combined with the ethnic patriotism of the Turkic migrants from the Balkans and the Russian empire to produce Turkish nationalism.[63] The possible multiethnic multireligious image of the empire was thus displaced by a Turkish nation-state structured around a Turkic-Muslim vision of the motherland.

Conclusion: The Emergence of a Bifurcated Ottoman Bourgeoisie

It was the interaction of internal and external factors and the subsequent emergence of a bifurcated bourgeoisie that led to the demise of the Ottoman empire. The Ottoman empire was structured into office-households that developed their own power bases and challenged the sultan's control. In response to this development and to increasing Ottoman defeats against Western-trained armies, the sultan introduced Western institutional innovations, mostly in military organization and education, to train a new corps of officials that would be loyal to his person. Yet, the Enlightenment ideas inherent in this Western education led Ottoman officials to develop ties with one another at the expense of the sultan. As these officials created social networks among themselves and acquired Western scientific expertise, they formed social resources that the sultan was unable to wrest away from them. These officials constituted the origins of the Ottoman bureaucratic bourgeoisie.

Concomitantly, increasing trade with the West intersected with the existing ethnic differentiation among Ottoman merchants to lead to the emergence of a new social group of Ottoman minorities who wrested economic resources away from the sultan by entering Western political protection. This protection also helped them escape the sultan's confiscation and control. As they developed networks among themselves and with the West and acquired wealth and Western goods, these minorities formed the origins of the Ottoman commercial bourgeoisie. It was this split within the Ottoman bourgeoisie in its formative stages, that which was structurally insurmountable, that led to the demise of the empire. This argument of the book is summarized in the table on page 139.

In the eighteenth and nineteenth centuries, Ottoman contact with the West through war and commerce interacted with the office-households and ethno-religious stratification contained in the Ottoman social structure to determine the parameters of Ottoman social change. The response of the sultan to this interaction also developed within boundaries set by the historical context: he employed Western-style education to train a new cadre of young officials loyal to his person and confiscation to curb surplus accumulation among Ottoman minority merchants. This reaction led to the unintended consequence of Ottoman bourgeois formation, which polarized and segmented along ethno-religious lines. During these two centuries, a Muslim Turkish bureaucratic bourgeoisie trained in Western-style schools formed to separate irretrievably from the minority, mostly Christian commercial bourgeoisie, which had developed through Western trade. Western ideas such as civiliza-

138

tion, equality, and national identity were particularly significant in securing this irretriev-able separation. The analysis offered in the book stops at this point on the table.

Ottoman Westernization and Social Change

Western contact	Ottoman social structure	Response of the sultan	Unintended consequences	Outcome
War	Office-households	Western-style education	Bureaucratic bourgeoisie	Atatürk and the rise of the Turkish nation-state
Commerce	Ethno-religious stratification	Confiscation and control	Commercial bourgeoisie	Segmented bourgeois formation and migrations

The next column on the table, that of outcome, anticipates the possible implications of the analysis: in the twentieth century, the labors of the Ottoman bureaucratic bour-geoisie under the guidance of Mustafa Kemal Atatürk create the Turkish nation-state. The process that leads to the formation of such a state, however, decimates the minority commercial bourgeoisie and eventually relegates Turkey to the semi-periphery of the world order. Yet, this stage also sets my next research agenda, that of analyzing the impact of Western-style education and nationalism on Ottoman society.

Implications of the Findings

What role did the West ultimately play in the demise of the Ottoman empire? Rather than deny the significance of the West in eighteenth- and nineteenth-century Ottoman social change, it is more productive to take issue with the assumed omnipotence of the West, its assumed agency in generating change in the rest of the world. The critique of this assumed agency ought to be a point of departure that would eventually lead to restoring the agency of the recipient societies. The role of the West in Ottoman change is better explained through analyzing the specific historical content of Western ideas, institutions, and econ-omies and the distinctive context of the Ottoman social structure within which such Westernization was interpreted by Ottoman social groups.

By doing so, the implied narrative in Ottoman social change of the overbearing determinacy of the West, the haphazardness of industrialization, and the dreadful failure to adapt is replaced with an analysis of Ottoman objective conditions and their subjective interpretations by social actors within the specific conjuncture of Westernization. Both the "otherness" of Eastern transformations and the primacy of Western change in explaining away the rest of the world are thus eliminated. Instead, the analysis through archival sources of external influences on and internal dynamics in Ottoman society reveals new conceptions, such as class segmentation, which produce fresh insights into patterns of late Ottoman and Republican social change.

Segmented Class Formation

Analyses of Ottoman inheritance records to approximate the adoption of Western goods, Western-style schools to analyze the diffusion pattern of Western institutions, and the growth of newspapers in the empire to estimate the pattern of circulation of Western ideas suggest possible novel measures of bourgeois class formation. The ensuing segmentation that occurs in Ottoman bourgeois class formation may provide additional insights into the growing literature on class fragmentation.

Marx's use of the concept of class fragments in the *Eighteenth Brumaire* (see Zeitlin 1984: 9; Roy 1984: 494–95) refers to which segments of bourgeoisie "actually [make] the laws, [are] at the head of the administration of the state, [have] command of all the organized public authorities" and which segments are excluded from political power. Hence, access to political power produces divisions within the emergent bourgeoisie. Among the recent applications of this approach, Maurice Zeitlin (1980, 1984) extends the tension between economic and political power in producing these fissions to determine who among the rival segments of the dominant bourgeois class in Chile lead social change, and David Abraham (1981) explains the emergence of the Nazi party through the sharpening internal tensions among the dominant class fractions of Weimar Germany.

The Role of Education

In the Ottoman context, Western-style education, which was introduced to unite society, instead deepened the existing gaps between segments into chasms. Analyzing this paradox will form the subject of my next volume. In it, I will study the Ottoman educational system to trace the production and reproduction of different Ottoman bourgeois visions and compare the different societal visions created by the Western-style state, missionary, and minority schools. The Ottoman group that emerged triumphant had, as Zeitlin proposes, the capacity to "fashion, as their conscious creation, a distinctive political culture for their class, one which simultaneously provides them with a contrary explanation of their common situation and an alternative vision of their possible future" (1980: 18). In late nineteenth- and early twentieth-century Ottoman society, the bureaucratic bourgeoisie educated in Western-style state schools emerged to fashion such a political culture; state-educated Muslim Turks thus triumphed over the missionary and minority school-educated minorities.

The Demise of the Ottoman Minority Bourgeoisie

The segmented bourgeois formation also provides insights into the processes that led to the demise of the Ottoman minority bourgeoisie. When the Ottoman state centralized power, and when, in addition, the nationalist vision became ascendant and gave precedence to the Turkish language and heritage, the minority bourgeoisie started to dwindle. Ottoman Armenians in Anatolia were forcefully transferred and decimated in the process—the rest left the empire. Most Ottoman Greeks departed when Greece and the new Turkish republic agreed to and enforced a population exchange across their borders. Ottoman Jews migrated to the West or to Jerusalem. Ottoman Arab Christians joined the emerging Arab national movements. Hence, the empire lost its cosmopolitan character and transformed itself into a homogenized nation-state.

The Constitution of the Turkish State

The social boundaries of the Turkish national bourgeoisie were also affected by the segmented Ottoman bourgeois formation. The modern nation-state of the Turkish republic was founded in 1923, on the remnants of the Ottoman empire, by Mustafa Kemal Atatürk, an Ottoman general. Mustafa Kemal and other members of the Ottoman bureaucratic bourgeoisie formed the new Turkish national bourgeoisie around the clearly defined social parameters of Westernism, secularism, and nationalism. Taking their cue from Ottoman segmentation, they included reformist Muslim Turks and excluded cosmopolitan non-Muslim Ottoman minorities from the national bourgeoisie.

Drawing the boundaries of the national bourgeoisie in accordance with this premise produced another unintended consequence for the Turkish republic, however: the new dominant class, by its premises, also created and excluded from power two significant segments of the population, those who still identified strongly with Islam and those who belonged to other ethnic groups, such as the Kurds. It is therefore not surprising that in contemporary Turkey, the two significant challenges to the Turkish national bourgeoisie coalesce around the Islamist and Kurdish movements, both of which attempt to generate an Islamist and Kurdish bourgeoisie in opposition to the dominant nationalist one.

New Frontiers

Moving beyond the Ottoman empire and the Turkish republic, the concept of bifurcated class formation may also provide insight into the structural weakness of the bourgeoisie throughout the Middle East, Asia, and Africa. For instance, in Kenya, one can argue that the British colonial policy of the importation of Asian Indians and the successful independence movement produced a similarly bifurcated bourgeoisie. Today, while Asian Indians and the British predominately comprise the Kenyan commercial bourgeoisie, indigenous Africans control the state and mostly staff the bureaucratic and political cadres. In Malaysia, the Chinese who had for centuries settled on the island for trade form the Malaysian commercial bourgeoisie and are still distinct from the Malays who control the state. In Uzbekistan, the experience of communist rule influences the current bourgeois structure as the former party leaders, capitalizing on their administrative expertise, staff the Uzbek bureaucratic bourgeoisie, and, at the same time, attempt to control the burgeoning commercial bourgeoisie. These observations may lead to new insights into the role of class segmentation as a vehicle for social change.

In the case of modern Turkey, bifurcated class formation provides a most intriguing way of thinking about the determinants of Turkey's current location in the world order. Had the Ottoman bureaucratic bourgeoisie not become nationalistic and eliminated the minority commercial bourgeoisie, then Turkey might today find itself closer to the center of the world order. However, had Atatürk, a member of this bureaucratic bourgeoisie and the subsequent founder of the Turkish republic, not emerged, Turkey might just as easily have been relegated to the periphery. In the post–cold war world order, if Turkey does not repeat its past experience, the Islamist and Kurdish segments could be accommodated on their own terms and incorporated into a pluralist democracy. Such an ideal, long-term, but difficult outcome might move Turkey toward the center of the new world order. Alternately, if Turkey opts for the other short-term, but destructive outcome, Islamist and Kurdish challenges could be repressed with force and contained within a bureaucratic authoritarian system, thus dooming Turkey to the periphery once again.

Appendix

Sample of an Inheritance Register (A5/104). (İstanbul Müftülüğü, Kısmet ve Beytülmal, Galata Mahkemesi [Archives of the Office of Religious Opinion, Register for the Inheritance Partitioner for the Populace of Constantinople, the Court of Galata], no. 14/268.)

Notes

Introduction

1. The first references to the idea of Europe can be traced to the Greeks. Europe was defined in opposition to the East. This East–West polarity also had an ideological dimension: the East implied lavish splendor, vulgarity, and arbitrary authority—all that was antithetical to Greece and Greek values. This perception persisted through the Roman period to acquire an emotional dimension with the emergence of Christianity (Hay 1968: 14).

2. In the sixteenth and seventeenth centuries, overseas expansion endowed the concept of Europe with an image. In cartography and geographical works, Europe was portrayed as "crowned, cuirassed, holding a spectre and orb, with weapons, scientific instruments, a palette, books, and Christian symbols." This image was contrasted to those of other continents: "Asia, garlanded and richly dressed, holding an incense burner and supported by camels and monkeys; Africa, naked with elephants and lions, snakes and palms, and often with the sun's rays like a halo on the head; America, naked with a feathered head-dress, holding a bow and arrow" (Hay 1968: 104–5).

3. Most explanations of the social processes that led to the rise of the West are based on the works of Karl Marx and Max Weber. Marx argued that the conjunction of three phenomena accounted for the rise of the West: a rural structure that allowed the peasantry to be set free at a certain point; urban craft development, which produced specialized, independent, nonagricultural commodity production in the form of crafts; and the accumulation of monetary wealth derived from trade and usury (Hobsbawm 1965: 46, 128). According to Weber, the rise of the West entailed a transition from traditional to legal authority and from social to rationally organized action. The nature of rule changed as traditional authority legitimated by tradition gave way to legal authority based on contractual law where members had clearly defined responsibilities and obligations. The bureaucratic organization played a crucial role in this Western transition as it transformed social action into rationally organized action (Weber 1978, I: 220, 226–31; II: 956–1005, 1028).

4. The demographic revolution helped France retain its military ascendancy on the continent as its population exceeded that of any other major power. The French monarchy carefully balanced its demographic ascendancy with political centralization. Yet, in the eighteenth century, due to increasing economic production, trade, and urbanization, the struggle for the control of the state widened to include, in addition to the monarchy and aristocracy, urban-based social groups defined in general as the bourgeoisie. The ideology of the Enlightenment questioned the basic assumptions inherited from the past and emphasized rationality in explaining the individual's existence and position in society. As this ideology interacted with the popular challenge, the subsequent political upheaval resulted in the 1789 French revolution.

5. The period 1740–70 was a crucial one in English history: the expansion of trade and production in terms of growing markets, increasing industrial output, and numerous technological inventions all coalesced to set the stage for the industrial revolution. England emphasized, in addition to agricultural production, trade and transportation of goods and bullion. It was the first

European society to inaugurate trade as a prime source of wealth; until then, land had been considered the primary source. This trade altered the societal organization in England as it produced a new, urban-based social group, the bourgeoisie.

6. The idea of a separate dining room did not become current in France until the sixteenth century and then only among the rich. Before, meals were taken in the kitchen. There was also no sophistication in European eating habits before the fifteenth or sixteenth centuries (Braudel 1981: 183, 187, 308; 1967: 139, 223–24): the use of a spoon, a fork, a knife, and individual glasses for each guest did not become widespread until the sixteenth century. When meals were moved to a separate dining room, the ceremonial attached to the meal increased.

7. The initial spatial differentiation of a dining room was then carried to the rest of the living quarters. By the mid-eighteenth century, pantry, kitchen, dining, drawing, and bedrooms were all separated from each other. This separation was made possible by the invention of the corridor, which helped divide space according to usage.

8. Reception rooms became immense with high ceilings and more open to the exterior; there was a superabundance of ornaments, sculptures, and decorative furniture such as buffets, heavily carved sideboards, which supported equally decorative pieces of silverware. Plates, dishes, pictures, and tapestries were now hung on the walls; the walls themselves were painted with complex motifs.

9. Austria and Germany, the other political powers in Europe, differentiated themselves through their *military* organization and innovations.

10. Its scope differentiates Westernization from former external influences such as Hellenization and Romanization (Momigliano 1975), Arabization, and Sinification. All these influences had been local.

11. For extensive criticisms of modernization theory, see Tipps 1973: 199; Smith 1973: 61–63.

12. As Edward Shils bluntly stated, however, "modern meant being Western without the onus of dependence on the West" (1965: 10).

13. He states that we need to "uncover the history of 'the people without history'—the active histories of 'primitives,' peasantries, laborers, immigrants, and besieged minorities" (Wolf 1982: x).

14. These assumptions were: (1) society is a thing apart; (2) mental events cause social behavior; (3) social change is a coherent phenomenon; (4) processes of change take societies through stages; (5) differentiation is a progressive master process; (6) social order depends on the balance between processes of differentiation and integration; (7) disapproved behavior results from strain and excessive change; (8) illegitimate and legitimate forms of conflict, coercion, and expropriation stem from different processes (Tilly 1984: 14).

15. Teodor Shanin applies Marx's historicity to Marx's work itself; he demonstrates how the late Marx "had a more complex and more realistic conceptualization of global heterogeneity of societal forms, dynamics and interdependence . . . due to four events" (1983: 6). These events were the Paris Commune, the discovery of prehistory, work on agricultural societies such as India, and Russian revolutionary populism. These events and other similar ones that showed change spreading through those societies considered backward led Marx to regard the multiple scenarios of change.

16. Marx did, after all, as Anthony Brewer (1980: 12, 37) argues, emphasize how much the pre-existing social structure affected the development of capitalism. And his explanation of the transition from feudalism to capitalism in Western Europe relied heavily on internal dynamics (Hilton 1978; Holton 1985) to demonstrate how societies produced the preconditions of their own transformation.

17. He could gather information solely through secondary sources, and, also, he could only define the social processes he read about his social system by negation—of what was not like in Western European change. In addition, his interest in the non-West was not systematic but derivative.

18. This, of course, is not to argue that the bourgeoisie cannot ever exist in fragmented form; the argument criticizes those analyses that epistemologically predetermine such a model before any empirical study.

19. Of course, the professed universalism of the bourgeoisie of itself as a class and the development and spread of bourgeois hegemony in the twentieth century have only fostered this skewed analysis. It is impossible to undertake a thorough analysis, as Koditschek argues, as long as

the bourgeoisie is depicted as a class "capable of acting collectively only defensively, in a negative sense" (1990: 13).

20. Yet, one can argue, as some have (for example, Koditschek 1990: 7), that since class formation entails the opposition between two social groups, an analysis of the working class necessitates a concomitant study of the oppressors of this class, namely, the bourgeoisie. One must admit, however, that such an approach is methodologically correct but empirically very challenging.

21. Of course, how this development took place is much debated. Most agree that the internal contradictions of the feudal mode of production caused the transformation (Hilton 1978, Holton 1985), but others like Sweezy and Pirenne (Hilton 1978: 26–29) point to the significance of the external force of trade.

22. The definition of this worth and the demarcation of the boundaries of status and income were historically contingent. The bourgeoisie became "structurally defined to include those who exercised control over large-scale capital or capitalist state or ideological apparatuses and derived their incomes primarily from interest, rent, and profit rather than from wages" (Aminzade 1981: 25). Aminzade's account of the formation of bourgeois hegemony in France is most articulate in its empirical historical depiction. He also explains how the universalist claims of the bourgeoisie, once formed, led to the development of bourgeois hegemony in France.

23. The French revolution was interpreted as a "bourgeois" one in the nineteenth century (Hobsbawm 1989: 29) by the first postrevolutionary generation. This generation rightfully coupled the revolution with its most significant social consequence, the bourgeoisie.

24. In middle-class formation, the British tradition also placed a much greater significance on the role of culture than the French (see, e.g., Thompson 1978; Calhoun 1982; Seed and Wolff 1984; Earle 1989).

25. There is, of course, also a political dimension to this debate (Gunn 1988: 18): pointing out the failure of the bourgeoisie calls for an inversion of the Marxist synthesis to the contrary. Marxists had depicted the industrial bourgeoisie, not the landed aristocracy, as the master of British society after the middle of the nineteenth century. Debating the role of the bourgeoisie meant challenging the Marxist thesis. Nevertheless, British Marxists themselves have concurred with the need for more extensive analysis of the British bourgeoisie before the debate can be brought to an end.

26. Yet, as Blackbourn (1977: 432) argues, such a "conservative" assessment is based more on prescription than explanation and makes gross overgeneralizations about the cohesion of the German bourgeoisie as a class.

27. There are three such assumptions made in particular: (1) about the bourgeoisie as a dynamic force for progressive social and political change; (2) about the characteristics of a strong and fully developed bourgeoisie; and (3) about conceptualizing the bourgeoisie's historical presence as that of a collective acting subject (Eley 1984: 44).

28. Marxist discussions of historical social change center predominantly on the inadequacies of the feudal and Asian modes of production in analyzing precapitalist societies. They increasingly highlight the significance of extra-economic forces in precapitalist societies; the debate, in particular, over the Western transition from feudalism to capitalism centers around the source of change (Hilton 1978). In studying the transformation of political rule in the West, the Weberians focus on the process of change and the role of political structure in structuring this change. They emphasize, in addition to economic factors, the significance of state initiative, nationalism, and the diffusion of ideas in generating change (Bendix 1978). Yet, their delineation of the sources of change is not adequately developed into a theoretical model, remaining descriptive at best.

29. Weber's analysis of social change derived from his theory of political action. Rational, traditional, and effectual orientations to political action gave rise to rational, traditional, or charismatic authority in societies. Weber located the source of change in the constant fluctuation among these three types of authority; the process of routinization of each authority type generated social change. The increasing differentiation and rationalization within administrative organizations affected the type of political rule. Weber perceived social change in the interplay of organizational processes that led society to fluctuate between different types of political organization.

30. This definition nicely dovetails with the Western European tradition of thought on social change in non-Western contexts—a tradition that identifies what is different from the West rather than empirically analyzing what is actually there.

31. The power "of the Turkish sultan and his administrative staff continued to be largely arbitrary despite all the rules and regulations" (Weber 1978: II, 1067–68, 1075).

32. As Turner paraphrases, the "mosaic structure of the Islamic city and the militaristic ethos of Islam inhibited the development of a creative middle class of industrialists and merchants" (1978: 46)—an inhibition that partially explains the absence of a capitalist democracy in the Middle East.

33. The patrimonial office lacked the bureaucratic separation of the "private" and the "official" spheres; patrimonial domination was based on authority, unlike the domination in the market, which was based on a constellation of interests. The patrimonial staff lacked the following features of a bureaucratic administrative staff: "a clearly defined sphere of competence subject to impersonal rules, a rationally established hierarchy, a regular system of appointment on the basis of free contract and orderly promotion, technical training as a regular requirement, and (frequently) fixed salaries." This general "lack" of articulation in patrimonialism is, in reality, a consequence of methodology, of using the emerging rational Western bureaucracies of the nineteenth century as a yardstick to measure other contemporary or historical societies (Weber 1978: I, 229; II, 942–43; 1028).

34. In patrimonialism, the ruler and his administrative staff seized upon, monopolized, and stifled new economic resources and innovations; capital formation of private economy is deprived of its sustenance. In spite of the presence of capitalist trading, tax-farming, lease and sale of offices, provision of supplies for the state, "the type of profit-making enterprise with heavy instruments in fixed capital and a rational organization of free labor which is oriented to the market purchases of private consumers did not and could not exist" (1978: I, 253).

35. These elements were (1) traditional economic relationships, where economic relationships were strictly tradition-bound, use of money primarily consumptive, and ruler's needs met in kind; (2) low economic production, where property and productive capacity of individual economic units were largely preempted for the ruler's needs; (3) economic appropriation, in which the resort to monopolistic want satisfaction, reliance on profit-making enterprises, and fee-taking or taxation provided important openings for profit in the hands of the ruler and his administrative staff, which almost resembled "political" capitalism; (4) economic arbitrariness, where the obligations placed on sources of direct taxation were arbitrary—they were bound by tradition and easily changeable by the ruler; (5) a lack of economic rationalization, wherein two bases of rationalization of economic activity—a basis for the calculability of obligations and the freedom to engage in private enterprise—were lacking; (6) restricted rational economic activity: the financial policy and general character of administrative practices tended to restrict the development of rational economic activity; (7) economic regulation: the inherent tendency to regulate economic activity in terms of utilitarian, welfare, or absolute values broke down *formal* rationality, hence the type of capitalism that developed was restricted to trading, tax-farming, provision of supplies for the state, and plantations and other colonial enterprises (Weber 1978, I: 238–40; II: 1094).

36. Hence patrimonial offices to administer society grew out of his household (Weber 1978, I: 228; II: 1013, 1025).

37. The ideological structure that reproduced these relations centered around legitimation and loyalty. Subjects rose from rags to riches by joining the ruler's service; they maintained this privileged position as long as they remained dependent on the ruler and regarded him as their master. This belief of a direct personal relationship with the ruler was shaped around the concept of filial piety to paternal power—thus the identification of the system as paternalistic. Piety toward the master was reinforced with piety toward tradition. The ruler's control over economic resources reproduced this ideological structure. The source of accumulation of wealth in patrimonialism was not acquisition by exchange but the exploitation of the tax capacities of the subjects. The patrimonial ruler did not like independent economic and social powers and controlled these through forming monopolies for state commercial enterprise. Yet he was constantly under the threat that his administrative staff might form such independent resources and challenge him (Weber 1978, II: 1007–8, 1092, 1106–7).

38. The third category, charismatic authority, is not systematically analyzed with respect to a set of societies but is used instead to account for all those sudden transformations realized throughout the world by charismatic leaders. Hence, oddly enough, this seems to be Weber's only category that cuts across the West/non-West divide.

39. Parsons states, "Islamic monotheism, despite its purity, is embedded in a good deal of archaic cultural content, particularly in the ad hoc, unsystematized Koranic law, much of which was parochial to Arab culture or even idiosyncratic to Mohammed himself. Perhaps still more fundamental, however, is the lack of a philosophical grounding for both theology and law" (1966: 85).

40. These range from segregative change (change in basic rules of social interaction that did not affect the system) to coalescent change (change within the political system) to exceptional change (exceptions to political rule still contained within the system) to revolutionary change (change *of* political systems, particularly of their mode of interaction). All are descriptive categories without much analytical power.

41. The boundaries of such change are drawn by two conditions: the nature of free-floating resources, and the presence of a politically autonomous ruler (Weber 1978, I: 73–75).

42. For example, the classical work on Islam and the West, that of Gibb and Bowen (1963), focuses almost exclusively on Islamic society to the exclusion of its relationship with the West; it argues that the deterioration of the religious spirit initiated Ottoman decline.

43. German Orientalist Carl Heinrich Becker (1876–1933) had argued this point before Turner. See his *Islamstudien; vom Werden und Wesen der islamischen Welt,* 2 vols. (Hildesheim: G. Olms, 1967), especially chapters 1, 2, 3, and 14, which focus on the cultural affinities between Christendom and Islamic civilizations that result from historical conjuncture and interaction.

44. In this religious context, learning a Western language and script could also carry the danger of bringing impiety to the Muslim. This necessitated the establishment of intermediaries, such as colonies of foreigners and Ottoman minorities, between the Ottoman empire and the West (Lewis 1982: 61).

45. A saying ascribed to the Prophet states that "whoever imitates a people becomes one of them." Imitating Western practices thus amounts in itself to an act of infidelity and consequently a betrayal of Islam. Hence, as innovation is assumed to be bad unless shown to be good, it implies a departure from the sacred precept and practice of Islam: by inference, such a departure from Islamic tradition is bad.

46. In addition, with the closing down of external markets for Ottoman goods, Muslim merchants turn to internal trade—they become artisans. They can no longer generate economic resources through trade (Ülgener 1981a: 132–40).

47. This point is best portrayed in the accounts by the Ottomans themselves of their decline. As early as 1541, the Ottoman grand vezir Lüfti Paşa observed decline and cited its characteristic signs as "inflation and speculation, venality and incompetence, multiplication of a useless and wasteful army and bureaucracy, vicious circle of financial stringency, fiscal rapacity and economic strangulation, decay of integrity and loyalty, and beyond them all the growing menacing shadow of maritime states of the West" (Lewis 1973: 201). Another treatise in 1630 attributes the decline to four causes: the withdrawal of the rulers from direct supervision of state affairs; the debasement and debilitation of the office of the grand vezir; the corruption of the imperial household and the Janissaries by outsiders; and the destruction of the military fief system and the military (Lewis 1973: 203–4; 207–8). Ibn Khaldun's idea of the rise and fall of societies is utilized by yet another treatise to demonstrate that the Ottoman empire was approaching the stage of decline and needed a strong ruler to stop this development. Other seventeenth- and eighteenth-century Ottoman thinkers make similar observations as they emphasize corruption, incompetence, and oppression as reasons for the Ottoman decline. As Lewis rightfully argues (1973: 212), there is another stylistic problem with this treatise literature. These political treatises are used to alert the sultan of the problems and induce him to consider recommendations. They can thus be stylized critiques, practiced regardless of contemporary problems.

48. Berkes (1964: 23–30) locates the source of change in the inability of these social groups to

confront and synthesize Western economic penetration into Ottoman society through its trade capitulations.

49. The role of the ideological has been specifically underlined in some current studies (Gorski 1993) that highlight the significance of the disciplinary revolution unleashed by ascetic religious movement in producing two different types of states in Holland and Prussia.

50. These decrees were issued by the sultan in the form of a manifesto strongly forbidding behavior contrary to law and justice, or any misuse of authority.

51. The following quote sums up İnalcık's view: "In the late sixteenth century, a profound transformation took place which may be attributed ultimately to economic and military changes in Western Europe. During this period, for example, in order to resist German infantrymen, the Ottomans discarded their fief cavalry in the provinces and increased the force of Janissaries, who were by this time equipped with firearms. This neglect of the fief holders within the army was followed by the disorganization of the land and taxation system upon which their status had been based. Simultaneously, the shift of international trade routes to the Atlantic Ocean and the invasion of the markets of the Levant by American silver resulted in the disorganization of the rigid Ottoman fiscal and economic structure" (1964: 45).

52. The Ottoman economic breakdown was general; it included "a drop in crop production, scarcity of precious metals, unfavorable balance of trade, excessive exploitation by the state and its agents of the populace in the provinces, population pressure, and the imbalance between population growth and production input" (İnalcık 1980: 285). Population pressure in fifteenth- through seventeenth-century Anatolia has been studied in detail (Cook 1972) to indeed reveal an increase.

53. The social origins of these notables were among religious officials, servants, and soldiery of the center stationed in or retired to urban centers, those who traded in precious goods, and leading guildsmen. Provincial notables were thus of urban, not rural origin; peasants were not a part of this group (İnalcık 1977: 36–38).

54. These notables were the most influential residents of the city, whom the government addressed in matters directly concerning the town population. They looked after the economic welfare of the city by safeguarding regulations and quality control, maintained and performed public services, used their power to influence decisions of the central government, and acted, in general, as intermediaries between the subjects and the government (İnalcık 1977: 43–51).

55. Their power culminated in 1808 in the signing of the Covenant of Union, which stated that "the division and conflicts within government and among provincial notables were the main causes of the desperate situation of the empire and this covenant proposed to revive it" (İnalcık 1964: 52–54).

56. One should also mention in this context the work of Jack Goldstone (1988a, 1991), who argues that political events in the East and West are all rooted in a wide-ranging ecological crisis. Although his effort to connect the Western/non-Western divide and develop a multi-causal model of change ought to be lauded, he downplays the agency of both institutions and actors in generating social change.

57. In his different works, Marx identified four variants of change (Holton 1985: 68). In *German Ideology,* he stated that the progressive universalization of the division of labor and exchange relations resulted in change. *The Poverty of Philosophy* defined change in terms of technological determinism: "The handmill gives you society with the feudal lord; the steam mill society with individual capitalist" ([1847] 1964: 95), Marx stated, identifying technology as the source of change. In the same work he also interpreted change in terms of a productive force embodying skills, knowledge, and experience, as well as material artifacts such as technology. *The Communist Manifesto* and historical sections of *Capital* ([1867] 1977: part 8) provided Marx's widely acknowledged definition of social change in terms of the internal contradictions between productive forces and social relations of production; this contradiction was to be resolved through class conflict.

58. The sketch of the Asian mode of production includes the following fundamental elements: "the absence of private property in land, the presence of large-scale irrigation systems in agriculture, the existence of autarchic village communities combining crafts with tillage and communal ownership of the soil, the stagnation of passively rentier or bureaucratic cities, and the domination of a

despotic state machinery cornering the bulk of the surplus and functioning not merely as the central apparatus of repression of the ruling class, but as its principal instrument of economic exploitation" (Anderson 1979: 483).

59. How did Marx come to form the Asian mode of production? His formulation of the Asiatic mode (Anderson 1979: 462–549; Turner 1984: 19–23) was built upon centuries-old comparisons of the West with the East. The theoretical juxtaposition and contrast of European and Asian state structures had its roots in the works of Aristotle, which portrayed Asians as more servile (than Europeans) and therefore enduring despotic rule without protest. During the Enlightenment, this connection was systematized; Montesquieu assumed that the lack of private property or a hereditary nobility in the East implied arbitrariness and tyranny of rule. As Islamic religion replaced legal codes, this arbitrariness was saddled with changelessness. Hence, Montesquieu was the first to define oriental societies through their arbitrary tyranny and changelessness. Adam Smith added the role of the absolute state to this formulation; he pointed out that the state in the East owned all land, irrigation, and transport. Marx's Asian mode of production merely summed up these separate intellectual traditions when he located the source of change as being external to the society, situated in the West.

60. Absolutism in Europe was the result of the intertwining of the feudal and capitalist modes of production, with an ascending urban bourgeoisie and a growing primitive accumulation of capital. This development of the bourgeoisie and economic capital was a by-product of the paradox of Western European absolutism: absolutism, by protecting aristocratic property and privileges, also indirectly guarded nascent mercantile and manufacturing interests. Yet such a by-product could have been easily curbed if property ownership had been constrained by social groups. Anderson limits the power of his explanation by using property ownership as the basic causal variable in the emergence of European absolutism (Anderson 1979: 40, 428–29).

61. Anderson's persistent focus on property and privileges stems from his attempts to combine the economic with the political in explaining historical change. His explanations, while informative, fail to present an alternative formulation to the Marxist paradigm.

62. Anderson's specific analysis of the Ottoman state repeated the same methodological mistakes he criticized. Anderson tied Ottoman decline to the military and economic superiority of absolutist Europe. The increase in Ottoman society of religiously endowed lands and the change of the land tenure system contributed to this decline. He portrayed the formal theoretical structure of sixteenth-century Ottoman society as the *actual* Ottoman structure throughout Ottoman rule. In addition, he failed to take into account the changes the Ottoman system went through during its seven centuries of the rule.

63. Marx's depiction of the Western European feudal mode of production may be a better analytical model than the Asian mode of production in ameliorating existing models of social change since it combines the analytical rigor of Marx's conception of Western European change with an indigenous empirical analysis of non-Western change.

64. The Asian mode of production was not the only source of inspiration; the persistent disjunctures between the economy and the polity in the Western European context also led many to question the innate tie between the state and ruling class. They then problematized the political sphere and moved the role of the state to the fore, often at the expense of the agency of other social groups in society.

65. In these interpretations, the source of change once more became endogenous to center on the social relations of production.

66. Skocpol generated the elements of change through comparisons rather than in-depth empirical studies of the internal dynamics of social change in each society, however. Because of the way she used the comparative historical method, societal elements entered the comparison only insofar as they could be compared with elements from other societies. Furthermore, upon entering the comparison, they were transformed, without explanation, from analytical categories to explanatory variables. Skocpol's state structure, the crucial variable in the transformation of France, China, and Russia, was an outgrowth of the same eighteenth-century European transformation. Skocpol mistook the variations in this state structure over time (as the Western model was imported to Russia and

China) as explanations of social change. This is due to the way Skocpol used historical sources. Skocpol treated historical evidence as a "thing"; she had no regard for or interest in its construction. She argued that "if a topic is too big for primary research and if excellent studies by specialists are already available in some profusion, secondary sources are appropriate as the basic source of evidence for a given study . . . (one) must resist the temptation to disappear forever into the primary evidence about each case" (1984: 382). Yet this nonempirical approach easily replicates the interpretive fallacies in the sources and reifies them, and the sociologist often finds what she expects to find as the source of historical change.

67. Ethnicity, which becomes a significant factor in non-Western transformations, is not adequately discussed in the Western European cases, which certainly entailed many ethnic divisions.

68. However, this is not to claim that the state would not have had a different development trajectory in the Middle Eastern context. Instead, it purports that the emphasis on the state as a social actor takes away from the significance of social groups and privileges institutions over human actors in causal explanations.

69. Wallerstein defines the Ottoman empire as a world-empire coming into contact with a capitalist world-economy, that of Europe; trade and warfare between the systems ended in the absorption of the Ottoman empire. The Ottoman empire then became a state within the world-economy as production within the Ottoman empire was peripheralized.

70. Wallerstein argues specifically that Ottoman state control over the means of production, circulation, violence, and administration decreases in this period; Ottoman exports of commercial crops to the West and new Ottoman imports such as coffee, sugar, and steel starting to flood Ottoman markets undermine domestic manufacture. This periodization and the evidence for it have been questioned by many scholars. Çizakça's (1985) Ottoman archival analysis of silk, wool, and cotton prices revealed two stages of incorporation, an early 1550–1650 stage followed by a full incorporation stage during the period 1830–1900. These periodizations are still open to criticism and await further archival documentation.

71. The variation in the reaction to capitalist penetration remains the most crucial criticism of Wallerstein's model, however (Chirot and Hall 1982: 99; Ragin and Chirot 1984: 290).

72. The fact that Wallerstein locates the source of global change in the exchange relations of Western societies does not at all ameliorate the image of the static non-West. Instead, the world-system itself becomes the source of change, covering all societies "like a powerful blanket, and pacifying all societal initiative" (Ragin and Chirot 1984: 277). Such a world-system also suffers from analytical rigor in explaining variations within the experiences of peripheries such as Eastern Europe and Latin America (Chirot 1981: 275).

73. This alteration (and concomitant Ottoman peripheralization) occurred when internal trade escaped administrative control in the sixteenth and seventeenth centuries due to incentives offered by contraband trade. Gradually internal trade articulated with external trade. Four sets of factors (two internal contradictions and two external factors) lay at the source of this peripheralization: internally, parcelization of economic and political control and the expansion of market realm with a concomitant weakening of political control over the economy; externally, price inflation and population increase (İslamoğlu and Keyder 1977: 41, 47).

74. The world-system approach thus underemphasizes what the state-centered approaches overemphasize: the significance of the Ottoman state as a social actor.

Chapter 1

1. Morocco encountered the rising West before the Ottoman empire did.

2. Mardin (1967: 120–23) alerts us to the possible difference between this ideal formulation and the real social structure. These elements simply form the organizing principles of the structure and may not directly correspond to the structure itself.

3. See *EI* "Askari" for a fuller discussion of this term.

4. There were special exceptions to religious minorities who joined the rulers without conver-

sion through the display of special skills: Greek Phanariots and Jewish physicians and military provisioners. In addition, there were also non-Muslim soldiers, even some feudal cavalry, during the earlier centuries of the empire. For further information on this group, see Kunt (1982).

5. They were aware that the household structure was differentiated into the sultan's immediate palace household and his extended administrative household.

6. See İnalcık (1973) and Findley (1980a, 1989) for detailed analyses of the Ottoman administrative structure.

7. Findley concurs that "the metaphorical integration of the entire state into a single household provided the sultans with a means by which to defend the state from the potentially divisive forces represented by the smaller kinship groups" (1980b: 227). Yet he goes on to include two additional organizational models, the autonomous confessional community and the guilds (1980b: 228; 1990: 867–68). I would argue that the organizations of Ottoman religious communities and guilds do not differ structurally from those of the administrative, military, and religious households.

8. This redefinition of the term "household" as the basic organizational unit is anticipated by Aristotle, who describes three kinds of government: Basilike, i.e., as a king rules his subjects; Politike, as citizens participate in ruling the city; and Despotike, as the Despotes, i.e., the master, rules his household. I am indebted to Bernard Lewis for providing me with this information.

9. The custom of calling the palace, court and/or government of a ruler a "gate" or "doorstep" was very prevalent in ancient times, for instance in Sassanid Iran, Pharaonic Egypt, and Japan. For a fuller discussion on the Ottoman usage of the term *bab*, see *EI* articles "Bab-ı 'Ali," "Bab-ı Hümayun," "Bab-ı Mashikhat," "Bab-ı Seraskeri," and *İslam Ansiklopedisi* articles "Bab" and "Babı 'Ali." The term used in the West for this Ottoman political organization was "Sublime Porte," a literal translation of *bab-ı ali*. The Ottoman term for office was *daire*, originally "circle," or "circumference," and in this context, "department" or "office."

10. See D9964 for one such inheritance register.

11. The sultan maintained communication (and thereby control) within his dominions through a well-maintained road network. In stations built along these roads, appointed subjects from nearby towns or villages kept fodder, extra horses, and supplies for the sultan's messengers traveling through (Halacoğlu 1981; Özkaya 1985: 291). Similarly, mountain passes, bridges, and roads within cities were built and maintained by the sultan (Orhonlu 1984). Such a communication network gave him the necessary swiftness in controlling and regulating his administration.

12. These religious scholars from the mosques who were invited to the palace to give sermons led to the development of another link between the sultan's household and society. The scholars, through these sermons, courses, and discussion groups, formed ties with the palace pages. Once these pages rose in stature, religious scholars could use their influence to procure favors, usually in the form of religious appointments, for themselves.

13. There was also the practice of religious debates (Ottoman term: *huzur dersleri)* established in the eighteenth century at the palace, in the presence of the sultan, among scholars to elicit opinion on religious texts.

14. The education of the sultans and their sons and daughters took place within the same framework (Ergin 1939: 2, 235). Basic calligraphy, reading, writing, and reciting the Qur'an were taught to the children together. Later on the sultan's sons were assigned personal tutors who trained them in specialized fields of knowledge and in one vocational skill, such as carpentry.

15. Although historical evidence indicates that this severing of relation with the past was never complete—for instance, many of them brought whole families with them to the capital—it nevertheless irretrievably restructured their position in society. See Patterson (1991, 1982) for a discussion, within the Western context, of identity formation and transformation in slavery.

16. The distinguishing characteristic of a patronage tie is that it is long term, not restricted to a single isolated transaction (Forand 1971; Gellner and Waterbury 1977: 1–6). The patronage tie between the sultan and his recruits was asymmetrical in terms of power; the sultan provided all and had the option to take back all.

17. When the sultan's household expanded in the eighteenth century, he could not establish this patronage tie in person. The members then started professing allegiance to his abstract position

rather than his physical self. This ultimately destroyed the exclusivity of the sultan's household and the sultan with it.

18. By using his personal ties with the sultan, the scholar then formed his own patronage ties, advanced the careers of all his sons, and married his daughters to influential Ottoman officials.

19. Findley (1980b: 228–29) specifies these fictitious kinships as forming through marriage, clientage, adoption, slavery, or milk brotherhood (lifelong bond among persons sharing the same wet nurse in infancy).

20. Refer to the Introduction for a critique of these terms as employed by Marx and Weber. Marx and Weber both use these terms as organizational structures, without giving any agency to the people in them.

21. For some periods of the eighteenth century, controlling for inflation, the Ottoman budget (in aspers) comprising these revenues and expenditure was:

Years	Revenue	Expenditure
1704–5	238,422,670	218,676,180
1710–11	299,164,010	231,158,210
1748–49	380,908,300	395,161,620

Source: Tabakoğlu 1981:398

During the second half of the eighteenth century, expenditures consistently exceeded incoming revenues.

22. The sultan's and state's revenues thus entered the same central treasury, without any differentiation.

23. Although Islamic law differentiates the public treasury from the private, both belonged to the Ottoman sultan (Velidedeoğlu 1940).

24. This orientation inhibited the development of economic resources outside state control.

25. Yet religious endowments owned land privately; urban land was also privately owned.

26. By the eighteenth century, Ottoman mines had started to dry up and eventually lost their significance as a revenue source.

27. Failure to pay was interpreted as a sign of rebellion against Ottoman sovereignty and quickly punished.

28. The salaries of the sultan's household members, ranging from those of his soldiers to the palace personnel, thereby including tens of thousands of people, was the most significant consistent expense among these items (Tabakoğlu 1981: 389–414).

29. These revenues had constituted 41 percent of the sultan's revenues in the sixteenth century and dwindled to 27–30 percent of those revenues in the seventeenth century (Cezar 1986: 38–40).

30. This commodification of offices and land also led to an increase in Ottoman expenditures during the eighteenth century (Cezar 1986: 301).

31. The essence of a religious endowment is a thing "restrained" to God that produces an income, the income being expended only upon the defined charitable purpose. Religious endowments conserved and propagated Ottoman society (Yediyıldız 1982b: 1–14).

32. Ottoman religious endowments developed economic life. They built caravanserais, inns, covered bazaars, market places, baths, shops, tenements, depots, workshops, bakeries, oil presses, mills, slaughterhouses, and tanneries to support the religious and charitable institutions of mosques, schools, hospices, and hospitals. They also provided public services through building and maintaining canals, dikes, roads, and bridges. By ensuring ease and safety of travel on the roads, the religious endowments also improved communication and trade networks within the empire. In addition, they supported the Ottoman educational system based on religious learning, with the aim of understanding God. Training centers for studying the Qur'an and learning to read and write for children

continued into a two-tiered college system for those who wanted to specialize; Ottoman religious dignitaries were recruited from these colleges. The graduates of these institutions had a dual role as interpreters and executors of Islamic law (İnalcık 1969: 132–35; 1970: 207–8; 1973: 140, 146–48, 165–75). Religious endowments also functioned as a credit institution for both Muslims and non-Muslims (Özdemir 1990: 745–46).

33. The analysis is based on 330 religious endowments that were randomly sampled from among the 6,000 founded during the eighteenth century (Yediyıldız 1982a, 1982b, 1982c, 1984). In this sample, religious endowment expenses were distributed as follows: 31 percent to religious functions, 28 percent to education and instruction, 14 percent to families of endowers, 11 percent to social services, 10 percent to administration of the endowment, and 6 percent to other miscellaneous expenses (1982b: 2).

34. The social composition of the endowers substantiates this conclusion. The sultan founded only 5 percent of these endowments; 58 percent were founded by his administrators, and 32 percent of the endowers' social origins were unidentified. Analysis of the sources of the endowed income again verifies this conclusion (Yediyıldız 1984: 25, 40): 32 percent of the endowed income consisted of hard cash (often lent out on interest running up to but not exceeding 15 percent); 30 percent of agricultural land, and another 30 percent of economic investments in inns, cellars, windmills, or manufactories. Of the cash endowments, 43 percent were once more bestowed by the sultan's officials; the social origin of 29 percent is unknown.

35. The sultan had the right to abolish the endowment if the revenues were not expended upon the defined charitable purpose, or if the endowment did not make a social contribution.

36. See Lewis (1988: 91–116) for a fuller discussion of the limits of obedience to the sultan that were set by Islamic law.

37. An analysis of hundreds of such lists reveals women, especially those left homeless after a fire, to be the most significant category of petitioners (İD38202, as cited in İpşirli 1991: 466).

38. Nevertheless, there is a lot of debate among scholars working on the Ottoman empire about this portrayal. All agree that this indeed was how the system was supposed to work in theory, but there is a lot of disagreement on the extent the system worked in this manner in practice. This theory–practice divide is a criticism that is equally valid for all legal systems, though. In addition, even the ideal construction invalidates Weber's and other European thinkers' assumptions about the "arbitrariness of Ottoman rule."

39. As Western observers, including Machiavelli, noted, by training the officials within the palace, the sultan was able to guarantee a loyal administration (İnalcık 1964: 43–44; 1970: 217–18; 1973: 68, 150; 1973: 54).

40. *Kaza* was the name given to the basic administrative as well as judicial unit within which these functions were executed.

41. A group of "exempted subjects" also received the tax immunity privileges of administrators in return for particular services to the state, such as those in mining, bridge, and road construction and upkeep.

42. It is difficult to assess how extensive the households of these officials, which I term "office households," were in Ottoman society; there are no existing studies on the topic. In this study, I presume that all members of the Ottoman administration had office-households in the eighteenth century.

43. For more detailed information on this social group, see Repp (1986, 1977), Ortaylı (1979), Gibb and Bowen (1963, II: 70–178), articles "Bab-ı Mashikhat," "Wakf" in *EI*2, and "Vakıf" and "Ulema" in *İslam Ansiklopedisi*.

44. There had been other precedents in Middle Eastern history to this Ottoman practice; the Abbasid state increased its control over religious dignitaries by conferring salaries upon them (*İslam Ansiklopedisi*, "Ulema," p. 23). For a fuller discussion of the dwindling role of the Ottoman religious dignitaries, see Lewis (1979: 97 ff.).

45. Yet there were considerable differences among guild organizations from one city to another. Usually the system was more comprehensive in large cities (Baer 1980: 16).

46. Two kinds of warrants could be issued, to the individual for the right to practice whatever he wanted, and for a man exercising a craft in a specific location (R. Lewis 1971: 145).

47. Gabriel Baer (1970b: 193–94) argues that in all periods there were more religiously separate guilds than mixed ones.

48. In the sixteenth century, 13 percent of state revenues came from customs, mines, and merchants in the cities (İnalcık 1970: 218; 1973: 109–11; 1974: 54).

49. The sultan only had full control over agricultural land. Even the property on such land could be owned privately, however. The sultan also had no control over religious endowments.

50. In Ottoman trade with Europe, the Italian states of Venice and Genoa were dominant until the end of the sixteenth century. The sixteenth-century trade of Venice with the Ottomans consisted, for example, of exporting woolens, silk brocades and satins, paper, glassware, and mirrors. In return, Venice imported from Egypt and Syria spices, drugs, dyestuffs, silk, and cotton, and from Asia Minor and the Balkans wheat, hides, wool, cotton, and silk.

51. The use of credit in economic transactions was widespread within Ottoman society. The principle of the letter of credit, the payment of a debt through the transfer of a claim, a significant variable in the emergence of capitalism in the West, was present in Ottoman society as well. Yet the pledging of valuables and of land became the most widely used security for loans and sales of credit.

52. In 1569, Ottoman trade capitulations were granted to the French. The English joined the competition in 1580, when they were also granted capitulations. The Ottoman sultan granted the capitulations with political, financial, and economic expectations; he used the capitulations to form political alliances, to obtain scarce goods such as woolen cloth, tin, steel, paper, and bullion, and to increase customs revenues. The Ottomans did not consider capitulations a contractual bilateral document. The Ottoman sultan retained the authority to decide unilaterally to void the capitulation when relations between states were broken. The main weapon of the European states to counter the bans of capitulations was the threat of boycotting Ottoman ports (İnalcık 1970: 211; 1973: 130–37; 1979: 55–56).

53. Yet Muslim merchants did indeed stay active in domestic trade. See, for example, the cases of the merchants Hace Hafız Ahmed Ağa and Hacı Ömer Ağa in 1817 (HH25433 and HH25311–12), the merchants Ahmed and Molla Mehmed, who engaged in pastrami, olive oil, and honey trade in 1825 (MM9731), and the merchant Elhac Mehmed Ağa in 1845 (CD5170, CD5218).

54. Sociologically, we define a minority as a social group that does not share equally in the societal power structure. Hence, a group can be numerically large, such as blacks in South Africa or women, but still not share in the power structure equally. The Ottoman term for religious minorities is *zimmi*, or *dhimmi*.

55. This book, focusing on the central lands of the empire rather than the Arab provinces, studies the Ottoman Greeks, Armenians, and Jews more than the Arab Christians. Yet, the Arab Christians were a significant social force in the provinces, particularly in the nineteenth century. For an extensive analysis of Arab Christians, see studies such as those of Bakhit (1972), Braude and Lewis (1982), Cohen (1984, 1973), Fawaz (1983), Hourani (1957), Hunter (1984), Masters (1988), Owen (1981), Rafeq (1977, 1966).

56. Although these decrees often gave the prevention of material shortages and increased consumption which developed when the minorities also purchased goods as the reason for issuing these decrees, the need to reproduce Ottoman social stratification was undoubtedly a significant concern.

57. These dress codes were periodically reissued and altered. Administrators issued the orders of the alterations to the minority communities by inviting their leaders to the room of the chief of the corps of halberdiers *(çavuşbaşı)*, as in the case of the 1748 decree (Özkaya 1985: 146).

58. Footwear colors were later spelled out in detail (Özkaya 1985: 155). The Jews and the Armenians had to wear black and purple, and the Greeks red. Yellow, the color that Muslims wore, was forbidden to the minorities.

59. Their dresses, for instance, had to be made from Bursa cotton or brightly colored cloth

(alaca), with head sashes that could only be red-yellow striped and underpants *(şalvar)* that could only be sky blue in color.

60. Yet such a social tie almost invariably resulted in the cooptation of the minority women into the dominant Muslim culture, since, upon such a marriage, they lost their rights to inherit from their kin.

61. In the sixteenth century, the sultan directly owned 50 percent of the land, and 37 percent of the revenues, most of it from the land, was distributed as fiefs to the mounted cavalry in return for their services. This distribution helped ease the constant cash crises in the payment of military salaries.

62. This book first defines Ottoman Westernization in terms of the adoption of goods, institutions, and ideas and then analyzes Westernization as it interacts with the Ottoman social structure and affects the agency of the Ottoman social groups.

63. Tradition is "that which is handed down—includes material objects, beliefs about all sorts of things, images of persons and events, practices and institutions. It includes buildings, monuments, landscapes, sculptures, paintings, books, tools, machines. It includes all that a society at a given time possesses and which already existed when its present possessors came upon it and which is not solely the product of physical processes in the external world or exclusively the result of ecological and physiological necessity" (Shils 1981: 12). Social reproduction in a society entails the reproduction of tradition; yet every time tradition is reproduced, it incorporates new elements from the environment and thus produces a new synthesis.

64. There were several exceptions to this perception of Western goods as status objects. One was the Ottoman utilization of European guns, a technological instrument, from early on. Another was the Ottoman use of tobacco, which was brought to the Ottoman empire during the early years of the seventeenth century (Göçek 1987: 104).

65. The studies of Douglas and Isherwood (1979) and Appadurai (1986) focus on the social meanings of goods and of goods consumption. Douglas focuses on consumption because "consumption is the very arena in which culture is fought over and licked into shape" (1979: 5, 57, 68, 70).

66. Material culture consists of "the totality of artifacts in a culture, the vast universe of objects used by humankind to cope with the physical world, to facilitate social intercourse, to delight our fancy, and to create symbols of meaning" (Schlereth 1983: 112).

67. The goods themselves were judged by their quality, which in turn was rated by the amount of time invested in producing them (Kınalızade, I: 157, in Ülgener 1981a: 85).

68. As one scholar states, it was "not the worldly goods that led people to sin, but the ambition and passion humans associated with them" (Ülgener 1981a: 55–56). See also Goldhizer, who argues, in relation to this point, that Islam strikes a balance between this and the other world by stating "the best among you is he who takes from both" (1981: 121).

69. This condition is not unique to Islam. Indeed, in history, there is rarely a correspondence between any religious prescription and social practice.

70. The Ottoman reward system, for example, was based on bestowing upon one another valuable robes; individuals also exchanged many luxury goods during ceremonial occasions.

71. Such fashions emerged in Ottoman society throughout the centuries, often taking the form of regional imitations; a clothing item from North Africa, or the Balkans, became popular at different periods. The trousers of North African sailors was one such item (Koçu 1969). The classical Western view of the changelessness of societies in the East and the nonexistence of fashion (Harte 1976: 155) seems to stem from a lack of knowledge about Ottoman society, not from a lack of fashion. The variations in Ottoman clothing were not discernable to Western observers but, as indicated here, they were nevertheless present.

72. According to the law, clothing had to be in accordance with custom and religious law.

73. One scholar (Ülgener 1981a: 123, 173–78, 180–8) argues that, in the Ottoman empire, wealth was not used as a medium to distribute goods and services but as a medium to distribute social prestige. Such an orientation enhanced the Ottoman consumption of Western goods while stunting the economic reproduction of these goods within Ottoman society. Islamic mysticism also

pacified and resigned the ruled to accept the exploitation of the rulers; it fueled the Ottoman consumption of Western goods by generating a double standard for rulers and subjects. The rulers differed in their moral standards from the ruled and consumed these Western luxury items without the need to justify their behavior on moral grounds. Kınalızade discussed and legitimized this stratification system. He stated that each stratum had to be content with its own standard of life, as "justice necessitates each person to engage in work that is fit, proper to his aptitude and not engage in more than one work as time is limited and he will not have the time to attain perfection in all and should therefore be contained and satisfied with some" (Kınalızade 1832, II:10, in Ülgener 1981b). Although this interpretation does indeed highlight significant aspects of Ottoman Western goods consumption, it overlooks structural factors such as internal competition among households and the effects of war and the world-economy on the empire. This book argues that a combination of such structural and ideational factors shaped Western goods use in Ottoman society.

74. For example, English cotton export into the Ottoman empire documents this accelerating economic penetration.

Year	Cotton Cloth	Cotton Thread (per thousand lbs.)
1825	3,578	557
1830	5,940	1,528
1835	25,692	3,272
1845	46,793	5,830
1850	31,124	2,384
1855	132,605	8,446
1860	229,201	22,824

Source: İnalcık 1979:48

75. One such notable, originally an employee of the Ottoman palace, returned to his place of birth upon retirement. He had a house built in 1825 decorated with Western forms, with scenes of Constantinople—as if to remind himself of the capital (Renda 1977: 103).

76. Mahmud II was not the first sultan to have his portrait painted; among the Ottoman sultans, the Italian painter Gentile Bellini painted the portrait of Mehmed II after the conquest of Constantinople (Lewis 1982: 242). The practice seems to have been discontinued after him until Mahmud II, however.

77. Women's fashion became visibly Western in the nineteenth century, especially following Empress Eugénie's reciprocal visit to Sultan Abdülaziz in Constantinople.

78. The Ottoman term is *Frenkler,* literally, the "Francs."

Chapter 2

1. I term this bourgeoisie "bureaucratic" because its most notable feature is the employment of the Western, predominantly French, administrative tradition in the complete restructuring of the Ottoman civil officialdom. Indeed, the "bureau" replaced the household as the administrative unit of the empire. For further discussion on the emergence of this Ottoman civil officialdom, see Findley (1980a, 1989).

2. During this time period, the French army increased, for instance, from 150,000 in the late seventeenth century to approximately 225,000 in the eighteenth, and the Russian army from 150,000 under Peter the Great to over 450,000 by the end of the reign of Catherine II (Yapp 1975: 331, 338–39).

3. As Yapp points out, "in 1870 Austria, Germany, Italy, and Russia each spent only about 25 new pence per head on their armies. Between 1874 and 1896 the average expenditure by Euro-

pean powers on their armies increased by slightly over 50 percent. Germany and Russia showed the largest increases with 79 percent and 75 percent respectively. The expenditure of France rose by 47 percent and that of Austria by only 21 percent" (1975: 342).

4. These were the Ottoman 1645–69 war of Crete, the 1663–76 war with Austria, the 1672–76 with Poland, the 1678–81 with Russia, and the 1683–99 with Austria, then joined by Russia, Poland, and Venice (Cezar 1986: 29–32).

5. These Ottoman wars were fought in 1708 with Austria, Russia, and Venice, in 1711 with Russia, in 1714–18 with Austria and Russia, in 1723–42 with Iran, in 1737–39 with Austria and Russia, in 1742–46 with Iran, and, in the second half of the eighteenth century, in 1768–74 with Russia, in 1787–92 with Russia and Austria, and in 1797–1801 with France over Egypt.

6. The costly wars in the nineteenth century were fought in 1806–7 with Russia, in 1807–9 with Britain, in 1809–12 with Russia, in 1828–29 with Allied forces over Greece and later with Russia, in 1853–56 with Russia, where the Ottomans received British and French help, and in 1877–78 with Russia.

7. See "Harb, Ottoman Empire," in *EI,* and Parry (1975: 218–56) for a fuller discussion of the Ottoman military transformation vis-à-vis innovations in European techniques of warfare.

8. These revolts took place in the Balkans, with the 1804–30 Serbian revolt, the 1821 Greek revolt and independence, and the 1797–1808 revolts in Albania and surrounding territories. Similar revolts ensued in the Arab provinces in the late nineteenth centuries.

9. The Ottoman treasury, too small to meet war expenses, could only finance limited projects. The sultan usually had to finance wars out of his resources.

10. One example of such goods is gunpowder. It was produced in the Ottoman empire but its declining quality and quantity in the late seventeenth and eighteenth centuries necessitated its import from the West. See "Barud, the Ottoman Empire," in *EI* for a fuller discussion of this transformation.

11. Some officials had suggested the possibility of imposing a similar mandatory loan on religious endowments. Yet, since the revenues of endowments were not clearly defined, it proved difficult to come up with an amount and to enforce it.

12. These scholars stated that the curse of the poor and the needy in their prayers would produce only harmful consequences for the Ottoman state. The response of the treasury officials was that "wars were won with the power of swords, not prayers." Nevertheless, an inauspicious event lending indirect support to the religious indeed occurred: the galley built at the shipyard with these pensions sank while being lowered to sea—causing the vezir in charge to weep bitterly and convincing everyone that it was the anguish of the poor and needy that caused the misfortune (Naima [1863] 1969, V: 2108–10).

13. Also, the empire was adversely affected by wars outside its boundaries. As the Ottoman economy became more and more incorporated into the world market, conflicts such as the 1860–65 U.S. Civil War increasingly affected the Ottoman financial system (Cevdet 1872: 128).

14. See "Duyun-u Umumiye" in *EI* for a fuller discussion of the establishment and administration of this organization. There is also an extensive literature on the Ottoman public debt; see, for instance, Pamuk (1987).

15. This time, the Ottoman administrators, who had become more experienced in borrowing, actually received 89 percent of this amount, totaling 107,858,796 gold coins.

16. The following discussion is based on "Asham" and "Kaime," both in *EI.*

17. Thus a new division was created between the "schooled men" and the "old troopers" (Findley 1980a: 59–60).

18. This was so much the case that one chronicler in the 1860s when commenting on the case of a person marrying the sultan's daughter, noted that "had this person been educated in the Western-style and had risen through the system gradually, there would have emerged an individual who would have been beneficial to the state" (Cevdet 1872: 69–71). Instead, the person had married into the sultan's household and had thus "wasted" his chances of success. Indeed, the sense of accomplishment shifted from the sultan's criteria to those established by the new Western-style educational institutions.

19. Increased Western influence in the empire also benefited another Ottoman social group, the minorities, who through their trade relations and subsequent legal protection by Western powers acquired resources independent of the sultan's control to form the seeds of the Ottoman commercial bourgeoisie.

20. By the late nineteenth century, these households had been so thoroughly replaced by the new Western-style institutions that one statesmen mourned, "there [no longer] are such households left in the capital. It was as if the capital had been a beautiful garden and these households its gorgeous flowers. Now all of these flowers have withered with the winds of autumn. The capital has turned into a vast empty autumn meadow" (Cevdet 1872: 18).

21. Whereas the sultan's household symbolically contained the hundreds of thousands to whom the sultan had delegated authority, the actual palace household ranged in the high thousands. Ottoman office-households varied in size from hundreds to low thousands of people, containing an agglomerate of individuals from foot soldiers to cooks to scribes (Findley 1980: 35). The provincial households were similarly in the low hundreds. For further information on households, see *EI* articles "Bab," "Bab-ı Ali," Bab-ı Hümayun, Bab-ı Meshikhat," "Bab-ı Seraskeri," and *İslam Ansiklopedisi* articles "Bab" and "Babıali."

22. This official looked after the financial administration of the Ottoman capital and provinces. His office was under the jurisdiction of the grand vezir; some members of his office also resided in the grand vezir's household. See "Maliyye" in *EI* for further information on the financial administration of the Ottoman empire.

23. This commodification of administrative offices, which began in the seventeenth century, actually extended beyond the fiefs over agricultural land to other administrative posts, such as judgeships: these also started to be auctioned off (Özkaya 1985: 206–7).

24. The seventeenth-century Ottoman chronicler Naima (1863) narrates many instances of this competition, which are cited later in this chapter. There are also archival documents referring to other instances; see, for instance, CM 27577, which summarizes an official's fight to retain his post.

25. Also, as the official remained behind, he purchased more property in the city, invested in social networks, got more entrenched in the capital, and often failed to leave for the administrative post in the provinces.

26. The Ottoman monetary system had two main currencies, aspers *(akçe)* and piasters *(guruş)*. In the eighteenth century, the exchange rate between the two was 120 aspers to 1 piaster (Lewis 1979: 111). For more information on these currencies and the transformation in their values over the centuries, see "Akçe" in *EI,* and "Kuruş" in *İslam Ansiklopedisi,* and Gibb and Bowen (1963, II: 49–59).

27. The average salary was five piasters a month. The cook received the highest salary of thirty piasters.

28. The valuable items in their registers were probably the periodic gifts, clothing, and goods their masters gave them. For example, the chief secretary of state *(reis-ül-küttab)* Raif İsmail Pasha (E37/4) gave his household yards of cloth and footwear during a religious holiday. Another vezir (KK749) distributed yearly supplies of cloth, robes, headgear, footwear, and some bonus *(bahşiş)* to his fifty household members.

29. Not all of these may be investments of the *paşa,* some could have been inherited or given as gifts.

30. The practice of moneylending with interest among the Ottoman Muslims raises a major legal problem since it was a practice rebuked by Islamic law. It is interesting to note, however, that although such transactions were clearly prohibited in the Qur'an, traditions and schools of interpretation all had different interpretations as to what forms of business came under such a prohibition. The tolerant Hanefite interpretation that the Ottoman Muslims followed gave them the necessary flexibility in practicing diverse forms of moneylending with interest. For a fuller discussion of this point, refer to "Rıba" in *EI*.

31. In the capital, geographical proximity intensified the existing interaction among office-households.

32. One might assume that the gift givers cultivated the vezir's interest in collecting horses by presenting him with some; horses were also valuable items of transportation and prestige in Ottoman society.

33. The sultan could only assert his position by expecting only the most valuable gifts and returning even more precious ones.

34. This is inferred from the honorific title *esseyyid,* which indicates such an ancestry, although one must add that there were many who made such claims without adequate proof.

35. The state could justify confiscation on the grounds that the official in question had accrued the wealth through the post. Previous wealth, especially that of the spouse, was therefore excluded.

36. In 1802, for example, upon Battal Hüseyin Pasha's death, his son inherited his wealth in return for paying the sultan 500,000 piasters, a substantial sum that the son had no trouble paying as he himself was the governor of Diyarbekir (CM25490). In 1808, the sons of Hasan Pasha purchased his inheritance in return for 30,900 purses of gold; these wealthy men were all listed as religious scholars *(müderris)* (MM9755/97–98). All the inheritances of officials theoretically belonged to the sultan because these officials had procured their wealth through and during their office tenure. The sultan often exercised his right, particularly when he was challenged by the strength of office-households. Yet, it was costly for the sultan to send his messengers to confiscate the inheritance. These messengers would spend money to travel, register the goods and properties, transfer these to the capital, and withhold some as service duties. Often, the sultan had to spend more on the process of confiscation than the total worth of the inheritance. In the eighteenth century, he therefore established the practice of letting heirs of officials purchase the inheritance for a cash value set by the sultan.

37. His full name was Softa Mahmud Pasha. One must note that the former steward was probably active in making his own fortunes as well; he probably acquired some cash and property while administering the office-household.

38. See "Waqf" in *EI,* and "Vakıf" in *İslam Ansiklopedisi* and Gibb and Bowen (1963, II:165–78) for a fuller discussion of this practice.

39. Officials endowed properties from all over the empire. Grand admiral Kaymak Mustafa Pasha (Aktepe 1969: 18–20, 26–35) used the revenues of his properties in Constantinople, Smyrna, Lesbos, Chios, and Kütahya to establish three endowments. The funds for the religious endowments grand vezir Damad İbrahim Pasha established came from his various shops, inns, and gardens in Constantinople, Smyrna, Antioch, Aydın, and Naksos island (Aktepe 1960: 152–53, 155–56).

40. Another archival document (KK2457) indicated that the deputy governor also owned 33 farms.

41. Archival registers contain lists of sultan's allocations to office-households. This information is extracted from *Hazariyye Defteri* 4/180, 280–82 in the Prime Minister's archives.

42. See "Musadara, the Ottoman Empire," in *EI* for further discussion of this measure.

43. The decree also reiterated that only inheritances of those who died without leaving any heirs would revert to the state treasury.

44. Originally, these officials were appointed by the Ottoman sultan. Initially elected by the native landowners, they were later chosen from among the Ottoman Greek families of the Phanar quarter in Constantinople (Gibb and Bowen 1963, I: 24–25). There usually were no Muslim officials appointed, except in some frontier fortresses occupied by permanent garrisons. The fact that this voivode was a Muslim indicates the presence of such a garrison. For further information on the office of the voivode, see "Boghdan," in *EI2.*

45. It was profitable to confiscate the inheritance of those who had ready cash. The confiscation of artisans' inheritances was not lucrative, however; artisans lacked large economic resources and often kept their wealth invested in goods, not in cash.

46. The late seventeenth century refers to the period Naima covered in his chronicles; Naima himself lived later.

47. Ottoman rule over this province was often indirect. In such provinces, the revenues that would elsewhere have accrued to the fief-holders were collected by agents for the local treasury (Gibb and Bowen 1963, I: 143, 147).

48. The same chronicler recounts how, for instance, one Sheik Salim, while sitting in his receiving room with prominent members of the city,

> would have two men dressed as palace officers come and greet him, bringing a letter presumably from the mother of the sultan. In addition, they would present a purse of gold as a gift from the sultan himself. The sheik would pretend to read the letter and send a reply. He would often repeat this trick, receiving letters presumably from the sultan, grand vezir, or other high officials. The dumb people in his audience, judging this correspondence to be an indication of the sheik's powerful position within Ottoman administration, would give him all they owned, all they possessed. (Naima [1863] 1969, VI: 2750)

49. For instance, Mirza Pasha, the ex-governor of Musul, unable to procure another post,

> cried at all the top level officials. Yet since he did not have the means to procure gifts, no one paid any attention to him. So he could not attain a post. Not having enough money to even pay the boatmen to cross the Bosphorus, [the ex-governor] used to live on the other side of the Bosphorus. He survived by constantly selling his goods. . . . (Naima [1863] 1969, VI: 2130–31)

50. According to an imperial decree of Sultan Mustafa III (1757–74), officials, upon appointment, had to pay the following (Özkaya 1985: 183, 186–87): those appointed governor-general *(beylerbeyi)* had to give one sable fur, one fully equipped horse, 29,000 aspers in tax (and 14,500 aspers if there was a change in their appointments). Governors of small districts *(sancakbeyi)* had to pay 7,000 in tax, and 3,500 upon the change of appointment. See Gibb and Bowen (1963, I: 259) for further information on this taxation system.

51. Household members tried hard to join another household upon the death of their household head since this often connoted a drop in their chances of advancement (Naima [1863] 1969, VI: 2614).

52. In the sixteenth century, provincial notables were (Ergenç 1982: 106–7) prominent people in towns such as rich merchants, experienced artisans, and religious scholars, who acted as mediators between the sultan and the subjects in their towns. They represented the subjects and helped execute the sultan's orders. The sultan's awareness of their significance can be deduced from imperial orders, which were always addressed to the official representative of the sultan and the local notables. Such provincial notables were also significant in the Arab provinces (Schilcher 1985).

53. The "prominent men of the town" appear in most petitions and court cases as a group whose opinion is assumed by all parties to reflect the interests of the town.

54. The eighteenth-century inheritance registers of provincial notables often cite their career history in describing the deceased. Among them one can find many retired officials from the capital. For instance, the tax-farmer of Bergos, Bekir Bey, who died in 1736, was a former chief officer *(müteferrikabaşı)*.

55. The 1858 Ottoman land law transformed approximately 70 percent of the land belonging to the sultan into private property (Ortaylı 1983: 158). This had been preceded by the 1845 and 1847 laws, which had issued title deeds to the owners of those private lands. By 1868, foreigners could own and inherit land in the empire. This transformation accompanied the shift from the household to the individual as the unit of analysis in nineteenth-century Ottoman society.

56. Ottoman chronicles refer to provincial notables as extensions of office-households, specifying that the main difference between office and provincial households was geographical location (Naima [1863] 1969, VI: 2507). Yet, given the centralized nature of Ottoman rule, this difference in location quickly became coupled with one of social power.

57. There also was a correlation between civil strife and the escalation of provincial notables as a social group. For instance, the 1744–81 period contained ten incidents of banditry in one region alone (Sakaoğlu 1984: 32–34). During the seventeenth and eighteenth centuries, strife in the empire

also escalated due to demographic and social factors. Population increases in the sixteenth and seventeenth centuries fostered unemployment; the movement of tribes through Asia Minor (Özkaya 1985: 164, 171) caused unrest.

58. The wealth of the Western Anatolian notables was based on land, farms, and the produce on newly cultivated land (Nagata 1976); twenty eighteenth-century Balkan notables had a similar wealth concentration pattern, except that, in their case, urban property was the more predominant form of investment (Nagata 1979).

59. *Keyl,* a measurement of volume, varied widely throughout the Ottoman empire. In Damascus, it was about twenty-two liters, in Aleppo, six and a half liters. For further information on the term, see *İslam Ansiklopedisi.*

60. The inheritance contained, in addition to his vast property, 394,786 gold coins. His revenues included the produce of sixty farms, mainly olive trees and corn.

61. He was the *serbevvabin* of the palace. He paid the substantial sum of 200,000 piasters to keep his father-in-law's confiscated inheritance.

62. Such appointments sometimes ended up in the official's defeat in a confrontation with the bandits. In 1784, one such official, the voivode of Uşak, Amcaoğlu İbrahim (MM9741/384–5), was murdered by the bandit Çevreoğlu Ahmed, who raided and burned the voivode's house and plundered his goods.

63. In the case of office-households, although their spatial proximity to the sultan had increased their access to large resources, it had also enabled the sultan to keep a vigilant watch over them. Yet the provincial notables, distant from the capital, escaped the control of the sultan due to the limited means of communication and transportation. Their popular nomination also often secured these notables the support of the populace against the sultan.

64. The confiscated inheritance, after being turned into cash, went directly into the sultan's treasury. This practice followed the initial custom of confiscating the resources of members of the sultan's household, which were all assumed to accumulate through the sultan's beneficence and therefore reverted to the sultan at the end of the appointment.

65. The imperial order specified that the "fine goods among his inheritance were to be sent to the center, the rest would be auctioned and the cash from that auction and from his debtors would all be sent to the center as well."

66. See, for instance, those of the notable of İzmir in 1825 (MM9731: 44), the notable of Beyşehir in 1823 (MM9731: 6), the notable of Bursa in 1824 (MM9731: 43), the notable of Havza in 1825 (MM9731: 16), the notable of Pazarköy in 1824 (MM9731: 40), the notable of Koziçe in 1824 (MM9731: 10), the notable of Zağra-i Cedid in 1824 (MM9731: 7), and the notable of Babadağ in 1826 (MM9731: 17). For the fiscal use of confiscation in history, see "Musadara, the Ottoman Empire," in *EI.*

67. There is a distinction made in Islamic law between "bandits" and "rebels" in terms of intent of the group and also in terms of the punishment awaiting them (Lewis 1988: 81–82). Bandits, including such groups as brigands, highwaymen, and pirates, were defined as mere criminals, whereas rebels were regarded as the contending armed forces of rival power. Bandits could thus be fought, captured and jailed, executed, and held accountable for the damage they caused; the taxes they collected would be considered theft, thereby making taxpayers still liable. Rebels, however, were often not pursued in flight, or jailed, or obliterated, or held accountable for the damage they caused. By being identified as "bandits," provincial notables thus had harsher punishment awaiting them.

68. This wealth consisted of 8 farms, 14 mills, 7 gardens, and 1,477 acres *(dönüm)* of land. It was sold by the treasury for 20,000 piasters to vezir Ragıb Mehmed Pasha, who had executed the rebels upon the sultan's orders.

69. Sepetçioğlu had many tax-farms, which he had farmed out to people at twice their value. When the sultan ordered him to give up the tax-farms, he rebelled. Another correspondence about this "bandit" (CM30330) reveals that his inheritance consisted of vast amounts of gold and aspers, at least 1,000 gold pieces and 5,000 white-silver aspers *(beyaz akçe).*

70. The document noted that the wealth, a mere 60,000 piasters, was small because of all the "scoundrels who he gathered around him for the fights" who had squandered his resources. Still, Karaosmanzade's wealth was immense. His listed properties included an inn with 59 rooms, mills, oil manufactories, 16 cloth shops, farms, and 15,000 sheep. The 194 camels, 1,843 ox, horse, and water buffalo yielded 27,370 piasters. The yearly revenue from his property was another 20,000: the tax-farms he had in his possession also sold up to 20,000.

71. Part of his confiscated goods, some cash, and a farm that was legally his wife's property were returned to her; the rest of his goods were sold and the cash sent to the sultan. His 428,840 piasters' worth of inheritance contained arms, ammunition, and some books: 81 percent of the inheritance was in cash. The notable was indeed a rich man.

72. The wealth consisted mostly of urban property and farms: two bathhouses, three shops, four mills, nine farms, seven gardens and vineyards, and two houses. Yet almost all of his wealth went to pay his debts to people whose property he had plundered.

73. The challenge of the provincial notables against the sultan was more successful in the distant Ottoman provinces, often leading to political independence movements (Hourani 1957: 100; Rafeq 1977: 57). The Ottoman North African provinces (Hess 1977) followed a similar pattern; local elements took over the Ottoman provincial administration. The distance from Constantinople enabled these provincial notables to exercise more autonomy than did those in Asia Minor and the Balkans.

74. Bayrakdar, who took part in the revolt of the Janissaries in Edirne against the newly founded military corps, later became a firm supporter of the sultan's reforms. Ironically, he ultimately lost his life during a rebellion of the Janissaries, who, opposing such changes, attacked his residence and burned it down. For a fuller account of Bayrakdar and his reforms, see "Mustafa Pasha, Bayrakdar," in *EI,* and Lewis (1979: 74–76).

75. The other three clauses were: one, the sultan's orders would be obeyed without reservation; two, the orders of the grand vezir would have the same stature as those of the sultan and therefore be immediately obeyed; and three, revenue collection in all parts of the empire would be conducted strictly in accordance with the laws of the state.

76. For a fuller discussion of this deed, see Berkes (1964), Davison (1963), Karal (1940), Lewis (1979), and Mardin (1960).

77. See D4936, for one such household.

78. There are even instances of confiscations of the inheritances of religious dignitaries—sheik-ül-islam Asım Efendi's case is an example in point (CA654). Another example is the confiscation of Kadı Abdurrahman Paşa's inheritance in 1810 (CM21554).

79. After the destruction of the Janissaries, the sultan gave the former residence of the agha of the Janissaries as a permanent residence to the sheik-ül-islam ("Bab-ı Mashikhat," in *EI*).

80. The other Ottoman reorganization occurred in the field of diplomacy. In the late eighteenth century, the Ottoman sultan sent permanent Ottoman ambassadors abroad (Kuran 1968), specifically to the states that comprised the West: one was sent to London in 1793; another to Paris in 1797. In 1795, resident ambassadors were also assigned to Berlin (Prussia) and Vienna (Austria), leaving only Russia out of this Ottoman diplomatic network. An Ottoman embassy was established in Russia much later, in 1857. These Ottoman ambassadors supplied information to the sultan on Western matters as they frequently dispatched messengers and sent the sultan translations of Western news and journal articles. They also recruited military officers to train the Ottoman army and procured some military supplies, such as tin for the Ottoman naval arsenal. When these ambassadors and their retinues returned home, they manned the new Ottoman institutions developing after the Western model.

81. In addition, the feudal cavalry had played a significant role in earlier centuries; sappers and gunners served a similar important role in later centuries.

82. Although religious scholars also opposed the sultan, so much so that about two thousand were deported to Eastern Anatolia in the 1890s, their participation has not yet been studied in a systematic manner (Mardin 1983: 59).

83. After 1827, the Ottoman sultan also sent Ottoman students to be trained in the West, particularly in France. In 1856, forty-six students were sent to Paris and a school was established there for them the following year. The mounting expenses of this school, in contrast to the success and economy of schools established in the Ottoman empire after Western models, led to its termination in 1864.

84. Between 1800 to 1900, due to the establishment of these schools, Ottoman literacy increased from 1 percent in 1800 to 5–10 percent in 1900 (Findley 1989: 139).

85. Napoleon Bonaparte was one of the applicants (Berkes 1964: 75).

86. Bonneval was the most influential among the earlier advisors. He married an Ottoman Greek woman, learned Turkish, and adopted the Ottoman style of life. Bonneval reorganized the Ottoman bombardiers corps, established a training school for them in 1734, and founded a school of military engineering the same year. He also modernized the cannon foundry, powder mill, arsenal, and miner-artillery transport corps.

87. These new military advisors were recruited mostly from France. Among them, a Hungarian nobleman, Baron de Tott (1730–93), who also learned Turkish, was most influential. He established a new artillery corps (Levy 1982: 235–36; Berkes 1964: 59; Shaw 1977, I: 250).

88. There were estimated to be around three hundred officials and engineers.

89. For instance, in 1734, when the first Western-style military school was established, two Western books, one on trigonometry and the other on military education, were immediately translated into Ottoman.

90. The translation in 1750 of a book on modern geography was followed in 1771 by another book on modern medicine. Translation efforts picked up in the years 1786–87, when the French embassy established an Ottoman printing press to print two works, one on fortifications, the other on naval maneuvers.

91. The teaching at the school of engineering in 1769 exemplifies this process (Berkes 1964: 59).

92. In 1805, to help finance naval reforms, the sultan founded a naval treasury from the revenues of his personal lands—these resources were separated from him in return for a cash payment. Similar treasuries for different activities within the military kept being founded throughout the nineteenth century (Cezar 1986: 151–53, 204–14, 289, 309).

93. Indeed, Volnay's *Les Ruines de Palmyre* and Voltaire's *Mahomet* were among the books banned by the Ottoman sultan. In this instance, even though the French instructor saw them reading these books, he encouraged them rather than denouncing them to the administration (Sağlam [1940] 1991: 57).

94. The sultan was actually aware of the problem but could not come up with an adequate solution. When dissenting voices started to be heard at the new school for civil servants, for instance, he altered the curriculum, replacing literature, philosophy, and mathematics with religion and Muslim jurisprudence (Mardin 1983: 44). Yet what was needed instead was a reinterpretation of the latter with respect to the challenges presented by the former.

95. One also noted (Ali Kemal 1913: 16–7) how, in middle school, for instance, "rather than taking turns in front of the teacher reciting sections of the lesson," the students now had to enter the teacher's room, sit on the floor according to one's knowledge capacity, with the most knowledgeable sitting at the front, and swiftly rotate out of position upon failing to answer the teacher's question. Hence the system became more interactive and more competitive.

96. The actual Ottoman term, *Padişahım Başaşağıya,* is a variation on *Padişahım Çok Yaşa,* "Long live my sultan."

97. Beşir Fuad was a graduate of the military academy and many students noted in their memoirs that they attended his funeral, as they were "very much affected by the contempt with which he had regarded life" (Ali Kemal [1913] 1985: 72).

98. The most intriguing, often comical, synthesis between the French and Ottoman forms of knowledge that structured these boundaries is recounted by one medical student who described (Sağlam [1940] 1991: 87, 112) how one instructor, İsmail Ali Bey, often read first from the collected

poems of a famous Muslim poet, Hafız, and then switched, often in mid-sentence, to the "exalted *[hazret-i]* Corneille," whose works he would then read, in the same poetic meter, sighing, after a few stanzas, "Allah, Allah," as he appreciated the depth of meaning in the work. Another instructor referred to the inventor of the stimulus theory of medical doctrines as "imam" Broussais.

99. In 1868, the Ottoman statesman Ziya Pasha noted in a newspaper editorial that "equality was a meaningless term as long as the upper classes of İstanbul would be steeped in wealth while the paupers in Smyrna had to drown their children because they were too poor to afford any" (Mardin 1962: 359).

100. For more detailed information on these secret societies and the subsequent legal organizations they led to, see the extensive literature on the topic, including Temo [1939] 1987), Mardin (1962, 1983), Ahmad (1980), Hanioğlu (1985).

101. When there was an altercation between the students and the soldiers who wanted to punish some politically active medical students, a rebellion erupted and the students wanted to fly the British flag over the school to demonstrate their support of those European countries that defended freedom (Nur [1928] 1992: 124).

102. These writers included Namık Kemal, Ziya Pasha, and Abdülhak Hamid. Hamid wrote the stanza that many memorized by heart, "They should chain the entire palace household from one end to the other/If they want to free this fatherland (insane with sorrow) from slavery." Similarly, another famous stanza was Namık Kemal's, "If I die without seeing enlightenment I hope to see in the nation/Let it be written to my tombstone that I am grieved as is the fatherland."

103. The Committee of Union and Progress (CUP), which ruled the empire from January 1913 to its dissolution in 1918, was engaged in a struggle for power with other contenders from 1908 on.

104. The name of the minister they allegedly were going to assassinate was Zeki Pasha. These arrested students were deported on the *Honor,* and thereafter were referred to as the "Victims of Honor."

105. The society referred to Salonica, where they were based, as "the temple of freedom" *(Kabe-i Hürriyet),* and to Constantinople, the abode of the sultan, as "the Byzantine harlot" *(Kahpe Bizans).*

106. The Ottoman term used here is *verem.* Even though it certainly was contacted due to other factors, and may even have been used figuratively rather than literally, it was nevertheless important in establishing a negative institutional culture around spying.

107. Indeed, even when they were hospitalized, some "kept on distributing within the hospital the seditious documents his friends brought him during their visits"; others "got (seditious) materials out from the French post offices and distributed them at night" (Mehmed Rauf 1911: 63, 91–92).

108. The accounts take into account the inflation that was rampant in this time period. According to "Akçe," in *EI,* this currency went through many debasements from its inception in 1327 during the reign of Orhan until the eighteenth century. The effect of these debasements was that "whereas 40 *akçes* went to the first Ottoman gold piece of sultan Mehmed II [in the mid-fifteenth century], by the reign of Mustafa II (1695–1703), when a currency reform resulted in the first coining of the Ottoman *kuruş,* the rate of the gold piece (whose own weight and standard had been pretty well maintained) had risen as much as 300 *akçes.*" The value of aspers declined steadily until the end of the empire. For more information on the Ottoman currency and its transformation in the Ottoman empire, see Gibb and Bowen (1963, II: 49–59).

109. Although social scientists have often recognized the significance of education in class formation (Parkin 1979; Collins 1982), few have situated it on an equal footing with economic production because of Marx's formulation that the educational system often reproduces the existing social structure and thereby inhibits change (Bourdieu and Passeron 1977).

110. For instance, Zaalouk argues that "the nineteenth century bourgeoisie, created by the state, . . . was dependent on education rather than property, and was patronized by foreign technicians, bankers, and merchants" (1989: 1). This implied suppression of the bureaucratic bourgeoisie to the advantage of the commercial bourgeoisie only holds if education is given more social valance than property. If, however, both are seen as being of equal worth, then the process of bourgeois class

formation becomes more evident. Only then can the current ambiguities of the nature and boundaries of the state bourgeoisie be resolved (Waterbury 1991: 9).

111. For instance, one notes the absence of the political power of the commercial society without articulating who actually has that power. Ahmad states that "in the Ottoman Empire there existed people who carried out the economic functions of a bourgeoisie, but never acquired the political power and influence of that class to mould the State in its own image and interests" (Ahmad 1980: 329).

112. Others who focus on the transformation of the Ottoman state argue and explore the development of the Ottoman political bourgeoisie in the mid-nineteenth century as reforms produced the first Western-educated cohort (Mardin 1962, 1983; Ortaylı 1983; Hanioğlu 1985; Keyder 1982; Georgeon 1986) without, at the same time, exploring the emergence of the Ottoman commercial bourgeoisie, or see the latter in dependent terms (Toprak 1982).

113. By 1914, there were 178 Islamic educational institutions training 7,000 students, as opposed to 2,119 students being trained in the new Western-style schools of the sultan (Aktar 1990: 41).

114. Also, as the clothing reform thus initiated in the military was extended to the civilians, it eliminated one of the pillars of the Ottoman social stratification system (Lewis 1979: 100–3).

115. Ottoman envoys to Europe had started observing the actual structures in government and society in the late eighteenth century (Lewis 1982: 207–8). Some reform suggestions ensued quickly thereafter but took time to implement because of the vastness of the task.

116. A civil servant in the office of the imperial chancery, he explained his refusal by stating, "the type of work I will be doing is similar to the one I had been performing, I therefore cannot accept a raise. Also, I heard that the treasury of the muslims is currently facing hardships, if I get more salary I will be contributing to the damage, so my old salary is sufficient for me."

117. Indeed, he noted that they tried to convince him "this salary and product is not specific to the individual, but instead to the position, hence, by deciding to do so, he will be harming whoever would occupy this position after him."

118. The term refers to the gift from a greater to a lesser person and, as such, differs from *pişkeş,* which denotes a present from an inferior to a superior. For further information on these practices, see "Pishkash," in *EI.*

119. Ottoman literacy had risen from 2 percent in 1868 to 5 percent in 1876, a remarkable achievement in a very short period of time (Issawi, in Findley 1989: 142).

120. Similarly, in 1842, when they were invited to join the newly founded midwifery school, none of the Ottoman Jews accepted (Bozkurt 1989: 158–59).

121. Two joined the foreign ministry, one urban administration, and one worked in trade courts.

122. The idea of *bedel,* a money payment in lieu of some personal service or contribution to the state, was old practice; the poll tax that minorities had to pay was abolished with the Imperial Rescript of 1856. In return for no longer having to pay this "protection tax," the minorities had to be recruited instead into Ottoman military service. When this recruitment failed because of the structural position of minorities in the Ottoman social system, the *bedel-i askeri* was introduced in lieu of such service, thereby reverting in practice to the old taxation system. It was abolished finally in 1908. For further information on this process, see "Djizya, the Ottoman" and "Badal," in *EI,* "Bedel-i Askeri," in *İslam Ansiklopedisi,* and Lewis (1979: 337–40).

123. These attempts are thoroughly documented by Yapp, who states that "one volunteer Christian cavalry brigade was raised, principally from Poles and Bulgarians, although, later, most of the Poles returned to Poland and were replaced by Muslims. The remaining Christian regiment apparently served in Syria . . . [When] the project of recruiting trustworthy Christians was revived . . . through a commission under Ömer Pasha which recommended the recruitment of Armenians and Bulgarians, but not Christians from Bosnia or Hercegovina, or Greeks" (1975: 351–52).

124. Of the 115 deputies, 67 (58.3 percent) were Muslims and 48 (41.7 percent) minorities (Karal 1982: 395).

125. The pledge was, "I pledge to respect my sultan, my country, and the laws of the Constitution and to perform no actions which might oppose them" (Karal 1982: 395).

126. As one scholar notes, the Western missionaries who established such schools throughout the empire "contributed to the development of a bourgeois stratum among the Christians of the empire. The schools the Protestants established in Anatolia and the Balkans became a training ground for new generations of more secular minded individuals who redefined the communal basis of orthodoxy" (Augustinos 1992: 121).

Chapter 3

1. The Ottoman expression used in this case was that the Europeans' "mold became too tight for their stature" *(kalıbları dar gelmeye başladı)*.

2. The Ottoman expression is *el hükmü lemen galebe kuvvetile*.

3. In a 1805 Ottoman report on paper production in Europe, Ottoman officials indicated how the Europeans regarded their economic policy seriously enough to develop protectionist measures around it and to wage war for its preservation (Genç 1990: 16).

4. Richards and Waterbury (1990: 47) make a similar argument for the contemporary political economy of the Middle East. They contend that contact with the West and increasing European involvement in the Middle East generated new class actors and strata, "a new merchant bourgeoisie from middlemen and foreigners." They add that "entrepreneurial functions were carried out by combinations of large foreign interests, nonnational intermediaries such as the Armenians, Jews, and Syro-Lebanese in Egypt, or by outright foreigners like the Greeks in Egypt" (1990: 402).

5. The change in pace of the Ottoman economy during this period is better appreciated if one cites the rates of growth in Ottoman–European trade during the period 1730–1873, which "expanded about half to approximately 3 million pounds between 1730–80, increased roughly eighty to ninety percent between 1780–1830, and the volume kept doubling every 11–13 years until the 1870's. Total value of the trade had surpassed 15 million pounds in 1850, and had reached 30 million pounds by the early 1870's" (Pamuk 1987: 29–30). Hence, Ottoman trade with Europe expanded tenfold in a century, and the Ottoman sultan lost control over this trade to the West. However, world trade patterns also increased during this period: it increased by 30 percent, from 300 million to 400 million pounds between 1800 and 1830, multiplied fivefold between 1840 and 1870, and passed 2,800 million pounds in the 1870s (Kasaba 1988: 44). Ottoman currency depreciated immensely during the same period; the rate of exchange of the Ottoman piaster vis-à-vis the pound sterling fell by approximately 20 percent between 1798 and 1803, and fell by another 50 percent between 1825 and 1834.

6. They had done so because Ottoman economic policy was based on provision (McGowan 1981: 11). The three traditional sectors of the Ottoman economy, namely, commerce, agriculture, and crafts (Masters 1988: 200), were all controlled by the state to guarantee the provisioning of the empire. The Ottoman sultan often used his bargaining power not to limit imports but to control and tax exports. Hence, what shaped Ottoman economic policy was "provisionism, namely, a consumer-oriented outlook to provide, to supply; traditionalism, that is, maintaining the status quo; and fiscalism, that is, maximizing state revenues" (Genç 1990: 14, 18).

7. This decrease was due to a number of economic factors that affected the entire Middle East (Issawi 1970: 266). The Middle Eastern region's productive power in agriculture and handicrafts had declined, and alternate sources of supply in the new colonies had also reduced Western demand for Middle Eastern products. The Middle East lost its control over trade in the Mediterranean and the Indian Ocean to the Europeans, and the spice trade dropped as a consequence. Yet, this decline in Middle Eastern trade with the West was mostly a decline in value as a crossroads trade. The Middle Eastern trade itself was not reduced to insignificance: the sheer size of the Ottoman empire guaranteed surplus production and exchange (Braudel 1984: 468–69).

8. In the eighteenth century, Ottoman trade goods consisted of silk, copper, animal hides,

boxwood, wax, furs, animal hair, wool, cotton, and deer horns (Özkaya 1985: 133). Ottoman exports to the West from Constantinople in 1750 consisted of buffalo hides, black ox hides, morocco, shagreen, goat's hair, camel hair, and wax; fine camlets, silk, and goat's hair processed for wigs were added later in the century (Braudel 1984: 471). Raw silk, mohair, carpets, raisins, raw cotton, rice, figs, lumber, dyes, olive oil, zinc, salt, and acorn were Ottoman exports from the port of Smyrna (Özkaya 1985: 144).

9. These were, specifically, textiles, mirrors, panes of glass, paper, pewter, sugar, brasil-wood and campeachy wood, English ales, mercury, drugs and spice, Indian indigo, and coffee. The new import items added and increased in quantity were cloth, silks, cottons from France, England, and Holland, steel, lead, furs, calicoes and indigo from St. Domingo, and coffee, Western imports from the French, English, and the Dutch arriving at the port of Smyrna were textiles, woolen cloth, tin cans, coffee, clocks and watches, glass, silver goods, ceramic ware, and lead (Özkaya 1985: 144). The French, in addition, exported lumber and headgear (purchased by foreign residents and minorities), and the English exported gloves, sugar, liquor, picture frames, paintings, wigs, firearms, and spices.

10. After 1580 (Davis 1970: 194), English traders traded with the Ottoman empire to find a way into Eastern markets and to secure themselves a share of the import to Europe of the roots and raw material for pharmaceutical use, pepper, spices, and Sumatran dyestuffs. By the seventeenth century, the volume of English woolen broadcloth sold at Ottoman ports equaled that of Venetian cloth.

11. In 1740, 700 French trade ships were engaged in trade with the Ottomans, as opposed to 10 English trade ships (Özkaya 1985: 127). By 1756, 60 percent of the European boats departing from Smyrna were French (Panzac 1980: 159). Their cargo consisted of Persian silk, angora wool, and Anatolian linen; wheat, oil, and cotton products were also of increasing importance.

12. The French had established many consulates at Ottoman ports, and these consulates actively interacted with Ottoman townsmen and tradesmen. By the end of the eighteenth century, the French had also established firms, trade centers in some of the ports: four in Alexandria, nine in Salonica, eleven in Constantinople, and twenty-nine in Smyrna (Özkaya 1985: 132).

13. Student vice consuls trained for six years, and recruitment of students was also regularized (Masson 1911: 181).

14. In 1774, of the 323,470 *livres* spent by the Marseille chamber, 277,000 went as salaries to consuls (Masson 1911: 66).

15. The Ottoman minorities had always retained their ties with their compatriots. For instance, during the second half of the eighteenth century, the Ottoman minorities in Constantinople had utilized their social networks with their coreligionists in many European cities and had drawn up bills of exchange with them. Specifically, "thirty percent of the drawees of the bills of exchange of Ottoman Greeks, Jews and Armenians were established in European cities such as Amsterdam, Leghorn or Vienna" (Eldem 1990: 589).

16. The Greeks did suffer a setback during the Greek War of Independence, 1821–28. The Ottoman Greeks participated in this war not as a community but as individuals fighting for their motherland (Frangakis-Syrett 1991b: 401). One can argue that the prosperity of the trade facilitated the success of nationhood. Kemal Karpat (1973) claims, for instance, that non-Muslim Ottoman intermediaries channeled the wealth they accumulated through the commercial expansion in the eighteenth century to the secessionist movements in the nineteenth century. Yet, as Clogg (1981) points out, more documentation is necessary to substantiate this connection between wealth and political activism.

17. For further discussion on this point, see, for instance, Lewis (1982: 107–9), who states that whereas Ottoman Muslims had preferred Jews, not often suspected of complicity with Western powers, for significant tasks, these Ottoman Jews lost their skills and contacts as they ceased to come from Europe and as Christian Europeans gained ascendancy in Mediterranean trade. Gibb and Bowen also assert that the commercial activities of Syrian Christians and Armenians expanded at the expense of the "other confessions, especially Jews, who were suddenly ousted by the European use

of legal protection favoring Christians" (1963, I: 310–11). Raymond also adds, in the case of Egypt, that "the Syrian Catholic community supplanted the Jews around the 1770s" (1974).

18. See Göçek (1987) for a fuller account of the Ottoman attempts and subsequent failure to counter Western expansion.

19. Municipal officials set a fixed price, purchased basic food staples, and stored them in the cities. This measure prevented food riots in the cities.

20. This penetration of the office-households into the Janissary corps changed the nature of the corps as the Janissaries became more and more involved in the political competition among the office-households over the allocation of offices.

21. The wealth of Janissaries was inherited by their kin, or, when there were no kin, by the Janissary corps (A427/38; A219/77; MM10232/11; B147/40; HH14109).

22. In Aleppo, for instance, tensions between the guilds and the Janissaries escalated as the Janissaries attempted to enter the trades without guild permission (Masters 1988: 46–47).

23. In the eighteenth century, there were 40,000 Janissaries in Constantinople, and throughout the empire 160,000 men were, or claimed to be, Janissaries. This large number also supports the contention that the Janissaries expanded into the ranks of the artisans. For more information, see "İstanbul," in *EI*.

24. Some such artisans in this military category were the skullcapper *(takkeci)* Mesut Agha, who died in 1796 (A679/31), stone-maker Hüseyin beşe son of Mehmed (A715/48), who died in 1799, and stone-maker Abdullah Ağa (A802/84), who died in 1805. All of the wealth of these artisans was concentrated in their raw material, products, and shops—it did not extend beyond the workplace. Most artisans' wealth was constrained to their job and profession. The heirs of these artisans often did not keep the goods or maintain partnership but received the cash equivalent instead.

25. He presumably had wealth over 200,000 piasters. The account then informs us that "his valuable goods were stolen, and, eventually, only 40,000 piasters including his documented loans to thirty people were recovered."

26. The liquid assets of the usurers and merchants also made this confiscation easier than those of the artisans, which were mostly goods or tools that could not be easily converted into cash.

27. Thus, technically, one can argue that the sultan was not confiscating their wealth but forcing a loan out of the heirs.

28. Muslim males, totaling 73,496, comprised 39 percent of the tax-paying population; there were also approximately 100,000 tax-exempt officials and their households in the capital. The actual minority figures were 54,500 Ottoman Greek males, 48,099 Ottoman Armenian males and 11,413 Ottoman Jewish males. Women, children, and students were not included in these figures. For further information, see "İstanbul," in *EI*.

29. Western travelers often commented on the interaction between minorities and foreign residents. One such traveler, for instance, noted that "all the Frankish merchants, i.e., French, British, Dutch, Venetians, Genoese, and others, live in Galata because of the residence of their ambassadors and because their ships land there. Galata also has a large population of Turks, Greeks, Armenians and Jews who have their own churches and synagogues" (in Davison 1982: 322).

30. In mid-seventeenth-century Galata, where the foreign residents lived, of the ninety-three districts, seventy were Greek, three Frankish, two Armenian, one Jewish, and seventeen Muslim. Hence the Ottoman Greeks held the population majority in this small but commercially significant district.

31. For further information on this practice, see "Beratlı," in *EI*.

32. Minorities had always traded with the West, but the West had not been powerful enough in the previous centuries to penetrate Ottoman society at large and to offer protection to minorities.

33. See (Göçek 1992) for a detailed analysis of Ottoman minority artisans, who, like all Ottoman artisans, failed to escape the sultan's control.

34. This was the term used to denote Ottoman Greeks residing in the quarter of Phanar, who

had monopolized the positions of dragomanship at the Sublime Porte, were often interpreters in foreign embassies, and often represented the Ottoman state in Europe and the Balkans.

35. His ability to do so as an official's son demonstrates how significant social position was in determining the boundaries of one's ties in society.

36. D'Ohsson's son followed him in the field of diplomacy to become a diplomat for the Swedes. After his education in Paris, Vienna, and Sweden, this son became a Swedish embassy secretary in Madrid and Paris. In 1835, he was made Swedish ambassador to Berlin. His career path indicates how fluid social boundaries were across states before the advent of nationalism: the son of an Ottoman subject represented Sweden in Europe.

37. In his memorandum, d'Ohsson suggested the foundation of a school of military sciences and outlined the courses, teachers, and schedule of the school. Such a school was indeed established in 1795, following his blueprint.

38. Specifically, it was the Swedish demand for money from the Ottoman empire and his support of the French revolutionaries in Constantinople against the royalists that put him at odds with the Ottomans.

39. He had accounts with the sultan's treasury, and this fact was used to justify the confiscation. He tried to evade confiscation by purchasing urban property under the names of his relatives rather than his own. His real estate investment was vast: it included two inns, eight houses, seventeen shops, six rooms, two ports, twelve vegetable gardens, and five plots of land.

40. He had not invested his wealth in property but kept it mostly in cash. His partner Abraham alone owed him 197,000 aspers. When all the money lent out to creditors was collected, his inheritance was determined (see D9976) at 4,476,481 aspers—a vast amount.

41. The Ottoman state often intervened on their behalf to guarantee their proper treatment in trade.

42. For example, Ottoman Armenians established themselves in Livorno in 1553, in Amsterdam in 1661–65 and 1701–5, and in Marseilles in 1612 (Frangakis-Syrett 1985: 32).

43. One study in particular (Masters 1988) demonstrates this eighteenth-century transition through a case study of the Muslin merchants of Aleppo, who switched, out of necessity, from being competitors in transit trade to sellers of locally produced agricultural products to the Europeans.

44. For further information on this treaty and its impact on the Ottoman empire, see "Küçük Kaynardja," in *EI*, and "Küçük Kaynarca," in *İslam Ansiklopedisi*.

45. This limitation by the sultan may have been due to the observation that Muslim merchants, who had more potential access to societal resources, could be more challenging to the sultan than minority merchants.

46. Indeed, many such confiscated inheritance registers of merchants appeared throughout the eighteenth and nineteenth centuries. For example, merchant Kara Mustafa of Candia in 1793 (MM9722/24–25), cloth merchant İbrahim Efendi of Constantinople in 1810 (MM9726/326–7), merchant Abdülaziz Ağa, who was also a money-changer, in 1809 (MM9755/189, 156–57, 174), and merchant Osman of Salonica in 1810 (MM9926/16) had all died leaving behind large fortunes that were all confiscated by the sultan. Yet the sultan could not engage in such a practice with minority merchants once they entered under foreign protection.

47. Eventually, in order to repatriate these former Ottoman subjects, the Ottoman sultan decreed in edicts in 1850, 1860, and 1863 that those claiming foreign citizenship ought to move to another country and forgo their inheritance rights from their Ottoman relatives, but to no avail (Bozkurt 1989: 145–46).

48. Ottoman provinces also witnessed a similar development in minority–West relations. The economic and social resources of minorities rose as a consequence (Hourani 1957: 103–5).

49. Their emigrations to Livorno, the center of Levant trade, and to Egypt to escape the persecution by the Orthodox on the Greek Catholics in Damascus and Aleppo, also helped expand their trade with Europe.

50. For a fuller discussion of this model, the regression, and its implications, see Göçek (1994).

51. For a thorough discussion of these earlier contacts between the Muslim world and Europe, see Lewis (1982), especially chapters 7, 9, and 10.

52. Once, when the sultan's Greek dragoman requested, on December 1733, two chairs for the kiosk of the Ottoman sultan, who "liked to sit in European fashion," the *bailo* took the dragoman into the best room in the embassy and let him select two chairs. These chairs with decorated frames were upholstered in velvet—the dragoman asked the *bailo* to have "some gold decoration and fringe put upon them." These chairs were then sent to the sultan's palace as gifts from the *bailo* (Shay 1944: 55). In the other instance, he sent two mirrors to the sultan's sons during their convalescence after their circumcisions.

53. They presented children's coffee-and-chocolate sets and opera glasses to the newly circumcised sultan's sons (Shay 1944: 45, 47, 48, 55).

54. Between 1726 and 1730, the grand vezir received 150 robes and the grand admiral a telescope. The grand admiral, for his building on the Bosphorus, also desired one thousand large pieces of glass and two thousand of average size.

55. In 1673, for example, when the French ambassador had an amateur theater group give performances in the embassy, the audience consisted of foreign residents and Ottoman minorities. When a new theater was built in the same embassy for ballet and theatrical performances in 1676, the audience now included some Ottoman officials (Renda 1977: 16–18; 1983: 15). In the eighteenth century, the Ottomans who had started to participate in these embassy functions became exposed to these Western forms (Tott [1785] 1973: 10–13). For a detailed discussion of the development of Ottoman theater, see And (1992).

56. The adoption of Western-style dress was one such instance. For example, upon his return from a visit to Paris, d'Ohsson started wearing "French-style costumes" in Constantinople (Beydilli 1983: 260).

57. Baron de Tott, a military advisor, married an Ottoman Greek woman himself and recounted the many visits he made to the houses of Ottoman officials as a consequence.

58. The advent of the water-frame machine and the mill cut production costs and reduced prices for English textiles to well below those of the Ottomans', and English textiles fully penetrated Ottoman domestic markets in the late nineteenth century (İnalcık 1979: 44–45).

59. The document refers to this official by his title, not his name; he is listed as Silahdar Ağa.

60. For example, in 1780, valuable swords, daggers, ring, gold watches, and many fur coats were sent directly to the sultan's treasury from the confiscated inheritance of the commander of Belgrade, İzzed Pasha (D4671).

61. One example is the 1798 inheritance register of the governor of Erzurum, Abdi Pasha (D694/677).

62. For example, the 1809 inheritance register of the head chamberlain *(kapucubaşı)* at the sultan's palace (D2277) contains a list of all the goods auctioned at this market and the names of those who purchased the auctioned goods. The officials at the treasury, the head physician, and the head eunuch of the Ottoman palace all purchased valuable goods from this inheritance.

63. The 1739 inheritance record drawn up after the death of the commander of Kefe, Mehmed Pasha (MM10338/315), indicates, for example, that he had sent his steward to Constantinople to purchase Western textiles for his household members. The steward had purchased large volumes of European broadcloth and satin cloth from the Frankish merchant Davidoci. Similarly, another governor, Cezzar Ahmed Pasha (CD7718), sent a couple of his household members to Constantinople in 1803 to procure many items, including textiles, Persian and Arabic dictionaries, ink, and paper. These goods were put in two saddlebags and given to his household members to transport. The expense register (KK791) of another vezir who held office in Belgrade in the period 1786–87 reveals that he had sent for textiles from Constantinople to clothe sixty to seventy members of his household. Many luxury items and Western goods such as watches and eyeglasses were present in the inheritance registers of tax-farmer Mehmed Efendi from an island in the Aegean (CM15918) in 1795 and of the governor of Jiddah Yusuf Pasha (MM9725/257-59) in 1800.

64. For studies based on Ottoman inheritance registers, see, for example, İnalcık (1953–54),

Fekete (1965), Barkan (1966), Mandeville (1966), Cohen (1971, 1973, 1984), Bakhit (1972), Cezar (1977), Jennings (1978), Veinstein (1981), Tucker (1981), Rafeq (1994).

65. In social science analysis, probate inventories have been used for a number of purposes (Schuurman 1980: 19–21), ranging from the study of wealth, wealth composition, forms of credit, and securities to consumer goods, consumption patterns, life style, material culture, to agricultural history entailing mechanization of agriculture, yield ratios, numbers of livestock, development of agricultural implements, economic activity of artisans, to women's history and their environment, history of the family, economic growth research, and the study of modernization, proto-industria- lization. With some exceptions, the origins of all inheritance registers (Woude and Schuurman 1980) in Europe can be traced to the period between the sixteenth and eighteenth centuries. This temporal location may have resulted from the general level of material culture, or the changing attitude of people toward the possession of material goods, or the changing structure of the family and inheritance during that period. The rise of a centralized government and, with it, a bureau- cracy, may also account for it. The rise of the general level of material wealth after the eighteenth century with the advent of individualization and mass manufacture may account for their disap- pearance; the relative value of goods decreased, and the drawing up of inheritance registers be- came very laborious.

66. The great bulk of what has been written throughout history has been by and for elites. Literacy among nonelites has been commonplace only for a few hundred years in the West, and literate common people have infrequently left any record of their actions, relationships, or attitudes (Roy 1984: 488). Inheritance registers balance historical accounts centering on the elite by providing material on the ordinary people. This new historical perspective has aided recent research on inheritance registers ranging from the peasant classes under the Habsburgs in the seventeenth century (Rebel 1983), to essays on popular culture in eighteenth-century Paris (Roche 1981), to the study of wills and wealth in medieval Genoa (Epstein 1984), to the study of society and economy in colonial Connecticut in the seventeenth and eighteenth centuries (Main 1985).

67. Inheritances maintain any separation of ownership and accentuate inequalities in the distribution of wealth and, through it, of social class, rank, and power (Rheinstein 1955: 4).

68. The extent of the use of the rules laid down in the Qur'an varies in practice (Schacht, 1964: 76): its hold is strongest on the law of family, inheritance, and religious endowments and weakest on penal law, taxation, constitutional law, and the law of war, with the law of contracts and obligations standing in the middle.

69. Wills are to be made with two witnesses when death draws unto them (Maide V: 106).

70. You "give unto orphans their wealth. Exchange not the goods for the bad in your marriage and thereof nor absorb their wealth into your own wealth—that would be a great sin" (Nisa IV: 2).

71. The section states, "give unto the women you marry free gift of their marriage portions" (Nisa IV: 4); it thus guarantees that women get their marriage portions back from the inheritance of their husbands.

72. Schacht states that the religious foundation was "construed as the withdrawal from circu- lation of the substance of a property owned by the founder where the spending of the proceeds only occurred for a charitable purpose" (1964: 125, 169). The legal issue of who becomes the owner of the substance remains unresolved in this formulation.

73. For example, according to Ottoman practice, creditors had to legally prove the debts the deceased owed them before being paid; they had to present a voucher or two witnesses. The wills the deceased made to his heirs, or wills made specifically to leave out certain heirs, were not considered valid. Wills could be made to a child still in the womb, to slaves, and to religious minorities—yet no inheritance could be partitioned among these parties. If there were no heirs but a will, the inheritance was given to the person specified by the will. If there was no will or some portion remained after the execution of the will, the inheritance reverted to the public treasury. If there were orphans involved in the inheritance as heirs, the state appointed a guardian over them to protect their share (Barkan 1966: 19–23). If upon the death, no heirs of the deceased emerged to claim their shares, the inheritance was given to the public treasury, where it was kept for a specified amount of time to be

reclaimed. If no such reclamation occurred, the public treasury retained the inheritance—as a 1760 case (MM9982/132) exemplified.

Two problems in application concerned the inheritance process of properties that formed a part of religious endowments and of fiefs. Properties belonging to religious endowments were distributed *equally* between male and female children—as opposed to the distribution of individual properties, where the male got twice the share of the female (B27/29). This may have provided an added incentive to establish religious endowments if one wanted to leave more to one's female heirs. In the case of fiefs, when the fief-holder died, the fief would be distributed to someone else—yet the produce in the cellars and movable goods belonged to the heirs (MM10211/41).

74. The extent of the judge's power and jurisdiction extended beyond matters of personal status such as marriage, divorce, inheritance, and child custody to include supervising and registering economic transactions, overseeing all religious institutions, including endowments, overseeing trade, fixing prices of goods and transportation costs, controlling weights and measures, supervising the currency, adjudicating criminal and civil cases, overseeing poll tax payments, endorsing heads of guilds, and approving construction of new buildings and renovations (Uzunçarşılı 1984b: 134; Doumani 1985: 156–57). Hence, the judge at once performed the functions of a legal executor, notary, and state official; he had to approve almost all societal transactions (Bayındır 1984).

75. The judges and religious court did not have separate work quarters; they operated out of the house of the judge.

76. See appendix in this book for one such register.

77. The division of shares into fractions in accordance with the Islamic law of inheritance became complex when some of the heirs died while the inheritance was still being drawn up. In 1765, for example, upon the immediate death of four of the heirs (perhaps because of a plague), the inheritance of Mehmed the fruit-seller (B25/234) was divided and redivided so many times that the denominator had become 61,440 for one share. Similarly, the 1803 inheritance of another Mehmed, the meat-seller (B80/19), was apportioned into shares of 1 in 1,152 upon the death of one of the heirs.

78. The idea that an institution, i.e., the Janissary corps, could inherit was highly unusual in Islamic legal practice. This practice may have resulted from the legal interpretation that qualifies the religious foundation, for instance, as an heir to an inheritance because it institutionally "withdraws from circulation of the substance of a property owned by the founder where the spending of the proceeds only occurs for a charitable purpose" (Schacht 1964: 125, 169). The same reasoning may apply to the Janissary corps, which also had ties with the religious Bektaşi order.

79. There were only two military judges, one overseeing the region of Rumelia, including Constantinople, and the other overseeing Anatolia, including Iraq, Syria, and Egypt. In addition to their daily salaries, these judges also took duties from their judicial transactions; these duties added up to from 8,000 aspers *(gurush)* a day for the military judge of Rumelia to 15,000 aspers a day for the military judge of Anatolia (Uzunçarşılı 1984b: 154–58).

80. In each judicial district, the local judge often executed military inheritances and saved the duties from them for the military inheritance partitioner; inspectors sent from Constantinople periodically collected these duties (Uzunçarşılı 1984b: 121–24, 230).

81. Court duties were fixed by imperial decree. The duty for each inheritance execution was fifteen for every thousand in the sixteenth and seventeenth centuries and twenty-five in the eighteenth (Uzunçarşılı 1984b: 136–37).

82. The judges broke these rules by

> farming out your judicial district to deputy-judges who would roam the villages, count and register the number of new graves; they would then go to the household asking when these people had died, what happened to their inheritance and why it was not reported, and how could the burial take place without permission. They would also not permit religious minorities to bury their dead without taking some money. And they would by force register the inheritance, even if all heirs were present and no one had asked the court to draw up the inheritance. When recording the inheritance, they would overvalue a 200 silver coin good as being worth a 1,000 (to increase their

proportional inheritance duties), would confiscate some goods in return for their services and would redraw the inheritance register by claiming that the distribution was unfair and that heirs had hidden goods away. They would thus apportion the inheritance over and over two or three times and reduce it so much so that the goods of the heirs were not even be sufficient to cover the duties accrued for the judge. (Mühimme 78/899)

83. Throughout the sixteenth and seventeenth centuries, many imperial decrees carefully spelled out (Uzunçarşılı 1984a: 240; 1984b: 123) who were subjects and who were not so as to reduce the emerging conflict over inheritance.

84. First, the population of inheritance registers listed for the years 1705 to 1809 was drawn out. Then, this population was classified in ascending twenty-year clusters. A random number aided the selection of the samples.

85. The confiscation system helped the Ottoman sultan to regain control over resources and to redistribute the resources contained in the inheritance. The Ottoman confiscation system originated in the emergence of the sultan's household. Ottoman officials were initially trained at the palace and then appointed to administrative posts by the sultan. Upon their death, their wealth reverted to the sultan through confiscation; the sultan who bestowed wealth thus took it away. Even when officials reduced their patronage ties with the sultan in the eighteenth century, the practice of confiscation continued and was legitimated by precedence. The inheritances of officials were confiscated either upon or before death, when there was a misuse of office. It is from among these confiscated inheritances that the sample of fifty-three is drawn.

86. See, for example, the inheritance register of Ali Ağa in 1763, which spreads, within MM9991, to pages 185, 190, 332, and 594–97.

87. Because the age of the deceased is unknown (although one can make an estimate from the number of heirs and their marital status) the acquisition pattern of the individual during his life cannot be estimated.

88. The wealth of the husband and wife are often separated in Ottoman society. It is therefore difficult to generalize the information about the deceased to his or her entire household.

89. The theoretical grounding of the Western goods penetration into pattern Ottoman society derives from diffusion theory and the early works of Gabriel Tarde (1969: 185–87). The theory states that imitation precedes from outer to inner man; people imitate one another by copying luxury before they become possessed of its tastes and literature, its aims and ideas, in a word, its spirit. Imitation of ends precedes the imitation of means. Contemporary research on the diffusion of innovations has improved these early generalizations. Woude and Schuurman state that "higher wealth groups, social groups and inhabitants of cities adopt new goods more readily than the lower wealth classes, the lower social classes, and rural inhabitants" (1979: 28).

90. One drawback of the analysis is the number of observations contained in each category. The total number of observations, 124, is a small sample for quantitative analysis. Yet it is nevertheless a sufficient stratified sample for historical research where data is limited by the availability of documents, time, and human power for collecting data. The number of observations is presented in each case to mitigate the bias that may result from relying on percentages and proportions.

91. The general form of a logit model is:

$$\log \frac{p}{1-p} = \text{CONSTANT} + \beta_1{}^*[\text{YEAR}] + \beta_2{}^*[\text{DUMMY VARIABLE FOR SOCIAL GROUP}] + \beta_3{}^*[\text{INTERACTION}]$$

When social group is broken down as dummies for Elite, Military, and Populace, and the groups are treated separately because samples are different from one another, the fitted equation is:

$$\text{Logit (Probability of Western Goods Present)} = a + \beta_1 (\text{Year}) + \beta_2 (\text{Social Group}) + \beta_3 (\text{Year} * \text{Social Group}) + e$$

The coefficient β_3 has three components: β_3 stands for the interaction between Year and top-level Officials; β_3' stands for the interaction between Year and Military; and β_3'' stands for interaction between Year and Populace.

92. In the second regression, the equation for "Elite" was:

$$X = .4798 + .0004116* (YEAR-1700), \text{ where}$$

$$p\,(\text{Western}) = \frac{e^x}{1 + e^x} = \frac{1}{e^{-x} - 1}$$

The equation for "Subjects" was:

$$X = -1.7972 + .0132116* (YEAR-1700),$$

where p(Western) was same as above. Note that the interaction term has been incorporated into each equation.

93. The absence of Western goods from some registers may be due to the partial nature of some registers, which only list properties, livestock, and debts of the deceased—at least these are the only portions of the registers that have survived.

94. Of the fifty-nine inheritances that contained Western goods, the values of only forty were known, and nineteen missing observations were all in the social group of officials (maybe due to confiscations). The average value of Western goods per inheritance was 39,571 aspers, and the average value of total goods per inheritance was 1,246,764; the average proportional value of Western goods was 3.2 percent in the inheritances.

95. For a detailed discussion of clocks, watches, binoculars, and other items of Western material culture diffusing into Ottoman society, see Göçek (1987), especially chapters 6 and 7. On clocks and watches, see also Davis (1984), Kurz (1975), Landes (1983), and Cipolla (1967). Although there were local productions of textiles, glassware, firearms, clocks, and watches (Kütükoğlu 1983), they varied greatly in quality.

96. The two dimensions of the growth of capitalism as an economic system and the bourgeoisie as its principal class were, in its Western historical formulation, the free accumulation of capital and the emancipation of labor from restrictions (Dobb 1947: 161, 185).

97. This is what makes the argument of Adam Smith that labor was the source of wealth, and that of John Locke, that labor was the true source of property, so powerful. Wealth, which had always been perceived as something derived from inheritance or conquest, was now regarded as a product of labor. Labor was no longer associated with poverty and the need to work. Two opposing views of labor emerged, that of the mercantilists, who emphasized industry as the site of productive work, and that of the physiocrats, for whom agricultural work was the only authentically productive type (Kaplan and Koepp 1986: 15–17).

98. Artisans became transformed into workers when skill became redefined and alienated from the artisan; industrial work, once formed, meant both mechanized factory work, domestic labor, the putting out system, and centralized manufactories (Bruland 1989: 157). This was also the case in transitional societies, such as the Russian empire (Bonnell 1983: 6).

99. Dehumanization of the productive citizen also set in at the same time, as workers "become docile automatons . . . portrayed as appendages to technology" (Sewell 1986: 276–77). The fuller quotation upon which this statement is drawn elucidates how the illustrations of the mechanical arts in the plates of Diderot's *Encyclopédie* "represent a scientized, individualized, utopian projection of the world of work as imagined by the philosophes. It is not an attractive vision . . . it is cold, analytical, and deadly serious. . . . Workers are docile automatons . . . portrayed as appendages to technology." A concomitant observation on the *Encyclopédie* contends (Koepp 1986: 232) that henceforth the alphabetical order starts to structure nature and society, instead of the tripartite division of history, philosophy, and poetry. Ironically, this Cartesian transformation was also accom-

panied by an optimism whereby it was believed that greater productivity would automatically lead to social happiness (Rabinbach 1986: 498).

100. The bourgeoisie formed into a class through acquiring the social vision of "leading humanity out of the darkness of their past" (Hobsbawm 1989: 23–24).

101. Another assumption that is less crucial for our purpose here, but nevertheless an important one, is that in form the bourgeoisie in non-Western contexts is often expected to replicate the Western one. This also is erroneous. The cosmopolitan bourgeoisie that was briefly created during the mid-nineteenth century in locations such as Buenos Aires and India (Jones 1987: 1–2) could not sustain itself as larger-scale business organization, managerial authority, and rapprochement with the state rendered it powerless. The belated development of the commercial capitalism that accompanied export agriculture left a very limited space for the formation, in its stead, of a local merchant bourgeoisie (Amin 1976: 338). Also, the collaboration of the large landowners and merchants in the production and export of agricultural goods obstructed the development of an industrial bourgeoisie (Allahar 1990: 226–27). The bourgeoisie in non-Western contexts was therefore dominated by merchants and not manufacturers and by a national bourgeoisie actively nurtured and sponsored by the state.

102. Of course, one can even argue that it did not even hold in the Western European context. More analysis needs to be conducted on this perspective to depict how Western divisions across race, religion, ethnicity, and gender affected class formation.

103. One can argue that the formation of the bureaucratic bourgeoisie from the Ottoman household structure was more of an example of change from within. Yet, this distinction is merely analytical. Empirically, as this book has attempted to demonstrate, "internal" and "external" elements of structure, agency, and historical conjuncture interact in creating both the Ottoman bureaucratic and the Ottoman commercial bourgeoisie.

104. Also, one scholar argues, the minorities did not invest this money in proto-industry because "many more attractive options, such as real estate, tax farming, religious foundations, trade and moneylending, existed for returning profits to investors" (Masters 1988: 147). Yet these attractive options were often contingent on the investor's religion. Another scholar's argument that the minorities "did not support the Ottoman state because it was economic disorder that helped them rise to power" (Kasaba 1988: 58–59) overlooks the eventual need for protection that the bourgeoisie needs to develop.

105. In Parkin's analysis, communal divisions are no longer "inherent attributes of the social system that tend to be residual and anachronistic in nature" (1974: 2–3) but the product of historically specific actors. Hence, all elements of class become historically constructed.

106. British exports to the Ottoman empire rose from 153,903 English pounds in 1814 to 2,515,821 pounds in 1850, an approximately fifteenfold increase (Owen 1981: 83–85).

107. For instance, Ahmed Lütfi noted that "with that treaty, even though the trade monopoly system was abolished, it was replaced by foreign monopoly . . . the foreigners participated in everything. They gradually pulled trade and commerce away [from the Ottomans]" ([1875] 1991, V: 112). Namık Kemal and Ziya Pasha also wrote in 1868 on the negative influence of the trade privileges given to the Europeans (cited in Önsoy 1988: 30).

108. This view has recently been challenged by one scholar (Pamuk 1987: 11–18), who argued that rather than singling out this one instance, one ought to look at the peripheralization of the Ottoman empire within the world economic system as a gradual process extending throughout the nineteenth century.

109. There was also substantial resistance to the trade treaty, mostly from Ottoman customs officials, who were also tax-farmers. For instance, in Smyrna, "in direct contravention to the newly applied treaty, [Ottoman] customs officials tried to impose extra dues on goods, did not release goods from customs until they were paid, forbade their circulation in the interior, or imposed additional taxes on the Ottoman purchases of these goods" (Frangakis-Syrett 1992: 93). Ottoman officials also resisted by "announcing a temporary prohibition on the export of a produce, claiming this to be an order of the government. Foreign merchants often attributed the zeal and promptness in

executing the order to the local authority's desire to drive incoming merchants out of the market so that local Ottoman Muslim merchants, who were also some of the local officials, could buy large quantities of wheat at low prices for speculation" (Frangakis-Syrett 1992: 103).

110. By the twentieth century, increased Habsburg influence led the Ottoman empire to enter World War I on the side of the Germans. This alliance was the end result of a long process of German penetration (Ortaylı 1981: 5, 32, 47, 52, 64). For instance, the Ottoman army started to employ German military officers, who, even though carrying Ottoman uniforms and ranks, maintained their advancement within the German military system. These were soon joined by civil administrators and educators. In 1850, Protestants were recognized as a minority group within the Ottoman empire. German engineers and professionals came to build the Baghdad railroad system in 1888. The German emperor Wilhelm II traveled twice to the Holy Lands and symbolically announced his commitment to protect the Muslims of the world. By the end of 1898, Germans had established more than 120 firms in Constantinople.

111. Those among them who accumulated enough capital to lend the Ottoman state were A. Baltazzi, Christaki Zographos, J. Camondo, and G. Zarifi (Eldem 1970: 229–30).

112. Banking in the empire was also established mainly as institutions through which to finance Ottoman state loans. The Ottoman state established the Istanbul Bank in 1847 with the bankers Alleon and Baltazzi with the latent function of lending 130 million piasters to the state and was abolished in 1852. The Ottoman Bank was established in 1856 with mostly British capital to finance the Crimean war, and other banks founded with British, French, Belgian, and Ottoman minority initiative continued (Eldem 1970: 231). Attempts to establish indigenous credit institutions, "to foster savings among the populace," dated back to the 1860s, yet the rumors of impending confiscation by the Ottoman state led to a major crisis whereby the effectiveness of these institutions was reduced significantly" (Eldem 1970: 232).

113. The Ottoman minority bankers who also had money owed to them were issued 8 million piasters' worth of PDA bonds at 5 percent interest in return for the owed amount.

114. The debts were 91.82 million Ottoman piasters in 1881, 78 million in 1898, and 131 million in 1913 (Eldem 1970: 266).

115. The net Public Debt Administration revenues (in English pounds) according to years were

1882–83/1886–87	19,520,000
1887–88/1891–92	19,360,000
1892–83/1896–97	21,570,000
1897–98/1901–92	21,200,000
1902–3/1906–7	25,380,000

116. One scholar (Kasaba 1988: 110) argues that Western imperialist policies of expansion to overcome the 1873–96 great depression in Europe led to direct foreign penetration whereby Europeans replaced the minorities. However, there is not yet adequate evidence to support this argument.

117. It administered the first Ottoman industrial exhibit in 1863, and formulated the Ottoman Commission for the Reform of the Industry in 1864.

118. The financing of these companies was often undertaken by Ottoman officials (İD 41/154).

119. Private industry mostly comprised silk production, printing presses, food processing, and bottling plants.

120. Between 1881 and 1903, the fifteen companies founded by domestic investment had a capital of 18.5 million piasters, as opposed to the 673.6 million piaster capital of the eighteen foreign companies—again, a dramatic thirty-five–fold difference (Eldem 1970: 121).

121. It mostly comprised textile production, cloth manufacturing for the military and civil officialdom, and some porcelain production (Eldem 1970: 117–21). The Ottoman state did invest in railroad production, a decision that increased agricultural production in the areas connected by rail twofold (Eldem 1970: 151–59).

122. The 1839 Noble Rescript of the Rose Chamber and the 1856 Imperial Rescript (Karal 1982: 388) were both based on the Western notions of human rights, proclaiming, meanwhile, such principles as the security of life, honor, and property and the equality of all, regardless of religion, in the application of its provisions. The former set the stage for these provisions and the latter one articulated them, whereby, Ottoman citizens, regardless of religion, could be accepted for government service and enroll in both military and civilian state schools. The reiteration of the second rescript demonstrated the inability of the first to surmount Ottoman ethnic segmentation between Muslims and minorities.

123. In the case of the Ottoman Greeks, Augustinos argues that these reforms "transformed the Greek confessional community into a national society" (1992: 6). This brings forth the issue of the relationship between nationalism and capitalism. Indeed, it is difficult to differentiate the national and bourgeois consciousness from one another since both appear to be conflated during the late nineteenth and early twentieth centuries.

124. Some of the minorities, namely, the Ottoman Greeks, were not happy to be placed on an equal footing with the others, the Armenians and the Jews, who had, in that order, always ranked below them socially.

125. One scholar (Gülsoy 1991: 447) argues that had the Ottoman Muslims been prepared for this rescript, which was suddenly foisted on them, they would have had more time to react peacefully rather than violently. The nature of the Muslim reactions, however, suggest that the reactions would have been just as strong had the Muslims been aware of the reform ahead of time.

126. Refer to (Goldstone 1991) for an erudite analysis of the interconnection between population movements and social change, including those in the Ottoman empire, but at an earlier period, the seventeenth century.

127. There has been no adequate study of Armenian labor migration patterns. My archival analysis on the Ottoman Armenians did indicate such a pattern, however (Göçek 1992).

128. These comprised migrations from the Crimea, the Caucasus, and the Balkans after the 1853–56 and the 1878 Ottoman–Russian wars; migrations from the Caucasus exceeded two million during the period 1862–70.

129. Note that even though these figures are based on the results of the first statistical compilations of information in the empire (Göçek and Hanioğlu 1992), nevertheless they probably did not include minorities under foreign protection and Ottoman palace members and their families who had tax-free status. So the figures are, at best, estimates, and therefore we base our argument on the ratio of Muslims to minorities in the empire rather than on actual figures. See also Göçek and Hanioğlu (1992) for other possible biases in Ottoman statistical data collection methods.

130. The only exception seems to be the Circassians and the Caucasians, who, after their defeat in 1859 at the hands of the Russians, were settled in Anatolia, namely, Kütahya and Ankara in one case, and Çukurova in the other (Eryılmaz 1990: 83).

131. The rest, consecutively 19 percent, 10 percent, and 20 percent, were identified as "others," probably Ottoman Jews, foreign merchants, and minorities that had attained foreign protection. One scholar conjectures that the Sephardic Jews were "unable to break into the trade of the Levant due to European mistrust and the Ottoman inability to award them special considerations" (Masters 1988: 90). For additional evidence on this point, refer to note 22 and Lewis (1982: 107–9), Gibb and Bowen (1963, I: 310–11), Raymond (1974: 282, 463, 490).

132. In another instance, a European company building an Ottoman port enhanced this polarization as it recruited nonguild workers among the Ottoman Christians to break the power of the largely Muslim porters' and boaters' guilds, which opposed the company's activities (Quatert 1983: 103).

133. These were mostly Ottoman Armenian students who were sent to one of the three educational institutions that epitomized Armenian education: the Nersesian Academy in Tiflis; the Kevorkian Academy in Echmiadzin; and the Lazarian Academy in Moscow.

134. Not all of this transformation was peaceful, however; there was often intracommunal conflict over the mode and pace of change. A case in point is the 1862 conflict within the Ottoman

Jewish community of Constantinople, between the religious conservatives and the Western modernizers, as the former accused the latter on grounds of "subverting the young minds with Christian propaganda" (Sevilla-Sharon 1992: 93–95). See also Dumont (1982) for other such instances.

135. This effect is best demonstrated in the case of one Armenian student, Sarkis Kukunyan, educated in St. Petersburg, who in 1890 formed an armed unit of 125 young Armenians and attempted to cross the Ottoman frontier. Even though all were destroyed, their bravery spread through the community in songs and iconographies (Minassian 1992: 35).

136. Such movements started among the Muslim Turks only after the loss of Central European provinces, the rise of independence movements among religious minorities, and the surge of Western intervention in Ottoman affairs.

137. These figures are based on the male populations only; female participation in the labor force, although substantial, was, of course, as in most other countries, not adequately reported.

138. The figures were somewhat similar in the rest of the empire as well (Issawi 1982: 261–63). In the European parts of the empire, of the thirty-two bankers and bank managers, none were Muslims, and of the ninety bankers in the Asian provinces (excluding the Arab provinces, where many Arab Christian names were found) only two were Muslims.

139. Although the pattern in the central lands of the empire may have been different, the research conducted so far, mainly in Smyrna (Kasaba 1988) and Constantinople (İnalcık 1973), supports the conjecture that the central pattern was similar to the provincial one.

Chapter 4

1. The Ottomans created this word and its meaning as referring to a political system by the mid-nineteenth century to introduce into the Ottoman language the concept of *civilisation,* a French word that emerged in the mid-eighteenth century (Baykara 1992: 1; "Medeniyyet," in *EI.)* It was coined on the basis of the old Arabic word *madina* to refer to the secular political system believed to be common in Europe. In the late fourteenth century, Ibn Khaldun, whose work was well known to Ottoman intellectuals, had discussed the unique style of life that emerged as a consequence of living in a town as opposed to the desert.

2. The term "cohort," employed here in its sociological sense, emphasizes that these individuals became a group, a unit, through sharing a life experience, that of undergoing socialization through the Ottoman Westernization era.

3. By the end of the nineteenth century, as Turkish nationalism took root in the Ottoman empire, the Turks became conscious of Western words incorporated into Turkish. Early in the twentieth century, the Turkish Republic started efforts to purify the language. The Turkish Language Association delineated Turkish words of foreign origin in an attempt to replace them with Turkish ones. See, for example, Demiray (1972) and Sinanoğlu (1972).

4. The content analysis comprised taking a proportional sample from each letter of the alphabet. Hence my research design (1) divided the dictionary into the number of pages contained under each letter; (2) randomly selected a proportional number of pages from each letter; and (3) counted and tallied up the number and specific place of origin of each word. I then calculated the proportional representation of each Western unit.

5. These were the two fifteenth-century works of Enveri and Nişancı, the sixteenth-century chronicle of Aşıkpaşazade, the works of an Ottoman chronicler, Peçevi, and a traveler, Evliya Çelebi, in the seventeenth century, and seven Ottoman embassy accounts from the eighteenth century.

6. French was the dominant language of discourse in eighteenth- and nineteenth-century Europe as well, as had been Italian in the late eighteenth century, particularly in the courts.

7. For one account of how an early Ottoman embassy to France diffused French language and culture into Ottoman society, see Göçek (1987).

8. The first translation started with François Fenelon's *Telemaque,* to be followed by Victor

Hugo's *Les Miserables*, Daniel Defoe's *Robinson Crusoe* (1864), *Monte Cristo* (1871–73) and "Atala" by Chateaubriand (1872), and "Paul et Virginie" in 1873 (Tanpınar 1982: 273).

9. These words contained those such as *asansör (ascenseur), şimendifer (chemin de fer), kalorifer (calorie fer)* and *telegraf (télégraphe)* (Ahmed Lüfti 1872, XIII: 13).

10. For example, "opinion publique" became *efkar-i umumiye*, "relations internationales" *münasebat-ı beynelmilel* (Özön 1962: v).

11. The intellectual was Abdülhak Hamid, and his play was based on the exile of Mithat Pasha, a very important Ottoman reformer, to Taif in 1884.

12. E. P. Thompson described how this vision was socially constructed as "working men formed a picture of the organization of society out of their own experience and with the help of their education, which was above all a political picture—of where their lives stood vis-à-vis others" (1963: 712–17).

13. This analogy is based on Frank Parkin's observation that "becoming class conscious, at least in the ideal-typical sense, could be likened to the learning of a foreign language: that is, it presents men with a new vocabulary and a new set of concepts which permit a different translation of the meaning of inequality from that encouraged by the conventional vocabulary of society" (1971: 90).

14. As Marx argues in the *German Ideology*, "the separate individuals form a class in so far as they have to carry on a common battle against another class; in other respects they are on hostile terms with each other as competitors" ([1846] 1964: 77).

15. In the late nineteenth century, as noted in Chapter Two, many intellectuals opposed to the sultan escaped to Europe and established newspapers and periodicals there. These Ottoman exiles were significant as a social group in articulating the identity of the Ottoman bourgeoisie vis-à-vis Western societies on the one hand and the sultan on the other.

16. These Ottoman intellectuals thus had their education and skills as their new cultural capital (Gouldner 1979: 19).

17. Of the ninety-three newspapers in the late nineteenth-century Ottoman empire, thirty-two were owned by Muslims (34 percent), twenty-one by Ottoman minorities (23 percent), three by foreign residents (3 percent), and the owners of thirty-seven (40 percent) were not stated. See Figure 5 for more information on these newspapers.

18. There was, for instance, a similar emphasis on physical and social separation of gender and on respect for the elderly.

19. An "opera theater" was established in 1874, and a "popular theater" in 1875 (And 1992: 66–67).

20. Among such plays, one can cite Nuri's *Zamane Şıkları* (Dandies of the Present) and *İşte Alafranga* (Here's Alla Franca), written under the pseudonym M.F.

21. The most significant among these plays were Namık Kemal's *Vatan Yahut Silistre* (Motherland or Silistre), based on an Ottoman general's valiant but futile defense of an Ottoman fort, which led many of the spectators to rally on the streets in support for their own motherland, their own empire, which was dwindling away.

22. The first plays in Turkish were Şinasi's (1826–71) *Şair Evlenmesi* (A Poet's Marriage), Namık Kemal's (1840–88) *Vatan Yahut Silistre* (Motherland or Silistre), Muallim Naci's (1852–1937) *Hazım Bey,* and Ebuzziya Tevfik's (1894–1913) adaptations from Victor Hugo.

23. Occasionally there were Muslims, such as Ahmed Necip and Hüsnü Efendi, who, when acting in Schiller's *Bandits,* refused to take off their turbans and shave off their beards in a scene taking place in the Bohemian forests. Contemporaneous theater performances in Europe contained many similar anachronisms.

24. For instance, two regulations included not smoking in the theater and sitting at the seats according to the numbers indicated on the tickets. Also, women were not permitted into theaters in 1859, a ban that lasted until 1879, where special shows for women, or covered theater boxes, were supplied. Since such companies also performed in the residences of the elite, women in the households may have had exposure to such performances before 1879. Interestingly enough, there were no such restrictions on children (And 1992: 52–53).

25. Such a bourgeoisie starts to dominate society in the Hegelian sense as it advocates property and legal rights, leads the process of professionalization, and develops a public sphere separate and independent from the state. Hegel's theory of civil society is "a response to the main danger of a natural right theory embodied in Jacobinism—namely, the absence of intermediary institutions between the individual and the state, and the possibility of terror precisely in the name of the people or citizen against the individual" (Cohen 1982: 26). Under such conditions, public identity, civic responsibility, and professional ethics rose to the forefront, as they indeed did in the Ottoman case.

26. Indeed, a critical mass of educated individuals, voluntary associations, journalistic media, professional societies, universities, patronage networks, cultural organizations and other structures that establish intermediate identities between the family and the state are crucial in the formation of a civil society and the bourgeoisie such a society fosters (Clowes, Kassow, and West 1991: 6).

27. Three different levels of such consciousness (Morris 1979: 37) can be differentiated depending on the level of organizational activity: consensus indicates the simple awareness of differences, rights, and duties; labor consciousness signifies the awareness of conflict and the organization to protect one's group against exploitation; and revolutionary class consciousness displays a sense of identity within an entire economic class, enabling the possibility of wholesale societal change in line with the interests of that particular class.

28. "Civil" refers to the rights and obligations individuals accrue through living in an urban setting, and its Western roots can be traced to the Greek *polis* and *politea*. The term appears in a medieval Latin translation of Aristotle's *Politics* and was discussed by St. Thomas Aquinas. The term was redefined in the eighteenth century during the Scottish and French Enlightenment and after the French revolution, which initiated a discussion of human rights and responsibilities and the role of the state in guaranteeing them. The current use of the term, shaped by Hegel and Gramsci, denotes those "interests, associations, organizations, loyalties, and authorities between the family and the state" (Lewis 1994: 47). Şerif Mardin, who discusses the concept of civil society in the Ottoman empire (1962: 232; 1990: 9–15), argues that such a social space emerged through Ottoman internal dynamics as political opposition to the sultan created new media and organizations.

29. This press mostly published general works, where historical chronicles and translations of Western science abound. There were printing presses established in the empire much earlier. Book printing was brought over in 1494 by Jewish exiles from Spain and Portugal, and the priest Apkar from Sivas founded the first Armenian press in 1568. The first Greek printing press was established in 1627 by Nikodemus Metaxas, a priest from Kafalonya (Göçek 1987: 108–15).

30. The first Ottoman post office open to the public was established in 1839 in Constantinople, and its diffusion to the rest of the empire continued in the next few decades. The postal systems of the European embassies and the private postal services of companies such as shipping lines had formed from the early eighteenth century, in accordance with the conditions of the Passarowitz Treaty in 1699. Accordingly, the Austrians established the first private postal service in 1719, and this and other similar services could not be abolished until 1914, when the trade capitulations were abolished. The first telegraph line was established in 1855 by the British and the French during the Crimean war (Lewis 1979: 185), tying the Ottoman empire to Europe through the Austrian communication network, and the telephone followed in 1909, thirty years after the Europeans.

31. Usually, each reading house was known in terms of the particular newspaper read aloud in it. By attending such a house during the week, one could easily follow the events of the empire. The office-households thus started to lose their allure as the hub of knowledge.

32. The guild system and the heterodox religious brotherhoods may be considered a third pattern; however, I argue that its organizational ethos is similar to the household.

33. Associations were thus crucial to the process of class formation, as "associational life was one of the principal means by which various constituent groups of the bourgeoisie came together as a class" (Bradley 1991: 133–34).

34. This development paralleled the European one, where the voluntary associations nurtured the printed media. In the West, in addition to newspapers, there were "books on merchant accounts and trade, geography and exploration, social etiquette and child rearing, history and law, gardening

and cookery, a well as the religious books which had previously dominated the output of the press" (Earle 1989: 11).

35. The first European newspaper was published in France in 1631, *La Gazette* (Nüzhet 1931: 8). The first London daily appeared in 1702 and the first literary magazine in 1709 (Earle 1989: 11).

36. For instance, in the eighteenth century, the French embassy published Ottoman translations of two French books on military sciences written by French military advisors to the empire and an Ottoman grammar book for the use of foreigners.

37. The number of such printing presses had almost doubled in the nineteenth century, from fifty-four to ninety-nine.

38. The first Ottoman newspaper to be closed down was the *Interpreter of Conditions (Tercüman-ı Ahval)* published by Şinasi, and it was closed for two weeks.

39. One such newspaper that was banned and its journalists deported was ironically entitled *İbret* (Admonition) (Ahmed Lütfi [1875] 1991: 46).

40. This quantitative information was derived from three separate sources on the history of printing in the Ottoman empire. I tabulated the number of newspapers established each year between 1830 and 1890 and mapped out the result in Figure 5. There may have been some newspapers that were not mentioned by these sources, but the graph nevertheless makes clear the *pattern* of the relationship between the establishment of newspapers and the sultan's censorship.

41. By 1875, there were twenty-seven newspapers published in Constantinople, three in French, one in English and French, nine in Greek, nine in Armenian, three in Bulgarian, and two in Hebrew (Alemdar 1980: 17).

42. Their circulation was often around fifteen to twenty thousand.

43. As the memoir of one medical students states, "he went to one of the many reading salons in the city after school on Thursday and there he read all types of periodicals and newspapers" (Nur [1928] 1992: 111). The nominal fee for entering such salons was one *gurush* for students.

44. Frank Parkin's (1971; 1974: 1–18; 1979) analyses of boundary formation among social groups through social exclusion and solidarism provide the two parameters around which a definition of a voluntary association can be formulated. Exclusion refers to the collective practices of groups to control entry to valued positions, and solidarism to the collective responses of excluded groups that are themselves unable to maximize resources by exclusion practices. Parkin contextualizes the process of social boundary formation by simultaneously analyzing the forces within and without the group in question. He bases his analysis on Max Weber's conception of social closure as "the process by which social collectivities seek to maximize rewards by restricting access to rewards and opportunities to a limited circle of eligibles" (Parkin 1974: 3). For another perspective on social closure, see also Murphy (1988).

45. Indeed, this venue of interaction formed one of the social resources through which officials could challenge the sultan's control. The mosque, bazaar, and coffee houses provided other, more public media of interaction.

46. The known members were (İhsanoğlu 1987c: 56–62) the president İsmail Ferruh Efendi, who had been the Ottoman ambassador to England between 1797 and 1800, Şanizade Ataullah Efendi, who was a chronicler, a physician, and the kadi of Eyüp, Melekpaşazade Abdülkadir Bey, the son of a prominent Ottoman statesman who had also been the sultan's son-in-law, and Kethüdazade Mehmed Arif Efendi. Noting the social backgrounds of these members, İhsanoğlu argues (1987c: 73–74) that had the Ottoman sultans tried to reform existing Ottoman institutions rather than bringing in alternate Western-style ones, they could have bridged the emerging gap between Westernized officials and traditional scholars. Such an argument dichotomizes the complex Ottoman social system and eludes the structural factors, such as wars with the West, that facilitated the development of Western-style military institutions and also diffused secular Enlightenment ideas. Change originating in the less religious, more heterodox Ottoman military thus set the tone for Ottoman transformation.

47. The Ottoman term used to define their activities was *bektaşilik*, referring to the Bektaşi religious order that is known for its "polite contempt of orthodoxy" (Redhouse 1890: 151).

48. An earlier attempt in this direction had been initiated by the Ottoman Grand Vezir Damad İbrahim Pasha, who formed, early in the eighteenth century, a committee to oversee the translation of significant Persian and Arabic works into Ottoman. This attempt ended abruptly in 1730 with a popular revolt (İhsanoğlu 1987b: 11). The chronicler Cevdet Pasha notes that the Ottoman Academy of Science was finally established in the 1870s with forty members that met once a month (Cevdet Pasha 1872: 46–47).

49. These were seven Englishmen, five Germans, four French, one Dane, one Swiss, one Sardinian, one American, two Greeks, and one Armenian.

50. A similar exception was drawn for the Ottoman Medical Society, which pledged that "it would not concern itself with religion and politics" (Unat 1987: 89).

51. The reading room was open 3–11 PM every day except Tuesday.

52. One paid a fee to use the library, but students were exempted from such payment.

53. Some articles from the journal have titles such as "Comparison between learning and ignorance," "The science of the wealth of nations," "Introduction to the science of geology," "History of the telegraph," "History of the sages of Greece," and "On the necessity of work" (Mardin 1962: 240). The journal also owned a small printing press to publish the material. The first issue had a circulation of three hundred, of which eighty-four were purchased by groups or organizations and two hundred and sixteen by individuals.

54. The nature and development of this polarization will be the subject of my next book.

55. Neale (1981: 68) concurs that these internal relations are often the key in assessing the extent of class formation in a particular context.

56. Culture is the first terrain upon which social groups elaborate the category of nation; nationality can then become defined as "a complex, uneven and unpredictable process, forged from an interaction of cultural coalescence and specific political intervention, which cannot be reduced to the static criteria of language, territory, ethnicity or culture" (Eley 1981: 91).

57. Miliband (1971: 23) even defined nationalism as false consciousness. Others have portrayed nationalism, community, and religion as "the most important enemies of class consciousness" (Neale 1981: 45).

58. The fact that there are not a corresponding number of such memoirs of Ottoman minorities is, in itself, very significant.

59. The student and later Ottoman deputy governor in the East during the Armenian incident, who committed suicide when he realized he would be tried and executed for his role in the Armenian incident, was Dr. Reşid Bey (Mehmetefendioğlu 1897).

60. If it did not, many reasoned, it was better to sacrifice one's life for the motherland rather than live under tyranny.

61. After this emphasis on the minorities, Kemal further notes the urban–rural divide, since the provinces provide both taxes and military conscripts while the urban centers supply neither.

62. Specifically, Arthur Lumley Davids, Arminius Vambery, and Leon Cahun studied the Asian roots of the Turkic language groups. Thomsen and Radloff deciphered the ancient Orhun inscriptions in Central Asia, thus revealing Turkic groups to have ancient literate origins.

63. Even though there is an extensive literature on the origins of Turkish nationalism, the recent works of Smith (1971, 1979, 1986), Gellner (1983), and Anderson (1983) bring new perspectives to the ethnic component of nationalism that have yet to be fully applied to the Ottoman context. Although I intend to study the social construction of Ottoman nationalism in more depth in my next volume, refer to Göçek (1993a, 1993b) for a preview of my interpretation.

References

Abbreviations of Archival Documents

A [Askeri Kassam] — Archives of the Office of Islamic Ruling—The Registers of the Military Inheritance Partitioner

Ayniyat — Prime Minister's Archives—Goods and Properties Accountancy Collection

B [Beledi Kassam] — Archives of the Office of Islamic Ruling—The Registers of the Urban Inheritance Partitioner

Buyruldu — Prime Minister's Archives—Rescript Collection

CA [Cevdet Adliye] — Prime Minister's Archives—Cevdet Classification, Juridical Section

CAsk [Cevdet Askeri] — Prime Minister's Archives—Cevdet Classification, Military Affairs Section

CD [Cevdet Dahiliye] — Prime Minister's Archives—Cevdet Classification, Internal Affairs Section

CH [Cevdet Hariciye] — Prime Minister's Archives—Cevdet Classification, Foreign Affairs Section

CI [Cevdet İktisat] — Prime Minister's Archives—Cevdet Classification, Economic Section

CM [Cevdet Maliye] — Prime Minister's Archives—Cevdet Classification, Finance Section

CS [Cevdet Saray] — Prime Minister's Archives—Cevdet Classification, Palace Affairs Section

D [Topkapı Defter] — Topkapı Palace Archives—Register

E [Topkapı Evrak] — Topkapı Palace Archives—Document

HH [Hattı Hümayun] — Prime Minister's Archives—The Classification of the Imperial Orders

İbnülemin — Prime Minister's Archives—İbnülemin Classification

İD [İrade Dahiliye] — Prime Minister's Archives—State Decrees Collection

KK [Kamil Kepeci] — Prime Minister's Archives—Kamil Kepeci Classification

ME [Milli Emlak] — Prime Minister's Archives—National Properties Collection

MM [Maliyeden Müdevver] — Prime Minister's Archives—The Registers of the Department of Finance

Mühimme — Prime Minister's Archives—The Registers of the Petitions to the Sultan

Abbott, Andrew. 1988. *The System of Professions: An Essay on the Division of Expert Labor.* Chicago: University of Chicago Press.

Abercrombie, Nicholas, S. Hill, and B. Turner. 1986. *Sovereign Individuals of Capitalism.* London: Allen and Unwin.

Abou-el-Haj, Rıfa'at 'Ali. 1991. *Formation of the Modern State: Ottoman Empire in the Sixteenth to Eighteenth Centuries.* Albany: SUNY Press.

———. 1984. *The 1703 Rebellion and the Structure of Ottoman Politics.* Leiden: Nederlands Historisch-Archaeologisch Instituut te Istanbul.

———. 1974. "The Ottoman vezir and pasha households, 1683–1703: a preliminary report." *Journal of the American Orientalist Society* 94: 438–47.

Abraham, David. 1981. *The Collapse of the Weimar Republic: Political Economy and Crisis.* Princeton, NJ: Princeton University Press.

Adam, Barbara. 1990. *Time and Social Theory.* London: Polity.

Adas, Michael. 1989. *Machines as the Measure of Men: Science, Technology and Ideologies of Western Dominance.* Ithaca, NY: Cornell University Press.

Ahmad, Aijaz. 1985. "Class, nation and the state: intermediate classes in peripheral societies." Pp. 43–65 in *Middle Classes in Dependent Countries,* ed. Dale Johnson. Beverly Hills, CA: Sage.

Ahmad, Feroz. 1980. "Vanguard of a nascent bourgeoisie: the social and economic policy of the Young Turks." Pp. 329–50 in *Social and Economic History of Turkey,* ed. O. Okyar and H. İnalcık. Ankara: Meteksan.

Ahmed İzzet Paşa. [1924] 1992. *Feryadım* (My Lamentation). Istanbul: Nehir.

Ahmed Lütfi Efendi. [1875] 1991. *Vak'a-Nüvis Ahmed Lütfi Efendi Tarihi* (The History of the Court Chronicler Ahmed Lütfi Efendi). Vols. 13 and 14. Ankara: Türk Tarih Kurumu.

Ahmed Rıza Bey. [1900] 1988. *Meclisi Mebusan ve Ayan Reisi Ahmed Rıza Beyin Anıları* (The Memoirs of Ahmed Rıza Bey, the President of the Chamber of Deputies and the Senate). Istanbul: Aba.

Akbayar, Nuri. 1984. "Ansiklopediciliğimizin İlk Seksen Yılı (The First Eighty Years of the Turkish Encyclopedic Tradition)." Pp. 219–34 in *Türkiye'de Dergiler ve Ansiklopediler, 1849–1984.* Istanbul. Gelişim.

Akçura, Yusuf. 1911. *Onsekiz ve Ondokuzuncu Asırlarda Osmanlı Devletinin Dağılma Devri* (The Decline of the Ottoman State in the Eighteenth and Nineteenth Centuries). Ankara: TTK.

Aktar, Yücel. 1990. *İkinci Meşrutiyet Dönemi Öğrenci Olayları, 1908–18* (Student Incidents During the Second Constitutional Period). Istanbul: İletişim.

Aktepe, Münir. 1969. "Onsekizinci yüzyıl vezirlerinden Kapdan-ı Derya Kaymak Mustafa Paşa'ya ait Vakfiyeler (Religious foundations established by Eighteenth-century vezir and admiral Kaymak Mustafa Paşa)." *Vakı flar Dergisi* 8: 15–35.

———. 1960. "Nevşehirli Damad İbrahim Paşa'ya Aid İki Vakfiye (Two religious foundations belonging to the Grand Vezir Nevşehirli Damad İbrahim Paşa)." *Tarih Dergisi* 11: 149–60.

———. 1954. "Ahmed IV. devrinde şark seferine iştirak eden Ordu Esnafı Hakkında Vesikalar (Documents on the artisans participating in the Eastern Campaign of Sultan Ahmed IV)." *Tarih Dergisi* 7: 17–30.

Alemdar, Korkmaz. 1980. *İstanbul (1875–1964): Türkiye'de Yayınlanan Fransızca bir Gazetenin Tarihi* (The History of a French newspaper Published in Turkey: Istanbul [1875–1964]). Ankara: Akademi Yayınları.

Alexander, Jeffrey C. 1988. "The new theoretical movement." Pp. 70–101 in *Handbook of Sociology,* ed. N. Smelser. Beverly Hills, CA: Sage.

Ali Kemal. [1913] 1985. *Ömrüm (1869–95)* (My Life, 1869–95). Istanbul: İsis.

Allahar, Anton. 1990. "The evolution of the Latin American bourgeoisie: an historical comparative study." *International Journal of Comparative Sociology* 31/3–4: 222–36.

Althusser, Louis, and E. Balibar. 1970. *Reading Capital.* London: New Left Books.

Amin, Samir. 1976. *Unequal Development: An Essay on the Social Formations of Peripheral Capitalism.* New York: Monthly Review press.

Aminzade, Ronald. 1992. "Historical sociology and time." *Sociological Methods and Research* 20/4: 456–80.

———. 1981. *Class, Politics and Early Industrial Capitalism: A Study of Mid-19th Century Toulouse, France.* Albany: SUNY Press.

And, Metin. 1992. *Türk Tiyatro Tarihi* (History of the Turkish Theater). Istanbul: İletişim.

Anderson, Benedict. 1983. *Imagined Communities.* London: Verso.

Anderson, Perry. 1979. *Lineages of the Absolutist State.* London: Verso.

Appadurai, Arjun (ed.). 1986. *The Social Life of Things: Commodities in Cultural Perspective.* Cambridge: Cambridge University Press.

Arık, Rüçhan. 1976. *Batılılaşma Dönemi Anadolu Tasvir Sanatı* (Anatolian Representational Art During the Era of Westernization). Ankara: İş Bankası.

Arjomand, Said. 1992. "Constitutions and the struggle for political order." *European Journal of Sociology* 33: 39–82.

———. 1988. *The Turban for the Crown: The Islamic Revolution in Iran.* New York: Oxford University Press.

———. 1986. "Religion, political order and societal change with special reference to Shi'ite Islam." In *Current Perspectives in Social Theory,* ed. S. G. McNall. Vol. 6. Greenwich, CT: JAI Press.

Augustinos, Gerasimos. 1992. *The Greeks of Asia Minor: Confession, Community and Ethnicity in the 19th Century.* Kent, OH: Kent State University Press.

Baer, G. 1980. "Patrons and clients in Ottoman Cairo." Pp. 11–18 in *Mémorial Ö. L. Barkan.* Paris: Librairie d'Amérique et d'Orient.

———. 1977. *Ottoman Guilds: A Reassessment.* Proceedings of the Conference on the Social and Economic History of Turkey. Ankara.

———. 1970a. "Guilds in Middle Eastern History." Pp. 11–30 in *Studies in the Economic History of the Middle East,* ed. M. A. Cook. London: Oxford University Press.

———. 1970b. "The structure of Turkish guilds and its significance for Ottoman social history." *The Israel Academy of Sciences and Humanities Proceedings* 4/10: 179–96.

Bağış, Ali İhsan. 1983. *Osmanlı Ticaretinde Gayrımüslimler* (Non-Muslims in Ottoman Trade). Ankara: Turhan.

Bailey, Anne, and Llobera, Joseph. 1981. "General introduction." Pp. 1–10 in *The Asian Mode of Production: Science and Politics,* ed. A. Bailey and J. Llobera. London: Routledge.

Bakhit, Adnan. 1972. "The Ottoman province of Damascus in the sixteenth century." Ph.D. dissertation. School of Oriental and African Studies, London University.

Barkan, Ömer Lütfi. 1966. "Edirne Askeri Kassamına ait Tereke Defterleri (1545–1659) (Inheritance registers of the military partitioner of Edirne, 1545–1659)." *Belgeler* 3: 19–123.

———. 1958. "Osmanlı İmparatorluğunda Esnaf Cemiyetleri (The artisanal organizations in the Ottoman Empire)." *İstanbul Üniversitesi İktisat Fakültesi Mecması* 41: 39–46.

———. 1940. "Türk Toprak Hukuku Tarihinde Tanzimat (Tanzimat within the history of the Turkish land law)." Pp. 321–41 in *Tanzimat I.* Istanbul: Maarif Matbaası.

Baudrillard, J. 1975. *The Mirror of Production.* St. Louis: Telos Press.

Bayındır, Abdülaziz. 1984. "Teorik ve Pratik Osmanlı Muhakeme Hukuku (The Ottoman legal system in theory and practice)." Ph.D. dissertation. Marmara University, Erzurum.

Baykara, Tuncer. 1992. *Osmanlılarda Medeniyet Kavramı ve 19. yüzyıla dair araştırmalar* (The Concept of Civilization in the Ottoman Empire and (Other) Research on Nineteenth-Century (Ottoman) History). Izmir: Akademi.

Beaujour, Felix. 1798. *Tableau du Commerce* II: 218.

Bechhofer, Frank, and B. Elliott. 1981. "Petty property: the survival of a moral economy." Pp. 182–200 in *The Petite Bourgeoisie: Comparative Studies of the Uneasy Stratum,* ed. F. Bechhofer and B. Elliott. London: Macmillan.

Becker, David. 1983. *The New Bourgeoisie and the Limits of Dependency: Mining, Class and Power in "Revolutionary" Peru.* Princeton, NJ: Princeton University Press.

Bendix, Reinhardt. 1988. *Embattled Reason: Essays on Sociology of Knowledge.* New Brunswick, NJ: Transaction Books.

———. 1978. *Kings or People: Power and the Mandate to Rule.* Berkeley: University of California Press.

Berdyaev, Nicolas. 1947. "The formation of the Russian intelligentsia and its character: Slavophilism and Westernization." Pp. 19–36 in *The Origin of Russian Communism.* London: Geoffrey Bles.

Berger, Morroe. 1950. "The Middle Class in the Arab World." Working paper. Princeton, NJ.

Bergere, Marie-Claire. 1986. *The Golden Age of the Chinese Bourgeoisie, 1911–37.* Cambridge: Cambridge University Press.

Berkes, Niyazi. 1964. *The Development of Secularism in Turkey.* Montreal: McGill University Press.

Beydilli, Kemal. 1983. "Ignatius Mouradgea d'Ohsson (Muradcan Tosunyan)."*İstanbul Üniversitesi Edebiyat Fakültesi Tarih Dergisi* 34: 247–314.

Blackbourn, David. 1984. "Germany in the 19th Century." Pp. 159–292 in *The Peculiarities of German History: Bourgeois Society and Politics in Nineteenth-Century Germany* by D. Blackbourn and G. Eley. Oxford: Oxford University Press.

———. 1977. "The *Mittelstand* in German society and politics, 1871–1914." *Social History* 4: 409–33.

Blackbourn, D., and G. Eley. 1984. *The Peculiarities of German History: Bourgeois Society and Politics in Nineteenth-Century Germany.* Oxford: Oxford University Press.

Bleda, Mithat Şükrü. [1950] 1979. *İmparatorluğun Çöküşü* (The Fall of the Empire). Istanbul: Remzi.

Bloch, Marc. 1961. *Feudal Society, vol. 1: The Growth of Ties of Dependence.* Chicago: University of Chicago Press.

Bonnell, Victoria. 1983. *Roots of Rebellion: Workers' Politics and Organizations in St. Petersburg and Moscow, 1900–14.* Berkeley: University of California Press.

Bourdieu, Pierre. 1989. "Social space and symbolic power." *Sociological Theory* 7/1: 14–25.

———. 1987. "What makes a social class? On the theoretical and practical existence of groups." *Berkeley Journal of Sociology* 22: 1–17.

———. 1985. "The social space and the genesis of groups." *Theory and Society* 14/6: 723–44.

———. 1977. *Outline of a Theory of Practice.* Cambridge: Cambridge University Press.

———, and J-C. Passeron. 1977. *Reproduction in Education, Society and Culture.* London: Sage.

Bowles, Samuel, and H. Gintis. 1986. *Democracy and Capitalism: Property, Community and the Contradictions of Modern Social Thought.* New York: Basic Books.

Bozkurt, Gülnihal. 1989. *Gayrımüslim Osmanlı Vatandaşlarının Hukuki Durumu, 1839–1914* (The Legal Status of Non-Muslim Ottoman Citizens, 1839–1914). Ankara: Türk Tarih Kurumu.

Bradley, Joseph. 1991. "Voluntary associations, civic culture and "obshchestvennost" in Moscow." Pp. 131–48 in *Between Tsar and People: Educated Society and the Quest for Public Identity in Late Imperial Russia,* ed. E. Clowes, S. Kassow, and J. West. Princeton, NJ: Princeton University Press.

Braude, Benjamin, and B. Lewis, eds. 1982. *Christians and Jews in the Ottoman Empire.* 2 vols. New York: Holmes and Meier.

Braudel, Fernand. 1984. *Civilization and Capitalism in the Fifteenth to Eighteenth Centuries, 3: The Perspective of the World.* New York: Harper and Row.

———. 1981. *The Structures of Everyday Life: The Limits of the Possible.* New York: Harper and Row.

Braudel, Fernand. 1967. *Capitalism and the Material Life, 1400–1800.* London: Weidenfeld and Nicholson.

Brewer, Anthony. 1980. *Marxist Theories of Imperialism: A Critical Survey.* London: Routledge.

Brinkmann, Carl. 1968. "Bourgeoisie." Pp. 654–56 in *International Encyclopedia of the Social Sciences*. New York: Macmillan.

Brubaker, Rogers. 1985. "Rethinking classical theory: the sociological vision of Pierre Bourdieu." *Theory and Society* 14: 723–44.

Bruland, Kristine. 1989. "The transformation of work in European industrialization." Pp. 154–69 in *The First Industrial Revolutions*, ed. Peter Mathias and J. Davis. London: Oxford University Press.

Bryant, Christopher, and D. Jary (eds.). 1991. "Introduction." Pp. 1–31 in *Giddens' Theory of Structuration: A Critical Appreciation*. London: Routledge.

Buckingham, J. S. 1827. *Travels in Mesopotamia*. London.

Burawoy, Michael. 1989. "Reflections on the class consciousness of Hungarian steelworkers." *Politics and Society* 17/1: 1–34.

———. 1985. *The Politics of Production: Factory Regimes Under Capitalism and Socialism*. London: Verso.

———. 1979. *Manufacturing Consent*. Berkeley: University of California Press.

Burrows, Matthew. 1986. "'Mission civilisatrice': French cultural policy in the Middle East, 1860–1914." *The Historical Journal* 29/1: 109–35.

Calhoun, Craig. 1982. *The Question of Class Struggle: Social Foundations of Popular Radicalism*. Chicago: University of Chicago Press.

Cantemir, Demetrius. 1737. *The History of the Othman Empire: The History of the Decay of the Othman Empire from the Reign of Mahomet IV to the Reign of Ahmed III Being the History of the Author's Own Times*. London.

———. 1734. *The History of the Growth and Decay of the Othman Empire*. London.

Çapanoğlu, Münir S. 1970. *Basın Tarihimizde Mizah Dergileri* (Satirical Journals in the History of the Turkish Press). Istanbul: Garanti.

Carchedi, Guglielmo. 1977. *On the Economic Identification of Social Classes*. London: Routledge.

Castles, Francis. 1973. "Barrington Moore's thesis and Swedish political development." *Government and Opposition* 8/3: 313–31.

Çetin, Atilla. 1981. "Maarif Nazırı Ahmed Zühdü Paşanın Osmanlı İmparatorluğundaki Yabancı Okullar Hakkındaki Raporu (The report of Minister of Education Ahmed Zühdü Paşa on the foreign schools in the Ottoman Empire)." *Güneydoğu Avrupa Araştırmaları Dergisi* 10–11: 189–220.

Cevdet Pasha. [1880] 1980. *Ma'ruzat* (Statements). Istanbul: Çağrı.

———. 1861. *Tarih-i Cevdet* (The Chronicle of Cevdet). Vols. 2, 3, 4, and 8. Constantinople.

———. 1872. *Tezakir* (Biographical Memoir). Ankara: Türk Tarih Kurumu.

Cezar, Yavuz. 1986. *Osmanlı Maliyesinde Bunalım ve Değişim Dönemi* (The Era of Crisis and Change in the Ottoman Financial Administration). Istanbul: Alan.

———. 1977. "Bir ayanın muhallefatı: Havza ve Köprü kazaları ayanı Kör İsmailoğlu Hüseyin (The inheritance register of an Ottoman provincial notable: Kör İsmailoğlu Hüseyin)." *Belleten* XLI: 41–78.

Chambers, Richard. 1968. "Notes on the *Mekteb-i Osmani* in Paris, 1857–1874." Pp. 313–32 in *Beginnings of Modernization in the Middle East*, ed. W. Polk and R. Chambers. Chicago: University of Chicago Press.

Chaumette, M. Amede. 1822. *Voyage en Bosnie dans les années 1807 et 1808*. Paris.

Chibbar, Y. P. 1967. *From Caste to Class: A Study of the Indian Middle Classes*. New Delhi: Associated.

Chirot, Daniel. 1981. "Changing fashions in the study of the social causes of economic and social change." Pp. 259–82 in *The State of Sociology: Problems and Prospects*, ed. J. F. Short. Beverly Hills, CA: Sage.

———. 1976. *Social Change in a Peripheral Society: The Creation of a Balkan Colony*. New York: Academic Press.

————, and T. D. Hall. 1982. "World-system theory." *Annual Review of Sociology* 8: 81–106.

Chmielowska, Danuta. 1990. "Osmanlı İmparatorluğunda Tanzimat Yazarlarının Sosyal Değişimlerdeki Rolü (The role of Tanzimat writers in Ottoman social change)." Pp. 233–8 in *V. Milletlerası Türkiye Sosyal ve İktisat Tarihi Kongresi Tebliğler.* Ankara: Türk Tarih Kurumu.

Chowdhury, Sultanul Alam. 1964. "The problem of representation in Muslim law of inheritance." *Islamic Studies* 3: 375–91.

Cipolla, Carlo. 1967. *Clocks and Culture, 1300–1700.* London: Walker.

Çizakça, Murat. 1985. "Incorporation of the Middle East into the European world-economy." *Review* 8: 353–78.

Clark, Blake. 1939. *Oriental England.* Shanghai.

Clogg, Richard. 1982. "The Greek millet in the Ottoman Empire." Pp. 185–207 in *Christians and Jews of the Ottoman Empire,* ed. B. Braude and B. Lewis. Vol. 1. New York: Holmes and Meier.

————. 1981. "The Greek mercantile Bourgeoisie: progressive or reactionary?" Pp. 85–110 in *Balkan Society in the Age of Greek Independence.* London: Macmillan.

Clowes, Edith, S. Kassow, and J. West. 1991. "Introduction: the problem of the middle in late imperial Russian society." Pp. 3–14 in *Between Tsar and People: Educated Society and the Quest for Public Identity in Late Imperial Russia,* ed. E. Clowes, S. Kassow, and J. West. Princeton, NJ: Princeton University Press.

Cohen, Amnon. 1984. *Jewish Life Under Islam: Jerusalem in the Sixteenth Century.* Cambridge, MA: Harvard University Press.

————. 1973. *Palestine in the Eighteenth Century: Patterns of Government and Administration.* Jerusalem: Magnes Press.

————. 1971. "The army in Palestine in the eighteenth century: sources of its weakness and strength." *British Society of Oriental and Asian Studies* 34: 36–55.

————, and B. Lewis. 1978. *Population and Revenue in the Towns of Palestine in the Sixteenth Century.* Princeton, NJ: Princeton University Press.

Cohen, G. A. 1978. *Karl Marx's Theory of History: A Defence.* Princeton, NJ: Princeton University Press.

Cohen, Jean L. 1982. *Class and Civil Society: The Limits of Marxian Critical Theory.* Amherst: University of Massachusetts Press.

Collins, R. 1982. *The Credential Society: A Historical Sociology of Education and Stratification.* New York: Academic Press.

Constantin, Gh. I. 1968. "La réactualisation de l'histoire de l'empire ottoman de Demetre Cantemir." *Cultura Turcica* 5: 55–66.

Cook, M. A. 1972. *Population Pressure in Rural Anatolia, 1450–1600.* London: Oxford University Press.

Corrigan, Philip, and Derek Sayer. 1985. *The Great Arch: English State Formation as Cultural Revolution.* Oxford: Basil Blackwell.

Coulson, N. J. 1971. *Succession in the Muslim Family.* Cambridge: Cambridge University Press.

Cvetkova, Bistra. 1977. "Problems of the Ottoman regime in the Balkans." Pp. 165–83 in *Studies in Eighteenth-Century Islamic History,* ed. T. Naff and R. Owen. Carbondale: Southern Illinois University Press.

————. 1975. "To the prehistory of the Tanzimat: an unknown Ottoman political treatise of the eighteenth century." *Etudes Historiques* 7: 133–46.

Dahrendorf, Ralf. 1967. *Society and Democracy in Germany.* New York: Doubleday.

Dallam, Thomas. 1893. "The diary of Master Thomas Dallam, 1599–1600." Pp. 1–98 in *Early Voyages and Travels in the Levant.* London: Hakluyt Society.

Darling, Frank C. 1979. *The Westernization of Asia: A Comparative Political Analysis.* Boston: G. K. Hall.

Davidoff, Leonore, and Catherine Hall. 1987. *Family Fortunes: Men and Women of the English Middle Class, 1780–1850.* London: Hutchinson.

Davis, Eric. 1983. *Challenging Colonialism: Bank Mısr and Egyptian Industrialization, 1920–41.* Princeton, NJ: Princeton University Press.

Davis, F. 1984. "The clocks and watches of the Topkapı Palace Museum." *Journal of Turkish Studies* 8: 41–55.

Davis, Howard. 1979. *Beyond Class Images: Explorations in the Structure of Social Consciousness.* London: Croom Helm.

Davis, R. 1970. "English imports from the Middle East, 1580–1780." Pp. 193–206 in *Studies in the Economic History of the Middle East,* ed. M. A. Cook. London: Oxford University Press.

Davison, Roderic. 1982. "Millets as agents of change in nineteenth-century Ottoman Empire." Pp. 319–37 in *Christians and Jews of the Ottoman Empire,* ed. B. Braude and B. Lewis. Vol. 1. New York: Holmes and Meier.

———. 1963. *Reform in the Ottoman Empire, 1856–76.* Princeton, NJ: Princeton University Press.

Demiray, Kemal. 1972. *Batı Dili Sözcüklerine Karşılıklar Kılavuzu* (A Guide of Turkish Synonyms for Words of Western Origin). Ankara: Türk Dil Kurumu.

Denel, Selim. 1982. *Batılılaşma Sürecinde İstanbul'da Tasarım ve Dış Mekanlarda Değişim ve Nedenleri* (The Transformation in Design and Construction of Façade During the Westernization Period). Ankara.

Derman, Hakan. 1984. "Mizah Dergleri ve Karikatür (Caricature and Satirical journals)." Pp. 71–84 in *Türkiye'de Dergiler ve Ansi klopediler, 1849-1984.* Istanbul: Gelişim.

Diyanet İşleri Başkanlığı. 1983. *Kur'an-ı Kerim ve Türkçe Anlamı (meal).* Ankara: Gaye.

Dobb, Maurice. 1947. *Studies in the Development of Capitalism.* New York: International.

Douglas, Mary, and B. Isherwood. 1979. *The World of Goods.* New York: Basic Books.

Doumani, B. B. 1985. "Palestinian Islamic court records: a source for socioeconomic history." *Middle Eastern Studies Association Bulletin* 19: 155–72.

Doyle, Michael W. 1986. *Empires.* Ithaca, NY: Cornell University Press.

Duben, Alan. 1990. "Household formation in late Ottoman history." *International Journal of Middle East Studies* 22: 419–35.

Dumont, Paul. 1982. "Jewish communities in Turkey during the last decades of the nineteenth century." Pp. 209–42 in *Christians and Jews of the Ottoman Empire,* ed. B. Braude and B. Lewis. Vol. 1. New York: Holmes and Meier.

Durkheim, Emile. 1956. *Education and Sociology.* Glencoe, IL: Free Press.

Dutemple, Edmond. 1883. *En Turquie d'Asie: Notes de Voyages.* Paris.

Düzdağ, M. E. 1983. *Şeyhülislam Ebussuud Efendi Fetvaları Işığında 16. asır Türk Hayatı* (Sixteenth Century Turkish Life According to the Religious Opinion of the Sheik-ul-Islam Ebussuud Efendi). Istanbul: Enderun.

Earle, Peter. 1989. *The Making of the English Middle Class: Business, Society, and Family Life in London, 1660–1730.* Berkeley: University of California Press.

Ehrenreich, Barbara and John. 1979. "The professional-managerial class." Pp. 5–45 in *Between Labor and Capital,* ed. Pat Walker. Boston: South End Press.

Eisenstadt, S. N. 1984. *Patrons, Clients and Friends: Interpersonal Relations and the Structure of Trust in Society.* Cambridge: Cambridge University Press.

———. 1977. "Patterns of stratification in the Middle East in a comparative framework." Pp. 1–19 in *Commoners, Climbers and Notables,* ed. C.A.D. van Nieuwenhuijze. Leiden: Brill.

———. 1963. *Political Systems of Empires.* London: Free Press of Glencoe.

Eldem, Edhem. 1990. "The trade of precious metals and bills of exchange in İstanbul during the second half of the eighteenth century." Pp. 579–89 in *V. Milleterarası Türkiye Sosyal ve İktisat Tarihi Kongresi Tebliğler.* Ankara: Türk Tarih Kurumu.

Eldem, Vedat. 1970. *Osmanlı İmparatorluğunun İktisadi Şartları Hakkında bir Tetkik* (An Investigation of the Economic Conditions of the Ottoman Empire). Istanbul: İş Bankası Yayınları.

Eley, Geoff. 1990. "Edward Thompson, social history and political culture: the making of a working class public, 1750–1850." Pp. 50–77 in *E. P. Thompson: Critical Perspectives,* ed. H. Kaye and K. McClelland. London: Polity.

————. 1984. "The British model and the German road." Pp. 39–158 in *The Peculiarities of German History: Bourgeois Society and Politics in Nineteenth-Century Germany* by D. Blackbourn and G. Eley. Oxford: Oxford University Press.

————. 1981. "Nationalism and social history." *Social History* 6/1: 83–107.

————, and D. Blackbourn. 1984. "Introduction." Pp. 1–39 in *The Peculiarities of German History: Bourgeois Society and Politics in Nineteenth-Century Germany* by D. Blackbourn and G. Eley. Oxford: Oxford University Press.

Elias, Norbert. 1978. *The Civilizing Process.* New York: Urizen.

Enault, L. 1855. *Constantinople et la Turquie.* Paris.

Encyclopedia of Islam (New Edition). 1960. Articles: "Akçe" by H. Bowen (1960), "Asham" by B. Lewis (1960), "Askari" by B. Lewis (1960), "Bab-ı 'Ali" by J. Denny (1960), "Bab-ı Hümayun" by U. Heyd (1960), "Bab-ı Mashikhat" and "Bab-ı Seraskeri" by B. Lewis (1960), "Badal" by H. Bowen (1960), "Barud, the Ottoman Empire" by V. J. Parry (1960), "Bayt al-Mal, Ottoman" by B. Lewis (1960), "Beratlı" by B. Lewis (1960), "Boghdan" by Halil İnalcık (1960), "Diwan-ı Humayun" by B. Lewis (1965), "Djizya, Ottoman" by H. İnalcık (1965), "Dustur: Turkey" by B. Lewis (1965), "Duyun-ı 'Umumiyye" by B. Lewis (1965), "Harb, Ottoman Empire" by V. J. Parry (1971), "Indonesia, history, the Islamic period" by S.M.N. al-Attas (1971), "Istanbul" by H. İnalcık (1971), "Kaime" by R. H. Davison (1971), "Küçük Kaynardja" by C. J. Heywood (1986), "Maliyye" by C. V. Findley (1987), "Medeniyyet" by N. Berkes (1989), "Mısr, the Ottoman period" by P. M. Holt (1991), "Musadara, the Ottoman Empire" by F. M. Göçek (1992), "Mustafa Pasha, Bayrakdar" by J. H. Kramers and C. E. Bosworth (1992), "Pishkash" by A.K.S. Lambton (1993), "Riba" by J. Schacht (1993), "Wakf" by Heffening (1934). Leiden: Brill.

Enver Paşa. [1913] 1989. *Kendi Mektuplarında Enver Paşa* (Enver Pasha Through his Personal Letters). Istanbul: Der.

Epstein, Steven. 1984. *Wills and Wealth in Medieval Genoa, 1150–1250.* Cambridge, MA: Harvard University Press.

Ercan, Yaşar. 1983. "Türkiye'de 15 ve 16. cı yüzyıllarda gayrı müslimlerin hukuki, içtimai ve iktisadi durumu (The legal, economic and social conditions of non-Muslims in fifteenth- and sixteenth-century Turkey)." *Belleten* 47: 1119–49.

Ergenç, Özer. 1982. "Osmanlı Klasik Dönemindeki 'Eşraf ve A'yan' üzerine bazı bilgiler (Some information on the provincial notables and elites during the Ottoman classical period)." *Journal of Ottoman Studies* 3: 105–13.

Ergin, O. Nuri. 1939. *Türkiye Maarif Tarihi: İslami devir mektep ve müesseseleri* (The History of Education in Turkey: Schools and Institutions of the Islamic Period). 5 vols. Istanbul: Osmanbey.

Eryılmaz, Bilal. 1990. *Osmanlı Devletinde Gayrımüslim Teba'anın Yönetimi* (The Administration of Non-Muslim Subjects in the Ottoman Empire). Istanbul: Risale.

Esenkova, Enver. 1959. *Türk Dilinde Fransiz Tesiri* (The French Influence in the Turkish Language). Istanbul: İstanbul Matbaacılık.

Esin, Emel. 1986. "Le Mahbubiye, un palais ottoman alla Franca." Pp. 73–86 in *L'Empire Ottoman, la République du Turquie et la France,* ed. H. Batu and L. Bacqué-Grammont. Istanbul: Isis.

Evans, Peter. 1982. "Reinventing the bourgeoisie: state entrepreneurship and class formation in dependent capitalist development." *American Journal of Sociology* 88: S210–S247.

Fahri Bey, Mabeynci. [1880] 1968. *İbretnüma* (Admonition). Ankara: Türk Tarih Kurumu.

Farley, J. Lewis. 1859. *Two Years in Syria.* London.

Farmayan, Hafiz. 1968. "The forces of modernization in nineteenth-century Iran: a historical survey." Pp. 119–51 in *Beginnings of Modernization in the Middle East,* ed. W. Polk and R. Chambers. Chicago: University of Chicago Press.

Faroqhi, Suraiya. 1985. "Civilian society and political power in the Ottoman Empire: a report on research in collective biography (1480–1830)." *International Journal of Middle East Studies* 17: 109–17.

Fawaz, Leila Tarazi. 1983. *Merchants and Migrants in Nineteenth-Century Beirut.* Cambridge, MA: Harvard University Press.

Fekete, L. 1965. "Taşralı bir Türk Efendisinin Evi (The House of a Provincial Turkish Gentleman)." *Belleten* 116: 615–38.

Findley, Carter Vaughn. 1990. "Decision making in the Ottoman Empire." Pp. 867–77 in *V. Milletlerarası Türkiye Sosyal ve İktisat Tarihi Kongresi Tebliğler.* Ankara: Türk Tarih Kurumu.

———. 1989. *Ottoman Civil Officialdom: A Social History.* Princeton, NJ: Princeton University Press.

———. 1986a. "Economic bases of revolution and repression in the late Ottoman Empire." *Comparative Studies in Society and History* 28/2: 81–106.

———. 1986b. "Factional Rivalry in Ottoman İstanbul: The Fall of Pertev Paşa, 1837." *Journal of Turkish Studies* 10: 127–34.

———. 1982. "The acid test of Ottomanism: the acceptance of non-Muslims in the late Ottoman bureaucracy." Pp. 339–68 in *Christians and Jews of the Ottoman Empire,*ed. B. Braude and B. Lewis. Vol. 1. New York: Holmes and Meier.

———. 1980a. *Bureaucratic Reform in the Ottoman Empire: the Sublime Porte, 1789–1922.* Princeton, NJ: Princeton University Press.

———. 1980b. "Patrimonial household organization and factional activity in the Ottoman ruling class." Pp. 227–33 in *Social and Economic History of Turkey,* ed. O. Okyar and H. İnalcık. Ankara: Meteksan.

Flachat, Jean-Claude. 1765. *L'Empire Ottoman: Observations sur le commerce et sur les Arts.* Lyon.

Forand, P. G. 1971. "The relation of the slave and the client to the master or patron in medieval Islam." *International Journal of Middle Eastern Studies* 2: 59–66.

Fowler, George. 1854. *Turkey, or a History of the Origin, Progress and Decline of the Ottoman Empire.* London.

Frangakis-Syrett, Elena. 1992. "Implementation of the 1838 Anglo-Turkish convention on İzmir trade: European and minority merchants." *New Perspectives on Turkey* 7: 91–112.

———. 1991a. "British economic activities in İzmir in the second half of the 19th and early 20th centuries." *New Perspectives on Turkey* 5–6: 191–227.

———. 1991b. "The Greek mercantile community of İzmir in the first half of the nineteenth century." *Les Villes dans l'Empire Ottoman: Activités et Sociétés* 1: 391–416.

———. 1988. "Trade between the Ottoman Empire and Western Europe: the case of İzmir in the eighteenth century." *New Perspectives on Turkey* 2/1: 1–18.

———. 1985. "The Raya communities of Smyrna in the eighteenth century (1690–1820): demographic and economic activities." Pp. 27–42 in *Actes du Colloque International d'Histoire. La Ville Néohellénique. Héritages Ottomans et État Grec.* Athens: Bibliotheca.

Frank, Andre Gunder. 1972. *Lumpenbourgeoisie, Lumpendevelopment: Dependence, Class and Politics in Latin America.* New York: Monthly Review press.

Fuad, Beşir. [1888] 1990.*İlk Türk Materyalisti Beşir Fuad'ın Mektupları* (The Letters of Beşir Fuad, the First Turkish Materialist Thinker). Istanbul: Aba.

Gellner, Ernest. 1983. *Nations and Nationalism.* London: Basil Blackwell.

———. 1981. *Muslim Society.* Cambridge: Cambridge University Press.

———, and J. Waterbury (eds.). 1977. *Patrons and Clients in Mediterranean Societies.* London: Duckworth.

Genç, Mehmet. 1990. "Osmanlı İmparatorluğunda Devlet ve Ekonomi (State and economy in the Ottoman Empire)." Pp. 13–25 in *V. Milletlerarası Türkiye Sosyal ve İktisat Tarihi Kongresi Tebliğler.* Ankara: Türk Tarih Kurumu.

———. 1984. "Onsekizinci yüzyılda Osmanlı ekonomisi ve savaş (War and the Ottoman economy in the eighteenth century." *Yapıt:* 52: 61.

Gencel, Şeyma. 1984. "Çocuk Dergileri (Children's journals)." Pp. 185–202 in *Türkiye'de Dergiler ve Ansiklopediler, 1849–1984.* Istanbul: Gelişim

Georgeon, François. 1986. *Türk Milliyetçiliğinin Kökenleri: Yusuf Akçura, 1876–1935* (originally published as *Aux Origines du Nationalisme Turc: Yusuf Akçura (1876–1935)*). Ankara: Yurt.

Gerber, Haim. 1987. *The Social Origins of the Modern Middle East.* Boulder, CO: Lynne Rienner.

Gibb, H.A.R., and H. Bowen. 1963. *Islamic Society and the West.* 2 vols. London: Oxford University Press.

Giddens, Anthony. 1987. "Out of the orrery: E. P. Thompson on consciousness and history." Pp. 203–24 in *Social Theory and Modern Sociology,* ed. A. Giddens. Palo Alto, CA: Stanford University Press.

———. 1985. *A Contemporary Critique of Historical Materialism, vol. 2, Nation-State and Violence.* Berkeley: University of California Press.

———. 1984. *The Constitution of Society: Outline of the Theory of Structuralism.* London: Polity.

———. 1982. "Power, the dialectic of control and class structuration." Pp. 29–45 in *Social Class and the Division of Labor,* ed. A. Giddens and G. Mackenzie. Cambridge: Cambridge University Press.

———. 1973. *The Class Structure of Advanced Societies.* New York: Harper and Row.

———. 1971. *Capitalism and Modern Social Theory: An Analysis of the Writings of Marx, Durkheim and Max Weber.* Cambridge: Polity.

Göçek, Fatma Müge. 1994a. "Empirical measurement of class formation in history: the case of the Ottoman Empire." Working paper. Ann Arbor, MI.

———. 1994b. "Ottoman Provincial Transformation in the Distribution of Power: The Tribulations of the Governor of Sivas in 1804 (A.H. 1219)." Pp. 31–41 in *Aspects of Ottoman History,* ed. A. Singer and A. Cohen. Jerusalem: Magnes.

———. 1993a. "Ethnic segmentation, Western education and political outcomes: nineteenth century Ottoman society." *Poetics Today* 14/3: 507–38.

———. 1993b. "Shifting the boundaries of literacy: the introduction of Western-style education to the Ottoman Empire." Pp. 267–88 in *Literacy: Interdisciplinary Conversations,* ed. D. Keller-Cohen. Princeton, NJ: Hampton Press.

———. 1992. "Reconstructing the lives of Ottoman Armenians in the eighteenth century." *Armenian Review* 45/3: 149.

———. 1987. *East Encounters West: France and the Ottoman Empire in the Eighteenth Century.* New York: Oxford University Press.

——— and M. D. Baer. 1994. "The legal recourse of minorities in history: eighteenth-century appeals to the Islamic court of Galata." Working paper. Ann Arbor, MI.

——— and Ş. Hanioğlu. 1992. "Western knowledge and imperial control: the first Ottoman social surveys, 1895–1897." *CRSO Working Paper Series* No. 500. Ann Arbor: MI.

Goldhizer, Ignaz. 1981. *Introduction to Islamic Theology and Law.* Princeton, NJ: Princeton University Press.

Goldstone, Jack. 1991. *Revolution and Rebellion in the Early Modern World.* Berkeley: University of California Press.

———. 1988a. "East and West in the 17th century: political crises in Stuart England, Ottoman Turkey and Ming China." *Comparative Studies in Society and History* 30/1: 103–42.

———. 1988b. "Sociology and history: reproducing comparative history." American Sociological Association Conference Paper.

Goodwin, Jeff, and T. Skocpol. 1989. "Explaining revolutions in the contemporary Third World." *Politics and Society* 17/4: 489–509.

Gordon, Alec. 1973. "The theory of the "progressive" national bourgeoisie." *Journal of Contemporary Asia* 3/2: 203.

Gorski, Philip. 1993. "The Protestant ethic revisited: disciplinary revolution and state formation in Holland and Prussia." *American Journal of Sociology* 99/2: 265–316.

Gouldner, Alvin. 1979. *The Future of Intellectuals and the Rise of the New Class.* New York: Seabury.

Göyünç, Nejat. 1983. "The procurement of labor and materials in the Ottoman Empire (sixteenth and eighteenth centuries)." Pp. 327–33 in *Economie et Sociétes dans l'Empire Ottoman*, ed. J. B. Grammont and P. Dumont. Paris: CNRS.

Grassi, Alfio. 1825. *Charte Turque en Organisation Religieuse, Civile et Militaire de l'Empire Ottoman*. Paris.

Gülsoy, Ufuk. 1991. "1856 Islahat Fermanına Tepkiler ve Maraş Olayları (Reactions to the 1856 reform rescript and the Maraş incidents)." Pp. 443–58 in *Bekir Kütükoğlu'na Armağan*. Istanbul: Edebiyat Fakültesi Basımevi.

Gunn, Simon. 1988. "The 'failure' of the Victorian middle class: a critique." Pp. 17–43 in *The Culture of Capital: Art, Power and the 19th Century Middle Class*. Manchester: Manchester University Press.

Guys, Henry. 1862. *Esquisse de l'Etat Politique et Commercial de la Syrie*. Paris.

Haidar, M. 1944. *Arabesque*. London: Hutchinson.

Halacoğlu, Yusuf. 1981. "Osmanlı İmparatorluğunda Menzil Teşkilatı hakkında bazı mülahazalar (Some reflections on the Ottoman communicaton organization)." *Journal of Ottoman Studies* 2: 123–32.

Hanagan, M., and C. Stephenson, eds. 1986. *Confrontation, Class Consciousness and the Labor Process: Studies in Proletarian Class Formation*. New York: Greenwood.

Hanioğlu, Şükrü. 1985. *Osmanlı İttihad ve Terakki Cemiyeti ve Jön Türklük, 1889–1902* (The Ottoman Union and Progress Committee and Young Turkism, 1889–1902). Istanbul: İletişim.

———. 1981. *Doktor Abdullah Cevdet ve Dönemi* (Dr. Abdullah Cevdet and His Time). Istanbul: Üçdal.

Harte, N. B. 1976. "Social control of dress and social change in pre-industrial England." Pp. 132–65 in *Trade, Government and Economy in Pre-industrial England*, ed. D. C. Coleman and A. H. John. London: Weidenfeld and Nicolson.

Hasan Amca. [1958] 1991. *Nizamiye Kapısı ve Yarı da Kalan İhtilal* (Entrance to the Barracks and an Incomplete Revolution). Istanbul: Arba.

Hatemi, Hüseyin. 1987. "Bilim Derneklerinin Hukuki Çerçevesi (Legal framework of the scientific societies)." Pp. 75–84 in *Osmanlı İlmi ve Mesleki Cemiyetleri*, ed. E. İhsanoğlu. Istanbul: Edebiyat Fakültesi.

Hay, D. 1968. *Europe: The Emergence of an Idea*. Edinburgh: Edinburgh University Press.

———. 1957. "'Europe' and 'Christendom': a problem in Renaissance terminology and historical semantics." *Diogenes* 17: 45–55.

Hell, Xavier Hommaire de. 1854. *Voyage en Turquie et en Perse (1846–8)*. Paris.

Hess, Andrew. 1977. "The forgotten frontier: The Ottoman North African provinces during the eighteenth century." Pp. 74–87 in *Studies in Eighteenth Century Islamic History*, ed. T. Naff and R. Owen. Carbondale: Southern Illinois University Press.

Heyd, Uriel. 1967. "Kanun and sharia' in old Ottoman criminal justice." *The Israel Academy of Sciences and Humanities Proceedings* 3/1: 1–18.

———. 1961. "The Ottoman ulema and Westernization in the time of Selim III and Mahmud II." *Scripta Hierosolymitana* 9: 63–96.

Hilton, Rodney. 1978. *The Transition from Feudalism to Capitalism*. London: Verso.

Hirschman, Albert O. 1970. *Exit, Voice and Loyalty: Responses to Declines in Firms, Organizations, and States*. Cambridge, MA: Harvard University Press.

Hobsbawm, E. J. 1989. "The making of a 'bourgeois' revolution." *Social Research* 56/1: 5–31.

———. 1984. "Notes on class consciousness." Pp. 15–32 in *Worlds of Labour*. London: Weidenfeld and Nicolson.

——— (ed.). 1965. *Karl Marx: Pre-Capitalist Economic Formations*. New York: International Publishers.

Holloway, John, and S. Picciotto. 1979. "Towards a materialist theory of the state." Pp. 1–31 in *State and Capital: A Marxist Debate*, ed. J. Holloway and S. Picciotto. Austin: University of Texas Press.

Holton, R. J. 1985. *The Transition from Feudalism to Capitalism.* London: Macmillan.

Hourani, Albert. 1957. "The changing face of the Fertile Crescent in the eighteenth century." *Studia Islamica* 8: 89–122.

Hroch, Miroslav. 1985. *Social Preconditions of the National Revival in Europe: A Comparative Analysis of the Social Composition of Patriotic Groups Among the Smaller European Nations.* Cambridge: Cambridge University Press.

Hunter, Robert. 1984. *Egypt Under the Khedives, 1805–79: From Household Government to Modern Bureaucracy.* Pittsburgh, PA: University of Pittsburgh Press.

İhsanoğlu, Ekmeleddin. 1987a. "Cemiyeti İlmiyei Osmaniyenin Kuruluş ve Faaliyetleri (The foundation and activities of the Ottoman Scientific Society." Pp. 197–220 in *Osmanlı İlmi ve Mesleki Cemiyetleri,* ed. E. İhsanoğlu. Istanbul: Edebiyat Fakültesi.

———. 1987b. "Modernleşme Süreci İçinde Osmanlı Devletinde İlmi ve Mesleki Cemiyetleşme Hareketlerine Genel bir Bakış (A general look at the scientific and professional institutionalization movements in the Ottoman Empire within its course of modernization)." Pp. 1–31 in *Osmanlı İlmi ve Mesleki Cemiyetleri,* ed. E. İhsanoğlu. Istanbul: Edebiyat Fakültesi.

———. 1987c. "19. yüzyıl başlarında-Tanzimat Öncesi-Kültür ve Eğitim Hayatı ve Beşiktaş Cemiyeti İlmiyesi olarak bilinen Ulema grubunun buradaki yeri (The location of the group of religious scholars known as the Beşiktaş Scientific Society within pre-Tanzimat cultural and educational life)." Pp. 43–74 in *Osmanlı İlmi ve Mesleki Cemiyetleri,* ed. E. İhsanoğlu. Istanbul: Edebiyat Fakültesi.

İlyasoğlu, A., and D. İnsel. 1984. "Kadın Dergilerinin Evrimi (The evolution of women's journals)." Pp. 163–84 in *Türkiye'de Dergiler ve Ansiklopediler, 1849–1984.* Istanbul: Gelişim.

İnalcık, Halil. 1990. "Köy, Köylü ve İmparatorluk ([The] village, the [peasant], and [the Ottoman] Empire)." Pp. 1–11 in *V. Milletlerarası Türkiye Sosyal ve İktisat Tarihi Kongresi Tebliğler.* Ankara: Türk Tarih Kurumu.

———. 1985. "The origin and definition of the circle of justice." Paper presented at the Islamic Law Conference, Princeton, NJ.

———. 1982. "The emergence of big farms, *çiftliks:* state, landlords and tenants." Pp. 105–26 in *Contributions à l'Histoire Economique et Sociale de l'Empire Ottoman,* ed. J. Bacqué-Grammont and P. Dumont. Louvain: Editions Peeters.

———. 1980. "Military and fiscal transformation in the Ottoman Empire, 1600–1700." *Archivum Ottomanicum* 6: 283–337.

———. 1979. "Osmanlı Pamuklu Pazarı, Hindistan ve İngiltere: Pazar Rekabetinde Emek Maliyetinin Rolü (Ottoman cotton textile market, India and England: the significance of labor cost in the competition for markets)." *Middle Eastern Technical University Studies in Development* (special Issue) (Ankara). Pp. 1–65.

———. 1977. "Centralization and decentralization in Ottoman administration." Pp. 27–52 in *Studies in Eighteenth Century Islamic History,* ed. T. Naff and R. Owen. Carbondale: Southern Illinois University Press.

———. 1975. "The Socio-political effects of diffusion of firearms in the Middle East." Pp. 195–217 in *War, Technology and Society in the Middle East,* ed. V. Parry and M. Yapp. London: Oxford University Press.

———. 1973. *The Ottoman Empire: The Classical Age, 1300–1600.* London: Weidenfeld and Nicolson.

———. 1972. "The Ottoman decline and its effects upon the Reaya." Pp. 341–54 in *Aspects of the Balkans, Continuity and Change,* ed. H. Birnbaum and S. Vryonis. The Hague: Mouton.

———. 1970. "The Ottoman economic mind and aspects of the Ottoman economy." Pp. 207–18 in *Studies in the Economic History of the Middle East,* ed. M. A. Cook. London: Oxford University Press.

———. 1969. "Capital formation in the Ottoman Empire." *Journal of Economic History* 19: 97–140.

———. 1968. "Ghulam: iv. Ottoman Empire." Pp. 1085–91 in *Encyclopedia of Islam.* Leiden: Brill.

———. 1968. "Istanbul." Pp. 224–48 in *Encyclopedia of Islam.* Leiden: Brill.

———. 1965. "Adaletnameler (Imperial rescripts of justice)." *Türk Tarih Kurumu Belgeler* 2: 49–145.

———. 1964. "The nature of traditional society: Turkey." Pp. 42–63 in *Political Modernization in Japan and Turkey*, ed. R. E. Ward and D. A. Rostow. Princeton, NJ: Princeton University Press.

———. 1953–55. "Documents on the economic and social history of Turkey in the fifteenth century." *Istanbul üniversitesi İktisat Fakültesi Mecmuası* 20: 44–8.

Iorga, N. 1925. *Points de Vue sur l'Histoire du Commerce de l'Orient à l'Epoque Moderne*. Paris.

İpşirli, Mehmed. 1991. "Osmanlılarda Cuma Selamlığı: Halk-Hükümdar Münasebetleri Açısından Önemi (The Friday audience in the Ottoman Empire: its significance in the populace–sovereign relationship)." Pp. 459–72 in *Bekir Kütükoğlu'na Armağan*. Istanbul: Edebiyat Fakültesi Basımevi.

İslam Ansiklopedisi. 1949. Articles: "Bab" by J. Hell (1949), "Bab-ı 'Ali" by T. Gökbilgin (1949), "Bedel-i Askeri" by S. S. Onar (1949), "Keyl" and "Kuruş" by E. V. Zambaur (1968), "Küçük Kaynarca" by C. Tukin (1968), "Ulema" by M. T. Gökbilgin (1979), "Vakıf" by B. Yediyıldız (1979). Istanbul: Milli Eğitim Matbaası.

İslamoğlu, Huri. 1987. "Introduction." Pp. 1–24 in *The Ottoman Empire and the World Economy*, ed. H. İ. İnan. New York: Cambridge University Press.

———, and Ç. Keyder. 1977. "Agenda for Ottoman history." *Review* 1: 31–56.

Issawi, Charles. 1982. "The transformation of the economic position of the millets in the nineteenth century." Pp. 261–85 in *Christians and Jews of the Ottoman Empire*, ed. B. Braude and B. Lewis. Vol. 1. New York: Holmes and Meier.

———. 1980. *The Economic History of Turkey, 1800–1914*. Chicago: University of Chicago Press.

———. 1970. "The decline of Middle Eastern trade, 1100–1850." Pp. 245–66 in *Islam and the Trade of Asia*, ed. D. S. Richard. Oxford: B. Cassirer.

———. 1968. "Asymmetrical development and transport in Egypt." Pp. 383–400 in *Beginnings of Modernization in the Middle East*, ed. W. Polk and R. Chambers. Chicago: University of Chicago Press.

Itzkowitz, N. 1977. "Men and ideas in the eighteenth century Ottoman Empire." Pp. 15–26 in *Studies in Eighteenth Century Islamic History*, ed. T. Naff and R. Owen. Carbondale: Southern Illinois University Press.

———. 1962. "Eighteenth-century Ottoman realities." *Studia Islamica* 16–18: 73–94.

Janowitz, Morris. 1975. "Some observations on the comparative analysis of Middle Eastern military institutions." Pp. 412–40 in *War, Technology and Society in the Middle East*, ed. V. J. Parry and M. E. Yapp. London: Oxford University Press.

Jennings, R. C. 1978. "Zimmis (non-Muslims) in early seventeenth century Ottoman judicial records: the sharia court of Anatolian Kayseri." *Journal of the Economic and Social History of the Orient* 21: 225–93.

Johnson, Dale. 1982a. "Class relations and middle classes." Pp. 87–107 in *Class and Social Development: A New Theory of the Middle Class*. Beverly Hills, CA: Sage.

———. 1982b. "Introduction." Pp. 11–25 in *Class and Social Development: A New Theory of the Middle Class*. Beverly Hills, CA: Sage.

Jones, Charles A. 1987. *International Business in the 19th Century: The Rise and Fall of a Cosmopolitan Bourgeoisie*. London: Wheatsheaf Books.

Jones, P.V.B. 1918. *The Household of a Tudor Nobleman*. Philadelphia.

Joyce, Patrick. 1987. "The historical meanings of work: an introduction." Pp. 1–30 in *The Historical Meanings of Work*, ed. P. Joyce. Cambridge: Cambridge University Press.

———. 1980. *Work, Society and Politics: The Culture of the Factory in later Victorian England*. London: Harvester.

Julliany, J. 1842. *Essai sur le Commerce de Marseille*. Paris.

Kafadar, Cemal. 1990. "A death in Venice (1575): Anatolian Muslim merchants trading in the Serenissima." *Journal of Turkish Studies* 13: 191–218.

————. 1981. "Yeniçeri-Esnaf relations: solidarity and conflict." M. A. thesis. McGill University, Montreal.

Kaplan, Steve Laurence. 1986. "Social classification and representation in the corporate world of 18th century France: Turgot's 'Carnival.'" Pp. 176–228 in *Work in France: Representations, Meaning, Organization and Practice,* ed. S. Kaplan and C. Koepp. Ithaca, NY: Cornell University Press.

————, and C. Koepp. 1986. "Introduction." Pp. 9–48 in *Work in France: Representations, Meaning, Organization and Practice,* ed. S. Kaplan and C. Koepp. Ithaca, NY: Cornell University Press.

Karal, Enver Ziya. 1983. *Osmanlı Tarihi* (Ottoman History). Ankara: Türk Tarih Kurumu.

————. 1982. "Non-Muslim representatives in the First Constitutional Assembly, 1876–7." Pp. 387–400 in *Christians and Jews of the Ottoman Empire,* ed. B. Braude and B. Lewis. Vol. 1. New York: Holmes and Meier.

————. 1940. "Tanzimattan Evvel Garplılaşma Hareketleri, 1718–1839 (Westernization movements before the Tanzimat)." Pp. 13–30 in *Tanzimat I.* Istanbul: Maarif Matbaası.

Karpat, Kemal. 1973. "An inquiry into the social foundations of nationalism in the Ottoman state." Princeton, NJ: Woodrow Wilson School Paper Series.

Kasaba, Reşat. 1988. *The Ottoman Empire and the World Economy: The Nineteenth Century.* Albany: SUNY Press.

Katznelson, Ira. 1986. "Working-class formation: constructing cases and comparisons." Pp. 3–41 in *Working-Class Formation: Nineteenth-Century Patterns of Western Europe,* ed. I. Katznelson and A. R. Zalberg. Princeton, NJ: Princeton University Press.

Katznelson, Ira, and A. R. Zalberg. 1986. *Working-Class Formation: Nineteenth-Century Patterns of Western Europe.* Princeton, NJ: Princeton University Press.

Kavcar, Cahit. 1985. *Batılılaşma Açısından Serveti Fünun Romanı* (The Novel of the Serveti Fünun from the Perspective of Westernization). Ankara: Sevinç.

Keyder, Çağlar. 1988. "Class and state in the transformation of modern Turkey." Pp. 191–221 in *State and Ideology in the Middle East and Pakistan.* New York: Macmillan.

————. 1982. *The Definition of a Peripheral Economy: Turkey, 1923–1929.* Cambridge: Cambridge University Press.

Khalaf, Samir. 1982. "Communal conflict in 19th century Lebanon." Pp. 107–34 in *Christians and Jews of the Ottoman Empire,* ed. B. Braude and B. Lewis. Vol. 2. New York: Holmes and Meier.

Kimeldorf, Howard. 1988. *Reds or Rackets? The Making of Radical and Conservative Unions of the Waterfront.* Berkeley: University of California Press.

Koçu, Reşat Ekrem. 1969. *Türk Giyim, Kuşam, Süslenme Sözlüğü* (Dictionary of Turkish Clothing Habits, Costumes and Accessories). Ankara: Basnur.

Koditschek, Theodore. 1990. *Class Formation and Urban-Industrial Society: Bradford, 1750–1850.* Cambridge: Cambridge University Press.

Koepp, Cynthia. 1986. "The alphabetical order: work in Diderot's *Encyclopédie.*" Pp. 229–57 in *Work in France: Representations, Meaning, Organization and Practice,* ed. S. Kaplan and C. Koepp. Ithaca, NY: Cornell University Press.

Kunt, I. Metin. 1983. *The Sultan's Servants: The Transformation of Ottoman Provincial Government, 1550–1650.* New York: Columbia University Press.

————. 1982. "Transformation of *Zimmi* into *Askeri.*" Pp. 55–67 in *Christians and Jews of the Ottoman Empire,* ed. B. Braude and B. Lewis. Vol. 1. New York: Holmes and Meier.

————. 1977. "Derviş Mehmed Paşa, vezir and entrepreneur: a study in Ottoman political-economic theory and practice." *Turcica* 9: 197–214.

Kuran, Abdullah. 1977. "Eighteenth-century Ottoman architecture." Pp. 303–27 in *Studies in Eighteenth Century Islamic History,* ed. T. Naff and R. Owen. Carbondale: Southern Illinois University Press.

Kuran, Ercümend. 1968. *Avrupa'da Osmanlı İkamet Elçiliklerinin Kuruluşu ve İlk Elçilerin Siyasi Faaliyetleri 1793–1821* (The Establishment of Ottoman Permanent Embassies in Europe and the Political Activities of the First Ambassadors, 1793–1821). Ankara: Türk Kültürünü Araştırma Enstitüsü.

Kurz, Otto. 1975. *The Decorative Arts of Europe and the Islamic East.* Leiden: Brill.

Kütükoğlu, Mübahat. 1983. *Osmanlılarda Narh Müessesesi ve 1640 tarihli Narh Defteri* (The Ottoman Institution of Setting Market Prices and the 1640 Register). Istanbul: Enderun.

———. 1974. *Osmanlı-İngiliz İktisadi Münasebetleri: 1580–1838* (Ottoman-English Economic Relations, 1580–1838). Istanbul: Enderun.

Landes, David. 1983. *Revolution in Time: Clocks and the Making of the Modern World.* Cambridge, MA: Belknap Press of Harvard University Press.

Langlois, Victor. 1856. "Du commerce de l'industrie et de l'agriculture de la karamanie." *Revue de l'Orient* 3: 270–5.

Layder, Derek. 1987. "Key issues in structuration theory: some critical remarks." *Current Perspectives in Social Theory* 8: 25–46.

Lazreg, Marnia. 1976. *The Emergence of Classes in Algeria: A Study of Colonialism and Sociopolitical Change.* Boulder, CO: Westview.

Le Roy Ladurie, Emmanuel. 1981. *The Mind and Method of the Historian.* Chicago: University of Chicago Press.

Leake, William Martin. 1835. *Travels in Northern Greece.* London.

Lenski, G. 1984. *Power and Privilege: A Theory of Social Stratification.* Chapel Hill: University of North Carolina Press.

Lerner, D., and J. S. Coleman. 1968. "Modernization." Pp. 386–408 in *International Encyclopedia of Social Sciences.* New York: Macmillan.

Levy, A. 1982. "Military reform and the problem of centralization in the Ottoman Empire in the eighteenth century." *Middle Eastern Studies* 18: 227–49.

———. 1971. "The officer corps in Sultan Mahmud II's new Ottoman army, 1826–39." *International Journal of Middle Eastern Studies* 2: 21–39.

Lewis, Bernard. 1994. "Why Turkey is the only Muslim democracy." *Middle East Quarterly* 1/1: 41–9.

———. 1988. *The Political Language of Islam.* Chicago: University of Chicago Press.

———. 1986. "Islam and the West." Pp. 16–30 in *National and International Politics in the Middle East: Essays in Honor of Elie Kedourie.* London: F. Cass.

———. 1982. *The Muslim Discovery of Europe.* New York: Norton.

———. 1979. *The Emergence of Modern Turkey.* London: Oxford University Press.

———. 1973. "Ottoman observers of Ottoman decline." Pp. 199–213 in *Islam in History.* London: Alcove.

———. 1958. "Some reflections on the decline of the Ottoman Empire." *Studia Islamica* 9: 111–27.

———. 1953. "The impact of the French Revolution on Turkey." *Journal of World History* 1/1: 105–26.

——— and P. Holt, eds. 1962. *Historians of the Middle East.* London: Oxford University Press.

Lewis, Raphaela. 1971. *Everyday Life in Ottoman Turkey.* New York: Dorset Press.

Lloyd, Christopher. 1986. *Explanation in Social History.* New York: Basil Blackwell.

Lukacs, Georg. 1971. *History and Class Consciousness: Studies in Marxist Dialectics.* London: Merlin.

M.A.B.D. 1801. *Voyage en Orient, ou Tableau Fidèle des Moeurs, du Commerce etc.* Paris.

Mackenzie, Gavin. 1982. "Class boundaries and the labor process." Pp. 63–86 in *Social Class and the Division of Labor,* ed. A. Giddens and G. Mackenzie. Cambridge: Cambridge University Press.

Mahmoud, Fatima Babiker. 1984. *The Sudanese Bourgeoisie: Vanguard of Development?* London: Zed.

Mahmut Şevket Paşa. [1913] 1988. *Mahmud Şevket Paşa'nın Günlüğü* (The Diary of Mahmud Shevket Pasha). Istanbul: Arba.

Main, Jackson Turner. 1985. *Society and Economy in Colonial Connecticut.* Princeton: NJ: Princeton University Press.

Mandeville, Jon. 1966. "The Ottoman court records of Syria and Jordan." *Journal of American Oriental Society* 86: 311–19.

Mann, Michael. 1993. *The Sources of Social Power, vol. 2: The Rise of Classes and Nation-States, 1760–1914.* Cambridge: Cambridge University Press.

———. 1986. *The Sources of Social Power, vol. 1: A History of Power from Beginning to A.D. 1760.* Cambridge: Cambridge University Press.

———. 1977. *Consciousness and Action Among the Western Working Class.* London: Macmillan.

Mantran, R. 1982. "Foreign merchants and the minorities in Istanbul during the sixteenth and seventeenth centuries." Pp. 127–84 in *Christians and Jews in the Ottoman Empire,* ed. B. Braude and B. Lewis. New York: Holmes and Meier.

Maoz, Moshe. 1982. "Communal conflicts in Ottoman Syria during the reform era." Pp. 91–105 in *Christians and Jews of the Ottoman Empire,* ed. B. Braude and B. Lewis. Vol. 2. New York: Holmes and Meier.

Mardin, Şerif. 1991. *Türk Modernleşmesi* (Turkish Modernization). Istanbul: İletişim.

———. 1990. *Türkiye'de Toplum ve Siyaset* (Society and Politics in Turkey). Istanbul: İletişim.

———. 1983. *Jön Türklerin Siyasi Fikirleri 1895–1908* (The Political Thoughts of the Young Turks, 1895–1908). Istanbul: İletişim.

———. 1967. "Historical determinants of stratification: social class and class consciousness in Turkey." *Review of the Faculty of the Political Sciences, Ankara* 22/4: 111–42.

———. 1962. *The Genesis of Young Ottoman Thought: A Study in the Modernization of Turkish Political Ideas.* Princeton, NJ: Princeton University Press.

———. 1960. "The mind of the Turkish reformer 1700–1900." *Western Humanities Review* 14: 413–36.

Maruyamo, Masao. 1980. "Fukuzawa, Uchimura and Okakura: Meiji intellectuals and Westernization." Pp. 233–47 in *Modern Japan: An Interpretive Anthology,* ed. I. Schneier. New York: Macmillan.

Marx, Karl. [1848] 1978. *The Communist Manifesto.* Translated by Samuel Moore. New York: Penguin.

———. [1867] 1977. *Capital.* Translated by Ben Fowkes. New York: International Publishers.

———. [1867] 1974. *Eighteenth Brumaire.* Translated by Eden and Cedar Paul. New York: International Publishers.

———. [1844] 1967. *Early Writings.* Translated by T. Bottomore. New York: McGraw-Hill.

———. [1847] 1964. *The Poverty of Philosophy.* Translated by C. P. Dutt. New York: International Publishers.

———. [1846] 1964. *German Ideology.* Translated by C. J. Arthur. New York: International Publishers.

Masson, Paul. 1911. *Histoire du Commerce Français dans le Levant au XVIIIe Siècle.* Paris.

Masters, Bruce. 1988. *The Origins of Western Economic Dominance in the Middle East: Mercantilism, and the Islamic Economy in Aleppo, 1600–1750.* New York: NYU Press.

McClelland, Keith. 1990. "Introduction." Pp. 1–11 in *E. P. Thompson: Critical Perspectives,* ed. H. Kaye and K. McClelland. London: Polity.

McGowan, Bruce. 1981. *Economic Life in the Ottoman Empire: Taxation, Trade and the Struggle for Land, 1600–1800.* London: Cambridge University Press.

McMichael, Philip. 1990. "Incorporating comparison within a world-historical perspective." *American Sociological Review* 55: 385–97.

Mehmed Memduh. [1910] 1990. *Tanzimattan Meşrutiyete: Mir'at-ı Şuunat* (From the Tanzimat to the Constitutional Period: The Mirror of Affairs). Istanbul: Nehir.

Mehmed Rauf, Leskovikli. [1911] 1991. *İttihat ve Terakki Ne İdi?* (What Was Union and Progress?). Istanbul: Arba.

Mehmetefendioğlu, Ahmet. [1897] 1993. *İttihat Terrakki'nin Kurucu Üyelerinden Dr. Reşid Bey'in Hatıraları* (The Memoirs of Dr. Reşid Bey, one of the Founders of Union and Progress). Istanbul: Arba.

Meiksins Wood, Ellen. 1982. "The politics of theory and the concept of class: E. P. Thompson and his critics." *Studies in Political Economy* 9: 45–75.

Merriman, John. 1979. "Introduction." Pp. 1–16 in *Consciousness and Class Experience in Nineteenth-Century Europe*, ed. J. Merriman. New York: Holmes and Meier.

Miliband, Ralph. 1971. "Barnave: a case of bourgeois class consciousness." Pp. 22–48 in *Aspects of History and Class Consciousness*, ed. I. Meszaros. London: Routledge.

Minassian, Anaide Ter. 1992. *Ermeni Devrimci Hareketinde Milliyetçilik ve Sosyalizm* (Socialism and Nationalism in the Armenian Revolutionary Movement). Istanbul: İletişim.

Momigliano, Arnoldo. 1975. *Alien Wisdom: The Limits of Hellenization*. London: Cambridge University Press.

Montagu, Lady Mary Wortley. 1965. *The Complete Letters of Lady Mary Wortley Montagu*, ed. R. Halsband. New York: Oxford University Press.

Moore, Barrington. 1967. *Social Origins of Dictatorship and Democracy: Lord and Peasant in the Making of the Modern World*. Boston: Beacon.

Morris, R. J. 1990a. *Class, sect and party: The Making of the British Middle Class Leeds, 1820–1850*. Manchester: Manchester University Press.

————. 1990b. "Clubs, societies, and associations." Pp. 395–443 in *The Cambridge Social History of Britain, 1750–1950, vol. 3: Social Agencies and Institutions*. Cambridge: Cambridge University Press.

————. 1979. *Class and Class Consciousness in the Industrial Revolution, 1780–1850*. London: Macmillan.

Murphey, Rhoads. 1983. "The Ottoman attitude towards the adoption of Western technology: the role of the *Efrenci* technicians in civil and military applications." Pp. 287–98 in *Contributions à l'Histoire Economique et Sociale de l'Empire Ottoman*, ed. J. Bacqué-Grammont and P. Dumont. Louvain: Editions Peeters.

Murphy, Raymond. 1988. *Social Closure: The Theory of Monopolization and Exclusion*. Oxford: Clarendon Press.

Mutaçiyeva, V. P. 1977. "Onsekizinci yüzyılın son on yılında ayanlık müessesesi (The institutions of provincial notables during the last ten years of the 18th century)." *Tarih Dergisi* 31: 163–82.

Nagata, Yuzo. 1979. *Some Documents on the Big Farms of the Notables in Western Anatolia*. Tokyo: Daiwa.

————. 1976. *Muhsinzade Mehmed Paşa ve Ayanlık Müessesesi* (The Institution of Local Notables and Muhsinzade Mehmed Pasha). Tokyo: Toyo Shuppon.

Naima. [1863] 1969. *Tarih-i Naima* (The Chronicle of Naima). 6 vols. Istanbul: Danışman.

Nazım Paşa. [1900] 1992. *Bir Devrin Tarihi* (History of an Era). Istanbul: Arba.

Neale, R. S. 1981. *Class in English History, 1680–1850*. Oxford: Blackwell.

Nijeholt, T. M. Chevalier. 1874. *Voyage en Russie au Caucase et en Perse (1866–8)*. Paris.

Nur, Rıza. [1928] 1992. *Hayat ve Hatıratım* (My Life and My Memoirs). Istanbul: İşaret.

Nüzhet, Selim (Gerçek). 1931. *Türk Gazeteciliği* (The Turkish Press). Istanbul.

Olivier, G. A. 1801. *Voyage dans l'Empire Ottoman, l'Egypte et le Perse*. Paris.

Önsoy, Rıfat. 1988. *Tanzimat Dönemi Osmanlı Sanayii ve Sanayileşme Politikası* (Industrialization Policy and the Ottoman Industry During the Tanzimat Era). Ankara: Doğuş.

Oppenheimer, Martin. 1982. "The political missions of the middle strata." Pp. 109–32 in *Class and Social Development: A New Theory of the Middle Class*. Beverly Hills, CA: Sage.

Orhonlu, Cengiz. 1984. *Osmanlı İmparatorluğunda Şehircilik ve Ulaşım* (Transportation and Urbanization in the Ottoman Empire). İzmir: Ege Üniversitesi Edebiyat Fakültesi.

Ortaylı, İlber. 1983. *İmparatorluğun En Uzun Yüzyılı* (The Longest Century of the [Ottoman] Empire). Istanbul: Hil.

————. 1981. *II. Abdülhamid döneminde Osmanlı İmparatorluğunda Alman Nüfuzu* (German Influence on the Ottoman Empire During the Reign of Abdülhamid II). Ankara: Ankara Üniversitesi.

————. 1979. "Onsekizinci yüzyılda İlmiyye Sınıfının Toplumsal Durumu üzerine Bazı Notlar (Some notes on the social condition of the class of religious scholars in the eighteenth century)." Pp. 155–9 in *Middle Eastern Technical University Studies in Development* (special issue) (Ankara).

Ossy, M. le comte André. 1818. *Voyage à l'Embouchure de la Mer Noire, ou Essai sur le Bosphore.* Paris.

Owen, Roger. 1981. *The Middle East in the World Economy, 1800–1914.* London: Methuen.

Özcan, Abdülkadir. 1991. "II. Mahmud'un Memleket Gezileri (Domestic voyages of Sultan Mahmud II)." Pp. 361–79 in *Bekir Kütükoğlu'na Armağan.* İstanbul: Edebiyat Fakültesi Basımevi.

Özdemir, Rıfat. 1990. "Ankara Hatuni Mahallesi Nakit Avarız Vakfının Kredi Kaynağı Açısından Önemi, 1785–1802 (The significance of the Ankara Hatuni neighborhood cash foundation as a source of credit. 1785–1802)." Pp. 733–54 in *V. Milletlerarası Türkiye Sosyal ve İktisat Tarihi Kongresi Tebliğler.* Ankara: Türk Tarih Kurumu.

Özkaya, Yücel. 1985. *Onsekizinci yüzyılda Osmanlı Kurumları ve Osmanlı Toplum Yaşantısı* (Ottoman Institutions and Social Life in the Eighteenth Century). Ankara: Kültür ve Turizm Bakanlığı.

——. 1983. *Osmanlı İmparatorluğunda Dağlı İsyanları* (The Dağlı Revolts in the Ottoman Empire). Ankara: Ankara Üniversitesi Dil Tarih Coğrafya Fakültesi.

——. 1977. *Osmanlı İmparatorluğunda Ayanlık* ([The Institution of Provincial] Notables in the Ottoman Empire). Ankara: Ankara Üniversitesi Dil Tarih Coğrafya Fakültesi.

Özön, Mustafa Nihat. 1962. *Türkçe-Yabancı Kelimeler Sözlüğü* (Dictionary of Turkish-Foreign Words). Istanbul: İnkilap.

Paige, Jeffrey. 1993. "Intimacy, identity and dignity: human needs and the primacy of production in Marxist social thought." *Working Paper.* Ann Arbor, MI.

Pak, Hyobom. 1974. *China and the West: Myths and Realities in History.* Leiden: Brill.

Pakalın, M. Zeki. 1983. *Osmanlı Terimleri ve Deyimleri Sözlüğü* (Dictionary of Ottoman Terminology). 3 vols. Istanbul: Milli Eğitim Basımevi.

Pamuk, Şevket. 1987. *The Ottoman Empire and European Capitalism, 1820–1913; Trade, Investment and Production.* London: Cambridge University Press.

Panzac, Daniel. 1980. "Activité et Diversité d'un grand port Ottoman: Smyrne dans la première moitié du XVIIIe siècle." Pp. 159–64 in *Ömer Lütfi Barkan.* Paris: Mémorial Librairie d'Amérique et d'Orient.

Parkin, Frank. 1979. *Marxism and Class Theory: A Bourgeois Critique.* New York: Columbia University Press.

——. 1974. "Strategies of social closure in class formation." Pp. 1–18 in *The Social Analysis of Class Structure,* ed. F. Parkin. London: Tavistock.

——. 1971. *Class Inequality and Political Order: Social Stratification in Capitalist and Communist Societies.* London: MacGibbon and Kee.

Parry, V. J. 1975. "Introduction," and "La manière de combattre." Pp. 1–31, 218–56 in *War, Technology and Society in the Middle East,* ed. V. J. Parry and M. E. Yapp. London: Oxford University Press.

——. 1969. "Elite elements in the Ottoman Empire." Pp. 50–73 in *Governing Elites: Studies in Training and Selection,* ed. R. Wilkinson. New York: Oxford University Press.

Parsons, Talcott. 1966. *Societies: Evolutionary and Comparative Perspectives.* Englewood Cliffs, NJ: Prentice-Hall.

Patterson, Orlando. 1991. *Freedom in the Making of Western Culture.* New York: Basic Books.

——. 1982. *Slavery and Social Death: A Comparative Study.* Cambridge, MA: Harvard University Press.

Perrot, Georges. 1864. *Souvenirs d'un Voyage en Asie Mineure.* Paris.

Pertusier, Charles. 1815. *Promenades Pittoresques dans Constantinople et sur les rives du Bosphore, suivies d'une notice sur la Dalmatie. Vol. 1.* Paris.

Pickthall, M. M. 1953. *The Meaning of the Glorious Koran.* New York: New American Library.

Pilbeam, Pamela. 1990. *The Middle Classes in Europe 1789–1914: France, Germany, Italy and Russia.* London: Macmillan.

Polanyi, K. et al. (eds.). 1957. *Trade and Market in the Early Empires.* Glencoe, IL: Free Press.

Porpora, Douglas V. 1987. *The Concept of Social Structure.* New York: Greenwood Press.

Poster, Mark. 1984. *Foucault, Marxism and History: Mode of Production Versus Mode of Information.* New York: Polity.

Poulantzas, Nicos. 1978. *Political Power and Social Classes.* London: Verso.

Przeworski, Adam. 1985. *Capitalism and Social Democracy.* London: Cambridge University Press.

———. 1977. "Proletariat into a class: the process of class formation from Karl Kautsky's *The Class Struggle* to recent controversies." *Politics and Society* 7/4: 343–401.

Quatert, Donald. 1983. *Social Disintegration and Popular Resistance in the Ottoman Empire, 1881–1908: Reactions to European Economic Penetration.* New York: NYU Press.

Rabinbach, Anson. 1986. "The European science of work: the economy of the body at the end of the 19th century." Pp. 475–513 in *Work in France: Representations, Meaning, Organization and Practice,* ed. S. Kaplan and C. Koepp. Ithaca, NY: Cornell University Press.

Rafeq, Abdul-karim. 1994. "Registers of succession and their importance for socio-economic history." Pp. 479–91 in *VII. CIEPO Symposium.* Ankara: Türk Tarih Kurumu.

———. 1977. "Changes in the relationship between the Ottoman central administration and the Syrian provinces from the sixteenth to the eighteenth centuries." Pp. 53–72 in *Studies in Eighteenth Century Islamic History,* ed. T. Naff and R. Owen. Carbondale: Southern Illinois University Press.

———. 1975. "The local forces in Syria in the seventeenth and eighteenth centuries." Pp. 277–307 in *War, Technology and Society in the Middle East,* ed. V. J. Parry and M. E. Yapp. London: Oxford University Press.

———. 1966. *The Province of Damascus, 1723–1783.* Beirut: Khayats.

Ragin, C., and D. Chirot. 1984. "The world-system of Immanuel Wallerstein: society and politics as history." Pp. 276–312 in *Vision and Method in Historical Society,* ed. T. Skocpol. New York: Cambridge University Press.

Raşid. 1865. *Tarih-i Raşid* (The Chronicle of Raşid). Constantinople.

Rasim, Ahmed. [1924] 1987. *Osmanlı İmparatorluğunun Batış Evreleri* (Decline Periods of the Ottoman Empire). Istanbul: Çağdaş.

Raymond, André. 1974. *Artisans et Commerçants au Caire au XVIIIe siècle.* 2 vols. Damas: Institut Français de Damas.

Rebel, Hermann. 1983. *Peasant Classes: The Bureaucratization of Property and Family Relations Under Early Habsburg Absolutism 1511–1636.* Princeton, NJ: Princeton University Press.

Redhouse, James W. 1890. *A Turkish and English Lexcon.* Constantinople: A.H. Boyajian.

Refik, Ahmed. 1930. *Hicri Onikinci Asırda İstanbul Hayatı (1100–1200)* (Life in Istanbul During the Twelfth Century of the Hijra). Istanbul.

Renda, Günsel. 1985. "Avrupa Sanatında Türk Modası (Turkish fashion in European art)." Pp. 39–50) in *Sanat Üzerine.* Istanbul: Cem.

———. 1983. "Europe and the Ottomans." Pp. 9–32 in *Europa und die Kundst des Islam 15. bis 18. Jahrhundert.* Vienna.

———. 1977. *Batılılaşma Döneminde Türk Resim Sanatı 1700–1850* (Turkish Painting During the Westernization Period). Ankara: Hacettepe Üniversitesi Yayınları.

Repp, R. C. 1986. *The Müfti of İstanbul: A Study in the Development of the Ottoman Learned Hierarchy.* London: Oxford University Press.

———. 1977. "The altered nature and role of the Ulema." Pp. 277–86 in *Studies in Eighteenth Century Islamic History,* ed. T. Naff and R. Owen. Carbondale: Southern Illinois University Press.

Resch, Robert P. 1989. "On the subject of class: history, politics, and economic determination." *Current Perspectives in Social Theory* 9: 91–121.

Rheinstein, Max. 1955. *Law of Decendents' Estates.* Indianapolis: Bobbs-Merrill.

Richards, Alan, and J. Waterbury. 1990. *A Political Economy of the Middle East: State, Class and Economic Development.* Boulder, CO: Westview.

Roche, D. 1981. *Le Peuple de Paris: Essai sur la Culture Populaire au XVIIIe Siècle.* Paris: Aubier.

Rodinson, Maxime. 1987. *Europe and the Mystique of Islam.* Seattle: University of Washington Press.

Rodinson, Maxime. 1972. *Marxisme et le Monde Musulman*. Paris: Editions du Sevil.

Rogers, Nicholas. 1979. "Money, land and lineage: the big bourgeoisie of Hanoverian London." *Social History* 4/3: 437–54.

Rolland, Charles. 1854. *La Turquie Contemporaire*. Paris.

Roseberry, William. 1989. *Anthropologies and Histories: Essays in Culture, History and Political Economy*. New Brunswick, NJ: Rutgers University Press.

Roy, William G. 1984. "Class conflict and social change in historical perspective." *Annual Review of Sociology* 10: 483–506.

Rudé, George. [1972] 1985. *Europe in the Eighteenth Century: Aristocracy and the Bourgeois Challenge*. London: Weidenfeld and Nicolson.

Rustow, Dankwart. 1975. "Political ends and military means in the late Ottoman and post Ottoman Middle East." Pp. 386–99 in *War, Technology and Society in the Middle East*, ed. V. J. Parry and M. E. Yapp. London: Oxford University Press.

Sadat, D. R. 1972. "Rumeli ayanları: eighteenth century." *Journal of Modern History* 44: 343–63.

Sağlam, Tevfik. [1940] 1991. *Nasıl Okudum* (How I Got Educated). Istanbul: Nehir.

Said, Edward. 1978. *Orientalism*. New York: Random House.

Sakaoğlu, Necdet. 1984. *Anadolu Derebeyi Ocaklarından Köse Paşa Hanedanı* (The Köse Pasha Dynasty Within the Organizations of the Anatolian Notables). Ankara: Yurt.

Sarc, Ö. Celal. 1940. "Tanzimat ve Sanayiimiz (Tanzimat and industry)." Pp. 423–40 in *Tanzimat I*. İstanbul: Maarif Matbaası.

Schacht, J. 1964. *An Introduction to Islamic Law*. Oxford: Clarendon.

Schilcher, Linda Schatkowski. 1985. *Families in Politics: Damascene Factions and Estates in the 18th and 19th Centuries*. Stuttgart: Franz Steiner.

Schlereth, T. J. 1983. "Material culture studies and social historical research." *Journal of Social History* 16: 111–44.

Schuurman, Anton, and V. D. Woude, eds. 1980. *Probate Inventories: A New Source for the Historical Study of Wealth, Material Culture and Agricultural Development*. Utrecht: Hes.

Seed, John and J. Wolff. 1984. "Class and culture in 19th century Manchester." *Theory, Culture and Society* 2/2: 38–53.

Sestini, Dominique. 1789. *Voyage dans la Grèce Asiatique, Cyzique, Brusse et Nicea*. Paris.

Sevilla-Sharon, Moshe. 1992. *Türkiye Yahudileri* (Turkish Jews). İstanbul: İletişim.

Sewell, William. 1991. "Three temporalities: toward an evenemental sociology." In *The Historic Turn in the Human Sciences*, ed. T. McDonald. Ann Arbor: University of Michigan Press.

———. 1990. "How classes are made: critical reflections on E. P. Thompson's theory of working class formation." Pp. 50–77 in *E. P. Thompson: Critical Perspectives*, ed. H. Kaye and K. McClelland. London: Polity.

———. 1987. "Theory of action, dialectic and history." *American Journal of Sociology* 93: 166–75.

———. 1986. "Visions of labor: illustrations of the mechanical arts before, in and after Diderot's *Encyclopédie*." Pp. 258–86 in *Work in France: Representations, Meaning, Organization and Practice*, ed. S. Kaplan and C. Koepp. Ithaca, NY: Cornell University Press.

———. 1985. *Structure and Mobility: The Men and Women of Marseille, 1820–70*. Cambridge: Cambridge University Press.

———. 1980. *Work and Revolution in France: The Language of Labor from the Old Regime to 1848*. Cambridge: Cambridge University Press.

———. 1979. "Property, labor and the emergence of socialism in France, 1789–1848." Pp. 45–63 in *Consciousness and Class Experience in Nineteenth-Century Europe*, ed. J. Merriman. New York: Holmes and Meier.

Shanin, Theodor. 1986. *Russia, 1905–7: Revolution as a Moment of Truth*. New Haven, CT: Yale University Press.

———. 1985. *Russia as a "Developing" Society*. New Haven, CT: Yale University Press.

——— (ed.). 1983. "Late Marx: gods and craftsmen." Pp. 3–39 in *Late Marx and the Russian Road: Marx and "the Peripheries of Capitalism."* New York: Monthly Review Press.

Shaw, Stanford. 1977. *History of the Ottoman Empire and Modern Turkey.* vols. 2 (Vol. 2 co-authored with Ezel Kural Shaw.) London: Cambridge University Press.

Shay, M. Lucille. 1944. *The Ottoman Empire from 1720 to 1734 as Revealed in Dispatches of Venetian Baili.* Urbana: University of Illinois Press.

Shils, Edward. 1981. *Tradition.* Chicago: University of Chicago Press.

———. 1965. *Political Development in the New States.* Gravenhage: Mouton.

Sinanoğlu, Samim, et al. 1972. *Batı Kaynaklı Sözcüklere Karşılık Bulma Denemesi* (An Exercise to Find Turkish Synonyms for Words of Western Origin). Ankara: Türk Dil Kurumu.

Şişman, Adnan. 1986. "Mekteb-i Osmani (1857–1864)." *Journal of Ottoman Studies* 5: 83–160.

Skocpol, Theda, ed. *Vision and Method in Historical Sociology.* Cambridge: Cambridge University Press.

———. 1979. *States and Social Revolutions: A Comparative Analysis of France, Russia and China.* London: Cambridge University Press.

Slade, Adolphus. 1837. *Turkey, Greece and Malta.* 2 vols. London: Saunders and Otley.

Smith, Anthony. 1986. *Ethnic Origins of Nations.* Oxford: Blackwell.

———. 1973. *The Concept of Social Change.* London: Routledge.

———. 1979. *Nationalism in the Twentieth Century.* Oxford: Martin Robertson.

———. 1971. *Theories of Nationalism.* London: Duckworth.

Smith, Dennis. 1982. *Conflict and Compromise: Class Formation in English Society 1830–1914, a Comparative Study of Birmingham and Sheffield.* London: Routledge.

Somers, Margaret. 1992. "Narrativity, narrative identity and social action: rethinking English working class formation." *University of Michigan CSST Working Paper Series.* Ann Arbor.

Springborg, Robert. 1990. "Agrarian bourgeoisie, semiproletariat, and the Egyptian state: lessons for liberalization." *International Journal of Middle East Studies* 22: 447–72.

Stavenhagen, Rodolfo. 1975. *Social Classes in Agrarian Societies.* Garden City, NY: Anchor.

Stedman Jones, Gareth. 1983. *Languages of Class: Studies in English Working Class History, 1832–1982.* Cambridge: Cambridge University Press.

Steinmetz, George. 1992. "Reflections on the role of social narratives in working-class formation." Working paper.

Steppat, F. 1968. "National education in Egypt before the British occupation." Pp. 281–97 in *Beginnings of Modernization in the Middle East,* ed. W. Polk and R. Chambers. Chicago: University of Chicago Press.

Stinchcombe, Arthur L. 1978. *Theoretical Methods in Social History.* New York: Academic Press.

Stone, Lawrence. 1985. "The bourgeois revolution in seventeenth-Century England revisited." *Past and Present* 109:44–54.

Suvla, Refii Şükrü. 1940. "Tanzimat Devrinde İstikrazlar ([Ottoman] state loans during the Tanzimat)." Pp. 263–88 in *Tanzimat I.* Istanbul: Maarif Matbaası.

Swanson, Glen. 1975. "War, technology and society in the Ottoman Empire from the reign of Abdülhamid II to 1913: Mahmud Şevket and the German military mission." Pp. 367–85 in *War, Technology and Society in the Middle East,* ed. V. J. Parry and M. E. Yapp. London: Oxford University Press.

Szyliowicz, J. S. 1973. *Education and Modernization in the Middle East.* Ithaca, NY: Cornell University Press.

Szymanski, Albert. 1983. *Class Structure: A Critical Perspective.* New York: Praeger.

Tabakoğlu, A. 1985. *Gerileme Dönemine Girerken Osmanlı Maliyesi* (Ottoman Financial System on the Eve of the Decline Period). Istanbul: Dergah.

———. 1981. "Onyedinci ve Onsekizinci Yüzyıl Osmanlı Bütçeleri (17th and 18th century Ottoman budgets)." *Istanbul Üniversitesi İktisat Fakültesi Mecmuası* 41: 389–414.

Tanpınar, Ahmed Hamdi. [1956] 1982. *Ondokuzuncu Asır Türk Edebiyatı Tarihi* (History of 19th-Century Turkish Literature). Istanbul: Çağlayan.

Tarde, Gabriel. 1969. *On Communication and Social Influence.* Chicago: University of Chicago Press.

Taylor, George. 1967. "Noncapitalist wealth and the origins of the French revolution." *American Historical Review* 72: 469–96.

———. 1964. "Types of capitalism in eighteenth-century France." *English Historical Review* 79: 478–97.

Temo, İbrahim. [1939] 1987. *İbrahim Temo'nun İttihat ve Terakki Anıları* (The Union and Progress Memoirs of İbrahim Temo). Istanbul: Aba.

Thompson, E. P. 1978. "Eighteenth-century English society: class struggle without class?" *Social History* 3/2: 133–65.

———. 1967. "Time, work discipline and industrial capitalism." *Past and Present* 38: 56–87.

———. 1963. *The Making of the English Working Class*. New York: Vintage.

Thomson, Ann. 1987. *Barbary and Enlightenment: European Attitudes Towards the Maghreb in the 18th Century*. Leiden: Brill.

Thomson, G. S. 1937. *Life in a Noble Household: 1641–1700*. New York.

Tietze, A. 1982. "Mustafia Ali on luxury and status symbols of Ottoman gentlemen." Pp. 577–90 in *Studia Turcologica Memoriae Alexii Bombaci Dicata*. Naples: Herder.

Tilly, Charles. 1990. *Coercion, Capital and the European States, AD 990–1990*. Cambridge: Blackwell.

———. 1986. *The Contentious French*. Cambridge: MA: Harvard University Press.

———. 1984. *Big Structures, Huge Processes, Large Comparisons*. New York: Russell Sage.

———. 1980. "Historical sociology." *Current Perspectives in Social Theory* 1: 55–9.

——— (ed.). 1975. *The Formation of National States in Western Europe*. Princeton, NJ: Princeton University Press.

Tilly, Louise and Charles (eds.). 1981. *Class Conflict and Collective Action*. Beverly Hills, CA: Sage.

Tilton, Timothy. 1974. "Social origins of liberal democracy: the Swedish case." *American Political Science Review* 68: 561–71.

Tipps, Dean C. 1973. "Modernization theory and the comparative study of societies: a critical perspective." *Comparative Studies in Society and History* 15: 199–226.

Toledano, Ehud. 1993. "Late Ottoman concepts of slavery, 1830–1880." *Poetics Today* 14/3: 477–506.

Toprak, Zafer. 1984. "Fikir Dergiciliğinin Yüz Yılı (A century of [Turkish] scholarly journals)." Pp. 13–54 in *Türkiye'de Dergiler ve Ansiklopediler, 1849–1984*. Istanbul: Gelişim.

———. 1982. *Türkiye'de "Milli İktisat," 1908–18* (The "National Economy" in Turkey, 1908–18). Istanbul: Yurt.

Tott, Baron de. [1785] 1973. *Memoires of Baron de Tott*. 2 vols. New York: Arno Press.

Touraine, Alain. 1988. *Return of the Actor: Social Theory in Postindustrial Society*. Minneapolis: University of Minnesota Press.

Trimberger, Ellen Kay. 1978. *Revolution from Above: Military Bureaucrats and Development in Japan, Turkey, Egypt and Peru*. New Brunswick, NJ: Transaction Books.

Tucker, R. 1981. *The Marx-Engels Reader*. New York: Norton.

Tumin, Jonathan. 1982. "The theory of democratic development: a critical revision." *Theory and Society* 12: 143–64.

Türek, A., and C. Derin. 1969. "Feyzullah Efendi'nin Kendi Kaleminden Hal Tercümesi (The autobiography of Feyzullah Efendi)." *Tarih Dergisi* 23: 205–18; 24: 69–72.

Turkish-English Lexicon. 1890. Ed. Sir J. Redhouse. Constantinople.

Turner, Bryan. 1984. *Capitalism and Class in the Middle East: Theories of Social Change and Economic Development*. London: Heinemann.

———. 1978. *Marx and the End of Orientalism*. London: Allen and Unwin.

Ülgener, S. F. 1981a. *Dünü ve Bugünü ile Zihniyet ve Din: İslam, Tasavvuf ve Çöpzülme Devri İktisat Ahlakı* (Ideology and Religon Yesterday and Today: Islam, Mysticism, and the Economic Ethnics of the [Ottoman] Decline Period). Istanbul: Der.

———.1981b. *İktisadi Çözülmenin Ahlak ve Zihniyet Dünyası:* (The Moral and Intellectual World of the [Ottoman] Economic Decline). Istanbul: Der.

Uluçay, Çağatay. 1985. *Padişahların Kadınları ve Kızları* (The Women and Daughters of the Sultan). Ankara: Türk Tarih Kurumu.

———. 1957. "The harem in the eighteenth century." Pp. 394–8 in *Twenty-Fourth International Congress of Orientalists*. London.

Unat, Ekrem Kadri. 1987. "Osmanlı Devletinde Tıp Cemiyetleri (Medical societies in the Ottoman Empire)." Pp. 85–110 in *Osmanlı İlmi ve Mesleki Cemiyetleri*, ed. E. İhsanoğlu. Istanbul: Edebiyat Fakültesi.

Uzunçarşılı, İ. H. 1984a. *Osmanlı Devletinin İlmiye Teşkilatı* (The Religious Organization of the Ottoman State). Ankara: Türk Tarih Kurumu.

———. 1984b. *Osmanlı Devletinin Saray Teşkilatı* (The Palace Organization of the Ottoman State). Ankara: Türk Tarih Kurumu.

———. 1984c. *Osmanlı Tarihi* (Ottoman History) Vol. 4, pt. 1. Ankara: Türk Tarih Kurumu.

Vartan Paşa. [1851] 1991. *Akabi Hikyayesi: İlk Türkçe Roman* (The Akabi Story: The First Turkish Novel). Istanbul: Eren.

Veinstein, G. 1981. "Les pélérins de la Mecque à travers quelques inventaires après deces Ottomans (XVIIe–XVIIIe siècles)." *Revue de l'Occident Musulman et de la Méditerranée* 31: 63–71.

———. 1979. "Trésor Public et Fortunes Privées dans l'Empire Ottoman (Milieu XVIe–début XIXe Siècles)." *Cahiers de la Méditerranée: L'Argent et al circulation des Capitaux dans les Pays Méditrranéens (XVI–XXe Siècles):* 121–34.

———, and Y. Triantafyllidou-Baladie. 1980. "Les inventaires après deces ottomans de Crète." Pp. 191–204 in *Afdeling Agrarische Geschiedanis Bijdragen*. Wageningen.

Velidedeoğlu, Hıfzı Veldet. 1940. "Kanunlaştırma Hareketleri ve Tanzimat (The [Ottoman] reform era and the legislative movements)." Pp. 139–209 in *Tanzimat I*. Istanbul: Maarif Matbaası.

Vilar, Pierre. 1973. "Marxist history, a history in the making: towards a dialogue with Althusser." *New Left Review* 80: 65–106.

Von Laue, Theodore H. 1987. *The World Revolution of Westernization: The Twentieth Century in Global Perspective*. New York: Oxford University Press.

Wacquant, Loic. 1991. "Making class: the middle class(es) in social theory and social structure." Pp. 39–64 in *Bringing Class Back In*, ed. S. McNall et al. Boulder, CO: Westview.

———. 1989. "Towards a reflexive sociology: a workshop with Pierre Bourdieu." *Sociological Theory* 7/1: 26–63.

Wada, Honuki. 1983. "Marx and revolutionary Russia." Pp. 40–75 in *Late Marx and the Russian Road: Marx and "the Peripheries of Capitalism."* New York: Monthly Review Press.

Wallerstein, Immanuel. 1991. *Unthinking Social Science: The Limits of 19th-Century Paradigms*. Oxford: Polity.

———. 1989. "The bourgeois(ie) as concept and reality." *New Left Review* 167: 91–106.

———. 1979. "The Ottoman Empire and the capitalist world-economy: some questions for research." *Review* 2: 389–98.

———. 1974. *The Modern World System I: Capitalist Agriculture and the Origins of the European World-Economy in the Sixteenth Century*. New York: Academic Press.

———, and R. Kasaba. 1983. "Incorporation into the world-economy: change in the structure of the Ottoman Empire, 1750–89." Pp. 335–54 in *Economie et Sociétés dans l'Empire Ottoman*. Paris: CNRS.

Waterbury, John. 1991. "Twilight of the state bourgeoisie?" *International Journal of Middle East Studies* 23: 1–17.

Weber, Max. 1978. *Economy and Society: An Outline of Interpretive Sociology,* ed. G. Roth and C. Wittich. 3 vols. Berkeley: University of California Press.

———. 1947. *The Theory of Social and Economic Organization*. New York: Free Press.

Weiss, Anita. 1991. *Culture, Class and Development in Pakistan: the Emergence of an Industrial Bourgeoisie in Punjab*. Boulder, CO: Westview.

White, Charles. 1845. *Three Years in Constantinople or Domestic Manners of the Turks in 1844*. London.

Williams, Raymond. 1983. *Culture and Society, 1780–1950.* New York: Columbia University Press.

———. 1973. "Base and superstructure in Marxist cultural theory." *New Left Review* 82: 3–16.

Wolf, Eric R. 1982. *Europe and the People Without History.* Berkeley: University of California Press.

Wolff, Janet, and J. Seed. 1988. "Introduction." Pp. 1–15 in *The Culture of Capital: Art, Power and the 19th Century Middle Class,* ed. J. Wolff and J. Seed. Manchester: Manchester University Press.

Wolff, P. 1984. *Understanding Marx.* Princeton, NJ: Princeton University Press.

Wolff, Richard, and S. Resnick. 1986. "What are class analyses?" *Research in Political Economy* 9: 1–32.

Wolpe, Harold (ed.). 1980. "Introduction." Pp. 1–43 in *The Articulation of Modes of Production,* ed. H. Wolpe. London: Routledge.

Woude, Van Der, and Anton Schuurman (eds.). 1980. *Probate Inventories: A New Source for the Historical Study of Wealth, Material Culture and Agricultural Development.* Utrecht: Hes.

Wright, Erik Olin. 1991. "The conceptual status of class structure in class analysis." Pp. 17–37 in *Bringing Class Back In,* ed. Scott McNall et al. Boulder, CO: Westview.

———. 1985. *Classes.* London: Verso.

———. 1980. "Varieties of Marxist conceptions of class structure." *Politics and Society* 9/3: 299–322.

Yapp, M. E. 1975. *War, Technology and Society in the Middle East.* London: Oxford University Press.

Yediyıldız, Bahaeddin. 1984. "Onsekizinci asır Türk vakıflarının iktisadi boyutu (The economic dimension of eighteenth-century Turkish religious foundations)." *Vakıflar Dergisi* 18: 5–42.

———. 1982a. "Müessee-Toplum Münasebetleri çerçevesinde Onsekizinci asır Türk Toplumu ve Vakıf Müessesesi (The eighteenth century institution of religious foundations and Turkish society within the framework of institution-society relations)." *Vakıflar Dergisi* 15: 23–54.

———. 1982b. "Türk Vakıf Kurucularının Sosyal Tabakalaşmadaki Yeri 1700–1800 (The location of the founders of religious establishments in the [Ottoman] social stratification system, 1700–1800)." *Journal of Ottoman Studies* 3: 143–64.

———. 1982c. "Vakıf Müessesesinin Onsekizinci asır Türk toplumundaki rolü (The significance of the institution of religious foundation in eighteenth-century Turkish society)." *Vakıflar Dergisi* 14: 1–28.

Yenişehirlioğlu, Filiz. 1983. "Western influence on the Ottoman architecture in the eighteenth century." Pp. 153–78 in *Das Osmanische Reich und Europa 1683 bis 1789: Konflikt, Entspannung und Austausch.* Munich: Oldenbourg.

Yüksel, Hasan. 1992. "Vakıf-Müsadere İlişkisi: Sam Valisi Vezir Süleyman Paşa Olayı (The religious foundation-confiscation connection: the incident of Vezir Süleyman Paşa, the governor of Damascus)." *Journal of Ottoman Studies* 12: 399–424.

Zaalouk, Malak. 1989. *Power, Class and Foreign Capital in Egypt: The Rise of the New Bourgeoisie.* London: Zed.

Zeitlin, Maurice. 1984. *The Civil Wars in Chile (or the Bourgeois Revolutions that Never Were).* Princeton, NJ: Princeton University Press.

———. 1980. "On classes, class conflict, and the state: an introductory note." Pp. 1–37 in *Classes, Class Conflict, and the State: Empirical Studies in Class Analysis.* Cambridge, MA: Winthrop.

———. 1968. "The social determinants of democracy in Chile." Pp. 220–34 in *Latin America: Reform or Revolution,* ed. James Petras and M. Zeitlin. Greenwich, CT: Fawcett.

Zilfi, Madeleine. 1983. "Elite circulation in the Ottoman Empire: great mollas of the eighteenth century." *Journal of Social and Economic History of the Orient* 26: 318–64.

Index

Abbasids, 155n.44
Abdülaziz I, 42, 62, 158n.77
Abdülaziz II, 80
Abdülhak Hamid, 166n.102, 181n.11
Abdülhamid II, 134
Abraham, David, 140
Absolutism, 15, 151n.60, 151n.62
Adas, Michael, 7–8
Africa, 141, 145n.2. *See also* North Africa
Ahmad, Aijaz, 16, 17, 167n.111
Ahmed İzzet Pasha, 119–20
Ahmed Lütfi, 177n.107
Ahmed Rıza, 79
Ahmed Vefik Pasha, 121
Ahmet Mithat, 122
Alafranga, 41
Albania, 64, 137, 159n.87
Algeria, 11, 49
Alleon, 178n.112
Allies, 159n.6
America. *See* United States
Amin, Samir, 16
Aminzade, Ronald, 147n.22
Anatolia: European economic penetration into, 112; mentioned, 3, 36, 63, 140, 164n.82, 179n.130; population growth in, 150n.52; Protestant schools in, 168n.126; rebellion in, 64; and Westernization, 115; world-economy joined by, 17
Anderson, Perry, 15, 151n.60, 151n.61, 151n.62
Appadurai, Arjun, 157n.65
Arab Christians. *See* Christians
Arabia, 11, 24, 115, 180n.136
Arabization, 146n.10
Aravelyan, 124
Architecture, 41–43, 158n.75
Aristotle, 15, 151n.59, 153n.8, 182n.28
Armenians, 34, 156n.55, 167n.123, 179n.124 (*see also* Minorities); commercial bourgeoisie among, 16, 19, 168n.4;

European education of, 115, 179n.133, 180n.135; in Galata, 170n.29, 170n.30; in the merchant group, 109, 116; migrations and transfers of, 19, 113, 140, 179n.127; numbers of, 92, 170n.28; printing presses established by, 182n.29; restrictions on, 156n.58; trade with the West by, 40, 89, 97, 109, 169n.15, 169–70n.17, 171n.42; in voluntary associations, 132, 184n.49
Army of the New Order, 72–73
Artisans, 32, 89, 111, 116, 149n.46; and confiscation, 161n.45; ethno-religious divisions of, 133; guild organization for, 33–34, 155n.45, 156n.46, 156n.47; integrated into the Janissaries, 90–91, 170n.23, 170n.24; as provincial notables, 162n.52; resources to challenge sultan lacked by, 90, 91–92, 170n.33; and social structure, 22, 32; voluntary associations of, 108, 176n.98
Asia, 97, 141, 145n.2; and Marx's analysis of social change, 14–16; mode of production in, 8–9, 14, 15–16, 17, 147n.28, 150–51n.58, 151n.59, 151n.63, 151n.64; Russia in, 125, 134
Asia Minor, 20, 28, 88, 156n.50, 164n.73
Aşıkpaşazade, 180n.5
Askeri, 21, 152n.3
Association for the Union of Ottoman Pharmacists, 133
Atatürk, Mustafa Kemal, 139, 141
Augustinos, Gerasimos, 179n.123
Austria, 6, 86, 96, 182n.30; military in, 68, 146n.9, 158–59n.3; Ottoman debt to, 111, 178n.114; warfare with Ottoman Empire and, 48, 61, 63, 159n.4, 159n.5
Ayan. See Provincial notables

Bab, 23, 153n.9, 160n.21; *bab-ı ali,* 23, 153n.9; *defteri,* 23; *hümayun,* 23, 153n.9; *meşihat,* 23, 153n.9; *seraskeri,* 23, 153n.9

209